Hockey Facts & Stats

2011–12

Hockey Facts & Stats

2011–12

Andrew Podnieks

Collins

Hockey Facts & Stats, 2011–12
Copyright © 2011 by Andrew Podnieks.
All rights reserved.

First edition

Published by Collins, an imprint of HarperCollins Publishers Ltd.

HarperCollins books may be purchased for educational, business, or sales promotional use through our Special Markets Department.

HarperCollins Publishers Ltd
2 Bloor Street East, 20th Floor
Toronto, Ontario, Canada
M4W 1A8

www.harpercollins.ca

ISBN: 978-1-44340-864-6

Library and Archives Canada Cataloguing in Publication data is available upon request.

Printed and bound in Canada
9 8 7 6 5 4 3 2 1

CONTENTS

INTRODUCTION

The 2010–11 season had a little of everything, but most of all it had plenty of drama, excitement and controversy. In other words, it was another thrilling hockey season—for the right and wrong reasons.

The Stanley Cup winner always takes centre stage, and this year was no exception. The Boston Bruins won the great silverware with a sensational run that included overcoming two home-ice losses to Montreal to start the playoffs; sweeping Philadelphia, the team that came back from a 3–0 deficit in games to eliminate the Bruins in game seven last year; shutting down Tampa Bay 1–0 in game seven of the conference finals; and producing an emphatic win in game seven in Vancouver to win the Cup. However, local fans promptly made idiots of themselves by rioting, creating headlines around the world for their heinous actions. Tim Thomas, the 37-year-old goalie with the heart of a kid, was the Conn Smythe Trophy winner for a playoff performance that was unmatched. And forward Milan Lucic, a Vancouver native, won the Cup with the enemy in an arena he had long been admired by hometown fans.

Canadian fans were given a greater treat, though, when NHL commissioner Gary Bettman reluctantly welcomed the Winnipeg Jets back to the league. The Jets left in 1995 for Arizona, and while many fans believed the Phoenix Coyotes would, indeed, be coming home, it soon became evident that the Atlanta Thrashers were in even worse shape and got to Winnipeg first.

The news wasn't all happy and good, though, as the NHL's marquee game in the United States, the so-called Winter Classic outdoor match on New Year's Day, in Pittsburgh, incurred major damage when Sidney Crosby suffered a season-ending, career-threatening concussion as the result of a blindside hit from Washington's David Steckel that resulted in no punishment, during the game or after. It was months before Crosby started exercising again, and even now the extent of the damage to his brain and his career is far from truly known.

Indeed, head hits and the NHL's Rule 48 dominated headlines as one player after another suffered serious concussions with little in the way of punishment from league disciplinarian Colin Campbell, who wisely stepped down at season's end. Brendan Shanahan was immediately named Campbell's successor, but it remains to be seen whether a power forward who liked rough play and who is only recently retired will have the brass tacks to mete out severe and unconditional punishment for hits to the head, deliberate or "accidental," as Bettman called many concussion-inducing hits during his annual press conference at the 2011 All-Star Game.

Internationally, Canada had a shockingly disappointing year. It started in the gold-medal game of the World Junior (U20) Championship. Leading Russia 3–0 to start the third period, and seemingly on their way to a record sixth straight gold, the Dave Cameron–coached team collapsed, losing 5–3.

The Canadian women then lost in overtime to the Americans at the World Women's Championship and the men lost in regulation to the Americans at the U18. At the World Championship, a strong start gave way to another loss to the Russians in the quarter-finals. And again, Canada held a 1–0 lead in the third, only to see Ken Hitchcock's team fail to hold the lead and lose 2–1, much as Hitchcock's team did at the gold-medal game of the 2008 Worlds.

Indeed, there was something for everyone in 2010–11, but it wasn't all good. Here's hoping the 2011–12 season sees the good get better and the bad get good. Perhaps Quebec City will get a team, Crosby will return to his old self, and head shots will be yesterday's news. Perhaps.

Andrew Podnieks
August 2011

GLOSSARY OF ABBREVIATIONS

NHL TEAMS

ANA=Anaheim Ducks, ATL=Atlanta Thrashers, BOS=Boston Bruins, BUF=Buffalo Sabres, CAL=Calgary Flames, CAR=Carolina Hurricanes, CHI=Chicago Blackhawks, COL=Colorado Avalanche, CBJ=Columbus Blue Jackets, DAL=Dallas Stars, DET=Detroit Red Wings, EDM=Edmonton Oilers, FLO=Florida Panthers, LA=Los Angeles Kings, MIN=Minnesota Wild, MON=Montreal Canadiens, NAS=Nashville Predators, NJ=New Jersey Devils, NYI=New York Islanders, NYR=New York Rangers, OTT=Ottawa Senators, PHI=Philadelphia Flyers, PHO=Phoenix Coyotes, PIT=Pittsburgh Penguins, STL=St. Louis Blues, SJ=San Jose Sharks, TB=Tampa Bay Lightning, TOR=Toronto Maple Leafs, VAN=Vancouver Canucks, WAS=Washington Capitals, WIN=Winnipeg Jets

International

AUT	Austria
BLR	Belarus
CAN	Canada
CRO	Croatia
CZE	Czech Republic
DEN	Denmark
FIN	Finland
FRA	France
GBR	Great Britain
GER	Germany
HUN	Hungary
ITA	Italy
JPN	Japan
KAZ	Kazakhstan
LAT	Latvia
LTU	Lithuania
NOR	Norway
POL	Poland
RUS	Russia
SOL	Slovenia
SUI	Switzerland
SVK	Slovakia
SWE	Sweden
USA	United States

NHL 2010–11

2011 STANLEY CUP FINALS GAME STORIES

GAME 1   JUNE 1   BOSTON 0 AT VANCOUVER 1

For the third time in four playoff series, the Vancouver Canucks started with a win thanks to a shutout from Roberto Luongo, and for the fourth time, they started with a win. The hero tonight was Raffi Torres, who scored the game's only goal with just 18.5 seconds left in the third period, the result of three quick, sensational plays. First, Ryan Kesler beat Johnny Boychuk to the puck at the Boston blue line. Then, he fired a cross-ice pass to winger Jannik Hansen, who had moved in on the play. Hansen then waited until defenceman Zdeno Chara fell to the ice, trying to block the pass or shot, and managed to get the puck to Torres streaking to the goal. Torres then got his stick down and redirected the hard pass beyond the reach of goalie Tim Thomas, who had been the best player for either side all night.

GAME 2   JUNE 4   BOSTON 2 AT VANCOUVER 3 (BURROWS 0:11 OT)

Alexandre Burrows capped a career night by scoring just 11 seconds into the first overtime period to give the Canucks a 3–2, come-from-behind win and take a controlling 2–0 lead in the Stanley Cup finals. Burrows also opened the scoring in the first and assisted on Daniel Sedin's tying goal midway through the third, which produced the overtime. It was Burrows's third OT winner in 2011 and came close to the all-time record for fastest overtime goal, set by Montreal's Brian Skrudland in 1986 against Calgary.

GAME 3   JUNE 6   VANCOUVER 1 AT BOSTON 8

This was a must-win game for the Bruins because a loss would have meant being down 3–0 in the series. Only once in Stanley Cup finals history has a team overcome such a deficit to win, and that was in 1942 (Toronto). The victory was fuelled by special teams, that part of the game that had been the Bruins' greatest nemesis all playoffs. The Bruins scored two power-play goals and two shorthanded goals, taking a scoreless game after twenty minutes and turning it into a rout by the end of the second period. But perhaps the most important moment in the game came early in the first period. Boston's Nathan Horton was the victim of a head shot from Aaron Rome after making a pass just inside the Vancouver blue line. Rome was given a five-minute major for interference and a game misconduct, and Horton was carried off on a stretcher. Boston didn't capitalize on the long power play but drew inspiration from the play and took it to the Canucks the rest of the way.

GAME 4   JUNE 8   VANCOUVER 0 AT BOSTON 4

The Boston Bruins finished their two-game home stand by doing exactly what Vancouver had done—winning the games on their own ice. They did so with another emphatic victory, making for an interesting lead-up to game five. Vancouver still had home-ice advantage in what was now a best-of-three series, but the Bruins had all the momentum. Again, it was a massive second period that proved the difference as they took a 1–0 lead after twenty minutes and turned it into a game-winning 3–0 lead. They added a goal early in the third, which forced Vancouver coach Alain Vigneault to pull goalie Roberto Luongo and give Cory Schneider his first taste of Stanley Cup finals action.

GAME 5   JUNE 10   BOSTON 0 AT VANCOUVER 1

After five games, this series could now clearly be divided into two—Vancouver home games, all won by the home team with dramatic and late goals, and two lopsided victories in Boston, also by the home side. More particularly, it might be divided into games in which the goalies did, or didn't do, their thing. Vancouver goalie Roberto Luongo was sensational at home, and he struggled miserably on the road. Tim Thomas was incredible in all games, but in the three Vancouver wins he allowed a decisive goal in each as a result of his aggressive style of play. In game five, the hero was Maxim Lapierre, who scored the only goal of the game at 4:35 of the third period. Kevin Bieksa had the puck at the right point and saw Thomas come well out to challenge him as he prepared to shoot. He fired a shot off the end boards that came out the other side of the net, right onto Lapierre's stick. Lapierre fired quickly, and Thomas dove back to snare the puck—but it had already crossed the goal line.

GAME 6   JUNE 13   VANCOUVER 2 AT BOSTON 5

Canucks goalie Roberto Luongo, virtually unbeatable at home, was nothing short of disastrous on the road. Again this night, he was chased from the crease, surrendering three early goals in a 5–2 loss. In all, the Bruins scored four times in 4:14 of the early part of the game and waltzed to an easy victory to force a decisive seventh game. Brad Marchand got some open ice down the right side, and as he barrelled in on goal he roofed a shot over the glove of Luongo at 5:35 to open the scoring. Just 35 seconds later, Milan Lucic knifed a shot that squirted between Luongo's pads and rolled over the goal line. Coach Alain Vigneault might have given his goalie the hook then, because it was clear Luongo wasn't on his game, but he waited one more goal. That came just two minutes later, when an Andrew Ference point shot beat the goalie cleanly. Cory Schneider came in and was sensational the rest of the way.

GAME 7   JUNE 15   BOSTON 4 AT VANCOUVER 0

Patrice Bergeron became just the 25th member of the Triple Gold Club, and he did so in style, scoring two goals in the first 40 minutes to take the Boston Bruins to a 4–0 victory and the Stanley Cup. Brad Marchand also scored twice for the victors. Most amazing, though, the Canucks, the highest-scoring team in the regular season, scored just eight goals in seven games against the sensational Tim Thomas, named Conn Smythe Trophy winner after the game. The Bruins, meanwhile, counted 22 goals against an often-shaky Roberto Luongo (who himself would have joined the TGC with a win). The Boston Bruins were Stanley Cup champions for the first time in 39 years. Bergeron has now won the Stanley Cup, Olympic gold and World Championship gold, the three requirements for Triple Gold Club membership.

2011 AWARD WINNERS—BIOGRAPHIES

DANIEL SEDIN—ART ROSS TROPHY, TED LINDSAY AWARD

Following his brother Henrik's Art Ross Trophy win with one of his own, Daniel ensured that he and his twin made NHL history, becoming the first brothers to win the scoring title in consecutive years. While Henrik was more of a scorer, Daniel was the passer. In 2010–11, for instance, he had only 29 goals but added 75 assists, his 104 total points making him the only player to break the century mark this season. He helped take his team to game seven of the Stanley Cup finals before losing to Boston.

COREY PERRY—HART TROPHY, ROCKET RICHARD TROPHY

Drafted 28th overall by Anaheim in 2003, Perry came by his hardware this year in surprising fashion. He was the only player in the league to hit 50 goals, but playing on a lesser-known team on the West Coast allowed him to fly under the radar for most of the season. Perry had an outstanding junior career, culminating with a Memorial Cup with the London Knights in 2005, just a few months after winning gold with Canada at the World Junior (U20) Championship. His 50 goals was by far his career best (his previous high was 32), and he also won gold with Canada at the 2010 Olympics.

MARTIN ST. LOUIS—LADY BYNG TROPHY

An incredible career started off in the worst way possible—St. Louis, small and skilled, was not even drafted. He signed as a free agent with Calgary in 1998 and was sent to the minors for the rest of the year, and two years later he was with Tampa Bay, his prospects for an NHL career hardly bright. But St. Louis developed and became a sensational player, leading the Lightning to an unlikely Stanley Cup in 2004 and winning the Art Ross and Hart trophies as well as the Lester B. Pearson Award. He then helped Canada win the World Cup in the fall of 2004. In addition to his incredible offensive talent, St. Louis is among the least penalized players in the game and never drops his gloves.

TIM THOMAS—VEZINA TROPHY, CONN SMYTHE TROPHY

An unlikely hero, Thomas reached his peak at age 37, at a time when most goalies have retired. He spent the better part of eight years in the minors and Europe, playing without fanfare or any chance of an NHL career. But the Boston Bruins gave him a chance, and Thomas responded. He not only was named the best goalie in the league, but he also took the Bruins to the Stanley Cup and was named MVP of the playoffs in the process.

JEFF SKINNER—CALDER MEMORIAL TROPHY

The most unlikely Calder winner in recent years, Skinner was the youngest player in the NHL during his rookie season, a season that should have been spent in junior. The trouble was that at Carolina's training camp in September 2010, he was so outstanding the team couldn't send him back to Kitchener to play with kids when his skills were clearly equal to those of grown men in the NHL. Skinner responded with 32 goals and 63 points, and when the Hurricanes didn't qualify for the playoffs, he represented Team Canada at the World Championship in Slovakia.

NICKLAS LIDSTROM—JAMES NORRIS TROPHY

By winning the Norris Trophy for the seventh time in his illustrious career, Lidstrom put himself in rare company. Only Doug Harvey has won as many Norrises, and only the great Bobby Orr has won more (eight). But what is doubly surprising is that Lidstrom did the deed at age 40. Soon after, he signed on with the Red Wings to play in his 20th NHL season. The four-time Stanley Cup champion has had the kind of unique career that will earn him a place in both the Hockey Hall of Fame and IIHF Hall of Fame as soon as he becomes eligible. In the meantime, he will try to improve on his four Stanley Cups and try to tie Orr for another place in history.

IAN LAPERRIERE—BILL MASTERTON TROPHY

Laperriere won the Masterton Trophy for 2010–11 despite not playing a single game all season. He was injured all year because of post-concussion syndrome, the result of blocking shots with his face twice during the previous campaign. In the first instance, he took a shot in the mouth, but after receiving dozens of stitches missed only one period of action and returned in the third period to finish the game. In the 2010 playoffs, he was hit in the cheek and broke his orbital bone, but after missing just a few games, he was back to help the Flyers reach the Cup finals. The two traumatic incidents caught up with him at training camp in September 2010, and he has been off ice ever since, trying to recover. He has refused to retire, but his career remains in jeopardy.

DAN BYLSMA—JACK ADAMS AWARD

Bylsma burst on the scene just a few years ago, taking the Penguins to the Cup finals after being hired midway through the 2007–08 season. But this year he earned coach-of-the-year honours for taking the Penguins to the playoffs while using a lineup that didn't include his two great stars, Sidney Crosby and Evgeni Malkin, for half the season. Somehow Bylsma got even more out of his role players, and the Penguins finished tied for third place overall with 106 points, an amazing total given the lack of star power on the team.

RYAN KESLER—FRANK J. SELKE TROPHY

This was a breakout year for Kesler, who emerged not only as a sensational checking forward but also a power forward who could make significant contributions to the team's offence. Playing in his seventh year with the Vancouver Canucks, he had a career-high 41 goals and was the team's best player in the playoffs as the Canucks marched all the way to game seven of the Cup finals.

ROBERTO LUONGO & CORY SCHNEIDER—WILLIAM M. JENNINGS TROPHY

Luongo and Schneider of Vancouver were first-time winners of the Jennings Trophy, awarded to the goalie(s) for the team that allowed the fewest goals over the course of the season. In all, the Canucks duo gave up only 185 goals in 82 games. Luongo played in the majority of the games (60 to 25), but Schneider was sensational for one stretch when Luongo was injured, and was reliable every time he started to give Luongo a rest during the long season.

DOUG WEIGHT—KING CLANCY MEMORIAL TROPHY

Being honoured in the final season of his 20-year career, Weight won a trophy given to a player for his leadership on the ice and community work away from the rink. Weight played his final three years with the New York Islanders, a persistent back injury finally forcing him to retire. He twice played at the Olympics for the United States (1998, 2002), and he also played at the 2004 World Cup and three World Championships.

WELCOME BACK, WINNIPEG!

KEY DATES IN THE NHL'S RETURN TO WINNIPEG

May 31, 2011	True North Sports and Entertainment buys the Atlanta Thrashers
June 8, 2011	Kevin Cheveldayoff hired as team general manager
June 21, 2011	NHL Board of Governors approves the sale
June 24, 2011	The Winnipeg franchise formally announces its nickname: Jets
June 24, 2011	The Jets select Mark Scheifele seventh overall in the 2011 Entry Draft
June 25, 2011	The Jets hire Claude Noel as head coach

THE WINNIPEG JETS' 2011–12 NHL SCHEDULE

October 9	vs. Montreal
October 13	at Chicago
October 15	at Phoenix
October 17	vs. Pittsburgh
October 19	at Toronto
October 20	at Ottawa
October 22	vs. Carolina
October 24	vs. NY Rangers
October 27	at Philadelphia
October 29	at Tampa Bay
October 31	at Florida
November 3	at NY Islanders
November 5	at New Jersey
November 6	at NY Rangers
November 8	at Buffalo
November 10	vs. Florida
November 12	at Columbus
November 14	vs. Florida
November 17	vs. Washington
November 19	vs. Philadelphia
November 23	at Washington
November 25	at Carolina
November 26	at Boston
November 29	vs. Ottawa
December 1	vs. Phoenix
December 3	vs. New Jersey

December 6	vs. Boston
December 9	vs. Carolina
December 10	at Detroit
December 13	vs. Minnesota
December 15	vs. Washington
December 17	vs. Anaheim
December 20	vs. NY Islanders
December 22	vs. Montreal
December 23	vs. Pittsburgh
December 27	at Colorado
December 29	vs. Los Angeles
December 31	vs. Toronto
January 4	at Montreal
January 5	at Toronto
January 7	at Buffalo
January 10	at Boston
January 12	vs. San Jose
January 14	vs. New Jersey
January 16	at Ottawa
January 17	at New Jersey
January 19	vs. Buffalo
January 21	vs. Florida
January 23	at Carolina
January 24	at NY Rangers
January 31	at Philadelphia
February 2	at Tampa Bay
February 3	at Florida
February 5	at Montreal
February 7	vs. Toronto
February 9	at Washington
February 10	at Pittsburgh
February 14	vs. NY Islanders
February 16	at Minnesota
February 17	vs. Boston
February 19	vs. Colorado
February 21	vs. Philadelphia
February 23	vs. Tampa Bay
February 25	vs. St. Louis
February 27	vs. Edmonton

March 1	vs. Florida
March 5	vs. Buffalo
March 8	at Vancouver
March 9	at Calgary
March 14	vs. Dallas
March 16	vs. Washington
March 18	vs. Carolina
March 20	at Pittsburgh
March 23	at Washington
March 24	at Nashville
March 26	vs. Ottawa
March 28	vs. NY Rangers
March 30	at Carolina
March 31	at Tampa Bay

April 3	at Florida
April 5	at NY Islanders
April 7	vs. Tampa Bay

TOP 10 LISTS

TOP 10 PLAYOFF GAMES OF 2011

1. May 17, 2011—Boston 6, Tampa Bay 5

Abandoning all systems and defence, teams exchanged scoring chances and leads and played thrilling, end-to-end hockey.

2. April 27, 2011—Tampa Bay 1, Pittsburgh 0

Stunning the Consol Energy Center crowd, the Lightning completed a comeback from a 3–1 deficit in the series to eliminate the Penguins, who had an incredible season despite the absence of Sidney Crosby and Evgeni Malkin for its last half.

3. April 20, 2011—Washington 4, NY Rangers 3

A terrible gaffe by Marian Gaborik at his own crease gave Jason Chimera the winner in double overtime and gave the Caps a 3–1 series lead. They eliminated New York three days later.

4. April 26, 2011—Vancouver 2, Chicago 1

Blowing a 3–0 series lead, the Canucks hung on and won game seven at home in OT to defeat the team that had eliminated them from the last two playoffs.

5. May 24, 2011—Vancouver 3, San Jose 2

Kevin Bieksa scored one of the strangest OT goals in Stanley Cup history as his wobbling point shot beat Pekka Rinne when the goalie and virtually every other player on the ice had lost sight of the puck on a shoot-in.

6. May 27, 2011—Boston 1, Tampa Bay 0

Despite an heroic performance from 41-year-old goalie Dwayne Roloson, the Lightning couldn't manage a goal on eventual Conn Smythe Trophy winner Tim Thomas, and the Bruins advanced to the Cup finals.

7. April 21, 2011—Boston 5, Montreal 4

Squandering the 2–0 road lead they had built in Boston, Montreal lost in game four of overtime on a goal by a former Habs player, Michael Ryder, eventually losing the series to Boston in seven games.

8. April 20, 2011—Detroit 6, Phoenix 3

In what many people thought would be the final game of the franchise's tenure in Arizona, the Coyotes were swept aside meekly by the dominant Red Wings, only to find new life in the postseason and linger for another year in the league.

9. June 10, 2011—Vancouver 1, Boston 0

A nearly perfect game from both sides saw the only goal come off a great bank pass from the point, off the other boards and out the back side from Kevin Bieksa to Maxim Lapierre.

10. June 15, 2011—Boston 4, Vancouver 0

Capitalizing on another poor showing from Vancouver goalie Roberto Luongo, the Bruins scored the first goal and cruised to victory behind the goaltending of Tim Thomas to win their first Stanley Cup since 1972.

TOP 10 SUMMER FREE-AGENT SIGNINGS

1. NY Rangers sign Brad Richards to a 9-year, $60-million contract
2. Philadelphia signs goalie Ilya Bryzgalov to a 9-year, $51-million contract
3. Buffalo signs Christian Ehrhoff to a 10-year, $40-million contract
4. Montreal signs Erik Cole to a 4-year, $18-million contract
5. Philadelphia signs Jaromir Jagr to a 1-year, $3.3-million contract
6. Columbus signs James Wisniewski to a 6-year, $33-million contract
7. Florida signs Ed Jovanovski to a 4-year, $16.5-million contract
8. Buffalo signs Ville Leino to a 6-year, $27-million contract
9. Florida signs Tomas Fleischmann to a 4-year, $18-million contract
10. Washington signs Joel Ward to a 4-year, $12-million contract

TOP 10 WINNIPEG JETS GAMES OF 2011–12

1. October 9, 2011—Season and home opener vs. Montreal
2. October 15, 2011—First game against the Phoenix Coyotes, the former Winnipeg Jets and the team long rumoured to be moving back, and whose captain Shane Doan played for the Jets in their final season, 1995–96
3. October 17, 2011—First visit by Sidney Crosby (assuming he's healthy by this time) and the Pittsburgh Penguins
4. October 19, 2011—First visit by the Toronto Maple Leafs, a team with much historical relevance in Winnipeg
5. November 26, 2011—First game against Stanley Cup champion Boston Bruins
6. February 27, 2012—First game against the Edmonton Oilers, the Jets' greatest playoff nemesis in the 1980s
7. December 3, 2011—First game against New Jersey, whose top star, Ilya Kovalchuk, was the only bright spot for a decade with the Atlanta Thrashers
8. October 13, 2011—First visit by the Chicago Blackhawks, whose captain, Jonathan Toews, is a native Winnipegger
9. October 27, 2011—First game at Philadelphia, whose goalie, Ilya Bryzgalov, played 2010–11 with Phoenix and who made headlines when it seemed the Coyotes might return to Winnipeg by declaring he would never sign with the Jets

10. December 13, 2011—First visit by Minnesota, whose star player, Dany Heatley, caused the death of Dan Snyder while both players were in Atlanta

TOP 10 TEAM CANADA MOMENTS OF 2010–11

1. Hayley Wickenheiser awarded the Order of Canada, July 1, 2011
2. Eighteen-year-old Jeff Skinner had a goal and two assists vs. France at the World Championship, May 1, 2011
3. Three-time all-star team forward Rick Nash accepted the invitation to captain Canada's World Championship team
4. Canada's juniors reached the gold-medal game for the 10th straight year
5. Canadian fans flocked to Buffalo and Lewiston to watch the U20 championship between Christmas and New Year's
6. Canada's U18 men staged an incredible comeback in the semifinals, trailing the U.S. 4–1 late in the third before losing 5–4 in overtime
7. Canada hammered the U.S. 4–1 in the U20 semifinals to earn a measure of vindication for the gold-medal loss the previous year
8. Canada's women overcame deficits of 1–0 and 2–1 to force overtime, only to lose gold medal to archrival United States at Women's World Championship
9. Joe Nieuwendyk, Doug Gilmour, Ed Belfour—all with Team Canada championship success—inducted into the Hockey Hall of Fame
10. Melody Davidson and Wickenheiser led a team of 15 people to act as ambassadors and mentors in the IIHF's most ambitious attempt to grow and support women's hockey

TOP 10 MOST LIKELY MEMBERS OF CANADA'S MEN'S OLYMPIC TEAM IN 2014

1. Sidney Crosby
2. Jonathan Toews
3. Steve Stamkos
4. Shea Weber
5. Carey Price
6. Corey Perry
7. Eric Staal
8. Ryan Getzlaf
9. Drew Doughty
10. Kris Letang

NHL TEAM INFORMATION, 2011–12

ANAHEIM DUCKS

(name changed from Mighty Ducks of Anaheim on June 22, 2006)
First Game Played: October 8, 1993
Detroit Red Wings 7 at Mighty Ducks of Anaheim 2
Nickname Provenance: Owners, Disney, named team after a popular kids' movie, *The Mighty Ducks* (1992)
Mascot: Wild Thing
Arena History: Arrowhead Pond, 1993–2006; Honda Center, 2006–present (capacity 17,174)
Retired Numbers: none
Hall of Famers: Players (1): Jari Kurri
Website: www.anaheimducks.com
Minor League Affiliate(s): Syracuse Crunch (AHL), Elmira Jackals (ECHL—shared with Ottawa)
Stanley Cups: (1) 2007
Hosted All-Star Game: none
1st Overall Draft Choices: none

BOSTON BRUINS

First Game Played: December 1, 1924
Montreal Maroons 1 at Boston Bruins 2
Nickname Provenance: Named by owner Art Ross for the brown bear
Mascot: Blades (b. October 9, 2000)
Arena History: Boston Arena, 1924–28; Boston Garden, 1928–95; FleetCenter, 1995–2003; TD Banknorth Garden (same building as the FleetCenter), 2005–2009; TD Garden, 2009–present (capacity 17,565)
Retired Numbers: Eddie Shore (2), Lionel Hitchman (3), Bobby Orr (4), Dit Clapper (5), Phil Esposito (7), Cam Neely (8), Johnny Bucyk (9), Milt Schmidt (15), Terry O'Reilly (24), Ray Bourque (77)
Hall of Famers: Players (47): Marty Barry, Bobby Bauer, Leo Boivin, Ray Bourque, Frank Brimsek, Johnny Bucyk, Billy Burch, Gerry Cheevers, Dit Clapper, Sprague Cleghorn, Paul Coffey, Roy Conacher, Bun Cook, Bill Cowley, Cy Denneny, Woody Dumart, Phil Esposito, Fern Flaman, Frank Fredrickson, Harvey Jackson, Tom Johnson, Duke Keats, Guy Lapointe, Brian Leetch, Harry Lumley, Mickey MacKay, Sylvio Mantha, Joe Mullen, Cam Neely, Harry Oliver, Bobby Orr, Bernie Parent, Brad Park, Jacques Plante, Babe Pratt, Bill Quackenbush, Jean Ratelle, Art Ross (inducted as Player, associated with Boston as Builder), Terry Sawchuk, Milt Schmidt, Eddie Shore, Babe Siebert, Hooley Smith, Allan Stanley, Nels Stewart, Tiny Thompson, Cooney Weiland; Builders (6):

Charles Adams, Weston Adams, Walter Brown, Bud Poile (played with Boston, inducted as Builder), Glen Sather (played with Boston, inducted as Builder), Harry Sinden
Website: www.bostonbruins.com
Minor League Affiliate(s): Providence Bruins (AHL), Reading Royals (ECHL—shared with Toronto)
Stanley Cups: (6) 1928–29, 1938–39, 1940–41, 1969–70, 1971–72, 2010–11
Hosted All-Star Game: (2) 1971, 1996
1st Overall Draft Choices: 1982 (Gord Kluzak), 1997 (Joe Thornton)

BUFFALO SABRES

First Game Played: October 10, 1970
Buffalo Sabres 2 at Pittsburgh Penguins 1
Nickname Provenance: a contest determined the name Sabres
Mascot: Sabre-Tooth
Arena History: Memorial Auditorium ("The Aud"), 1970–96; Marine Midland Bank Arena, 1996–2000; HSBC Arena (same building as the Marine Midland Bank Arena), 2000–present (capacity 18,690)
Retired Numbers: Tim Horton (2), Rick Martin (7), Gilbert Perreault (11), Rene Robert (14), Pat LaFontaine (16), Danny Gare (18)
Hall of Famers: Players (9): Dick Duff, Doug Gilmour, Tim Horton, Gilbert Perreault, Dale Hawerchuk, Clark Gillies, Grant Fuhr, Pat LaFontaine, Marcel Pronovost (inducted as Player, associated with Buffalo as Builder); Builders (4): Scotty Bowman, Punch Imlach, Seymour Knox III, Roger Neilson
Website: www.sabres.com
Minor League Affiliate(s): (AHL)
Stanley Cups: none
Hosted All-Star Game: 1978
1st Overall Draft Choices: 1970 (Gilbert Perreault), 1987 (Pierre Turgeon)

CALGARY FLAMES

First Game Played:
As Atlanta Flames: October 7, 1972
Atlanta Flames 3 at New York Islanders 2
As Calgary Flames: October 9, 1980
Quebec Nordiques 5 at Calgary Flames 5
Nickname Provenance: Flames was chosen by contest, representative of Atlanta during the Civil War, when much of it was burned to the ground
Mascot: Harvey the Hound
Arena History: The Omni (Atlanta), 1972–80; Stampede Corral, 1980–83; Olympic Saddledome, 1983–95; Canadian Airlines Saddledome, 1995–2001; Pengrowth

Saddledome, 2001–2010; Scotiabank Saddledome, 2010–present (same building as previous three Saddledomes—capacity 19,289)
Retired Numbers: Lanny McDonald (9), Mike Vernon (30)
Hall of Famers: Players (7): Lanny McDonald, Joe Mullen, Grant Fuhr, Brett Hull, Al MacInnis, Doug Gilmour, Joe Nieuwendyk; Builders (3): Cliff Fletcher, Harley Hotchkiss, Daryl "Doc" Seaman
Website: www.calgaryflames.com
Minor League Affiliate(s): Abbotsford Heat (AHL), Utah Grizzlies (ECHL)
Stanley Cups: (1) 1988–89
Hosted All-Star Game: 1985
1st Overall Draft Choices: none

CAROLINA HURRICANES

First Game Played:
As Hartford Whalers: October 11, 1979
Hartford Whalers 1 at Minnesota North Stars 4
As Carolina Hurricanes: October 1, 1997
Carolina Hurricanes 2 at Tampa Bay Lightning 4
Nickname Provenance: Whalers adopted because it contained the letters of the WHA and it was emblematic of the region
Mascot: Stormy
Arena History: Springfield Civic Center (Springfield, Mass.), 1979–80; Hartford Civic Center (Hartford), 1980–97; Greensboro Coliseum, 1997–99; Raleigh Entertainment & Sports Arena, 1999–2003; RBC Center (same building as the Raleigh Entertainment & Sports Arena), 2003–present (capacity 18,730)
Retired Numbers: Glen Wesley (2), Ron Francis (10), Rod Brind'Amour (17)
Hall of Famers: Players (6): Paul Coffey (Hartford/Carolina), Gordie Howe (Hartford), Mark Howe (Hartford), Bobby Hull (Hartford), Dave Keon (Hartford), Ron Francis (Hartford/Carolina)
Website: www.carolinahurricanes.com
Minor League Affiliate(s): Charlotte Checkers (AHL), Florida Everblades (ECHL—shared with Tampa Bay)
Stanley Cups: 2005–06
Hosted All-Star Game: (2) 1986 (as Hartford Whalers), 2011
1st Overall Draft Choices: none

CHICAGO BLACKHAWKS

First Game Played: November 17, 1926
Toronto St. Pats 1 at Chicago Blackhawks 4
Nickname Provenance: (spelling changed from "Black Hawks" to "Blackhawks" in 1986)

Mascot: Tommy the Hawk
Arena History: Chicago Coliseum, 1926–29, 1932; Chicago Stadium, 1929–94; United Center, 1995–present (opening of United Center delayed by disruption of 1994–95 NHL season, capacity 20,500)
Retired Numbers: Glenn Hall (1), Keith Magnuson (3), Pierre Pilote (3), Bobby Hull (9), Denis Savard (18), Stan Mikita (21), Tony Esposito (35)
Hall of Famers: Players (41): Sid Abel, Ed Belfour, Doug Bentley, Max Bentley, Georges Boucher, Frank Brimsek, Billy Burch, Paul Coffey, Lionel Conacher, Roy Conacher, Art Coulter, Babe Dye, Phil Esposito, Tony Esposito, Bill Gadsby, Charlie Gardiner, Herb Gardiner, Doug Gilmour, Michel Goulet, Glenn Hall, George Hay, Bobby Hull, Duke Keats, Hugh Lehman, Ted Lindsay, Harry Lumley, Mickey MacKay, Stan Mikita, Howie Morenz, Bill Mosienko, Bert Olmstead, Bobby Orr, Pierre Pilote, Denis Savard, Earl Seibert, Clint Smith, Allan Stanley, Barney Stanley, Jack Stewart, Carl Voss (played for Chicago, inducted as Builder), Harry Watson; Builders (12): Al Arbour, Emile Francis (played for Chicago, inducted as Builder), Dick Irvin (played for Chicago, inducted as Builder), Tommy Ivan, John Mariucci (also played for Chicago), Major Frederic McLaughlin, James Norris, James Norris, Jr., Rudy Pilous, Bud Poile (played for Chicago, inducted as Builder), Arthur Wirtz, William Wirtz
Website: www.chicagoblackhawks.com
Minor League Affiliate(s): Rockford IceHogs (AHL), Toledo Walleye (ECHL—shared with Detroit)
Stanley Cups: (4) 1933–34, 1937–38, 1960–61, 2009–10
Hosted All-Star Game: (4) 1948, 1961, 1974, 1991
1st Overall Draft Choices: 2007 (Patrick Kane)

COLORADO AVALANCHE

First Game Played:
As Quebec Nordiques: October 10, 1979
Atlanta Flames 5 at Quebec Nordiques 3
As Colorado Avalanche: October 6, 1995
Detroit Red Wings 2 at Colorado Avalanche 3
Nickname Provenance: Team owners polled fans. Out of eight names offered, Avalanche was the most popular.
Mascot: Howler
Arena History: McNichols Sports Arena, 1995–99; Pepsi Center, 1999–present (capacity 18,007)
Retired Numbers: J-C Tremblay (3), Marc Tardif (8), Michel Goulet (16), Joe Sakic (19), Peter Stastny (26), Patrick Roy (33), Ray Bourque (77)
Hall of Famers: Players (6): Ray Bourque, Patrick Roy, Michel Goulet (Quebec), Jari Kurri, Guy Lafleur (Quebec), Peter Stastny (Quebec)
Website: www.coloradoavalanche.com

Minor League Affiliate(s): Lake Erie Monsters (AHL), Tulsa Oilers (CHL)
Stanley Cups: (2) 1995–96, 2000–01
Hosted All-Star Game: 2001
1st Overall Draft Choices: 1989 (Mats Sundin—Quebec Nordiques), 1990 (Owen Nolan—Quebec), 1991 (Eric Lindros—Quebec)

COLUMBUS BLUE JACKETS

First Game Played: October 7, 2000
Chicago Blackhawks 5 at Columbus Blue Jackets 3
Nickname Provenance: Reflects patriotism and history of the Civil War
Mascot: Stinger
Arena History: Nationwide Arena, 2000–present (capacity 18,136)
Retired Numbers: none
Hall of Famers: none
Website: www. bluejackets.com
Minor League Affiliate(s): Springfield Falcons (AHL), Chicago Express (ECHL)
Stanley Cups: none
Hosted All-Star Game: none
1st Overall Draft Choices: 2002 (Rick Nash)

DALLAS STARS

First Game Played:
As Minnesota North Stars: October 11, 1967
Minnesota North Stars 2 at St. Louis Blues 2
As Dallas Stars: October 5, 1993
Detroit Red Wings 4 at Dallas Stars 6
Nickname Provenance: Shortening of North Stars, consistent with Texas as the Lone Star state
Mascot: none
Arena History: Metropolitan Sports Center (also known as the Met Center), 1967–93; Reunion Arena, 1993–2001; American Airlines Center, 2001–present (capacity 18,532)
Retired Numbers: Neal Broten (7), Bill Goldsworthy (8), Bill Masterton (19)
Hall of Famers: Players (9): Mike Gartner (Minnesota), Harry Howell (Minnesota), Brett Hull, Larry Murphy (Minnesota), Gump Worsley (Minnesota), Leo Boivin (Minnesota), Dino Ciccarelli (Minnesota), Ed Belfour, Joe Nieuwendyk; Builders (3): Herb Brooks (coached Minnesota), Glen Sather (played for University of Minnesota), John Mariucci
Website: www.dallasstars.com
Minor League Affiliate(s): Allen Americans (CHL), Idaho Steelheads (ECHL), Texas Stars (AHL)

Stanley Cups: (1) 1998–99
Hosted All-Star Game: (2) 1972 (as North Stars); 2007
1st Overall Draft Choices: 1978 (Bobby Smith—Minnesota North Stars), 1983
(Brian Lawton—Minnesota), 1988 (Mike Modano—Minnesota)

DETROIT RED WINGS

First Game Played:
As Detroit Cougars: November 18, 1926
Boston Bruins 2 at Detroit Cougars 0
As Detroit Falcons: November 13, 1930
New York Rangers 0 at Detroit Falcons 1
As Detroit Red Wings: November 10, 1932
Chicago Blackhawks 1 at Detroit Red Wings 3
Nickname Provenance: Owner James Norris, a Montreal native, used the Winged Wheel
from his hometown team and combined it with Detroit's place in America as a car-
making centre
Mascot: Al the Octopus
Arena History: Windsor Arena (Border Cities Arena), 1926–27; Olympia, 1929–79;
Joe Louis Arena, 1979–present (capacity 20,066)
Retired Numbers: Terry Sawchuk (1), Ted Lindsay (7), Gordie Howe (9), Alex
Delvecchio (10), Sid Abel (12), Steve Yzerman (19)
Hall of Famers: Players (53): Sid Abel, Jack Adams (inducted as Player, associated
with Detroit as builder), Marty Barry, Andy Bathgate, Johnny Bucyk, Dino Ciccarelli,
Paul Coffey, Charlie Conacher, Roy Conacher, Alec Connell, Alex Delvecchio, Marcel
Dionne, Bernie Federko, Slava Fetisov, Frank Foyston, Frank Fredrickson, Bill Gadsby,
Ed Giacomin, Ebbie Goodfellow, Glenn Hall, Doug Harvey, George Hay, Harry Holmes,
Gordie Howe, Mark Howe, Syd Howe, Brett Hull, Duke Keats, Red Kelly, Brian Kilrea
(played for Detroit, inducted as Builder), Igor Larionov, Herbie Lewis, Ted Lindsay,
Harry Lumley, Frank Mahovlich, Larry Murphy, Reg Noble, Brad Park, Bud Poile
(played for Detroit, inducted as Builder), Marcel Pronovost, Bill Quackenbush, Luc
Robitaille, Borje Salming, Terry Sawchuk, Earl Seibert, Darryl Sittler, Jack Stewart,
Tiny Thompson, Norm Ullman, Jack Walker, Harry Watson, Cooney Weiland, Steve
Yzerman; Builders (9): Al Arbour (played for Detroit, inducted as Builder), Leo Boivin
(played for Detroit, inducted as Builder), Scotty Bowman, Jimmy Devellano, Tommy
Ivan, Bruce Norris, James Norris, James Norris, Jr., Carl Voss (played for Detroit,
inducted as Builder)
Website: www.detroitredwings.com
Minor League Affiliate(s): Grand Rapids Griffins (AHL), Toledo Walleye
(ECHL—shared with Chicago)
Stanley Cups: (11) 1935–36, 1936–37, 1942–43, 1949–50, 1951–52, 1953–54,
1954–55, 1996–97, 1997–98, 2002–02, 2007–08

Hosted All-Star Game: (5) 1950, 1952, 1954, 1955, 1980
1st Overall Draft Choices: 1977 (Dale McCourt), 1986 (Joe Murphy)

EDMONTON OILERS

First Game Played: October 10, 1979
Edmonton Oilers 2 at Chicago Black Hawks 4
Nickname Provenance: From Alberta Oilers and later Edmonton Oilers of WHA, to refer to Alberta's place as an oil capital in Canada
Mascot: none
Arena History: Northlands Coliseum, 1979–99; Skyreach Centre, 1999–2003; Rexall Place, 2005–present (all three are the same building, capacity 16,839)
Retired Numbers: Al Hamilton (3), Paul Coffey (7), Glenn Anderson (9) Mark Messier (11), Jari Kurri (17), Grant Fuhr (31), Wayne Gretzky (99—leaguewide recognition)
Hall of Famers: Players (6): Glenn Anderson, Paul Coffey, Grant Fuhr, Wayne Gretzky, Jari Kurri, Mark Messier; Builders (1): Glen Sather
Website: www.edmontonoilers.com
Minor League Affiliate(s): Oklahoma City Barons (AHL), Stockton Thunder (ECHL—shared with San Jose)
Stanley Cups: (5) 1983–84, 1984–85, 1986–87, 1987–88, 1989–90
Hosted All-Star Game: (1) 1989
1st Overall Draft Choices: 2010 (Taylor Hall), 2011 (Ryan Nugent-Hopkins)

FLORIDA PANTHERS

First Game Played: October 6, 1993
Florida Panthers 4 at Chicago Blackhawks 4
Nickname Provenance: Named for the animal, which is common in Florida
Mascot: Stanley C. Panther
Arena History: Miami Arena, 1993–99; National Car Rental Center, 1999–2002; Office Depot Center, 2002–03; BankAtlantic Center, 2005–present (previous three are the same building, capacity 19,250)
Retired Numbers: none
Hall of Famers: Players (4): Ed Belfour, Dino Ciccarelli, Igor Larionov, Joe Nieuwendyk
Website: www.floridapanthers.com
Minor League Affiliate(s): San Antonio Rampage (AHL), Cincinnati Cyclones (ECHL—shared with Nashville)
Stanley Cups: none
Hosted All-Star Game: (1) 2003
1st Overall Draft Choices: 1994 (Ed Jovanovski)

LOS ANGELES KINGS

First Game Played: October 14, 1967
Philadelphia Flyers 2 at Los Angeles Kings 4
Nickname Provenance: Named by owner Jack Kent Cooke to give the team a royal (i.e., important) sound to it
Mascot: Bailey
Arena History: Long Beach Arena, October 1967; Los Angeles Sports Arena, November–December 1967; The Forum, 1967–88; Great Western Forum, 1988–99 (same building as The Forum); Staples Center, 1999–present (capacity 18,118)
Retired Numbers: Marcel Dionne (16), Dave Taylor (18), Luc Robitaille (20), Rogie Vachon (30), Wayne Gretzky (99—leaguewide recognition)
Hall of Famers: Players (14): Paul Coffey, Marcel Dionne, Dick Duff, Grant Fuhr, Wayne Gretzky, Harry Howell, Jari Kurri, Larry Murphy, Bob Pulford, Larry Robinson, Luc Robitaille, Terry Sawchuk, Steve Shutt, Billy Smith; Builders (1): Brian Kilrea (played for Los Angeles, inducted as Builder)
Website: www.lakings.com
Minor League Affiliate(s): Manchester Monarchs (AHL), Ontario Reign (ECHL)
Stanley Cups: none
Hosted All-Star Game: (2) 1981, 2002
1st Overall Draft Choices: none

MINNESOTA WILD

First Game Played: October 6, 2000
Minnesota Wild 1 at Mighty Ducks of Anaheim 3
Nickname Provenance: Selected by fan contest
Mascot: Nordy
Arena History: Xcel Energy Center, 2000–present (capacity 18,064)
Retired Numbers: none
Hall of Famers: none
Website: www.wild.com
Minor League Affiliate(s): Houston Aeros (AHL), Bakersfield Condors (ECHL)
Stanley Cups: none
Hosted All-Star Game: (1) 2004
1st Overall Draft Choices: none

MONTREAL CANADIENS

First Game Played:
In NHA: January 19, 1910
Montreal Canadiens 4 at Renfrew Millionaires 9

In NHL: December 19, 1917

Ottawa Senators 4 at Montreal Canadiens 7

Nickname Provenance: As a Canadian team based in Quebec, simply called Canadians in French (they are also known as "the Habs," short for "*les habitants*," a name given to the early settlers of the province)

Mascot: Youppi

Arena History: Westmount Arena, 1909–1918; Jubilee Arena, 1918–20; Mount Royal Arena, 1920–24; Montreal Forum, 1924–96 (refurbished in 1968); Molson Centre, 1996–2002; Bell Centre, 2002–present (same building as Molson Centre, capacity 21,273)

Retired Numbers: Jacques Plante (1), Doug Harvey (2), Emile "Butch" Bouchard (3), Jean Beliveau (4), Bernie Geoffrion (5), Howie Morenz (7), Maurice Richard (9), Guy Lafleur (10), Yvan Cournoyer (12), Dickie Moore (12), Henri Richard (16), Elmer Lach (16), Serge Savard (18), Larry Robinson (19), Bob Gainey (23), Ken Dryden (29), Patrick Roy (33)

Hall of Famers: Players (51): Marty Barry, Harry Cameron, Gord Drillon, Dick Duff, Tony Esposito, Rod Langway, Roy Worters, Dick Irvin (inducted as Player, associated with Montreal as Builder), Howie Morenz, Georges Vezina, Aurel Joliat, Newsy Lalonde, Joe Malone, Sprague Cleghorn, Herb Gardiner, Sylvio Mantha, Joe Hall, George Hainsworth, Maurice Richard, Jack Laviolette, Didier Pitre, Bill Durnan, Babe Siebert, Toe Blake, Emile Bouchard, Elmer Lach, Ken Reardon, Tom Johnson, Jean Beliveau, Bernie Geoffrion, Doug Harvey, Dickie Moore, Jacques Plante, Henri Richard, Patrick Roy, Gump Worsley, Frank Mahovlich, Yvan Cournoyer, Ken Dryden, Jacques Lemaire, Bert Olmstead, Serge Savard, Jacques Laperriere, Guy Lafleur, Buddy O'Connor, Bob Gainey, Guy Lapointe, Steve Shutt, Larry Robinson, Denis Savard, Doug Gilmour; Builders (12): Cliff Fletcher, William Northey, Hon. Donat Raymond, Frank Selke, Ambrose O'Brien, Leo Dandurand, Tommy Gorman, Hon. Hartland de Montarville Molson, Joseph Cattarinich, Sam Pollock, Scotty Bowman, Glen Sather (played with Montreal, inducted as Builder)

Website: www.canadiens.com

Minor League Affiliate(s): Hamilton Bulldogs (AHL)

Stanley Cups: (23) 1923–24, 1929–30, 1930–31, 1943–44, 1945–46, 1952–53, 1955–56, 1956–57, 1957–58, 1958–59, 1959–60, 1964–65, 1065–66, 1967–68, 1968–69, 1970–71, 1972–73, 1975–76, 1976–77, 1977–78, 1978–79, 1985–86, 1992–93

Hosted All-Star Game: (12) 1953, 1956, 1957, 1958, 1959, 1960, 1965, 1967, 1969, 1975, 1993, 2009

1st Overall Draft Choices: 1969 (Rejean Houle), 1971 (Guy Lafleur), 1980 (Doug Wickenheiser)

NASHVILLE PREDATORS

First Game Played: October 10, 1998
Florida Panthers 1 at Nashville Predators 0
Nickname Provenance: selected by fans
Mascot: Gnash
Arena History: Nashville Arena, 1998–99, 2007; Gaylord Entertainment Center, 1999–2007; Sommet Centre, 2007–2010; Bridgestone Arena, 2010–present (all refer to the same building, capacity 17,113)
Retired Numbers: none
Hall of Famers: none
Website: www.nashvillepredators.com
Minor League Affiliate(s): Milwaukee Admirals (AHL), Cincinnati Cyclones (ECHL—shared with Florida)
Stanley Cups: none
Hosted All-Star Game: none
1st Overall Draft Choices: none

NEW JERSEY DEVILS

First Game Played:
As Kansas City Scouts: October 9, 1974
Kansas City Scouts 2 at Toronto Maple Leafs 6
As Colorado Rockies: October 5, 1976
Toronto Maple Leafs 2 at Colorado Rockies 4
As New Jersey Devils: October 5, 1982
Pittsburgh Penguins 3 at New Jersey Devils 3
Nickname Provenance: Selected by fans in reference to legend of a demonic baby produced by one Mrs. Leeds in 1735, her 13th child
Mascot: The Devil
Arena History: Kemper Arena (Kansas City), 1974–76; McNichols Sports Arena (Colorado), 1976–82; Brendan Byrne Arena, 1982–83; Byrne Meadowlands Arena, 1983–92 (same building as Brendan Byrne Arena); Meadowlands Arena (same building as Byrne Meadowlands Arena), 1992–96; Continental Airlines Arena (same building as Meadowlands Arena), 1996–2007; Prudential Center, 2007–present (capacity 17,625)
Retired Numbers: Ken Daneyko (3), Scott Stevens (4)
Hall of Famers: Players (7): Slava Fetisov, Doug Gilmour, Igor Larionov, Lanny McDonald (Colorado Rockies), Joe Nieuwendyk, Peter Stastny, Scott Stevens; Builders (2): Herb Brooks, Lou Lamoriello
Website: www.newjerseydevils.com
Minor League Affiliate(s): Albany Devils (AHL), Trenton Devils (ECHL)
Stanley Cups: (3) 1994–95, 1999–2000, 2002–03

Hosted All-Star Game: (1) 1984
1st Overall Draft Choices: 1979 (Rob Ramage—Colorado Rockies)

NEW YORK ISLANDERS

First Game Played: October 7, 1972
Atlanta Flames 3 at New York Islanders 2
Nickname Provenance: Named, simply, because the team is located on Long Island, New York
Mascot: none
Arena History: Nassau Veterans' Memorial Coliseum, 1972–present (capacity 16,234)
Retired Numbers: Denis Potvin (5), Clark Gillies (9), Bryan Trottier (19), Mike Bossy (22), Bob Nystrom (23), Billy Smith (31)
Hall of Famers: Players (6): Mike Bossy, Pat LaFontaine, Denis Potvin, Billy Smith, Bryan Trottier, Clark Gillies; Builders (2): Al Arbour, Bill Torrey
Website: www.newyorkislanders.com
Minor League Affiliate(s): Bridgeport Sound Tigers (AHL), Kalamazoo Wings (ECHL), Odessa Jackalopes (CHL)
Stanley Cups: (4) 1979–80, 1980–81, 1981–82, 1982–83
Hosted All-Star Game: (1) 1983
1st Overall Draft Choices: 1972 (Billy Harris), 1973 (Denis Potvin), 2000 (Rick DiPietro), 2009 (John Tavares)

NEW YORK RANGERS

First Game Played: November 16, 1926
Montreal Maroons 0 at New York Rangers 1
Nickname Provenance: Emerged when sportswriters in New York called the new franchise Tex's Rangers, in reference to Tex Rickard, the president of Madison Square Garden and the man who assembled the executive for the team in 1926
Mascot: none
Arena History: Madison Square Garden, 1926–68; Madison Square Garden, 1968–present (newly built, capacity 18,200)
Retired Numbers: Ed Giacomin (1), Brian Leetch (2), Harry Howell (3), Rod Gilbert (7), Andy Bathgate (9), Adam Graves (9) Mark Messier (11), Mike Richter (35)
Hall of Famers: Players (47): Glenn Anderson, Dick Duff, Howie Morenz, Lester Patrick, Bill Cook, Frank Boucher, Ching Johnson, Babe Siebert, Earl Seibert, Doug Bentley, Max Bentley, Babe Pratt, Neil Colville, Bryan Hextall, Bill Gadsby, Terry Sawchuk, Bernie Geoffrion, Doug Harvey, Charlie Rayner, Art Coulter, Johnny Bower, Tim Horton, Andy Bathgate, Jacques Plante, Harry Howell, Lynn Patrick, Pat LaFontaine, Harry Lumley, Gump Worsley, Allan Stanley, Rod Gilbert, Phil Esposito, Jean Ratelle, Ed Giacomin, Guy Lafleur, Buddy O'Connor, Brad Park, Clint Smith,

Marcel Dionne, Edgar Laprade, Bun Cook, Wayne Gretzky, Mike Gartner, Jari Kurri, Mark Messier, Brian Leetch, Luc Robitaille; Builders (9): Herb Brooks, Bud Poile (played with Rangers, inducted as Builder), Emile Francis (also played for Rangers), William Jennings, John Kilpatrick, Roger Neilson, Craig Patrick, Glen Sather (played with Rangers, inducted as Builder), Carl Voss (played with Rangers, inducted as Builder)
Website: www.newyorkrangers.com
Minor League Affiliate(s): Connecticut Whale (AHL), Greenville Road Warriors (ECHL—shared with Philadelphia)
Stanley Cups: (4) 1927–28, 1932–33, 1939–40, 1993–94
Hosted All-Star Game: (2) 1973, 1994
1st Overall Draft Choices: none

OTTAWA SENATORS

First Game Played: October 8, 1992
Montreal Canadiens 3 at Ottawa Senators 5
Nickname Provenance: From original team of same name from 1917–34
Mascot: Spartacat
Arena History: Civic Centre, 1992–96; Palladium, 1996; Corel Centre, 1996–2006; Scotiabank Place, 2006–present (same building as Palladium and Corel Centre, capacity 19,153)
Retired Numbers: Frank Finnigan (8)
Hall of Famers: none
Website: www.ottawasenators.com
Minor League Affiliate(s): Binghamton Senators (AHL), Elmira Jackals (ECHL—shared with Anaheim)
Stanley Cups: none
Hosted All-Star Game: (1) 2012
1st Overall Draft Choices: 1993 (Alexandre Daigle), 1995 (Bryan Berard), 1996 (Chris Phillips)

PHILADELPHIA FLYERS

First Game Played: October 11, 1967
Philadelphia Flyers 1 at Oakland Seals 5
Nickname Provenance: Named by a nine-year-old in a fan contest
Mascot: none
Arena History: The Spectrum, 1967–96; CoreStates Center, 1996–98; First Union Center, 1998–2003 (same building as CoreStates Center); Wachovia Center, 2003–2010 (same building as First Union Center); Wells Fargo Center, 2010–present (same building as Wachovia Center, capacity 19,537)
Retired Numbers: Bernie Parent (1), Barry Ashbee (4), Bill Barber (7), Bobby Clarke (16)

Hall of Famers: Players (8): Paul Coffey, Bernie Parent, Bobby Clarke, Bill Barber, Dale Hawerchuk, Mark Howe, Darryl Sittler, Allan Stanley; Builders (2): Ed Snider, Keith Allen
Website: www.philadelphiaflyers.com
Minor League Affiliate(s): Adirondack Phantoms (AHL), Greenville Road Warriors (ECHL—shared with NY Rangers)
Stanley Cups: (2) 1973–74, 1974–75
Hosted All-Star Game: (2) 1976, 1992
1st Overall Draft Choices: 1975 (Mel Bridgman)

PHOENIX COYOTES

First Game Played:
As Winnipeg Jets: October 10, 1979
Winnipeg Jets 2 at Pittsburgh Penguins 4
As Phoenix Coyotes: October 5, 1996
Phoenix Coyotes 0 at Hartford Whalers 1
Nickname Provenance: Logo depicts a Kachina coyote, indigenous to the region
Mascot: Howler
Arena History: Winnipeg Arena (Winnipeg), 1979–96; America West Arena, 1996–98; Cellular One Ice Den (same building as America West Arena), 1998–99; America West Arena, 1999–2000; Alltel Ice Den, 2000–03 (same building as America West Arena); Glendale Arena, 2003–2008; Jobing.com Arena (same building as Glendale Arena, capacity 17,799)
Retired Numbers: Bobby Hull (9—Winnipeg), Dale Hawerchuk (10—Winnipeg), Thomas Steen (25—Winnipeg), Teppo Numminen (27)
Hall of Famers: Players (5): Mike Gartner, Brett Hull, Bobby Hull (Winnipeg), Dale Hawerchuk (Winnipeg), Serge Savard (Winnipeg)
Website: www.phoenixcoyotes.com
Minor League Affiliate(s): Portland Pirates (AHL), Las Vegas Wranglers (ECHL), Arizona Sundogs (CHL)
Stanley Cups: none
Hosted All-Star Game: none
1st Overall Draft Choices: 1981 (Dale Hawerchuk—Winnipeg Jets)

PITTSBURGH PENGUINS

First Game Played: October 11, 1967
Montreal Canadiens 2 at Pittsburgh Penguins 1
Nickname Provenance: After the Pittsburgh arena opened in 1961, it was dubbed "The Igloo" for its shape. As a result, when Pittsburgh was awarded an NHL team in 1967, owners opted for a nickname compatible with "Igloo" and decided on "Penguins."
Mascot: Iceburgh

Arena History: Civic Arena ("The Igloo"), 1967–2000; Mellon Arena, 2000–2010 (same building as Civic Arena); Consol Energy Center, 2010–present (capacity 18,087)
Retired Numbers: Michel Briere (21), Mario Lemieux (66)
Hall of Famers: Players (11): Leo Boivin, Paul Coffey, Tim Horton, Red Kelly (inducted as Player, associated with Pittsburgh as Builder), Andy Bathgate, Mario Lemieux, Larry Murphy, Bryan Trottier, Joe Mullen, Ron Francis, Luc Robitaille; Builders (4): Scotty Bowman, Bob Johnson, Craig Patrick, Glen Sather (played for Pittsburgh, inducted as Builder)
Website: www.pittsburghpenguins.com
Minor League Affiliate(s): Wilkes-Barre/Scranton Penguins (AHL), Wheeling Nailers (ECHL)
Stanley Cups: (3) 1990–91, 1991–92, 2008–09
Hosted All-Star Game: 1990
1st Overall Draft Choices: 1984 (Mario Lemieux), 2003 (Marc-Andre Fleury), 2005 (Sidney Crosby)

ST. LOUIS BLUES

First Game Played: October 11, 1967
Minnesota North Stars 2 at St. Louis Blues 2
Nickname Provenance: Named to remember the city's place in the history of music
Mascot: Louie
Arena History: St. Louis Arena, 1967–94; Kiel Center, 1994–2000; Savvis Center, 2000–2008, Scottrade Center, 2008–present (same building as Kiel Center and Savvis Center, capacity 19,022)
Retired Numbers: Al MacInnis (2), Bob Gassoff (3), Barclay Plager (8), Brian Sutter (11), Brett Hull (16), Bernie Federko (24)
Hall of Famers: Players (16): Glenn Anderson, Grant Fuhr, Bernie Federko, Doug Gilmour, Dale Hawerchuk, Joe Mullen, Wayne Gretzky, Peter Stastny, Guy Lapointe, Jacques Plante, Glenn Hall, Dickie Moore, Doug Harvey, Al MacInnis, Scott Stevens, Brett Hull; Builders (7): Roger Neilson, Al Arbour, Scotty Bowman, Emile Francis, Craig Patrick (played for St. Louis, inducted as Builder), Lynn Patrick, Glen Sather (played for St. Louis, inducted as Builder)
Website: www.stlouisblues.com
Minor League Affiliate(s): Peoria Rivermen (AHL), Alaska Aces (ECHL)
Stanley Cups: none
Hosted All-Star Game: (2) 1970, 1988
1st Overall Draft Choices: none

SAN JOSE SHARKS

First Game Played: October 4, 1991
San Jose Sharks 3 at Vancouver Canucks 4
Nickname Provenance: named by team owners after a fan contest
Mascot: S.J. Sharkie (b. January 1992)
Arena History: Cow Palace, 1991–93; San Jose Arena, 1993–2001; Compaq Center, 2001–03; HP Pavilion, 2003–present (same building as Compaq Center and San Jose Arena, capacity 17,496)
Retired Numbers: none
Hall of Famers: (2) Ed Belfour, Igor Larionov
Website: www.sjsharks.com
Minor League Affiliate(s): Worcester Sharks (AHL), Stockton Thunder (ECHL—shared with Edmonton)
Stanley Cups: none
Hosted All-Star Game: 1997
1st Overall Draft Choices: none

TAMPA BAY LIGHTNING

First Game Played: October 7, 1992
Chicago Blackhawks 3 at Tampa Bay Lightning 7
Nickname Provenance: Tampa Bay is, statistically, the lightning capital of the world.
Mascot: Thunder Bug
Arena History: Expo Hall, 1992–93; ThunderDome, 1993–96 (five home games played at Orlando Arena); Ice Palace, 1998–2003; *St. Petersburg Times* Forum, 2003–present (same building as Ice Palace, capacity 19,758)
Retired Numbers: none
Hall of Famers: Players (2): Dino Ciccarelli, Denis Savard
Website: www.tampabaylightning.com
Minor League Affiliate(s): Norfolk Admirals (AHL), Florida Everblades (ECHL—shared with Carolina)
Stanley Cups: (1) 2003–04
Hosted All-Star Game: (1) 1999
1st Overall Draft Choices: 1992 (Roman Hamrlik), 1998 (Vincent Lecavalier), 2008 (Steve Stamkos)

TORONTO MAPLE LEAFS

First Game Played:
As Toronto Arenas: December 19, 1917
Toronto Arenas 9 at Montreal Wanderers 10

As Toronto St. Pats: December 23, 1919
Toronto St. Pats 0 at Ottawa Senators 3
As Toronto Maple Leafs: February 17, 1927
New York Americans 1 at Toronto Maple Leafs 4
Nickname Provenance: Named by owner Conn Smythe after a World War I regiment
Mascot: Carlton the Bear
Arena History: Arena Gardens (Mutual Street Arena), 1917–31; Maple Leaf Gardens, 1931–99; Air Canada Centre, 1999–present (capacity 18,819)
Retired Numbers: Bill Barilko (5), Ace Bailey (6)
Honoured Numbers: Turk Broda (1), Johnny Bower (1), Red Kelly (4), King Clancy (7), Tim Horton (7), Charlie Conacher (9), Ted Kennedy (9), Syl Apps (10), George Armstrong (10), Wendel Clark (17), Borje Salming (21), Frank Mahovlich (27), Darryl Sittler (27), Doug Gilmour (93)
Hall of Famers: Players (62): Jack Adams, Glenn Anderson, Syl Apps, Al Arbour, George Armstrong, Ace Bailey, Andy Bathgate, Ed Belfour, Max Bentley, Leo Boivin, Johnny Bower, Turk Broda, Harry Cameron, Gerry Cheevers, King Clancy, Sprague Cleghorn, Charlie Conacher, Rusty Crawford, Hap Day, Gord Drillon, Dick Duff, Babe Dye, Fern Flaman, Grant Fuhr, Mike Gartner, Eddie Gerard, Doug Gilmour, George Hainsworth, Harry Holmes, Red Horner, Tim Horton, Syd Howe, Harvey Jackson, Red Kelly, Ted Kennedy, Dave Keon, Brian Leetch, Harry Lumley, Frank Mahovlich, Lanny McDonald, Dickie Moore, Larry Murphy, Joe Nieuwendyk, Frank Nighbor, Reg Noble, Bert Olmstead, Bernie Parent, Pierre Pilote, Jacques Plante, Babe Pratt, Joe Primeau, Marcel Pronovost, Bob Pulford, Borje Salming, Terry Sawchuk, Sweeney Schriner, Darryl Sittler, Allan Stanley, Norm Ullman, Carl Voss, Harry Watson, Ron Francis; Builders (12): Harold Ballard, J.P. Bickell, Cliff Fletcher, Foster Hewitt, William Hewitt, Punch Imlach, Dick Irvin (played for Toronto, inducted as Builder), Frank Mathers (played for Toronto, inducted as Builder), Rudy Pilous, Bud Poile (played for Toronto, inducted as Builder), Frank Selke, Conn Smythe
Website: www.torontomapleleafs.com
Minor League Affiliate(s): Toronto Marlies (AHL), Reading Royals (ECHL—shared with Boston)
Stanley Cups: (13) 1917–18, 1921–22, 1931–32, 1941–42, 1944–45, 1946–47, 1947–48, 1948–49, 1950–51, 1961–62, 1962–63, 1963–64, 1966–67
Hosted All-Star Game: (8) 1947, 1949, 1951, 1962, 1963, 1964, 1968, 2000
1st Overall Draft Choices: 1985 (Wendel Clark)

VANCOUVER CANUCKS

First Game Played: October 9, 1970
Los Angeles Kings 3 at Vancouver Canucks 1
Nickname Provenance: Continuation of WHL franchise nickname
Mascot: Fin the Whale

Arena History: Pacific Coliseum, 1970–95; General Motors (GM) Place, 1995–2010; Rogers Arena, 2010–present (same building as GM Place, capacity 18,810)
Retired Numbers: Wayne Maki (11, unofficial, later worn by Mark Messier but not before or since), Stan Smyl (12), Trevor Linden (16), Markus Naslund (19)
Hall of Famers: (3) Igor Larionov, Cam Neely, Mark Messier
Website: www.canucks.com
Minor League Affiliate(s): Manitoba Moose (AHL), Victoria Salmon Kings (ECHL)
Stanley Cups: none
Hosted All-Star Game: (2) 1977, 1998
1st Overall Draft Choices: none

WASHINGTON CAPITALS

First Game Played: October 9, 1974
Washington Capitals 3 at New York Rangers 6
Nickname Provenance: So called because the team plays in the capital city of the USA
Mascot: Slapshot
Arena History: Capital Centre, 1974–93; US Air Arena, 1993–97 (same building as Capital Centre); US Airways Arena, 1997 (same building as US Air Arena); MCI Center, 1997–2006; Verizon Center, 2006–present (same building as MCI Center—capacity 18,277)
Retired Numbers: Rod Langway (5), Yvon Labre (7), Mike Gartner (11), Dale Hunter (32)
Hall of Famers: Players (5): Dino Ciccarelli, Mike Gartner, Rod Langway, Larry Murphy, Scott Stevens; Builders (1): Craig Patrick (played for Washington, inducted as Builder)
Website: www.washingtoncaps.com
Minor League Affiliate(s): Hershey Bears (AHL), South Carolina Stingrays (ECHL)
Stanley Cups: none
Hosted All-Star Game: (1) 1982
1st Overall Draft Choices: 1974 (Greg Joly), 1976 (Rick Green), 2005 (Alexander Ovechkin)

WINNIPEG JETS

First Game Played:
As Atlanta Thrashers: October 2, 1999
New Jersey Devils 4 at Atlanta Thrashers 1
Nickname Provenance: Jets was the name of the previous WHA/NHL franchise
Arena History: Philips Arena, 1999–2011 (capacity 18,545); MTS Centre, 2011–present (capacity 15,015)
Retired Numbers: Dan Snyder (37, unofficial)
Hall of Famers: none

Website: www.winnipegjets.com
Minor League Affiliate(s): St. John's IceCaps (AHL)
Stanley Cups: none
Hosted All-Star Game: (1) 2008 (as Thrashers)
1st Overall Draft Choices: 1999 (Patrik Stefan), 2001 (Ilya Kovalchuk)

FINAL STANDINGS, REGULAR SEASON, 2010–11

EASTERN CONFERENCE

Atlantic Division	GP	W	L	OT	GF	GA	Pts
Philadelphia	82	47	23	12	259	223	106
Pittsburgh	82	49	25	8	238	199	106
NY Rangers	82	44	33	5	233	198	93
New Jersey	82	38	39	5	174	209	81
NY Islanders	82	30	39	13	229	264	73

Northeast Division							
Boston	82	46	25	11	246	195	103
Montreal	82	44	30	8	216	209	96
Buffalo	82	43	29	10	245	229	96
Toronto	82	37	34	11	218	251	85
Ottawa	82	32	40	10	192	250	74

Southeast Division							
Washington	82	48	23	11	224	197	107
Tampa Bay	82	46	25	11	247	240	103
Carolina	82	40	31	11	236	239	91
Atlanta	82	34	36	12	223	269	80
Florida	82	30	40	12	195	229	72

WESTERN CONFERENCE

Central Division	GP	W	L	OT	GF	GA	Pts
Detroit	82	47	25	10	261	241	104
Nashville	82	44	27	11	219	194	99
Chicago	82	44	29	9	258	225	97
St. Louis	82	38	33	11	240	234	87
Columbus	82	34	35	13	215	258	81

Northwest Division							
Vancouver	82	54	19	9	262	185	117
Calgary	82	41	29	12	250	237	94
Minnesota	82	39	35	8	206	233	86
Colorado	82	30	44	8	227	288	68
Edmonton	82	25	45	12	193	269	62

Pacific Division							
San Jose	82	48	25	9	248	213	105
Anaheim	82	47	30	5	239	235	99
Phoenix	82	43	26	13	231	226	99
Los Angeles	82	46	30	6	219	198	98
Dallas	82	42	29	11	227	233	95

SCORING LEADERS & GOALIE LEADERS, 2010–11

(Nationality and NHL team in parentheses)

SCORING LEADERS, 2010–11

Points

Daniel Sedin (SWE-VAN)	104
Martin St. Louis (CAN-TB)	99
Corey Perry (CAN-ANA)	98
Henrik Sedin (SWE-VAN)	94
Steve Stamkos (CAN-TB)	91
Jarome Iginla (CAN-CAL)	86
Alexander Ovechkin (RUS-WAS)	85
Teemu Selanne (FIN-ANA)	80
Henrik Zetterberg (SWE-DET)	80
Brad Richards (CAN-DAL)	77

Goals

Corey Perry (CAN-ANA)	50
Steve Stamkos (CAN-TB)	45
Jarome Iginla (CAN-CAL)	43
Ryan Kesler (CAN-VAN)	41
Daniel Sedin (SWE-VAN)	41
Patrick Marleau (CAN-SJ)	37
Jeff Carter (CAN-PHI)	36
Daniel Briere (CAN-PHI)	34
Michael Grabner (AUT-NYI)	34
Bobby Ryan (USA-ANA)	34
Patrick Sharp (CAN-CHI)	34

Assists

Henrik Sedin (SWE-VAN)	75
Martin St. Louis (CAN-TB)	68
Daniel Sedin (SWE-VAN)	63
Ryan Getzlaf (CAN-ANA)	57
Henrik Zetterberg (SWE-DET)	56
Alexander Ovechkin (RUS-WAS)	53
Mike Ribeiro (CAN-DAL)	52
Claude Giroux (CAN-PHI)	50
Lubomir Visnovsky (SVK-ANA)	50
David Krejci (CZE-BOS)	49

Brad Richards (CAN-DAL)	49
Teemu Selanne (FIN-ANA)	49
Joe Thornton (CAN-SJ)	49

Penalty Minutes

Zenon Konopka (CAN-TB)	307
Chris Neil (CAN-OTT)	210
Theo Peckham (CAN-EDM)	198
Cody McLeod (CAN-COL)	189
Derek Dorsett (CAN-CBJ)	184
Steve Ott (CAN-DAL)	183
Jared Boll (CAN-CBJ)	182
Sean Avery (CAN-NYR)	174
Brad Staubitz (CAN-MIN)	173
Steve Downie (CAN-TB)	171
George Parros (USA-ANA)	171

WINS, GOALIE

Roberto Luongo (CAN-VAN)	38
Carey Price (CAN-MON)	38
Jimmy Howard (USA-DET)	37
Miikka Kiprusoff (FIN-CAL)	37
Cam Ward (CAN-CAR)	37
Ilya Bryzgalov (RUS-PHO)	36
Marc-Andre Fleury (CAN-PIT)	36
Henrik Lundqvist (SWE-NYR)	36
Antti Niemi (FIN-SJ)	35
Jonathan Quick (USA-LA)	35
Tim Thomas (USA-BOS)	35

LOSSES, GOALIE

Nikolai Khabibulin (RUS-EDM)	32
Carey Price (CAN-MON)	28
Tomas Vokoun (CZE-FLO)	28
Brian Elliott (CAN-OTT/COL)	27
Henrik Lundqvist (SWE-NYR)	27
Martin Brodeur (CAN-NJ)	26
Cam Ward (CAN-CAR)	26
Dwayne Roloson (CAN-NTI/TB)	25
Miikka Kiprusoff (FIN-CAL)	24
Kari Lehtonen (FIN-DAL)	24

MINUTES PLAYED

Cam Ward (CAN-CAR)	4,317:35
Carey Price (CAN-MON)	4,206:08
Miikka Kiprusoff (FIN-CAL)	4,155:39
Kari Lehtonen (FIN-DAL)	4,119:11
Ilya Bryzgalov (RUS-PHO)	4,059:52
Henrik Lundqvist (SWE-NYR)	4,006:40
Ryan Miller (USA-BUF)	3,829:18
Pekka Rinne (FIN-NAS)	3,789:15
Marc-Andre Fleury (CAN-PIT)	3,695:10
Jimmy Howard (USA-DET)	3,615:15

SHUTOUTS

Henrik Lundqvist (SWE-NYR)	11
Tim Thomas (USA-BOS)	9
Carey Price (CAN-MON)	8
Ilya Bryzgalov (RUS-PHO)	7
Jaroslav Halak (SVK-STL)	7
Martin Brodeur (CAN-NJ)	6
Miikka Kiprusoff (FIN-CAL)	6
Antti Niemi (FIN-CHI)	6
Jonathan Quick (USA-LA)	6
Pekka Rinne (FIN-NAS)	6
Tomas Vokoun (CZE-FLO)	6

GOALS-AGAINST AVERAGE

Tim Thomas (USA-BOS)	2.00
Roberto Luongo (CAN-VAN)	2.11
Pekka Rinne (FIN-NAS)	2.12
Jonathan Quick (USA-LA)	2.24
Henrik Lundqvist (SWE-NYR)	2.28
Corey Crawford (CAN-CHI)	2.30
Marc-Andre Fleury (CAN-PIT)	2.32
Carey Price (CAN-MON)	2.35
Antti Niemi (FIN-CHI)	2.38
Michal Neuvirth (CZE-WAS)	2.45

PLAYERS WHO PLAYED IN 2009–10, BUT NOT IN 2010–11

PLAYER	2010–11 STATUS
Afinogenov, Maxim	played for St. Petersburg (KHL)
Armstrong, Derek	did not play
Arsene, Dean	played for Peoria (AHL)
Artyukin, Evgeni	played for St. Petersburg (KHL)
Backlund, Johan	played for Adirondack (AHL)
Baumgartner, Nolan	played for Manitoba (AHL)
Bitz, Byron	did not play
Blake, Rob	retired
Bochenski, Brandon	played for Astana Barys (KHL)
Bodnarchuk, Andrew	played for Providence (AHL)
Borer, Casey	played for Charlotte (AHL)
Bourque, Chris	played in Swiss league and KHL
Brashear, Donald	retired
Brind'Amour, Rod	retired
Brunnstrom, Fabian	played for Texas/Toronto (AHL)
Byers, Dane	played for Springfield/San Antonio (AHL)
Calder, Kyle	played in ECHL & KHL
Cheechoo, Jonathan	played for Worcester (AHL)
Chelios, Chris	retired
Cliché, Marc-Andre	played for Manchester (AHL)
Clune, Rich	played for Manchester (AHL)
Conboy, Tim	played for Portland (AHL)
Cote, Riley	retired
Cowen, Jared	played in WHL & AHL
Curry, John	played for Wilkes-Barre (AHL)
Danis, Yann	played for Khabarovsk (KHL)
Daugavins, Kaspars	played for Binghamton (AHL)
Davis, Patrick	played for Albany/Worcester (AHL)
Davison, Rob	played for Albany (AHL)
Demitra, Pavol	played for Yaroslavl (KHL)
Deveaux, Andre	played for Chicago (AHL)
Donovan, Shean	did not play—free agent
Drouin-Deslauriers, Jeff	played for Oklahoma (AHL)
Dubielewicz, Wade	played for Cologne (DEL)
Duchesne, Jeremy	played for St. Georges (NAHL)
Durno, Chris	played for Norfolk (AHL)
Elkins, Corey	played for Manchester (AHL)

Eriksson, Anders	played for Timra/MoDo (SEL)
Ersberg, Erik	played in AHL & KHL
Exelby, Garnet	played for Rockford (AHL)
Fedoruk, Todd	did not play—free agent
Finger, Jeff	played for Toronto (AHL)
Flood, Mark	played for Manitoba (AHL)
Fortunus, Maxime	played for Texas (AHL)
Frischmon, Trevor	played for Springfield (AHL)
Goertzen, Steve	played for Springfield (AHL)
Grant, Triston	played for Rochester (AHL)
Grebeshkov, Denis	played for St. Petersburg (KHL)
Greiss, Thomas	played for Brynas (SEL)
Guerin, Bill	retired
Guite, Ben	played for Springfield (AHL)
Harding, Josh	did not play—injured
Haydar, Darren	played for Chicago (AHL)
Heikkinen, Ilkka	played for Novosibirsk (AHL)
Helminen, Dwight	played for Pelicans (Finland)
Hennessy, Josh	played for Lugano (Switzerland)
Heshka, Shaun	played for Salzburg (Austria)
Hilbert, Andy	did not play
Hoggan, Jeff	played for Wolfsburg (DEL)
Huet, Cristobal	played for Fribourg (Switzerland)
Irmen, Danny	played for Bolzano (Italy)
Irwin, Brayden	played for Toronto (AHL)
Jackson, Scott	played for Norfolk (AHL)
Jaffray, Jason	played for Manitoba (AHL)
Johnson, Aaron	played for Milwaukee (AHL)
Johnsson, Kim	did not play—injured
Junland, Jonas	played for Farjestad (SEL)
Kalinski, Jon	played for Adirondack (AHL)
Kalus, Petr	played for Springfield (AHL)
Kana, Tomas	played for Springfield (AHL)
Kane, Boyd	played for Hershey (AHL)
Kariya, Paul	did not play—injured
Keller, Ryan	played for Binghamton (AHL)
Klementyev, Anton	played for Bridgeport (AHL)
Kohn, Dustin	played for Bridgeport (AHL)
Koistinen, Ville	played for Skelleftea (SEL)
Kozlov, Vyacheslav	played for CSKA/Ufa (KHL)
Krajicek, Lukas	played for Trinec (Czech Republic)
Kreps, Kamil	played for Karpat (Finland)

Kronwall, Staffan	played in AHL & SEL
Laing, Quintin	played in ECHL & AHL
Laliberte, David	played in AHL
Lang, Robert	did not play—unsigned free agent
Laperriere, Ian	retired
Laraque, Georges	retired
Larman, Drew	played for Florida (ECHL)
Lefebvre, Guillaume	played for Bakersfield (ECHL)
Legace, Manny	played for Iserlohn (DEL)
Lehtinen, Jere	retired
Lindgren, Perttu	played for Lukko Rauma (Finland)
Linglet, Charles	played for Nizhny Novgorod (KHL)
Lisin, Enver	played for Magnitogorsk (KHL)
Lundmark, Jamie	played in AHL & SEL
Maltby, Kirk	retired
May, Brad	retired
McAmmond, Dean	did not play—free agent
McDonald, Colin	played for Oklahoma (AHL)
McGrattan, Brian	played for Providence/Syracuse (AHL)
McKee, Jay	retired
Meech, Derek	played for Grand Rapids (AHL)
Mercier, Justin	played for Lake Erie (AHL)
Metropolit, Glen	played for Zug (Switzerland)
Mihalik, Vladimir	played for Norfolk (AHL)
Minard, Chris	played for Grand Rapids (AHL)
Moore, Greg	played for Adirondack/Springfield (AHL)
Motin, Johan	played in AHL & ECHL
Mueller, Peter	did not play—injured
Murphy, Cory	played for Zurich (Switzerland)
Nabokov, Evgeni	played for St. Petersburg (KHL)
Niedermayer, Scott	retired
Nilsson, Robert	played for Ufa (KHL)
Nokelainen, Petteri	played for Jokerit (Finland)
Nolan, Owen	played for Zurich (Switzerland)
Olvecky, Peter	played for KalPa (Finland)
O'Neill, Wes	played in AHL & ECHL
Osala, Oskar	played for Charlotte (AHL)
Paetsch, Nathan	played for Rochester/Syracuse (AHL)
Pandolfo, Jay	played for Springfield (AHL)
Park, Richard	played for Geneva (Switzerland)
Pechurski, Alexander	played in WHL & CHL
Peltier, Derek	played for Peoria (AHL)

Penner, Jeff	played for Providence/Houston (AHL)
Peters, Andrew	played for Rochester (AHL)
Pettinger, Matt	played for Cologne (DEL)
Picard, Alexandre	played for San Antonio (AHL)
Pikkarainen, Ilkka	played for Timra (SEL)
Popovic, Mark	played for Lugano (Switzerland)
Pothier, Brian	played for Geneva (Switzerland)
Preissing, Tom	played for Astana Barys (KHL)
Primeau, Wayne	retired
Pyorala, Mika	played for Frolunda (SEL)
Ranger, Paul	did not play—free agent
Rechlicz, Joel	played for Hershey (AHL)
Redden, Wade	played for Hartford (AHL)
Ross, Jared	played for Chicago (AHL)
Salak, Alexander	played for Farjestad (SEL)
Salvador, Bryce	did not play—injured
Sanguinetti, Bobby	played for Charlotte (AHL)
Satan, Miroslav	played for Moscow (KHL)
Sauer, Kurt	did not play—injured
Schneider, Mathieu	retired
Schubert, Christoph	played in SEL & DEL
Sharp, MacGregor	played for Syracuse/Abbotsford (AHL)
Sheppard, James	did not play—injured
Sifers, Jaime	played for Chicago (AHL)
Skoula, Martin	played for Avangard Omsk (KHL)
Smith, Nathan	played for Augsburg (DEL)
Smolenak, Radek	played for Sparta/Kladno (Czech Republic)
Souray, Sheldon	played for Hershey (AHL)
Stastny, Yan	played for CSKA (KHL)
Stewart, Gregory	played for Oklahoma City (AHL)
Stone, Ryan	played for Abbotsford (AHL)
St. Pierre, Martin	played in Austria, Finland, KHL
Streit, Mark	did not play—injured
Sydor, Darryl	retired
Sykora, Petr	played in Czech Republic, KHL
Szczechura, Paul	played for Norfolk (AHL)
Tarnasky, Nick	played in ECHL & AHL
Tkachuk, Keith	retired
Tokarski, Dustin	played for Norfolk (AHL)
Tollefsen, Ole-Kristian	played for MoDo (SEL)
Toskala, Vesa	played for AIK (SEL)
Trotter, Brock	played for Riga (KHL)

Tucker, Darcy	retired
Valabik, Boris	played for Chicago/Providence (AHL)
Valiquette, Stephen	played for CSKA (KHL)
Veilleux, Stephane	played in Finland, Switzerland
Vesce, Ryan	played for Nizhny Novgorod (KHL)
Vishnevskiy, Ivan	played for Rockford (AHL)
Walker, Scott	retired
Wallin, Rickard	played for Farjestad (SEL)
Walter, Ben	played for Lake Erie (AHL)
Ward, Aaron	retired
Whitfield, Trent	played for Providence (AHL)
Witt, Brendan	retired
Wozniewski, Andy	played for Zug (Switzerland)
Wyman, J.T.	played for Hamilton (AHL)
Yelle, Stephane	retired
Zaba, Matt	played for Bolzano (Italy)
Zalewski, Steven	played for Worcester/Albany (AHL)

PLAYERS SUSPENDED IN 2010–11

September 24, 2010	Nick Boynton (Chicago)	1 game (inappropriate gesture)
October 4, 2010	Mike Cammalleri (Montreal)	1 game (slashing)
October 10, 2010	Pierre-Luc Letourneau-Leblond (New Jersey)	1 game (late-game instigator)
October 12, 2010	James Wisniewski (NY Islanders)	2 games (obscene gesture)
October 12, 2010	Niklas Hjalmarsson (Chicago)	2 games (boarding)
October 18, 2010	Shane Doan (Phoenix)	3 games (head hit)
October 22, 2010	Rick Rypien (Vancouver)	6 games (contact with a fan)
October 27, 2010	Stephane Robidas (Dallas)	1 game (two game misconducts)
November 1, 2010	Daniel Briere (Philadelphia)	3 games (head hit)
November 5, 2010	Joe Thornton (San Jose)	2 games (head hit)
November 13, 2010	Brent Burns (Minnesota)	2 games (butt-ending)
November 18, 2010	Mattias Ritola (Tampa Bay)	2 games (boarding)
November 18, 2010	Olli Jokinen (Calgary)	3 games (head hit)
December 13, 2010	Jody Shelley (Philadelphia)	2 games (boarding)
December 19, 2010	Matt Martin (NY Islanders)	2 games (head hit)
December 29, 2010	Jody Shelley (Philadelphia)	2 games (sucker punch)
January 8, 2011	Ben Eager (Atlanta)	4 games (sucker punch)
January 9, 2011	Tom Kostopoulos (Calgary)	6 games (head hit)
January 14, 2011	Shane O'Brien (Nashville)	2 games (high-sticking)
January 14, 2011	Mike Brown (Toronto)	3 games (head hit)
January 18, 2011	Scott Nichol (San Jose)	4 games (head hit)
February 4, 2011	Daniel Paille (Boston)	4 games (head hit)
February 9, 2011	Artem Volchenkov (New Jersey)	3 games (head hit)
February 9, 2011	Matt Cooke (Pittsburgh)	4 games (boarding)
February 12, 2011	Eric Godard (Pittsburgh)	10 games (leaving the bench to fight)
February 12, 2011	Matt Martin (NY Islanders)	4 games (sucker punch)
February 12, 2011	Trevor Gillies (NY Islanders)	9 games (head hit)
February 23, 2011	Scottie Upshall (Phoenix)	2 games (boarding)
March 4, 2011	Trevor Gillies (NY Islanders)	2 games (boarding)
March 10, 2011	Pavel Kubina (Tampa Bay)	3 games (head hit)
March 16, 2011	Dany Heatley (San Jose)	2 games (head hit)
March 17, 2011	Brad Marchand (Boston)	2 games (head hit)
March 21, 2011	Matt Cooke (Pittsburgh)	17 games (head hit)
April 7, 2011	Raffi Torres (Vancouver)	4 games (elbowing)

MILESTONES TO WATCH FOR IN 2011–12

Daniel Alfredsson	11 goals to 400
Jason Arnott	28 games to 1,200
Martin Biron	21 games to 500
Jay Bouwmeester	starts season with Iron Man streak at 424 games
Daniel Briere	36 goals to 300
Martin Brodeur	68 games to 1,200
Ilya Bryzgalov	1,306 minutes played to 20,000
Zdeno Chara	72 games to 1,000
Sidney Crosby	28 points to 600
Matt Cullen	42 games to 1,000
Rick DiPietro	2,331 minutes played to 20,000
Shane Doan	4 goals to 300
Patrik Elias	39 games to 1,000; 19 assists to 500
Marc-Andre Fleury	16 wins to 200
Marian Gaborik	17 goals to 300
J-S Giguere	221 minutes played to 30,000
Hal Gill	6 games to 1,000
Sergei Gonchar	42 games to 1,100
Roman Hamrlik	29 assists to 500
Tomas Holmstrom	48 games to 1,000
Jarome Iginla	16 goals to 500
Jaromir Jagr	1 point to 1,600
Olli Jokinen	40 games to 1,000
Miikka Kiprusoff	24 wins to 300
Mike Knuble	32 games to 1,000
Saku Koivu	62 games to 1,000
Ilya Kovalchuk	31 goals to 400
Vincent Lecavalier	62 games to 1,000
Nicklas Lidstrom	6 games to 1,500
Roberto Luongo	1,474 minutes played to 40,000
Todd Marchant	5 games to 1,200
Patrick Marleau	65 games to 1,100
Derek Morris	54 games to 1,000
Rick Nash	41 goals to 300
Rob Niedermayer	47 games to 1,200
Sean O'Donnell	27 games to 1,200
Chris Phillips	55 games to 1,000
Chris Pronger	46 games to 1,200
Vaclav Prospal	22 games to 1,000
Brian Rolston	14 games to 1,200

Teemu Selanne	41 games to 1,300; 60 points to 1,400
Ryan Smyth	31 games to 1,100
Tim Thomas	39 wins to 200
Joe Thornton	5 games to 1,000
Marty Turco	27 wins to 300
Thomas Vokoun	38 wins to 300
Ray Whitney	74 points to 1,000

2011 PLAYOFF RESULTS

EASTERN CONFERENCE QUARTERFINALS

(1) Washington vs. (8) NY Rangers

April 13	NY Rangers 1 at Washington 2 (Semin 18:24 OT)
April 15	NY Rangers 0 at Washington 2 [Neuvirth]
April 17	Washington 2 at NY Rangers 3
April 20	Washington 4 at NY Rangers 3 (Chimera 32:36 OT)
April 23	NY Rangers 1 at Washington 3

Washington wins best-of-seven 4–1

(2) Philadelphia vs. (7) Buffalo

April 14	Buffalo 1 at Philadelphia 0 [Miller]
April 16	Buffalo 4 at Philadelphia 5
April 18	Philadelphia 4 at Buffalo 2
April 20	Philadelphia 0 at Buffalo 1 [Miller]
April 22	Buffalo 4 at Philadelphia 3 (Ennis 5:31 OT)
April 24	Philadelphia 5 at Buffalo 4 (Leino 4:43 OT)
April 26	Buffalo 2 at Philadelphia 5

Philadelphia wins best-of-seven 4–3

(3) Boston vs. (6) Montreal

April 14	Montreal 2 at Boston 0 [Price]
April 16	Montreal 3 at Boston 1
April 18	Boston 4 at Montreal 2
April 21	Boston 5 at Montreal 4 (Ryder 1:59 OT)
April 23	Montreal 1 at Boston 2 (Horton 29:03 OT)
April 26	Boston 1 at Montreal 2
April 27	Montreal 3 at Boston 4 (Horton 5:43 OT)

Boston wins best-of-seven 4–3

(4) Pittsburgh vs. (5) Tampa Bay

April 13	Tampa Bay 0 at Pittsburgh 3 [Fleury]
April 15	Tampa Bay 5 at Pittsburgh 1
April 18	Pittsburgh 3 at Tampa Bay 2
April 20	Pittsburgh 3 at Tampa Bay 2 (Neal 23:38 OT)
April 23	Tampa Bay 8 at Pittsburgh 2
April 25	Pittsburgh 2 at Tampa Bay 4
April 27	Tampa Bay 1 at Pittsburgh 0 [Roloson]

Tampa Bay wins best-of-seven 4–3

WESTERN CONFERENCE QUARTERFINALS

(1) Vancouver vs. (8) Chicago

April 13	Chicago 0 at Vancouver 2 [Luongo]
April 15	Chicago 3 at Vancouver 4
April 17	Vancouver 3 at Chicago 2
April 19	Vancouver 2 at Chicago 7
April 21	Chicago 5 at Vancouver 0 [Crawford]
April 24	Vancouver 3 at Chicago 4 (B. Smith 15:30 OT)
April 26	Chicago 1 at Vancouver 2 (Burrows 5:22 OT)

Vancouver wins best-of-seven 4–3

(2) San Jose vs. (7) Los Angeles

April 14	Los Angeles 2 at San Jose 3 (Pavelski 14:44 OT)
April 16	Los Angeles 4 at San Jose 0 [Quick]
April 17	San Jose 6 at Los Angeles 5 (Setoguchi 3:09 OT)
April 21	San Jose 6 at Los Angeles 3
April 23	Los Angeles 3 at San Jose 1
April 25	San Jose 4 at Los Angeles 3 (Thornton 2:22 OT)

San Jose wins best-of-seven 4–2

(3) Detroit vs. (6) Phoenix

April 13	Phoenix 2 at Detroit 4
April 16	Phoenix 3 at Detroit 4
April 18	Detroit 4 at Phoenix 2
April 20	Detroit 6 at Phoenix 3

Detroit wins best-of-seven 4–0

(4) Anaheim at (5) Nashville

April 13	Nashville 4 at Anaheim 1
April 15	Nashville 3 at Anaheim 5
April 17	Anaheim 3 at Nashville 4
April 20	Anaheim 6 at Nashville 3
April 22	Nashville 4 at Anaheim 3 (Smithson 1:57 OT)
April 24	Anaheim 2 at Nashville 4

Nashville wins best-of-seven 4–2

EASTERN CONFERENCE SEMIFINALS

(1) Washington vs. (5) Tampa Bay
April 29	Tampa Bay 4 at Washington 2
May 1	Tampa Bay 3 at Washington 2 (Lecavalier 6:19 OT)
May 3	Washington 3 at Tampa Bay 4
May 4	Washington 3 at Tampa Bay 5

Tampa Bay wins best-of-seven 4–0

(2) Philadelphia vs. (3) Boston
April 30	Boston 7 at Philadelphia 3
May 2	Boston 3 at Philadelphia 2 (Krejci 14:00 OT)
May 4	Philadelphia 1 at Boston 5
May 6	Philadelphia 1 at Boston 5

Boston wins best-of-seven 4–0

WESTERN CONFERENCE SEMIFINALS

(1) Vancouver vs. (5) Nashville
April 28	Nashville 0 at Vancouver 1 [Luongo]
April 30	Nashville 2 at Vancouver 1 (Halischuk 34:51 OT)
May 3	Vancouver 3 at Nashville 2 (Kesler 10:45 OT)
May 5	Vancouver 4 at Nashville 2
May 7	Nashville 4 at Vancouver 3
May 9	Vancouver 3 at Nashville 1

Vancouver wins best-of-seven 4–2

(2) San Jose vs. (3) Detroit
April 29	Detroit 1 at San Jose 2 (Ferriero 7:03 OT)
May 1	Detroit 1 at San Jose 2
May 4	San Jose 4 at Detroit 3 (Setoguchi 9:21 OT)
May 6	San Jose 3 at Detroit 4
May 8	Detroit 4 at San Jose 3
May 10	San Jose 1 at Detroit 3
May 12	Detroit 2 at San Jose 3

San Jose wins best-of-seven 4–3

EASTERN CONFERENCE FINALS

(3) Boston vs. (5) Tampa Bay

May 14	Tampa Bay 5 at Boston 2
May 17	Tampa Bay 5 at Boston 6
May 19	Boston 2 at Tampa Bay 0 [Thomas]
May 21	Boston 3 at Tampa Bay 5
May 23	Tampa Bay 1 at Boston 3
May 25	Boston 4 at Tampa Bay 5
May 27	Tampa Bay 0 at Boston 1 [Thomas]

Boston wins best-of-seven 4–3

WESTERN CONFERENCE FINALS

(1) Vancouver vs. (2) San Jose

May 15	San Jose 2 at Vancouver 3
May 18	San Jose 3 at Vancouver 7
May 20	Vancouver 3 at San Jose 4
May 22	Vancouver 4 at San Jose 2
May 24	San Jose 2 at Vancouver 3 (Bieksa 30:18 OT)

Vancouver wins best-of-seven 4–1

STANLEY CUP FINALS

June 1	Boston 0 at Vancouver 1 [Luongo]
June 4	Boston 2 at Vancouver 3 (Burrows 0:11 OT)
June 6	Vancouver 1 at Boston 8
June 8	Vancouver 0 at Boston 4 [Thomas]
June 10	Boston 0 at Vancouver 1 [Luongo]
June 13	Vancouver 2 at Boston 5
June 15	Boston 4 at Vancouver 0 [Thomas]

Boston wins best-of-seven 4–3

PLAYER STATISTICS BY TEAM, 2011 PLAYOFFS

ANAHEIM DUCKS

	GP	G	A	P	Pim
Corey Perry	6	2	6	8	4
Teemu Selanne	6	6	1	7	12
Saku Koivu	6	1	6	7	6
Ryan Getzlaf	6	2	4	6	9
Bobby Ryan	4	3	1	4	2
Jason Blake	6	3	1	4	0
Cam Fowler	6	1	3	4	2
Lubomir Visnovsky	6	0	3	3	2
Brandon McMillan	6	1	1	2	0
Francois Beauchemin	6	0	2	2	2
Matt Beleskey	6	1	0	1	4
Luca Sbisa	6	0	1	1	8
Todd Marchant	6	0	1	1	4
George Parros	6	0	0	0	16
Sheldon Brookbank	4	0	0	0	14
Jarkko Ruutu	3	0	0	0	12
Brad Winchester	3	0	0	0	4
Toni Lydman	6	0	0	0	2
Nick Bonino	4	0	0	0	2
Dan Sexton	1	0	0	0	2
Andy Sutton	1	0	0	0	2
Ray Emery	6	0	0	0	0
Andreas Lilja	3	0	0	0	0
Dan Ellis	1	0	0	0	0
Kyle Palmieri	1	0	0	0	0

In Goal	GP	W-L	Mins	GA	SO	GAA
Ray Emery	6	2–3	319:20	17	0	3.20
Dan Ellis	1	0–1	40:56	4	0	5.85

BOSTON BRUINS

	GP	G	A	P	Pim
David Krejci	25	12	11	23	10
Patrice Bergeron	23	6	14	20	28
Brad Marchand	25	11	8	19	40
Nathan Horton	21	8	9	17	35
Michael Ryder	25	8	9	17	8
Mark Recchi	25	5	9	14	8

Chris Kelly	25	5	8	13	6
Milan Lucic	25	5	7	12	63
Rich Peverley	25	4	8	12	17
Dennis Seidenberg	25	1	10	11	31
Tomas Kaberle	25	0	11	11	4
Andrew Ference	25	4	6	10	37
Johnny Boychuk	25	3	6	9	12
Zdeno Chara	24	2	7	9	34
Tyler Seguin	13	3	4	7	2
Daniel Paille	25	3	3	6	4
Gregory Campbell	25	1	3	4	4
Adam McQuaid	23	0	4	4	14
Shawn Thornton	18	0	1	1	24
Shane Hnidy	3	0	0	0	7
Tim Thomas	25	0	0	0	4

In Goal	GP	W-L	Mins	GA	SO	GAA
Tim Thomas	25	16–9	1,541:53	51	4	1.98

BUFFALO SABRES

	GP	G	A	P	Pim
Marc-Andre Gragnani	7	1	6	7	4
Tyler Myers	7	1	5	6	16
Thomas Vanek	7	5	0	5	0
Tyler Ennis	7	2	2	4	4
Rob Niedermayer	7	1	3	4	2
Jason Pominville	5	1	3	4	2
Patrick Kaleta	6	1	2	3	6
Drew Stafford	7	1	2	3	2
Nathan Gerbe	7	2	0	2	18
Paul Gaustad	7	0	2	2	13
Tim Connolly	6	0	2	2	2
Andrej Sekera	2	1	0	1	4
Cody McCormick	7	1	0	1	2
Brad Boyes	7	1	0	1	0
Chris Butler	7	0	1	1	10
Steve Montador	6	0	1	1	8
Mike Weber	7	0	1	1	6
Jordan Leopold	5	0	1	1	4
Ryan Miller	7	0	1	1	2
Mike Grier	7	0	1	1	0
Jochen Hecht	1	0	1	1	0

Derek Roy	1	0	1	1	0
Shaone Morrisonn	1	0	0	0	2
Matt Ellis	1	0	0	0	0
Jhonas Enroth	1	0	0	0	0
Mark Mancari	1	0	0	0	0

In Goal	**GP**	**W-L**	**Mins**	**GA**	**SO**	**GAA**
Ryan Miller	7	34	409:42	20	2	2.93
Jhonas Enroth	1	00	17:11	1	0	3.53

CHICAGO BLACKHAWKS

	GP	**G**	**A**	**P**	**Pim**
Duncan Keith	7	4	2	6	6
Dave Bolland	4	2	4	6	4
Marian Hossa	7	2	4	6	2
Patrick Kane	7	1	5	6	2
Patrick Sharp	7	3	2	5	2
Michael Frolik	7	2	3	5	2
Bryan Bickell	5	2	2	4	0
Jonathan Toews	7	1	3	4	2
Ben Smith	7	3	0	3	0
Brian Campbell	7	1	2	3	6
Niklas Hjalmarsson	7	0	2	2	2
Corey Crawford	7	0	2	2	0
Viktor Stalberg	7	1	0	1	5
Brent Seabrook	5	0	1	1	6
Chris Campoli	7	0	1	1	2
Ryan Johnson	6	0	1	1	2
Marcus Kruger	5	0	1	1	0
John Scott	4	0	0	0	22
Troy Brouwer	7	0	0	0	11
Nick Leddy	7	0	0	0	0
Fernando Pisani	3	0	0	0	0
Jake Dowell	2	0	0	0	0
Tomas Kopecky	1	0	0	0	0

In Goal	**GP**	**W-L**	**Mins**	**GA**	**SO**	**GAA**
Corey Crawford	7	3–4	435:12	16	1	2.21

DETROIT RED WINGS

	GP	**G**	**A**	**P**	**Pim**
Pavel Datsyuk	11	4	11	15	8
Nicklas Lidstrom	11	4	4	8	4

Henrik Zetterberg	7	3	5	8	2
Valtteri Filppula	11	2	6	8	6
Tomas Holmstrom	11	3	4	7	8
Darren Helm	11	3	3	6	8
Todd Bertuzzi	11	2	4	6	15
Daniel Cleary	11	2	4	6	6
Niklas Kronwall	11	2	4	6	4
Patrick Eaves	11	3	1	4	6
Johan Franzen	8	2	1	3	6
Brian Rafalski	11	2	1	3	4
Jiri Hudler	10	1	2	3	6
Jonathan Ericsson	11	1	2	3	4
Drew Miller	9	1	1	2	4
Brad Stuart	11	0	2	2	8
Ruslan Salei	11	1	0	1	0
Kris Draper	8	0	1	1	2
Mike Modano	2	0	1	1	0
Justin Abdelkader	11	0	0	0	22
Jimmy Howard	11	0	0	0	2

In Goal	**GP**	**W-L**	**Mins**	**GA**	**SO**	**GAA**
Jimmy Howard	11	7–4	673:22	28	0	2.50

LOS ANGELES KINGS

	GP	**G**	**A**	**P**	**Pim**
Kyle Clifford	6	3	2	5	7
Brad Richardson	6	2	3	5	2
Ryan Smyth	6	2	3	5	0
Jack Johnson	6	1	4	5	0
Justin Williams	6	3	1	4	2
Drew Doughty	6	2	2	4	8
Trevor Lewis	6	1	3	4	2
Wayne Simmonds	6	1	2	3	20
Jarret Stoll	5	0	3	3	0
Dustin Brown	6	1	1	2	6
Willie Mitchell	6	1	1	2	4
Justin Penner	6	1	1	2	4
Michal Handzus	6	1	1	2	0
Rob Scuderi	6	0	2	2	0
Kevin Westgarth	6	1	2	2	14
Alexei Ponikarovsky	4	1	0	1	0
Alec Martinez	6	0	1	1	2

Matt Greene	6	0	0	0	14
Jonathan Quick	6	0	0	0	0
Scott Parse	2	0	0	0	0
Oscar Moller	1	0	0	0	0

In Goal	**GP**	**W–L**	**Mins**	**GA**	**SO**	**GAA**
Jonathan Quick	6	2–4	380:15	20	1	3.16

MONTREAL CANADIENS

	GP	**G**	**A**	**P**	**Pim**
Mike Cammalleri	7	3	7	10	0
Brian Gionta	7	3	2	5	0
Tomas Plekanec	7	2	3	5	2
P.K. Subban	7	2	2	4	2
Scott Gomez	7	0	4	4	2
Roman Hamrlik	7	0	3	3	6
Andrei Kostitsyn	6	2	0	2	6
Yannick Weber	3	2	0	2	0
Mathieu Darche	7	1	1	2	0
James Wisniewski	6	0	2	2	7
Lars Eller	7	0	2	2	4
Brent Sopel	7	1	0	1	2
Jeff Halpern	4	1	0	1	0
Travis Moen	7	0	1	1	2
David Desharnais	5	0	1	1	2
Benoit Pouliot	3	0	0	0	7
Jaroslav Spacek	7	0	0	0	4
Hal Gill	7	0	0	0	2
Ryan White	7	0	0	0	2
Carey Price	7	0	0	0	0
Tom Pyatt	7	0	0	0	0
Paul Mara	1	0	0	0	0

In Goal	**GP**	**W–L**	**Mins**	**GA**	**SO**	**GAA**
Carey Price	7	3–4	455:29	16	1	2.11

NASHVILLE PREDATORS

	GP	**G**	**A**	**P**	**Pim**
Joel Ward	12	7	6	13	6
David Legwand	12	6	3	9	8
Mike Fisher	12	3	4	7	11
Nick Spaling	12	2	4	6	0
Jordin Tootoo	12	1	5	6	28

Ryan Suter	12	1	5	6	6
Martin Erat	10	1	5	6	6
Cody Franson	12	1	5	6	0
Shea Weber	12	3	2	5	8
Sergei Kostitsyn	12	0	5	5	2
Patric Hornqvist	12	2	1	3	6
Steve Sullivan	9	2	1	3	2
Kevin Klein	12	1	2	3	6
Matt Halischuk	12	2	0	2	0
Jerred Smithson	11	1	1	2	8
Blake Geoffrion	12	0	2	2	4
Jonathon Blum	12	0	2	2	0
J-P Dumont	3	0	1	1	2
Pekka Rinne	12	0	1	1	0
Shane O'Brien	12	0	0	0	18
Colin Wilson	3	0	0	0	0
Anders Lindback	1	0	0	0	0

In Goal	**GP**	**W-L**	**Mins**	**GA**	**SO**	**GAA**
Pekka Rinne	12	6–6	748:28	32	0	2.57
Anders Lindback	1	0–0	13:14	0	0	0.00

NEW YORK RANGERS

	GP	**G**	**A**	**P**	**Pim**
Brandon Dubinski	5	2	1	3	2
Wojtek Wolski	5	1	2	3	0
Marian Gaborik	5	1	1	2	2
Bryan McCabe	5	0	2	2	14
Ruslan Fedotenko	5	0	2	2	4
Erik Christensen	5	1	0	1	2
Matt Gilroy	5	1	0	1	2
Artem Anisimov	5	1	0	1	0
Vinny Prospal	5	1	0	1	0
Sean Avery	4	0	1	1	12
Brandon Prust	5	0	1	1	4
Chris Drury	5	0	1	1	2
Michael Sauer	5	0	1	1	0
Marc Staal	5	0	1	1	0
Brian Boyle	5	0	0	0	6
Ryan McDonagh	5	0	0	0	4
Derek Stepan	5	0	0	0	2
Mats Zuccarello	1	0	0	0	2

Dan Girardi	5	0	0	0	0
Henrik Lundqvist	5	0	0	0	0

In Goal	**GP**	**W-L**	**Mins**	**GA**	**SO**	**GAA**
Henrik Lundqvist	5	1–4	345:35	13	0	2.25

PHILADELPHIA FLYERS

	GP	**G**	**A**	**P**	**Pim**
Claude Giroux	11	1	11	12	8
Daniel Briere	11	7	2	9	14
James van Riemsdyk	11	7	0	7	4
Mike Richards	11	1	6	7	15
Andrej Meszaros	11	2	4	6	8
Kimmo Timonen	11	1	5	6	14
Kris Versteeg	11	1	5	6	12
Ville Leino	11	3	2	5	0
Scott Hartnell	11	1	3	4	23
Matt Carle	11	0	4	4	2
Daniel Carcillo	11	2	1	3	30
Braydon Coburn	11	1	2	3	6
Nikolai Zherdev	8	1	2	3	2
Jeff Carter	6	1	1	2	2
Sean O'Donnell	11	0	2	2	5
Darroll Powe	11	0	1	1	4
Chris Pronger	3	0	1	1	4
Zac Rinaldo	2	0	0	0	12
Brian Boucher	9	0	0	0	2
Jody Shelley	2	0	0	0	2
Blair Betts	11	0	0	0	0
Danny Syvret	10	0	0	0	0
Sergei Bobrovsky	6	0	0	0	0
Michael Leighton	2	0	0	0	0
Andreas Nodl	2	0	0	0	0

In Goal	**GP**	**W-L**	**Mins**	**GA**	**SO**	**GAA**
Brian Boucher	9	4–4	422:22	22	0	3.13
Sergei Bobrovsky	6	0–2	185:37	10	0	3.23
Michael Leighton	2	0–1	69:43	4	0	3.43

PHOENIX COYOTES

	GP	**G**	**A**	**P**	**Pim**
Shane Doan	4	3	2	5	6
Radim Vrbata	4	2	3	5	0

Keith Yandle	4	0	5	5	0
Martin Hanzal	4	1	2	3	8
Kyle Turris	4	1	2	3	2
Ray Whitney	4	1	2	3	2
David Schlemko	4	1	0	1	4
Taylor Pyatt	4	1	0	1	0
Mikkel Bodker	4	0	1	1	2
Ed Jovanovski	4	0	1	1	2
Lauri Korpikoski	4	0	1	1	2
Rostislav Klesla	4	0	0	0	7
Adrian Aucoin	4	0	0	0	2
Eric Belanger	4	0	0	0	2
Michal Roszival	4	0	0	0	2
Ilya Bryzgalov	4	0	0	0	0
Vernon Fiddler	4	0	0	0	0
Lee Stempniak	4	0	0	0	0
Andrew Ebbett	3	0	0	0	0
Paul Bissonnette	1	0	0	0	0

In Goal	**GP**	**W-L**	**Mins**	**GA**	**SO**	**GAA**
Ilya Bryzgalov	4	0–4	233:43	17	0	4.36

PITTSBURGH PENGUINS

	GP	**G**	**A**	**P**	**Pim**
Arron Asham	7	3	1	4	2
Maxime Talbot	7	1	3	4	14
Kris Letang	7	0	4	4	10
Tyler Kennedy	7	2	1	3	2
Jordan Staal	7	1	2	3	2
Brooks Orpik	7	0	3	3	14
Alex Kovalev	7	1	1	2	10
James Neal	7	1	1	2	6
Michael Rupp	7	1	1	2	4
Ben Lovejoy	7	0	2	2	4
Paul Martin	7	0	2	2	2
Chris Kunitz	6	1	0	1	6
Craig Adams	7	1	0	1	2
Pascal Dupuis	7	1	0	1	2
Chris Conner	7	1	0	1	0
Mark Letestu	7	0	1	1	0
Zbynek Michalek	7	0	1	1	0

Matt Niskanen	7	0	1	1	0
Brent Johnson	1	0	0	0	2
Marc-Andre Fleury	7	0	0	0	0
Eric Tangradi	1	0	0	0	0

In Goal	**GP**	**W-L**	**Mins**	**GA**	**SO**	**GAA**
Marc-Andre Fleury	7	3–4	405:12	17	1	2.52
Brent Johnson	1	0–0	34:29	4	0	7.06

SAN JOSE SHARKS

	GP	**G**	**A**	**P**	**Pim**
Joe Thornton	18	3	14	17	16
Dan Boyle	18	4	12	16	8
Ryane Clowe	17	6	9	15	32
Logan Couture	18	7	7	14	2
Patrick Marleau	18	7	6	13	9
Devin Setoguchi	18	7	3	10	12
Joe Pavelski	18	5	5	10	10
Dany Heatley	18	3	6	9	12
Ian White	17	1	8	9	8
Kyle Wellwood	18	1	6	7	0
Torrey Mitchell	18	1	4	5	10
Niclas Wallin	18	1	3	4	10
Jason Demers	13	2	1	3	8
Marc-Edouard Vlasic	18	0	3	3	4
Ben Eager	10	1	0	1	41
Benn Ferriero	8	1	0	1	6
Andrew Desjardins	3	1	0	1	4
Jamie McGinn	7	0	1	1	30
Douglas Murray	18	0	1	1	8
Kent Huskins	5	0	1	1	2
Scott Nichol	15	0	0	0	26
Jamal Mayers	12	0	0	0	12
Antti Niemi	18	0	0	0	0
Antero Niittymaki	2	0	0	0	0
Justin Braun	1	0	0	0	0

In Goal	**GP**	**W-L**	**Mins**	**GA**	**SO**	**GAA**
Antti Niemi	18	8–9	1,044:06	56	0	3.22
Antero Niittymaki	2	1–0	91:29	1	0	0.66

TAMPA BAY LIGHTNING

	GP	G	A	P	Pim
Marin St. Louis	18	10	10	20	4
Vincent Lecavalier	18	6	13	19	16
Teddy Purcell	18	6	11	17	2
Steve Downie	17	2	12	14	40
Steve Stamkos	18	6	7	13	6
Simon Gagne	15	5	7	12	4
Sean Bergenheim	16	9	2	11	8
Dominic Moore	18	3	8	11	18
Eric Brewer	18	1	6	7	14
Ryan Malone	18	3	3	6	24
Victor Hedman	18	0	6	6	8
Adam Hall	18	1	4	5	8
Nate Thompson	18	1	3	4	4
Pavel Kubina	8	2	1	3	10
Marc-Andre Bergeron	14	2	1	3	9
Brett Clark	18	1	2	3	8
Mattias Ohlund	18	1	2	3	8
Mike Lundin	18	0	2	2	2
Randy Jones	5	0	1	1	2
Blair Jones	7	0	0	0	2
Dana Tyrell	7	0	0	0	2
Dwayne Roloson	17	0	0	0	0
Mike Smith	3	0	0	0	0
Mattias Ritola	1	0	0	0	0

In Goal	GP	W-L	Mins	GA	SO	GAA
Dwayne Roloson	17	10–6	981:49	41	1	2.51
Mike Smith	3	1–1	120:09	2	0	1.00

VANCOUVER CANUCKS

	GP	G	A	P	Pim
Henrik Sedin	25	3	19	22	16
Daniel Sedin	25	9	11	20	32
Ryan Kesler	25	7	12	19	47
Alexandre Burrows	25	9	8	17	34
Christian Ehrhoff	23	2	10	12	16
Alexander Edler	25	2	9	11	8
Kevin Bieksa	25	5	5	10	51
Jannik Hansen	25	3	6	9	18
Chris Higgins	25	4	4	8	2

	GP	G	A	P	Pim
Mason Raymond	24	2	6	8	6
Raffi Torres	23	3	4	7	28
Dan Hamhuis	19	1	5	6	6
Maxim Lapierre	25	3	2	5	56
Sami Salo	21	3	2	5	2
Mikael Samuelsson	11	1	2	3	8
Aaron Rome	14	1	0	1	37
Cody Hodgson	12	0	1	1	2
Tanner Glass	20	0	0	0	18
Victor Oreskovich	19	0	0	0	12
Keith Ballard	10	0	0	0	6
Andrew Alberts	9	0	0	0	6
Jeff Tambellini	6	0	0	0	2
Roberto Luongo	25	0	0	0	0
Manny Malhotra	6	0	0	0	0
Christopher Tanev	5	0	0	0	0
Cory Schneider	4	0	0	0	0
Alexandre Bolduc	3	0	0	0	0

In Goal	**GP**	**W-L**	**Mins**	**GA**	**SO**	**GAA**
Roberto Luongo	25	15–10	1,427:10	61	4	2.56
Cory Schneider	5	0–0	162:39	7	0	2.58

WASHINGTON CAPITALS

	GP	G	A	P	Pim
Alex Ovechkin	9	5	5	10	10
Brooks Laich	9	1	6	7	2
Alexander Semin	9	4	2	6	8
Marcus Johansson	9	2	4	6	0
Mike Green	8	1	5	6	8
Jason Arnott	9	1	5	6	2
Jason Chimera	9	2	2	4	2
John Carlson	9	2	1	3	4
Marco Sturm	9	1	2	3	4
Mike Knuble	6	2	0	2	8
John Erskine	9	1	1	2	6
Nicklas Backstrom	9	0	2	2	4
Eric Fehr	5	1	0	1	0
Scott Hannan	9	0	1	1	2
Karl Alzner	9	0	1	1	0
Boyd Gordon	9	0	0	0	6
Jeff Schultz	9	0	0	0	6

Matt Bradley	9	0	0	0	4
Matt Hendricks	7	0	0	0	4
Michal Neuvirth	9	0	0	0	0
Sean Collins	1	0	0	0	0

In Goal	**GP**	**W-L**	**Mins**	**GA**	**SO**	**GAA**
Michal Neuvirth	9	4-5	590:27	23	1	2.34

ALL REGULAR-SEASON SCORES, 2010–11

OCTOBER 7

Carolina 4, Minnesota 3 (at Helsinki, Finland)
Montreal 2 at Toronto 3 (Leafs led 2–0 midway through 1st)
Philadelphia 3 at Pittsburgh 2 (Flyers led 2–0 after 2nd)
Chicago 3 at Colorado 4 (Stastny 3:40 OT)
Calgary 0 at Edmonton 4 [Khabibulin]

OCTOBER 8

Minnesota 1, Carolina 2 (at Helsinki, Finland) (SO)
Columbus 3, San Jose 2 (at Stockholm, Sweden)
Dallas 4 at New Jersey 3 (Eriksson 1:36 OT)
Anaheim 0 at Detroit 4 [Howard]
Buffalo 2 at Ottawa 1 (one goal in each period)
Washington 2 at Atlanta 4 (E. Kane two goals)

OCTOBER 9

Phoenix 5, Boston 2 (at Prague, Czech Republic)
San Jose 3, Columbus 2 (at Stockholm, Sweden) (Moreau 1:56 OT)
NY Rangers 6 at Buffalo 3 (Stepan (NYR) hat trick)
Ottawa 1 at Toronto 5 (Leafs led 5–0 early in 3rd)
Dallas 5 at NY Islanders 4 (SO)
Montreal 3 at Pittsburgh 2 (Penguins led 2–1 late in 3rd)
New Jersey 2 at Washington 7 (Ovechkin (WAS) two goals)
Atlanta 3 at Tampa Bay 5 (Stamkos (TB) two goals)
Philadelphia 1 at St. Louis 2 (SO)
Anaheim 1 at Nashville 4 (Predators scored three goals in 2nd)
Detroit 3 at Chicago 2 (Red Wings scored only goal of 3rd)
Los Angeles 2 at Vancouver 1 (SO)

OCTOBER 10

Boston 3, Phoenix 0 (at Prague, Czech Republic)
Los Angeles 1 at Calgary 3 (Calgary had empty-net goal)
Florida 2 at Edmonton 3 (all goals in 2nd)

OCTOBER 11

Pittsburgh 3 at New Jersey 1 (Penguins had empty-net goal)
NY Rangers 4 at NY Islanders 6 (game tied 3–3 after 2nd)
Anaheim 1 at St. Louis 5 (D'Agostini two goals)
Chicago 4 at Buffalo 3 (Sabres led 2–0 early in 1st)
Colorado 2 at Philadelphia 4 (Carter (PHI) two goals)
Ottawa 2 at Washington 3 (Ovechkin 4:28 OT)
Florida 1 at Vancouver 2 (D. Sedin two goals)

OCTOBER 12

Colorado 5 at Detroit 4 (SO)
Atlanta 1 at Los Angeles 3 (Smyth two goals)

OCTOBER 13

New Jersey 1 at Buffalo 0 (Kovalchuk 0:53 OT)
NY Islanders 1 at Washington 2 (Islanders led 1–0 late in 2nd)
Tampa Bay 4 at Montreal 3 (Malone 4:09 OT)
Toronto 4 at Pittsburgh 3 (Leafs led 4–2 late in 2nd)
Nashville 3 at Chicago 2 (Predators scored only two goals of final two periods)
Vancouver 3 at Anaheim 4 (seven different scorers)

OCTOBER 14

Tampa Bay 3 at Philadelphia 2 (Lightning scored in each period)
Carolina 2 at Ottawa 3 (Fisher (OTT) two goals)
St. Louis 3 at Nashville 4 (Predators led 2–0 early in 1st)
Edmonton 2 at Minnesota 4 (M. Koivu two goals)
Detroit 1 at Dallas 4 (Red Wings scored only goal of 3rd)
Florida 3 at Calgary 0 [Vokoun]

OCTOBER 15

Colorado 3 at New Jersey 2 (Avs led 2–0 midway through 2nd)
Toronto 4 at NY Rangers 3 (Kessel 3:08 OT)
NY Islanders 2 at Pittsburgh 3 (Goligoski 1:51 OT)
Chicago 5 at Columbus 2 (Sharp (CHI) two goals)
Montreal 2 at Buffalo 1 (Habs led 2–0 after 2nd)
Atlanta 5 at Anaheim 4 (SO)
Vancouver 1 at Los Angeles 4 (D. Brown two goals)

OCTOBER 16

Ottawa 3 at Montreal 4 (Habs scored only goal of 3rd)
Boston 4 at New Jersey 1 (all goals in 2nd)
Colorado 2 at NY Islanders 5 (Jurcina (NYI) two goals)
Pittsburgh 5 at Philadelphia 1 (Flyers led 1–0 early in 1st)
Tampa Bay 0 at Florida 6 [Vokoun]
Washington 3 at Nashville 2 (Laich 1:44 OT)
Columbus 3 at Minnesota 2 (Blue Jackets scored only goal of 3rd)
St. Louis 2 at Dallas 3 (SO)
Buffalo 3 at Chicago 4 (Hawks scored only two goals of 3rd)
Detroit 2 at Phoenix 1 (Kronwall 4:44 OT)
Edmonton 3 at Calgary 5 (Oilers led 3–2 after 2nd)
Atlanta 4 at San Jose 2 (two goals in each period)

OCTOBER 17

Phoenix 2 at Anaheim 3 (game tied 2–2 midway through 3rd)
Carolina 1 at Vancouver 5 (Raymond two goals)

OCTOBER 18

NY Islanders 2 at Toronto 1 (Tavares 3:26 OT)
Colorado 3 at NY Rangers 1 (game tied 1–1 after 1st & 2nd)
Ottawa 2 at Pittsburgh 5 (Penguins led 3–0 early in 2nd)
Dallas 4 at Tampa Bay 5 (Moore (TB) two goals)
St. Louis 2 at Chicago 3 (Sharp 3:50 OT)

OCTOBER 19

Boston 3 at Washington 1 (Bruins led 2–0 after 1st)
Calgary 1 at Nashville 0 (Bourque 2:10 OT) [Kiprusoff]
Vancouver 2 at Minnesota 6 (Wild scored three goals in 1st & 2nd)
Carolina 5 at San Jose 2 (Marleau both goals for SJ)

OCTOBER 20

Buffalo 4 at Atlanta 1 (Sabres led 3–0 after 2nd)
Anaheim 1 at Columbus 3 (Nash two goals)
Vancouver 1 at Chicago 2 (SO)
Carolina 3 at Los Angeles 4 (Kings scored only goal of 3rd)

OCTOBER 21

Washington 1 at Boston 4 (Bruins led 3–0 midway through 2nd)
NY Rangers 2 at Toronto 1 (Rangers led 2–0 after 1st & 2nd)
Anaheim 3 at Philadelphia 2 (game tied 1–1 early in 1st)
Calgary 2 at Detroit 4 (game tied 1–1 late in 1st)
New Jersey 3 at Montreal 0 [Brodeur]
NY Islanders 3 at Tampa Bay 2 (Moulson 1:56 OT)
Dallas 4 at Florida 1 (Wandell two goals)
Pittsburgh 4 at Nashville 3 (Letang 3:49 OT)
San Jose 4 at Colorado 2 (Pavelski (SJ) two goals)
Minnesota 4 at Edmonton 2 (Wild led 2–0 midway through 1st)
Los Angeles 2 at Phoenix 4 (Stempniak hat trick)

OCTOBER 22

Calgary 6 at Columbus 2 (Bourque hat trick)
Ottawa 4 at Buffalo 2 (game tied 2–2 early in 2nd)
Tampa Bay 5 at Atlanta 2 (Stamkos hat trick)
Chicago 2 at St. Louis 4 (Blues scored only two goals of 3rd)
Minnesota 1 at Vancouver 5 (Malhotra two goals)

OCTOBER 23

NY Rangers 3 at Boston 2 (no scoring in 3rd)
Montreal 3 at Ottawa 0 [Price]
Buffalo 6 at New Jersey 1 (Sabres led 5–0 midway through 3rd)
Toronto 2 at Philadelphia 5 (Flyers led 2–1 early in 2nd)
Atlanta 3 at Washington 4 (Fleischmann 1:37 OT)
NY Islanders 3 at Florida 4 (Panthers scored only goal of 3rd)
Anaheim 4 at Detroit 5 (Zetterberg (DET) two goals)
Pittsburgh 0 at St. Louis 1 (E. Johnson 0:50 OT) [Halak]
Nashville 1 at Dallas 0 (C. O'Reilly 0:42 1st) [Rinne]
Columbus 3 at Chicago 2 (Hawks led 2–0 after 1st)
Los Angeles 6 at Colorado 4 (Richardson (LA) hat trick)
Carolina 4 at Phoenix 3 (Babchuk 2:52 OT)
San Jose 6 at Edmonton 1 (Oilers led 1–0 early in 1st)

OCTOBER 24

Nashville 4 at Tampa Bay 3 (seven different scorers)
New Jersey 1 at NY Rangers 3 (Rangers had empty-net goal)
San Jose 0 at Calgary 4 [Kiprusoff]

OCTOBER 25

Philadelphia 1 at Columbus 2 (one goal in each period)
Phoenix 2 at Montreal 3 (A. Kostitsyn 1:25 OT)
Los Angeles 3 at Minnesota 2 (SO)

OCTOBER 26

Florida 1 at Toronto 3 (Leafs scored only two goals of 3rd)
Buffalo 3 at Philadelphia 6 (nine different scorers)
Phoenix 2 at Ottawa 5 (Kovalev (OTT) two goals)
Edmonton 4 at Calgary 5 (SO)
Anaheim 5 at Dallas 2 (game tied 1–1 early in 2nd)
Colorado 3 at Vancouver 4 (Raymond 0:28 OT)

OCTOBER 27

Atlanta 6 at NY Rangers 4 (ten different scorers)
Washington 3 at Carolina 0 [Neuvirth]
NY Islanders 3 at Montreal 5 (Habs had empty-net goal)
Pittsburgh 3 at Tampa Bay 5 (Penguins scored all goals in 1st)
Los Angeles 1 at Chicago 3 (game tied 1–1 midway through 1st)
New Jersey 2 at San Jose 5 (Thornton hat trick)

OCTOBER 28

Toronto 0 at Boston 2 [Thomas]
Phoenix 4 at Detroit 2 (Coyotes had empty-net goal)
Edmonton 2 at Columbus 3 (SO)
Florida 3 at Ottawa 5 (eight different scorers)
St. Louis 3 at Nashville 0 [Halak]
Washington 1 at Minnesota 2 (one goal in each period)
Los Angeles 5 at Dallas 2 (game tied 1–1 after 1st)
Colorado 6 at Calgary 5 (Stewart scored first three Avs goals)

OCTOBER 29

Montreal 3 at NY Islanders 1 (game tied 1–1 after 2nd)
Carolina 4 at NY Rangers 3 (Hurricanes scored only goal of 3rd)
Philadelphia 3 at Pittsburgh 2 (Penguins led 1–0 early in 2nd)
Buffalo 3 at Atlanta 4 (Byfuglien 4:31 OT)
Edmonton 7 at Chicago 4 (game tied 1–1 early in 1st)
New Jersey 2 at Anaheim 1 (no scoring in 1st)

OCTOBER 30

NY Rangers 2 at Toronto 0 [Lundqvist]
Florida 3 at Montreal 1 (game tied 1–1 early in 2nd)
Boston 4 at Ottawa 0 [Thomas]
NY Islanders 1 at Philadelphia 6 (Carter & Pronger two goals each)
Pittsburgh 3 at Carolina 0 [Johnson]
Nashville 2 at Detroit 5 (Datsyuk (DET) two goals)
Atlanta 3 at St. Louis 4 (SO)
Chicago 3 at Minnesota 1 (Hawks had empty-net goal)
Buffalo 0 at Dallas 4 [Raycroft]
Columbus 1 at Colorado 5 (Avs scored only three goals of 2nd)
Tampa Bay 3 at Phoenix 0 [Ellis]
Washington 7 at Calgary 2 (Caps scored only six goals of 2nd)
New Jersey 1 at Los Angeles 3 (no scoring in 3rd)
Anaheim 2 at San Jose 5 (Heatley (SJ) two goals)

OCTOBER 31

No games

NOVEMBER 1

Chicago 2 at NY Rangers 3 (game tied 2–2 early in 3rd)
Carolina 2 at Philadelphia 3 (Hurricanes scored in final minute)
New Jersey 0 at Vancouver 3 [Luongo]

NOVEMBER 2

Ottawa 3 at Toronto 2 (Leafs scored only two goals of 3rd)
Montreal 0 at Columbus 3 [Garon]
San Jose 0 at Minnesota 1 (Brunette 13:19 2nd) [Backstrom]
Vancouver 4 at Edmonton 3 (Torres (VAN) hat trick)

NOVEMBER 3

Boston 5 at Buffalo 2 (Bruins led 4–0 early 2nd)
Toronto 4 at Washington 5 (SO)
NY Islanders 2 at Carolina 7 (Matsumoto (CAR) two goals)
Atlanta 4 at Florida 3 (game tied 3–3 midway through 3rd)
New Jersey 5 at Chicago 3 (Devils led 2–0 late in 2nd)
Pittsburgh 2 at Dallas 5 (Stars led 2–1 early in 2nd)
Detroit 2 at Calgary 1 (Flames led 1–0 after 1st)

Nashville 3 at Phoenix 4 (Jovanovski (PHO) hat trick)
Tampa Bay 2 at Anaheim 3 (Getzlaf 2:53 OT)

NOVEMBER 4

NY Rangers 1 at Philadelphia 4 Flyers scored three goals in 2nd)
Columbus 3 at Atlanta 0 [Garon]
NY Islanders 1 at Ottawa 4 (Senators had empty-net goal)
San Jose 0 at St. Louis 2 [Halak]
Vancouver 3 at Colorado 1 (Canucks scored in each period)
Tampa Bay 0 at Los Angeles 1 (Williams 5:20 3rd) [Quick]

NOVEMBER 5

NY Rangers 3 at New Jersey 0 [Lundqvist]
Boston 3 at Washington 5 (eight different scorers)
Montreal 3 at Buffalo 2 (no scoring in 3rd)
Carolina 4 at Florida 7 (Weiss (FLO) two goals)
Calgary 1 at Minnesota 2 (Wild scored only goal of last two periods)
Phoenix 3 at Dallas 6 (Eriksson & Richards (DAL) two goals each)
Detroit 3 at Edmonton 1 (game tied 1–1 early in 2nd)
Pittsburgh 2 at Anaheim 3 (Crosby both PIT goals)

NOVEMBER 6

Nashville 1 at Los Angeles 4 (Predators scored only goal of 3rd)
St. Louis 2 at Boston 1 (SO)
Buffalo 3 at Toronto 2 (SO)
Ottawa 3 at Montreal 2 (Habs scored late goal)
Philadelphia 2 at NY Islanders 1 (one goal in each period)
Florida 2 at Carolina 3 (Hurricanes led 1–0 after 2nd)
Chicago 5 at Atlanta 4 (SO)
Minnesota 3 at Columbus 2 (game tied 2–2 after 2nd)
Dallas 0 at Colorado 5 [Budaj]
Pittsburgh 4 at Phoenix 3 (SO)
Detroit 4 at Vancouver 6 (Red Wings led 4–3 early in 3rd)
Tampa Bay 2 at San Jose 5 (game tied 1–1 midway through 1st)

NOVEMBER 7

Philadelphia 2 at Washington 3 (Green 0:29 OT)
St. Louis 2 at NY Rangers 0 [Conklin]
Edmonton 2 at Chicago 1 (Hawks led 1–0 after 1st & 2nd)
Nashville 4 at Anaheim 5 (Ducks outscored Predators 3–2 in 3rd)

NOVEMBER 8

Phoenix 2 at Detroit 3 (Zetterberg 1:23 OT)

NOVEMBER 9

Washington 5 at NY Rangers 3 (Capitals had empty-net goal)
Edmonton 1 at Carolina 7 (Oilers trailed 6–0 early in 3rd)
Vancouver 0 at Montreal 2 [Price]
Atlanta 2 at Ottawa 5 (Thrashers led 1–0 early in 1st)
Toronto 0 at Tampa Bay 4 [Ellis]
Calgary 4 at Colorado 2 (Glencross (CAL) two goals)
Anaheim 3 at San Jose 2 (Visnovsky 4:27 OT)

NOVEMBER 10

Buffalo 5 at New Jersey 4 (SO)
Boston 7 at Pittsburgh 4 (eleven different scorers)
St. Louis 1 at Columbus 8 (Clark & Voracek two goals each)
Toronto 1 at Florida 4 (Panthers led 2–0 after 2nd)
Phoenix 2 at Chicago 1 (no scoring in 3rd)
NY Islanders 0 at Anaheim 1 (S. Koivu 3:40 3rd) [McElhinney]

NOVEMBER 11

Montreal 3 at Boston 1 (game tied 1–1 after 1st & 2nd)
Buffalo 2 at NY Rangers 3 (Anisimov 1:32 OT)
Tampa Bay 3 at Washington 6 (Caps led 2–1 after 2nd)
Philadelphia 8 at Carolina 1 (Carter hat trick)
Minnesota 1 at Atlanta 5 (Thrashers led 3–0 early in 3rd)
Edmonton 2 at Detroit 6 (Cleary (DET) two goals)
Vancouver 6 at Ottawa 2 (game tied 1–1 after 1st)
Nashville 3 at St. Louis 2 (SO)
Dallas 1 at Los Angeles 3 (game tied 1–1 after 1st & 2nd)
NY Islanders 1 at San Jose 2 (SO)

NOVEMBER 12

Edmonton 3 at New Jersey 4 (Kovalchuk 3:27 OT)
Tampa Bay 1 at Pittsburgh 5 (Penguins led 2–1 early in 3rd)
Colorado 5 at Columbus 1 (Jones two goals)
Minnesota 1 at Florida 2 (all goals in 1st)
Calgary 4 at Phoenix 5 (Flames scored twice in final minute)
Dallas 2 at Anaheim 4 (game tied 1–1 after 1st & 2nd)

NOVEMBER 13

Ottawa 2 at Boston 0 [Elliott]
Washington 2 at Buffalo 3 (Vanek 4:00 OT)
Vancouver 5 at Toronto 3 (Canucks scored only two goals of 3rd)
Carolina 2 at Montreal 7 (game tied 2–2 midway through 2nd)
Florida 2 at Philadelphia 5 (Flyers led 5–0 midway through 2nd)
Pittsburgh 4 at Atlanta 2 (game tied 1–1 after 2nd)
Colorado 1 at Detroit 3 (Avs scored only goal of 3rd)
Chicago 3 at Nashville 4 (SO)
St. Louis 3 at Phoenix 5 (Coyotes had empty-net goal)
Calgary 3 at San Jose 4 (Flames scored in final minute)
NY Islanders 1 at Los Angeles 5 (Kings led 2–1 early in 1st)

NOVEMBER 14

Edmonton 2 at NY Rangers 8 (Gaborik hat trick)
Atlanta 4 at Washington 6 (game tied 4–4 after 2nd)
Minnesota 4 at Tampa Bay 1 (game tied 1–1 midway through 1st)
Anaheim 2 at Chicago 3 (Stalberg 4:32 OT)

NOVEMBER 15

New Jersey 0 at Boston 3 [Thomas]
Vancouver 3 at Buffalo 4 (Myers 4:37 OT)
Ottawa 1 at Philadelphia 5 (game tied 1–1 midway through 1st)
NY Rangers 3 at Pittsburgh 2 (Callahan 3:38 OT)
St. Louis 3 at Colorado 6 (both teams scored in all periods)
Los Angeles 3 at San Jose 6 (nine different scorers)

NOVEMBER 16

Nashville 4 at Toronto 5 (no scoring in 3rd)
Philadelphia 0 at Montreal 3 [Price]
Anaheim 1 at Dallas 2 (Stars scored only goal of 3rd)

NOVEMBER 17

Tampa Bay 4 at NY Islanders 2 (Lightning had empty-net goal)
Boston 3 at NY Rangers 2 (Rangers led 1–0 midway through 2nd)
Vancouver 1 at Pittsburgh 3 (no scoring in 3rd)
Buffalo 2 at Washington 4 (Capitals had empty-net goal)
Ottawa 1 at Carolina 7 ('Canes led 4–0 after 1st)
Florida 2 at Atlanta 1 (no scoring in 3rd)
St. Louis 3 at Detroit 7 (Red Wings scored only four goals of 3rd)
Anaheim 1 at Minnesota 2 (Miettinen 3:36 OT)
San Jose 3 at Colorado 4 (Porter 2:07 OT)
Phoenix 3 at Calgary 1 (Coyotes had empty-net goal)
Chicago 5 at Edmonton 0 (Turco)
Columbus 5 at Los Angeles 3 (Nash (CBJ) two goals)

NOVEMBER 18

Florida 0 at Boston 4 [Rask]
New Jersey 1 at Toronto 3 (Leafs led 2–0 midway through 2nd)
Tampa Bay 8 at Philadelphia 7 (Flyers led 5–4 after 1st)
Nashville 3 at Montreal 0 (Rinne)
San Jose 4 at Dallas 5 (Ribeiro 2:52 OT)

NOVEMBER 19

Carolina 4 at Pittsburgh 5 (SO)
Minnesota 4 at Detroit 3 (Madden 4:18 OT)
Los Angeles 2 at Buffalo 4 (Sabres scored only two goals of 3rd)
Washington 0 at Atlanta 5 [Pavelec]
Ottawa 2 at St. Louis 5 (Senators led 1–0 midway through 2nd)
NY Rangers 1 at Colorado 5 (Avs scored only four goals of 2nd)
Chicago 2 at Calgary 7 (Iginla hat trick)
Phoenix 4 at Edmonton 3 (SO)
Columbus 4 at Anaheim 3 (Blue Jackets outscored Ducks 3–2 in 2nd)

NOVEMBER 20

Los Angeles 4 at Boston 3 (SO)
Tampa Bay 2 at Buffalo 1 (no scoring in 3rd)
Toronto 0 at Montreal 2 (Price)
Florida 4 at NY Islanders 1 (Panthers scored all goals in 2nd)
Philadelphia 5 at Washington 4 (SO)
Nashville 2 at Carolina 1 (SO)
New Jersey 2 at St. Louis 3 (Blues scored only goal of 3rd)
NY Rangers 5 at Minnesota 2 (Rangers led 4–0 early in 3rd)
Colorado 4 at Dallas 3 (SO)
Chicago 7 at Vancouver 1 (Pisani two goals)
Columbus 3 at San Jose 0 (Jackets scored in each period)

NOVEMBER 21

NY Islanders 1 at Atlanta 2 (Byfuglien 1:30 OT)
Calgary 4 at Detroit 5 (Lidstrom 1:38 OT)
Edmonton 4 at Anaheim 2 (Oilers scored only two goals of 3rd)
Phoenix 3 at Vancouver 2 (game tied 2–2 after 2nd)

NOVEMBER 22

Dallas 1 at Toronto 4 (Leafs led 2–1 late in 2nd)
Washington 0 at New Jersey 5 [Hedberg]
Calgary 1 at NY Rangers 2 (all goals in 2nd)
Montreal 2 at Philadelphia 3 (Habs led 2–0 after 1st)
Nashville 0 at Columbus 2 [S. Mason]
Los Angeles 2 at Ottawa 3 (Sens got only goal of 3rd)
Boston 1 at Tampa Bay 3 (Lightning scored only three goals of 2nd)
Pittsburgh 3 at Florida 2 (Penguins scored only goal of 3rd)

NOVEMBER 23

Edmonton 0 at Phoenix 5 [Bryzgalov]

NOVEMBER 24

Pittsburgh 1 at Buffalo 0 (Dupuis 15:04 1st) [Enroth]
Columbus 4 at NY Islanders 3 (Voracek 2:31 OT)
Washington 3 at Carolina 2 (Backstrom (WAS) two goals)
Detroit 1 at Atlanta 5 (Thrashers led 2–1 after 1st)
Los Angeles 1 at Montreal 4 (Habs led 2–1 early in 2nd)

Dallas 2 at Ottawa 1 (Stars scored only goal of 3rd)
Calgary 1 at New Jersey 2 (SO)
NY Rangers 3 at Tampa Bay 5 (Rangers scored only goals of 3rd)
Boston 3 at Florida 1 (Panthers led 1–0 after 2nd)
St. Louis 2 at Nashville 1 (SO)
Philadelphia 6 at Minnesota 1 (Flyers led 2–1 late in 2nd)
Colorado 2 at Vancouver 4 (game tied 1–1 midway through 2nd)
Chicago 2 at San Jose 5 (Sharks led 2–1 early in 2nd)

NOVEMBER 25

Colorado 2 at Edmonton 3 (Oilers scored only goal of 3rd)

NOVEMBER 26

Carolina 3 at Boston 0 [Ward]
New Jersey 0 at NY Islanders 2 [DiPietro]
Calgary 3 at Philadelphia 2 (SO)
Ottawa 1 at Pittsburgh 2 (Penguins trailed 1–0 after 1st)
Nashville 2 at Minnesota 5 (Havlat (MIN) two goals)
Chicago 4 at Anaheim 1 (game tied 1–1 after 2nd)
Tampa Bay 0 at Washington 6 [Varlamov]
Detroit 2 at Columbus 1 (Red Wings led 1–0 early in 3rd)
Toronto 1 at Buffalo 3 (Sabres led 2–0 after 1st & 2nd)
Montreal 0 at Atlanta 3 [Pavelec]
NY Rangers 3 at Florida 0 [Lundqvist]
St. Louis 2 at Dallas 3 (Stars trailed 2–1 after 2nd)
San Jose 1 at Vancouver 6 (game tied 1–1 after 1st)

NOVEMBER 27

Philadelphia 1 at New Jersey 2 (SO)
Calgary 1 at Pittsburgh 4 (Crosby hat trick)
Buffalo 1 at Montreal 3 (Sabres scored only goal of 3rd)
Toronto 0 at Ottawa 3 [Elliott]
Florida 4 at Tampa Bay 3 (SO)
Dallas 2 at St. Louis 1 (Stars trailed 1–0 after 2nd)
NY Rangers 2 at Nashville 1 (SO)
Anaheim 6 at Phoenix 4 (game tied 3–3 after 2nd)
Minnesota 4 at Colorado 7 (game tied 2–2 early in 2nd)
San Jose 4 at Edmonton 3 (game tied 1–1 early in 1st)
Chicago 2 at Los Angeles 1 (Hawks led 2–0 early in 3rd)

NOVEMBER 28

Carolina 2 at Washington 3 (SO)
Boston 1 at Atlanta 4 (Thrashers led 3–0 after 1st)
Columbus 2 at Detroit 4 (Blue Jackets led 1–0 midway through 2nd)

NOVEMBER 29

Pittsburgh 3 at NY Rangers 1 (no scoring in 3rd)
Dallas 4 at Carolina 1 (Stars led 3–1 early in 2nd)
Edmonton 4 at Ottawa 1 (Oilers scored only three goals of 3rd)
Minnesota 0 at Calgary 3 [Kiprusoff]
Los Angeles 0 at Anaheim 2 [Hiller]

NOVEMBER 30

Tampa Bay 4 at Toronto 3 (OT)
Phoenix 0 at Nashville 3 [Rinne]
St. Louis 5 at Chicago 7 (Toews and Kane (CHI) two goals each)
Atlanta 3 at Colorado 2 (Stewart 1:49 OT)
Detroit 5 at San Jose 3 (Zetterberg (DET) two goals)

DECEMBER 1

Edmonton 4 at Montreal 3 (Penner 2:28 OT)
Boston 3 at Philadelphia 0 [Thomas]
Nashville 4 at Columbus 3 (SO)
Washington 4 at St. Louis 1 (Caps scored only two goals of 3rd)
Phoenix 4 at Minnesota 2 (Coyotes led 2–1 late in 3rd)
Vancouver 7 at Calgary 2 (Raymond hat trick)
Florida 3 at Anaheim 5 (Ducks led 3–2 early in 3rd)

DECEMBER 2

Tampa Bay 1 at Boston 8 (Bruins led 3–1 late in 2nd)
Edmonton 5 at Toronto 0 [Khabibulin]
Montreal 5 at New Jersey 1 (Devils scored only goal of 3rd)
NY Rangers 6 at NY Islanders 5 (Rangers scored twice in each period)
Atlanta 2 at Pittsburgh 3 (Crosby hat trick)
San Jose 4 at Ottawa 0 [Niemi]
Washington 1 at Dallas 2 (no scoring in 1st)
Florida 2 at Los Angeles 3 (Kings scored only two goals in 3rd)

DECEMBER 3

NY Islanders 0 at NY Rangers 2 [Lundqvist]
Colorado 1 at Carolina 2 (B. Sutter 1:16 OT)
Columbus 0 at Buffalo 5 [Miller]
Calgary 3 at Minnesota 2 (SO)
Vancouver 3 at Chicago 0 [Luongo]
Detroit 4 at Anaheim 0 [Howard]

DECEMBER 4

New Jersey 3 at Philadelphia 5 (game tied 2–2 after 2nd)
San Jose 1 at Montreal 3 (game tied 1–1 midway through 1st)
Boston 2 at Toronto 3 (SO)
Buffalo 1 at Ottawa 0 (SO)
Atlanta 3 at Washington 1 (Thrashers led 2–0 midway through 2nd)
Pittsburgh 7 at Columbus 2 (Penguins led 4–0 after 1st)
Colorado 5 at Tampa Bay 6 (eleven different scorers)
Carolina 2 at Nashville 5 (game tied 1–1 early in 1st)
Minnesota 3 at Dallas 4 (Robidas 3:37 OT)
Florida 2 at Phoenix 1 (SO)
St. Louis 1 at Edmonton 2 (Hall 0:23 OT)
Detroit 2 at Los Angeles 3 (Kopitar 4:04 OT)

DECEMBER 5

Philadelphia 3 at NY Islanders 2 (Flyers led 1–0 after 1st & 2nd)
Ottawa 3 at NY Rangers 1 (Kelly all Senators goals)
Calgary 2 at Chicago 4 (Hawks led 2–1 midway through 1st)
Phoenix 3 at Anaheim 0 (Coyotes scored in each period)
St. Louis 3 at Vancouver 2 (Blues scored only goal of 3rd)

DECEMBER 6

New Jersey 1 at Pittsburgh 2 (no scoring in 3rd)
Toronto 5 at Washington 4 (SO)
Nashville 2 at Atlanta 3 (Bogosian 2:11 OT)
San Jose 5 at Detroit 2 (Couture (SJ) two goals)
Dallas 2 at Columbus 3 (SO)

DECEMBER 7

Buffalo 2 at Boston 3 (Recchi 2:11 OT)
Ottawa 1 at Montreal 4 (game tied 1–1 after 1st & 2nd)
Colorado 3 at Florida 4 (Weiss 0:43 OT)
Tampa Bay 2 at Calgary 4 (Flames led 3–0 early in 2nd)
Anaheim 3 at Edmonton 2 (SO)

DECEMBER 8

San Jose 5 at Philadelphia 4 (SO)
Toronto 2 at Pittsburgh 5 (Letestu & Crosby (PIT) two goals each)
Nashville 3 at Detroit 2 (Predators led 2–0 early in 2nd)
Dallas 3 at Chicago 5 (Hawks led 3–0 early in 2nd)
Anaheim 4 at Vancouver 5 (SO)

DECEMBER 9

NY Islanders 2 at Boston 5 (Bruins scored three goals in 3rd)
San Jose 3 at Buffalo 6 (Gaustad & Vanek (BUF) two goals each)
Philadelphia 4 at Toronto 1 (Briere two goals)
Florida 3 at Washington 0 [Vokoun]
NY Rangers 5 at Ottawa 3 (Rangers trailed 3–2 after 2nd)
Columbus 1 at St. Louis 4 (Blues had empty-net goal)
Minnesota 3 at Phoenix 2 (game tied 1–1 late in 1st)
Calgary 1 at Los Angeles 2 (Flames scored late in 3rd)

DECEMBER 10

Montreal 2 at Detroit 4 (Red Wings had empty-net goal)
New Jersey 2 at Ottawa 3 (no scoring in 3rd)
Colorado 4 at Atlanta 2 (Avs scored only two goals of 3rd)
Carolina 1 at Dallas 2 (SO)
Tampa Bay 3 at Edmonton 4 (SO)
Calgary 2 at Anaheim 3 (SO)

DECEMBER 11

Philadelphia 2 at Boston 1 (Richards 4:57 OT)
Pittsburgh 5 at Buffalo 2 (Penguins led 2–1 after 1st & 2nd)
Montreal 1 at Toronto 3 (Leafs had empty-net goal)
Detroit 4 at New Jersey 1 (Red Wings led 3–0 after 2nd)
Atlanta 5 at NY Islanders 4 (Thrashers scored four goals in 3rd)

Colorado 3 at Washington 2 (game tied 1–1 midway through 1st)
NY Rangers 1 at Columbus 3 (game tied 1–1 after 2nd)
Carolina 2 at St. Louis 1 (SO)
Florida 0 at Nashville 3 [Lindback]
Dallas 2 at Phoenix 5 (Coyotes led 3–0 after 1st)
Tampa Bay 5 at Vancouver 4 (Stamkos 0:34 OT)
Minnesota 3 at Los Angeles 2 (Burns 2:50 OT)
Chicago 1 at San Jose 2 (Clowe 3:52 OT)

DECEMBER 12

Washington 0 at NY Rangers 7 [Lundqvist]
Vancouver 2 at Edmonton 1 (Oilers scored only goal of 3rd)
Minnesota 2 at Anaheim 6 (Perry hat trick)

DECEMBER 13

Los Angeles 5 at Detroit 0 [Quick]
Atlanta 4 at Ottawa 3 (Little 1:09 OT)
NY Islanders 0 at Nashville 5 [Lindback]
Chicago 5 at Colorado 7 (game tied 4–4 after 2nd)
Columbus 2 at Calgary 3 (Iginla 3:49 OT)
Dallas 3 at San Jose 2 (SO)

DECEMBER 14

Pittsburgh 2 at Philadelphia 3 (Hartnell broke 2–2 tie midway through 3rd)
Toronto 4 at Edmonton 1 (Leafs led 2–0 midway through 1st)

DECEMBER 15

Boston 2 at Buffalo 3 (Stafford all Sabres goals)
Phoenix 0 at New Jersey 3 [Brodeur]
NY Rangers 4 at Pittsburgh 1 (Penguins led 1–0 after 1st & 2nd)
Anaheim 2 at Washington 1 (Getzlaf 4:03 OT)
St. Louis 2 at Detroit 5 (Lidstrom hat trick)
Philadelphia 5 at Montreal 3 (van Riemsdyk (PHI) two goals)
Atlanta 1 at Tampa Bay 2 (SO)
Carolina 4 at Florida 3 (Panthers led 3–1 after 2nd)
San Jose 2 at Nashville 3 (Predators scored only two goals of 3rd)
Colorado 4 at Chicago 3 (Fleischmann (COL) hat trick)
Columbus 2 at Vancouver 3 (Kesler 3:30 OT)

DECEMBER 16

Anaheim 2 at NY Islanders 3 (Islanders led 3–0 late in 1st)
Phoenix 3 at NY Rangers 4 (SO)
Carolina 3 at Atlanta 2 (SO)
Boston 3 at Montreal 4 (Habs led 2–1 late in 1st)
Los Angeles 4 at St. Louis 6 (Blues scored only two goals of 3rd)
Ottawa 3 at Minnesota 1 (Wild led 1–0 after 1st)
San Jose 4 at Dallas 3 (Couture 1:20 OT)
Toronto 2 at Calgary 5 (Flames scored only three goals of 2nd)
Columbus 3 at Edmonton 6 (Huselius (CBJ) hat trick)

DECEMBER 17

Nashville 3 at New Jersey 1 (Devils scored final goal)
Buffalo 2 at Florida 6 (Panthers led 4–0 after 1st)
Detroit 1 at Chicago 4 (Kopecky two goals)
Ottawa 5 at Colorado 6 (Duchene 2:36 OT)

DECEMBER 18

NY Rangers 1 at Philadelphia 4 (Flyers scored three goals in 3rd)
Washington 2 at Boston 3 (Bruins led 3–0 after 1st)
Phoenix 4 at NY Islanders 3 (SO)
Anaheim 2 at Carolina 4 (E. Staal hat trick)
New Jersey 1 at Atlanta 7 (Boulton hat trick)
Dallas 2 at Columbus 1 (Stars scored only goal of 3rd)
Buffalo 1 at Tampa Bay 3 (Lightning scored only goal of 3rd)
San Jose 4 at St. Louis 1 (Sharks led 3–0 midway through 2nd)
Los Angeles 6 at Nashville 1 (no scoring in 3rd)
Minnesota 3 at Calgary 1 (Flames scored final goal)
Toronto 1 at Vancouver 4 (Canucks led 2–1 early in 3rd)

DECEMBER 19

Washington 3 at Ottawa 2 (no scoring in 3rd)
Dallas 4 at Detroit 3 (Eriksson 4:18 OT)
Los Angeles 2 at Chicago 3 (game tied 1–1 early in 2nd)
Montreal 2 at Colorado 3 (no scoring in 3rd)

DECEMBER 20

Anaheim 3 at Boston 0 [Hiller]
Atlanta 6 at Toronto 3 (Thrashers led 5–1 early in 3rd)
Florida 5 at Philadelphia 0 [Vokoun]
Phoenix 1 at Pittsburgh 6 (Malkin two goals)
Carolina 1 at Tampa Bay 5 (game tied 1–1 late in 1st)
Vancouver 3 at St. Louis 1 (Canucks led 2–0 midway through 2nd)
Calgary 1 at Minnesota 4 (game tied 1–1 after 2nd)

DECEMBER 21

Anaheim 2 at Buffalo 5 (Sabres led 4–0 late in 3rd)
New Jersey 1 at Washington 5 (game tied 1–1 early in 2nd)
St. Louis 4 at Atlanta 2 (game tied 1–1 early in 1st)
Calgary 1 at Columbus 3 (Blue Jackets scored in each period)
Montreal 2 at Dallas 5 (Stars led 3–0 early in 2nd)
Los Angeles 5 at Colorado 0 [Quick]
Edmonton 1 at San Jose 2 (Sharks led 2–0 after 2nd)

DECEMBER 22

Tampa Bay 1 at NY Islanders 2 (Tavares 3:23 OT)
Florida 2 at Pittsburgh 5 (seven different scorers)
Vancouver 4 at Detroit 5 (Zetterberg 2:59 OT)
Nashville 1 at Chicago 4 (Skille two goals)

DECEMBER 23

Atlanta 1 at Boston 4 (S. Thornton two goals)
Florida 4 at Buffalo 3 (Panthers led 3–0 after 1st)
NY Islanders 5 at New Jersey 1 (Bailey two goals)
Tampa Bay 4 at NY Rangers 3 (SO)
Pittsburgh 3 at Washington 2 (SO)
Montreal 3 at Carolina 2 (all goals in 2nd)
Vancouver 7 at Columbus 3 (Canucks led 6–0 midway through 2nd)
Detroit 3 at St. Louis 4 (Berglund (STL) two goals)
Ottawa 2 at Nashville 1 (no scoring in 3rd)
Calgary 3 at Dallas 2 (SO)
Minnesota 3 at Colorado 1 (no scoring in 3rd)
Edmonton 2 at Los Angeles 3 (SO)
Phoenix 1 at San Jose 4 (Marleau two goals)

DECEMBER 26

Pittsburgh 1 at Ottawa 3 (Karlsson two goals)
Toronto 4 at New Jersey 1 (Leafs led 3–0 after 2nd)
Montreal 1 at NY Islanders 4 (Habs scored final goal)
Washington 3 at Carolina 2 (game tied 1–1 early in 2nd)
Tampa Bay 3 at Atlanta 2 (Lecavalier 1:13 OT)
Columbus 1 at Chicago 4 (Hawks scored three goals in 3rd)
Nashville 0 at St. Louis 2 [Halak]
Detroit 4 at Minnesota 1 (Wild scored only goal of 3rd)
Phoenix 1 at Dallas 0 (Turris 10:46 2nd) [LaBarbera]
Edmonton 2 at Vancouver 3 (Canucks scored only two goals of 3rd)
Anaheim 1 at Los Angeles 4 (all goals in 2nd)

DECEMBER 27

NY Islanders 2 at NY Rangers 7 (game tied 2–2 after 1st)
Minnesota 3 at Columbus 4 (SO)
Boston 3 at Florida 2 (SO)
Detroit 4 at Colorado 3 (Kronwall 3:42 OT)
Buffalo 2 at Calgary 5 (Sabres led 1–0 after 1st)
Los Angeles 4 at San Jose 0 (0–0 after 2nd) [Quick]

DECEMBER 28

Carolina 4 at Toronto 3 (game tied 3–3 after 2nd)
Atlanta 3 at Pittsburgh 6 (Crosby (PIT) two goals)
Montreal 0 at Washington 3 [Varlamov]
Boston 4 at Tampa Bay 3 (both teams scored in all periods)
Chicago 1 at St. Louis 3 (Blues scored only two goals of 3rd)
Dallas 4 at Nashville 2 (game tied 1–1 after 2nd)
Buffalo 4 at Edmonton 2 (Weber (BUF) two goals)
Anaheim 3 at Phoenix 1 (no scoring in 3rd)
Philadelphia 2 at Vancouver 6 (Kesler (VAN) two goals)

DECEMBER 29

NY Rangers 3 at New Jersey 1 (game tied 1–1 early in 1st)
Pittsburgh 1 at NY Islanders 2 (SO)
Carolina 4 at Ottawa 0 [Ward]
San Jose 3 at Minnesota 5 (Wild scored only three goals of 3rd)
Detroit 7 at Dallas 3 (Eaves (DET) hat trick)
Los Angeles 3 at Phoenix 6 (Doan (PHO) two goals)

DECEMBER 30

Columbus 3 at Toronto 2 (Huselius (CBJ) two goals)
Boston 2 at Atlanta 3 (SO)
Montreal 1 at Tampa Bay 4 (Stamkos two goals)
San Jose 5 at Chicago 3 (Sharks scored only two goals of 3rd)
Colorado 4 at Edmonton 3 (SO)
Philadelphia 7 at Los Angeles 4 (Flyers led 4–3 midway through 2nd)

DECEMBER 31

Atlanta 1 at New Jersey 3 (Devils led 2–0 after 2nd)
Montreal 3 at Florida 2 (Wisniewski 3:41 OT)
Nashville 4 at Minnesota 1 (Predators had empty-net goal)
NY Islanders 4 at Detroit 3 (Parenteau 3:57 OT)
Ottawa 3 at Columbus 4 (Voracek 2:06 OT)
Phoenix 3 at St. Louis 4 (Coyotes scored all goals in 3rd)
Philadelphia 2 at Anaheim 5 (Ducks led 3–0 midway through 2nd)
Vancouver 4 at Dallas 1 (Canucks led 4–0 after 2nd)
Colorado 3 at Calgary 4 (Flames scored all goals in 2nd)

JANUARY 1

Washington 3 at Pittsburgh 1 (played at Heinz Field—Crosby suffered concussion)
Boston 6 at Buffalo 7 (SO)
Toronto 5 at Ottawa 1 (no scoring in 3rd)
New Jersey 3 at Carolina 6 (both teams scored in all periods)
NY Rangers 1 at Tampa Bay 2 (Thompson 0:19 OT)
San Jose 1 at Los Angeles 0 (Setoguchi 18:54 2nd) [Niemi]
Calgary 2 at Edmonton 1 (no scoring in 3rd)

JANUARY 2

Atlanta 4 at Montreal 3 (Byfuglien 3:43 OT)
NY Rangers 0 at Florida 3 [Vokoun]
Philadelphia 3 at Detroit 2 (Red Wings scored only two goals of 3rd)
Dallas 4 at St. Louis 2 (Stars scored only three goals of 3rd)
Columbus 1 at Nashville 4 (Blue Jackets led 1–0 after 1st)
Phoenix 5 at Minnesota 6 (Barker 0:46 OT)
Vancouver 2 at Colorado 1 (Canucks led 1–0 after 1st & 2nd)
Chicago 1 at Anaheim 2 (no scoring in 3rd)

JANUARY 3

Boston 2 at Toronto 1 (Leafs led 1–0 after 1st)
Florida 4 at Carolina 3 (Allen 1:16 OT)
NY Islanders 5 at Calgary 2 (Islanders led 2–1 midway through 1st)
Chicago 4 at Los Angeles 3 (both teams scored in all periods)
Vancouver 4 at San Jose 3 (Sharks scored all goals in 2nd)

JANUARY 4

Minnesota 2 at New Jersey 1 (one goal in each period)
Tampa Bay 1 at Washington 0 (St. Louis 2:54 OT) [Roloson]
Buffalo 3 at Colorado 4 (D. Jones 4:17 OT)
Detroit 5 at Edmonton 3 (game tied 1–1 after 1st)
Columbus 2 at Phoenix 4 (no scoring in 1st)

JANUARY 5

Carolina 1 at NY Rangers 2 (Zuccarello 3:09 OT)
Tampa Bay 1 at Pittsburgh 8 (Kunitz hat trick)
Atlanta 3 at Florida 2 (Peverley (ATL) two goals)
Dallas 4 at Chicago 2 (Ribeiro (DAL) two goals)
Calgary 1 at Vancouver 3 (Flames scored only goal of 3rd)
Nashville 4 at Anaheim 1 (Predators had empty-net goal)

JANUARY 6

Minnesota 3 at Boston 1 (no scoring in 1st)
St. Louis 5 at Toronto 6 (SO)
Philadelphia 4 at New Jersey 2 (game tied 2–2 after 2nd)
Pittsburgh 1 at Montreal 2 (SO)
Phoenix 2 at Colorado 0 [LaBarbera]
NY Islanders 1 at Edmonton 2 (Oilers led 2–0 after 1st)
Nashville 5 at Los Angeles 2 (teams combined for five goals in 2nd)
Buffalo 3 at San Jose 0 [Miller]

JANUARY 7

Toronto 9 at Atlanta 3 (Leafs scored only six goals of 2nd)
Carolina 5 at Florida 3 (game tied 2–2 after 2nd)
Ottawa 2 at Chicago 3 (SO)
NY Rangers 3 at Dallas 2 (SO)

Detroit 5 at Calgary 4 (SO)
Edmonton 1 at Vancouver 6 (Canucks scored only three goals of 3rd)
Columbus 0 at Anaheim 6 [Hiller]

JANUARY 8

New Jersey 1 at Philadelphia 2 (no scoring in 3rd)
NY Islanders 4 at Colorado 3 (Tavares 3:52 OT)
Boston 2 at Montreal 3 (Pacioretty 3:43 OT)
Tampa Bay 2 at Ottawa 1 (Senators led 1–0 after 2nd)
Minnesota 4 at Pittsburgh 0 [Theodore]
Florida 2 at Washington 3 (game tied 1–1 after 2nd)
NY Rangers 2 at St. Louis 1 (all goals in 2nd)
Buffalo 2 at Phoenix 1 (Stafford 3:12 OT)
Nashville 2 at San Jose 1 (one goal in each period)
Detroit 2 at Vancouver 1 (SO)
Columbus 4 at Los Angeles 6 (Kings led 4–0 midway through 2nd)

JANUARY 9

Atlanta 3 at Carolina 4 (Cole 2:09 OT)
Tampa Bay 3 at New Jersey 6 (Devils scored five goals in 3rd)
Dallas 4 at Minnesota 0 [Raycroft]
NY Islanders 0 at Chicago 5 [Crawford]
San Jose 0 at Anaheim 1 (Ryan 14:29 2nd) [Hiller]

JANUARY 10

Boston 4 at Pittsburgh 2 (Bruins trailed 2–0 after 2nd)
Phoenix 4 at St. Louis 3 (Blues led 1–0 after 1st)
Detroit 4 at Colorado 5 (Avs led 4–2 after 1st)
Toronto 3 at Los Angeles 2 (game tied 1–1 midway through 2nd)

JANUARY 11

Ottawa 0 at Boston 6 [Thomas]
Philadelphia 5 at Buffalo 2 (Hartnell (PHI) two goals)
Vancouver 4 at NY Islanders 3 (SO)
Montreal 2 at NY Rangers 1 (one goal in each period)
Calgary 5 at Carolina 6 (SO)
Phoenix 4 at Columbus 3 (Coyotes scored only two goals of 3rd)
Washington 3 at Florida 4 (Wideman 2:51 OT)

Minnesota 1 at Nashville 5 (Spaling two goals)
Edmonton 2 at Dallas 3 (game tied 2–2 midway through 3rd)
Toronto 4 at San Jose 2 (Leafs scored all goals in 3rd)

JANUARY 12

Pittsburgh 5 at Montreal 2 (Goligoski (PIT) two goals)
Washington 0 at Tampa Bay 3 [Roloson]
Colorado 0 at Chicago 4 [Crawford]
St. Louis 4 at Anaheim 7 (Ducks scored four goals in 3rd)

JANUARY 13

Philadelphia 5 at Boston 7 (Flyers led 3–2 after 2nd)
Carolina 2 at Buffalo 3 (Sabres scored in each period)
Ottawa 6 at NY Islanders 4 (ten different scorers)
Vancouver 0 at NY Rangers 1 (Wolski 7:18 2nd) [Lundqvist]
Nashville 2 at Florida 3 (game tied 1–1 after 1st & 2nd)
Toronto 1 at Phoenix 5 (Coyotes scored four goals in 3rd)
St. Louis 3 at Los Angeles 1 (no scoring in 3rd)
Edmonton 5 at San Jose 2 (Sharks scored its two goals in 3rd)

JANUARY 14

Vancouver 4 at Washington 2 (Caps led 1–0 early in 1st)
Detroit 2 at Columbus 3 (SO)
Calgary 3 at Ottawa 2 (Flames scored all goals in 2nd)
Philadelphia 5 at Atlanta 2 (game tied 2–2 after 2nd)
New Jersey 5 at Tampa Bay 2 (Lightning led 1–0 early in 1st)
Colorado 4 at Minnesota 1 (Avalanche had empty-net goal)

JANUARY 15

Pittsburgh 3 at Boston 2 (Penguins scored only goal of 3rd)
Calgary 2 at Toronto 1 (SO)
NY Rangers 2 at Montreal 3 (Habs led 3–1 after 1st)
Buffalo 3 at NY Islanders 5 (no scoring in 1st)
Tampa Bay 4 at Carolina 6 (game tied 2–2 after 1st)
New Jersey 2 at Florida 3 (Kulikov 3:36 OT)
Columbus 5 at Detroit 6 (Franzen 0:45 OT)
Chicago 2 at Nashville 3 (SO)
Atlanta 1 at Dallas 6 (Stars scored only three goals of 3rd)

Anaheim 2 at Phoenix 6 (game tied 1–1 after 1st)
Edmonton 2 at Los Angeles 5 (game tied 2–2 after 1st)
St. Louis 2 at San Jose 4 (game tied 2–2 after 2nd)

JANUARY 16

Ottawa 1 at Washington 3 (Senators led 1–0 after 1st & 2nd)
Vancouver 0 at Minnesota 4 (no scoring in 1st)
Philadelphia 3 at NY Rangers 2 (Rangers scored only two goals of 3rd)
Nashville 3 at Chicago 6 (Hawks scored four goals in 3rd)
Edmonton 2 at Anaheim 3 (Selanne (ANA) two goals)

JANUARY 17

Carolina 0 at Boston 7 [Thomas]
New Jersey 5 at NY Islanders 2 (no scoring in 3rd)
San Jose 4 at Phoenix 2 (game tied 1–1 after 1st)
Calgary 4 at Montreal 5 (Subban 1:06 OT)
Atlanta 3 at Florida 2 (SO)
Los Angeles 1 at Dallas 2 (Kings led 1–0 after 1st)

JANUARY 18

Montreal 1 at Buffalo 2 (Pominville 1:09 OT)
Washington 2 at Philadelphia 3 (Meszaros 1:07 OT)
Detroit 1 at Pittsburgh 4 (Penguins led 2–1 late in 2nd)
Boston 3 at Carolina 2 (game tied 1–1 after 1st & 2nd)
Anaheim 2 at Ottawa 1 (SO)
Columbus 2 at Tampa Bay 3 (SO)
Los Angeles 1 at St. Louis 2 (one goal in each period)
Vancouver 3 at Colorado 4 (D. Jones 2:52 OT)
Minnesota 4 at Edmonton 1 (Wild led 2–0 after 1st & 2nd)
Nashville 5 at Phoenix 2 (Dumont hat trick)

JANUARY 19

Toronto 0 at NY Rangers 7 [Lundqvist]
Columbus 3 at Florida 2 (Umberger 4:06 OT)
Minnesota 6 at Calgary 0 [N. Backstrom]

JANUARY 20

Buffalo 4 at Boston 2 (Sabres scored only two goals of 3rd)
Anaheim 2 at Toronto 5 (game tied 1–1 after 1st)
Pittsburgh 0 at New Jersey 2 (both goals in 1st)
Washington 2 at NY Islanders 1 (no scoring in 3rd)
Ottawa 2 at Philadelphia 6 (Flyers scored only three goals of 3rd)
NY Rangers 1 at Carolina 4 (Hurricanes led 2–0 after 1st)
Tampa Bay 3 at Atlanta 2 (SO)
Detroit 4 at St. Louis 3 (Helm 1:51 OT)
Nashville 5 at Colorado 1 (Predators led 2–0 after 1st & 2nd)
Dallas 4 at Edmonton 2 (game tied 1–1 midway through 1st)
San Jose 2 at Vancouver 1 (SO)
Phoenix 2 at Los Angeles 0 (both goals in 2nd)

JANUARY 21

NY Islanders 5 at Buffalo 2 (Islanders had empty-net goal)
Montreal 7 at Ottawa 1 (Senators' only goal came in 1st)
Tampa Bay 2 at Florida 1 (SO)
Dallas 4 at Calgary 7 (both teams scored in all periods)

JANUARY 22

New Jersey 3 at Philadelphia 1 (Elias two goals)
Chicago 4 at Detroit 1 (game tied 1–1 after 1st)
Boston 6 at Colorado 2 (Bruins scored twice in each period)
Washington 4 at Toronto 1 (Capitals led 1–0 after 1st & 2nd)
Anaheim 4 at Montreal 3 (SO)
Carolina 2 at Pittsburgh 3 (both teams scored twice in 3rd)
NY Rangers 3 at Atlanta 2 (SO)
Columbus 5 at St. Louis 2 (Jackets scored only three goals of 3rd)
Los Angeles 4 at Phoenix 3 (game tied 3–3 after 2nd)
Calgary 4 at Vancouver 3 (SO)
Minnesota 3 at San Jose 4 (Burns scored late in 3rd to break 3–3 tie)

JANUARY 23

Florida 2 at New Jersey 5 (Arnott (NJ) two goals)
Buffalo 5 at NY Islanders 3 (game tied 2–2 after 2nd)
Philadelphia 4 at Chicago 1 (Flyers led 1–0 after 2nd)
Atlanta 1 at Tampa Bay 7 (Lighting scored only five goals of 2nd)
Nashville 3 at Edmonton 2 (SO)

JANUARY 24

NY Rangers 2 at Washington 1 (SO)
Toronto 4 at Carolina 6 (Hurricanes outscored Leafs 4–3 in 3rd)
Nashville 1 at Calgary 3 (game tied 1–1 midway through 2nd)
St. Louis 3 at Colorado 4 (game tied 2–2 after 2nd)
Dallas 1 at Vancouver 7 (eight different scorers)
Boston 0 at Los Angeles 2 [Quick]

JANUARY 25

Florida 4 at NY Rangers 3 (Weaver broke 3–3 tie midway through 3rd)
Montreal 2 at Philadelphia 5 (Flyers led 2–0 after 1st)
NY Islanders 0 at Pittsburgh 1 (C. Adams 8:35 3rd) [Fleury]
Anaheim 3 at Columbus 2 (Ducks led 2–0 early in 1st)
Buffalo 3 at Ottawa 2 (SO)
Toronto 0 at Tampa Bay 2 (both goals in 1st)
Minnesota 4 at Chicago 2 (Hawks led 2–1 after 1st)
Edmonton 4 at Phoenix 3 (Oilers scored three goals in 3rd)

JANUARY 26

Florida 1 at Boston 2 (one goal in each period)
Carolina 4 at NY Islanders 2 (E. Staal (CAR) two goals)
Washington 0 at Atlanta 1 (Antropov 11:21 2nd) [Pavelec]
New Jersey 1 at Detroit 3 (game tied 1–1 after 1st & 2nd)
Edmonton 1 at Dallas 3 (no scoring in 3rd)
Phoenix 5 at Colorado 2 (Belanger (PHO) two goals)
St. Louis 1 at Calgary 4 (Moss two goals)
Nashville 1 at Vancouver 2 (all goals in 3rd)
San Jose 2 at Los Angeles 3 (SO)

JANUARY 30

2011 NHL All-Star Game (at Carolina)
Team Lidstrom 11—Team Staal 10

FEBRUARY 1

Florida 3 at Toronto 4 (SO)
Ottawa 1 at New Jersey 2 (Devils got only goal of 3rd)
Pittsburgh 4 at NY Rangers 3 (SO)
Montreal 3 at Washington 2 (SO)

Boston 3 at Carolina 2 (game tied 1–1 after 2nd)
NY Islanders 4 at Atlanta 1 (Islanders scored only three goals of 2nd)
Chicago 7 at Columbus 4 (eleven different scorers)
Philadelphia 0 at Tampa Bay 4 [Roloson]
Calgary 3 at Nashville 2 (SO)
Los Angeles 0 at Minnesota 1 (SO) [N. Backstrom]
Vancouver 4 at Dallas 1 (Canucks led 2–0 early in 2nd)
Phoenix 3 at San Jose 5 (Sharks scored only four goals of 3rd)

FEBRUARY 2

Detroit 7 at Ottawa 5 (Franzen (DET) five goals)
NY Islanders 0 at Pittsburgh 3 [Johnson/Fleury]
Florida 2 at Montreal 3 (Panthers led 1–0 early in 2nd)
Vancouver 6 at Phoenix 0 [Luongo]
Los Angeles 3 at Edmonton 1 (Kings led 2–1 after 2nd)
San Jose 4 at Anaheim 3 (Sharks led 3–0 after 1st)

FEBRUARY 3

Dallas 3 at Boston 6 (Bruins led 4–0 after 1st)
Carolina 0 at Toronto 3 [Reimer]
New Jersey 3 at NY Rangers 2 (Devils led 3–0 late in 2nd)
Nashville 2 at Philadelphia 3 (game tied 1–1 after 1st & 2nd)
Calgary 4 at Atlanta 2 (Flames had empty-net goal)
Minnesota 4 at Colorado 3 (Wild led 2–1 late in 2nd)

FEBRUARY 4

Florida 4 at New Jersey 3 (Olesz 2:00 OT)
Buffalo 2 at Pittsburgh 3 (no scoring in 3rd)
Columbus 3 at Detroit 0 (one goal in each period)
Washington 5 at Tampa Bay 2 (Backstrom (WAS) two goals)
Edmonton 3 at St. Louis 5 (game tied 1–1 midway through 1st)
Chicago 3 at Vancouver 4 (D. Sedin broke 3–3 tie late in 3rd)

FEBRUARY 5

San Jose 2 at Boston 0 [Niemi]
NY Rangers 0 at Montreal 2 [Price]
Anaheim 3 at Colorado 0 [McElhinney]
Toronto 2 at Buffalo 6 (Stafford (BUF) two goals)

Ottawa 3 at NY Islanders 5 (game tied 3–3 after 1st & 2nd)
Dallas 1 at Philadelphia 3 (Flyers score in each period)
Atlanta 3 at Carolina 4 (OT)
Edmonton 3 at Columbus 4 (Huselius broke 3–3 tie late in 3rd)
Detroit 0 at Nashville 3 (one goal in each period)
Minnesota 0 at Phoenix 1 (Pyatt 2:20 3rd) [Bryzgalov]
Los Angeles 4 at Calgary 3 (SO)

FEBRUARY 6

Pittsburgh 0 at Washington 3 (one goal in each period)
New Jersey 4 at Montreal 1 (Devils led 2–0 after 1st)
St. Louis 3 at Tampa Bay 4 (Lecavalier 4:53 OT)

FEBRUARY 7

Atlanta 4 at Toronto 5 (Leafs scored three goals in 2nd)
NY Rangers 2 at Detroit 3 (Red Wings led 1–0 after 2nd)
Edmonton 4 at Nashville 0 [Dubnyk]
Chicago 1 at Calgary 3 (game tied 1–1 after 2nd)
Colorado 0 at Phoenix 3 [Bryzgalov]
Ottawa 2 at Vancouver 4 (Canucks led 3–0 early in 2nd)

FEBRUARY 8

Carolina 2 at New Jersey 3 (Tedenby 2:42 OT)
Toronto 5 at NY Islanders 3 (Leafs scored three goals in 3rd)
Columbus 4 at Pittsburgh 1 (Blue Jackets led 3–0 after 2nd)
San Jose 2 at Washington 0 [Niemi]
Buffalo 7 at Tampa Bay 4 (Sabres scored five goals in 3rd)
St. Louis 2 at Florida 1 (one goal in each period)

FEBRUARY 9

Montreal 6 at Boston 8 (both teams scored four goals in 2nd)
Nashville 4 at Detroit 1 (no scoring in 3rd)
San Jose 3 at Columbus 2 (Blue Jackets led 2–0 after 1st)
Colorado 2 at Minnesota 3 (game tied 1–1 late in 1st)
Phoenix 3 at Dallas 2 (Vrbata 1:13 OT)
Ottawa 2 at Calgary 5 (Flames scored twice in 2nd & 3rd)
Chicago 4 at Edmonton 1 (Hawks led 2–0 after 2nd)
Anaheim 4 at Vancouver 3 (Canucks scored in final minute)

FEBRUARY 10

New Jersey 2 at Toronto 1 (Kovalchuk 4:36 OT)
Carolina 1 at Philadelphia 2 (all goals in 3rd)
Los Angeles 1 at Pittsburgh 2 (J. Staal 4:41 OT)
NY Islanders 4 at Montreal 3 (SO)
Buffalo 3 at Florida 2 (Myers 4:55 OT)

FEBRUARY 11

Detroit 6 at Boston 1 (Red Wings scored only three goals of 2nd)
San Jose 1 at New Jersey 2 (all goals in 3rd)
Pittsburgh 3 at NY Islanders 9 (Islanders scored four goals in 1st & 2nd)
Colorado 1 at Columbus 3 (Avs led 1–0 after 1st)
NY Rangers 2 at Atlanta 3 (game tied 1–1 after 2nd)
Minnesota 5 at St. Louis 4 (SO)
Chicago 3 at Dallas 4 (SO)
Anaheim 5 at Calgary 4 (Fowler 4:41 OT)

FEBRUARY 12

Los Angeles 4 at Washington 1 (Kings scored only three goals of 3rd)
Ottawa 5 at Edmonton 3 (game tied 2–2 after 2nd)
Toronto 0 at Montreal 3 [Price]
Carolina 3 at Tampa Bay 4 (Bergeron 1:32 OT)
Colorado 3 at Nashville 5 (game tied 2–2 after 2nd)
Chicago 2 at Phoenix 3 (SO)
St. Louis 1 at Minnesota 3 (no scoring in 3rd)
Calgary 2 at Vancouver 4 (Samuelsson (VAN) two goals)

FEBRUARY 13

NY Islanders 7 at Buffalo 6 (Grabner 2:55 OT)
Pittsburgh 3 at NY Rangers 5 (game tied 2–2 after 1st)
Columbus 2 at Dallas 1 (no scoring in 3rd)
Boston 2 at Detroit 4 (Bruins led 2–1 in 1st)
Los Angeles 1 at Philadelphia 0 (Doughty 0:17 2nd) [Quick]
Carolina 3 at Atlanta 2 (Ladd both Thrashers goals)
San Jose 2 at Florida 3 (game tied 1–1 after 2nd)
Anaheim 4 at Edmonton 0 [Hiller]

FEBRUARY 14

Vancouver 2 at St. Louis 3 (game tied 1–1 midway through 1st)
Calgary 9 at Colorado 1 (Flames led 5–0 after 1st)
Washington 2 at Phoenix 3 (Caps led 1–0 midway through 2nd)

FEBRUARY 15

Toronto 4 at Boston 3 (game tied 2–2 after 2nd)
Buffalo 3 at Montreal 2 (SO)
NY Islanders 4 at Ottawa 3 (SO)
Philadelphia 4 at Tampa Bay 3 (SO)
San Jose 2 at Nashville 1 (Marleau 3:53 OT)
Vancouver 4 at Minnesota 1 (game tied 1–1 after 1st)
Dallas 1 at Edmonton 4 (Oilers scored only goal of 3rd)

FEBRUARY 16

Toronto 2 at Buffalo 1 (Sabres scored last goal)
Carolina 2 at New Jersey 3 (no scoring in 1st)
Los Angeles 4 at Columbus 3 (SO)
Philadelphia 4 at Florida 2 (Panthers scored both goals in 3rd)
Minnesota 1 at Chicago 3 (Hawks led 1–0 after 1st & 2nd)
Pittsburgh 3 at Colorado 2 (Kennedy 4:10 OT)
Dallas 2 at Calgary 4 (Flames scored only two goals of 3rd)
Washington 7 at Anaheim 6 (Semin (WAS) hat trick)

FEBRUARY 17

Boston 6 at NY Islanders 3 (Bruins led 3–0 after 1st)
Los Angeles 3 at NY Rangers 4 (SO)
Detroit 6 at Tampa Bay 2 (Red Wings scored two goals in each period)
Vancouver 1 at Nashville 3 (all goals in 2nd)
Montreal 1 at Edmonton 4 (Oilers scored only three goals of 3rd)
Atlanta 3 at Phoenix 4 (no scoring in 3rd)
Washington 2 at San Jose 3 (Caps scored late goal)

FEBRUARY 18

NY Rangers 0 at New Jersey 1 (Kovalchuk 8:18 2nd) [Hedberg]
Philadelphia 2 at Carolina 3 (Hurricanes broke 2–2 tie late in 3rd)
St. Louis 3 at Buffalo 0 [Conklin]
Boston 4 at Ottawa 2 (game tied 1–1 after 2nd)

Detroit 4 at Florida 3 (both teams scored in all periods)
Anaheim 1 at Minnesota 5 (Ducks led 1–0 early in 1st)
Columbus 4 at Chicago 3 (Hawks led 2–1 after 1st)

FEBRUARY 19

Atlanta 3 at Edmonton 6 (Oilers scored four goals in 3rd)
Ottawa 1 at Toronto 0 (SO)
Los Angeles 0 at NY Islanders 3 [Montoya]
New Jersey 4 at Carolina 1 (Devils led 3–0 after 1st & 2nd)
Florida 3 at Tampa Bay 2 (SO)
Anaheim 3 at St. Louis 9 (Blues scored four goals in 1st & 2nd)
Phoenix 3 at Nashville 2 (Predators scored goal in final minute)
Dallas 2 at Vancouver 5 (game tied 1–1 after 2nd)
Colorado 0 at San Jose 4 [Niemi]

FEBRUARY 20

Washington 2 at Buffalo 1 (game tied 1–1 after 2nd)
Philadelphia 4 at NY Rangers 2 (Rangers led 1–0 midway through 1st)
Pittsburgh 2 at Chicago 3 (SO)
Detroit 2 at Minnesota 1 (SO)
Montreal 0 at Calgary 4 [Kiprusoff]

FEBRUARY 21

Florida 1 at NY Islanders 5 (Moulson hat trick)
Chicago 5 at St. Louis 3 (Blues led 2–0 after 1st)
Washington 1 at Pittsburgh 0 (Ovechkin 16:38 2nd) [Neuvirth]

FEBRUARY 22

NY Islanders 1 at Toronto 2 (one goal in each period)
Phoenix 3 at Philadelphia 2 (Doan 2:41 OT)
NY Rangers 4 at Carolina 3 (SO)
San Jose 4 at Detroit 3 (game tied 1–1 early in 2nd)
Nashville 0 at Columbus 4 [S. Mason]
Edmonton 1 at Minnesota 4 (game tied 1–1 after 1st)
New Jersey 1 at Dallas 0 (Palmieri 14:23 3rd) [Hedberg]
Boston 3 at Calgary 1 (Bruins led 1–0 after 1st & 2nd)
Colorado 4 at St. Louis 3 (game tied 2–2 after 2nd)
Montreal 3 at Vancouver 2 (Habs led 2–1 early in 2nd)

FEBRUARY 23

Atlanta 1 at Buffalo 4 (game tied 1–1 late in 2nd)
Florida 1 at Ottawa 5 (Butler two goals)
San Jose 3 at Pittsburgh 2 (Marleau 4:56 OT)
Phoenix 3 at Tampa Bay 8 (Lightning led 5–0 after 1st)
Edmonton 5 at Colorado 1 (Oilers led 3–0 late in 2nd)
Los Angeles 3 at Anaheim 2 (Kings scored only goal of 3rd)

FEBRUARY 24

NY Islanders 3 at Philadelphia 4 (Meszaros 4:42 OT)
Dallas 4 at Detroit 1 (Red Wings had empty-net goal)
Toronto 5 at Montreal 4 (Habs led 1–0 early in 1st)
Chicago 3 at Nashville 0 [Crawford]
St. Louis 2 at Vancouver 3 (Canucks scored only goal of 3rd)
Minnesota 2 at Los Angeles 4 (Kings scored only two goals of 3rd)

FEBRUARY 25

NY Rangers 6 at Washington 0 [Lundqvist]
Pittsburgh 1 at Carolina 4 (Hurricanes led 3–0 midway through 2nd)
Phoenix 3 at Columbus 5 (game tied 2–2 after 1st)
Ottawa 2 at Buffalo 4 (Sabres led 2–0 midway through 2nd)
Florida 2 at Atlanta 1 (SO)
New Jersey 1 at Tampa Bay 2 (Devils scored only goal of 3rd)
San Jose 4 at Calgary 3 (SO)
St. Louis 5 at Edmonton 0 [Bishop]
Minnesota 3 at Anaheim 2 (Bouchard 4:53 OT)

FEBRUARY 26

Nashville 2 at Dallas 3 (Predators led 2–1 after 2nd)
Colorado 3 at Los Angeles 4 (Jones (COL) two goals)
Detroit 3 at Buffalo 2 (SO)
Pittsburgh 6 at Toronto 5 (SO)
Carolina 3 at Montreal 4 (Habs scored only goal of 3rd)
Philadelphia 1 at Ottawa 4 (Flyers led 1–0 after 1st)
Washington 3 at NY Islanders 2 (Islanders led 2–1 after 2nd)
Boston 3 at Vancouver 1 (Canucks led 1–0 after 1st)

FEBRUARY 27

Tampa Bay 2 at NY Rangers 1 (one goal in each period)

Columbus 2 at Nashville 3 (Predators scored all goals in 3rd)

Toronto 2 at Atlanta 3 (Hainsey 2:31 OT)

New Jersey 2 at Florida 1 (no scoring in 1st)

Phoenix 3 at Chicago 4 (SO)

St. Louis 0 at Calgary 1 (Moss 5:39 3rd) [Kiprusoff]

Boston 3 at Edmonton 2 (Oilers led 1–0 midway through 1st)

Colorado 2 at Anaheim 3 (Ducks broke 2–2 tie midway through 3rd)

FEBRUARY 28

Chicago 4 at Minnesota 2 (Hawks scored only three goals of 2nd)

Detroit 7 at Los Angeles 4 (both teams scored three goals in 3rd)

MARCH 1

Buffalo 3 at NY Rangers 2 (Sabres scored in each period)

NY Islanders 1 at Washington 2 (Ovechkin 1:55 OT)

Florida 1 at Carolina 2 (no scoring in 3rd)

Montreal 3 at Atlanta 1 (Habs had empty-net goal)

Boston 3 at Ottawa 0 [Rask]

Calgary 6 at St. Louis 0 [Kiprusoff]

Nashville 1 at Edmonton 2 (SO)

Dallas 3 at Phoenix 2 (Benn broke 2–2 tie at 19:55 of 3rd)

Columbus 1 at Vancouver 2 (SO)

Colorado 1 at San Jose 2 (SO)

MARCH 2

Pittsburgh 2 at Toronto 3 (Grabovski 0:42 OT)

Tampa Bay 1 at New Jersey 2 (game tied 1–1 after 2nd)

Minnesota 1 at NY Islanders 4 (Wild scored its only goal in 3rd)

Calgary 4 at Chicago 6 (Hawks had empty-net goal)

Detroit 1 at Anaheim 2 (Ryan 2:50 OT)

MARCH 3

Tampa Bay 1 at Boston 2 (Boston had only goal of 3rd)

Minnesota 3 at NY Rangers 1 (Rangers led 1–0 early in 2nd)

Toronto 3 at Philadelphia 2 (Leafs scored only goal of 3rd)

St. Louis 2 at Washington 3 (Capitals scored only goal of 3rd)

Buffalo 2 at Carolina 3 (McBain 0:26 OT)
Ottawa 3 at Atlanta 1 (Senators led 1–0 after 1st & 2nd)
Montreal 4 at Florida 0 [Price]
Columbus 2 at Edmonton 4 (Oilers led 2–0 after 1st)
Nashville 3 at Vancouver 0 [Rinne]
Phoenix 0 at Los Angeles 1 (Stoll 12:13 3rd) [Bernier]
Detroit 1 at San Jose 3 (game tied 1–1 after 1st)

MARCH 4

Pittsburgh 1 at New Jersey 2 (Kovalchuk 4:35 OT)
NY Rangers 4 at Ottawa 1 (Senators scored final goal)
Carolina 2 at Chicago 5 (seven different scorers)
Columbus 3 at Calgary 4 (game tied 2–2 early in 2nd)
Dallas 3 at Anaheim 4 (Visnovsky 4:56 OT)

MARCH 5

St. Louis 2 at NY Islanders 5 (Blues scored their goals in 3rd)
Buffalo 5 at Philadelphia 3 (Flyers led 2–0 after 1st)
Vancouver 3 at Los Angeles 1 (game tied 1–1 after 1st & 2nd)
Pittsburgh 3 at Boston 2 (Jeffrey 1:52 OT)
Chicago 5 at Toronto 3 (Hawks led 3–0 midway through 2nd)
Florida 3 at Atlanta 4 (Ladd 0:25 OT)
Montreal 4 at Tampa Bay 2 (Habs led 2–0 after 1st)
Detroit 4 at Phoenix 5 (SO)
Edmonton 5 at Colorado 1 (Oilers led 2–0 after 1st)
Dallas 3 at San Jose 2 (Sharks led 2–1 after 2nd)

MARCH 6

New Jersey 3 at NY Islanders 2 (SO)
Philadelphia 0 at NY Rangers 7 [Lundqvist]
Washington 3 at Florida 2 (Semin 0:48 OT)
Buffalo 3 at Minnesota 2 (Stafford 0:46 OT)
Nashville 2 at Calgary 3 (Predators led 2–1 after 1st)
Vancouver 3 at Anaheim 0 [Schneider]

MARCH 7

Washington 2 at Tampa Bay 1 (SO)
Columbus 4 at St. Louis 5 (SO)
Dallas 4 at Los Angeles 3 (Morrow 0:38 OT)

MARCH 8

Ottawa 2 at New Jersey 1 (Condra both Senators goals)
Toronto 3 at NY Islanders 4 (Comeau 4:02 OT)
Edmonton 1 at Philadelphia 4 (Flyers led 2–0 after 1st)
Buffalo 1 at Pittsburgh 3 (Sabres led 1–0 early in 2nd)
Boston 1 at Montreal 4 (Eller two goals)
Chicago 2 at Florida 3 (Panthers led 3–0 after 1st)
Colorado 2 at Minnesota 5 (Wild scored only three goals of 3rd)
Vancouver 4 at Phoenix 3 (Hamhuis 2:13 OT)
Nashville 2 at San Jose 3 (Marleau 3:24 OT)

MARCH 9

Edmonton 0 at Washington 5 [Holtby]
Atlanta 3 at Carolina 2 (Stapleton 1:38 OT)
Los Angeles 2 at Detroit 1 (no scoring in 3rd)
St. Louis 4 at Columbus 3 (Stewart 0:54 OT)
Chicago 3 at Tampa Bay 4 (SO)
Calgary 4 at Dallas 3 (SO)
NY Rangers 2 at Anaheim 5 (Rangers led 1–0 early in 1st)

MARCH 10

Buffalo 4 at Boston 3 (Boyes 3:44 OT)
Philadelphia 3 at Toronto 2 (Flyers led 2–0 midway through 2nd)
Ottawa 2 at Florida 1 (all goals in 3rd)
Montreal 1 at St. Louis 4 (game tied 1–1 after 1st)
Minnesota 0 at Nashville 4 [Rinne]
Calgary 0 at Phoenix 3 [Bryzgalov]
Vancouver 5 at San Jose 4 (SO)

MARCH 11

Boston 2 at NY Islanders 4 (Islanders scored only three goals of 3rd)
Carolina 1 at Washington 2 (Hurricanes led 1–0 after 2nd)
Edmonton 1 at Detroit 2 (Datsyuk 4:18 OT)
Los Angeles 4 at Columbus 2 (Kopitar hat trick)
New Jersey 3 at Atlanta 2 (Zajac 4:18 OT)
Ottawa 2 at Tampa Bay 1 (Senators led 2–0 after 2nd)
Minnesota 0 at Dallas 4 [Lehtonen]
Anaheim 6 at Colorado 2 (Ducks scored four goals in 2nd)

MARCH 12

Montreal 3 at Pittsburgh 0 [Price]
Buffalo 3 at Toronto 4 (seven different scorers)
NY Islanders 2 at New Jersey 3 (Salmela 3:09 OT)
Atlanta 5 at Philadelphia 4 (Hainsey 1:17 OT)
Columbus 3 at Carolina 2 (Jackets led 2–0 after 2nd)
Tampa Bay 3 at Florida 4 (Garrison 4:44 OT)
Detroit 5 at St. Louis 3 (eight different scorers)
Colorado 2 at Nashville 4 (Predators had empty-net goal)
Vancouver 4 at Calgary 3 (no scoring in 3rd)
NY Rangers 3 at San Jose 2 (SO)

MARCH 13

Edmonton 1 at Pittsburgh 5 (Penguins led 3–1 early in 3rd)
Chicago 3 at Washington 4 (Knuble 3:51 OT)
Los Angeles 3 at Dallas 2 (Handzus broke 2–2 tie at 19:39 of 3rd)
Ottawa 4 at Buffalo 6 (game tied 2–2 after 1st)
Phoenix 5 at Anaheim 2 (Coyotes had empty-net goal)

MARCH 14

Tampa Bay 6 at Toronto 2 (Ritola (TB) two goals)
San Jose 3 at Chicago 6 (Blackhawks scored five goals in 2nd)
Minnesota 2 at Vancouver 4 (Canucks led 3–0 midway through 1st)

MARCH 15

Carolina 1 at Buffalo 0 (B. Sutter 19:17 1st) [Ward]
Atlanta 2 at New Jersey 4 (Devils scored only two goals of 3rd)
NY Islanders 3 at NY Rangers 6 (Gaborik (NYR) two goals)
Boston 3 at Columbus 2 (SO)
Washington 4 at Montreal 2 (game tied 2–2 after 2nd)
Pittsburgh 5 at Ottawa 1 (Penguins led 2–1 early in 2nd)
Philadelphia 3 at Florida 2 (no scoring in 3rd)
Los Angeles 4 at Nashville 2 (game tied 1–1 after 1st)
San Jose 6 at Dallas 3 (Sharks scored four goals in 3rd)
Phoenix 4 at Calgary 3 (seven different scorers)

MARCH 16

Toronto 3 at Carolina 1 (game tied 1–1 after 1st)
Washington 2 at Detroit 3 (Red Wings scored only goal of 3rd)
Colorado 2 at Vancouver 4 (Avs led 2–0 after 1st)
St. Louis 1 at Anaheim 2 (Ducks scored only goal of 3rd)

MARCH 17

Philadelphia 3 at Atlanta 4 (SO)
Detroit 2 at Columbus 0 [MacDonald]
Tampa Bay 2 at Montreal 3 (SO)
New Jersey 1 at Ottawa 3 (Neil two goals)
Toronto 0 at Florida 4 [Clemmensen]
Boston 3 at Nashville 4 (Weber 3:37 OT)
Chicago 0 at Dallas 5 [Lehtonen]
Colorado 2 at Calgary 5 (Flames led 3–1 after 1st)
Phoenix 3 at Edmonton 1 (Coyotes led 2–0 after 2nd)
St. Louis 4 at Los Angeles 0 [Halak]
Minnesota 2 at San Jose 3 (Sharks scored only goal of 3rd)

MARCH 18

Washington 3 at New Jersey 0 [Neuvirth]
Montreal 3 at NY Rangers 6 (Rangers led 5–1 after 1st)
NY Islanders 2 at Carolina 3 (Pitkanen 3:58 OT)
Phoenix 3 at Vancouver 1 (all goals in 3rd)

MARCH 19

Columbus 5 at Minnesota 4 (Vermette 4:26 OT)
Atlanta 2 at Buffalo 8 (game tied 1–1 midway through 1st)
Boston 2 at Toronto 5 (Leafs scored only three goals of 2nd)
Tampa Bay 2 at Ottawa 3 (Spezza 3:28 OT)
NY Islanders 4 at Florida 3 (SO)
Detroit 1 at Nashville 3 (game tied 1–1 after 2nd)
Philadelphia 3 at Dallas 2 (SO)
Colorado 3 at Edmonton 2 (SO)
Anaheim 2 at Los Angeles 1 (Perry 1:32 OT)
St. Louis 3 at San Jose 5 (Sharks scored only three goals of 1st)

MARCH 20

NY Rangers 5 at Pittsburgh 2 (game tied 1–1 after 1st & 2nd)
Nashville 4 at Buffalo 3 (Erat 0:27 OT)
New Jersey 3 at Columbus 0 [Brodeur]
Montreal 8 at Minnesota 1 (Subban hat trick)
Chicago 2 at Phoenix 1 (one goal in each period)
Calgary 4 at Anaheim 5 (Perry 2:38 OT)

MARCH 21

Pittsburgh 5 at Detroit 4 (SO)
Calgary 1 at Los Angeles 2 (SO)

MARCH 22

New Jersey 1 at Boston 4 (Devils led 1–0 midway through 1st)
Florida 0 at NY Rangers 1 (Dubinsky 7:49 3rd) [Lundqvist]
Washington 5 at Philadelphia 4 (SO)
Ottawa 3 at Carolina 4 (Larose (CAR) two goals)
Buffalo 2 at Montreal 0 [Miller]
NY Islanders 5 at Tampa Bay 2 (seven different scorers)
Edmonton 1 at Nashville 3 (no scoring in 3rd)
Toronto 3 at Minnesota 0 [Reimer]
Columbus 4 at Colorado 5 (SO)
St. Louis 1 at Phoenix 2 (Blues led 1–0 after 1st)

MARCH 23

Vancouver 2 at Detroit 1 (no scoring in 1st)
Florida 0 at Chicago 4 [Crawford]
Anaheim 4 at Dallas 3 (Fowler 1:42 OT)
Calgary 3 at San Jose 6 (Sharks led 4–2 after 1st)

MARCH 24

Montreal 0 at Boston 7 [Thomas]
Atlanta 2 at NY Islanders 1 (no scoring in 3rd)
Ottawa 2 at NY Rangers 1 (SO)
Pittsburgh 2 at Philadelphia 1 (SO)
Edmonton 0 at St. Louis 4 [Halak]
Anaheim 4 at Nashville 5 (Predators led 4–1 after 2nd)
Toronto 4 at Colorado 3 (both teams scored in all periods)

Columbus 0 at Phoenix 3 [Bryzgalov]
San Jose 3 at Los Angeles 4 (SO)

MARCH 25

New Jersey 0 at Pittsburgh 1 (SO)
Florida 2 at Buffalo 4 (Stafford (BUF) two goals)
Washington 0 at Ottawa 2 [Anderson]
Vancouver 3 at Atlanta 1 (Canucks had empty-net goal)
Carolina 4 at Tampa Bay 3 (Cole (CAR) & Gagne (TB) two goals each)

MARCH 26

NY Rangers 1 at Boston 0 (Stepan 6:39 1st) [Lundqvist]
Colorado 1 at Los Angeles 4 (Kings led 2–0 after 1st)
New Jersey 0 at Buffalo 2 [Miller]
Washington 2 at Montreal 0 [Holtby]
Philadelphia 4 at NY Islanders 1 (Flyers led 3–1 after 1st)
Tampa Bay 4 at Carolina 2 (game tied 2–2 after 1st)
Toronto 2 at Detroit 4 (game tied 2–2 early in 3rd)
Dallas 2 at Nashville 4 (Legwand & Fisher (NAS) two goals each)
St. Louis 6 at Minnesota 3 (Blues scored twice in each period)
Anaheim 2 at Chicago 1 (Hawks led 1–0 after 1st & 2nd)
San Jose 4 at Phoenix 1 (game tied 1–1 early in 2nd)
Calgary 5 at Edmonton 4 (SO)

MARCH 27

Florida 1 at Pittsburgh 2 (SO)
Ottawa 4 at Atlanta 5 (SO)
Vancouver 4 at Columbus 1 (Higgins two goals)
Boston 2 at Philadelphia 1 (Bruins scored only goal of 3rd)

MARCH 28

Chicago 3 at Detroit 2 (Hossa 0:51 OT)
Colorado 4 at Anaheim 5 (game tied 3–3 after 2nd)

MARCH 29

Chicago 0 at Boston 3 [Thomas]
Buffalo 3 at Toronto 4 (no scoring in 3rd)
Philadelphia 5 at Pittsburgh 2 (game tied 1–1 after 1st)
Carolina 3 at Washington 2 (SO)

Florida 2 at Columbus 3 (SO)
Atlanta 1 at Montreal 3 (Habs led 2–0 after 1st & 2nd)
Ottawa 2 at Tampa Bay 5 (Lightning led 3–0 midway through 3rd)
Minnesota 3 at St. Louis 2 (SO)
Vancouver 3 at Nashville 1 (Canucks scored only three goals of 3rd)
Los Angeles 2 at Edmonton 0 [Bernier]
Dallas 1 at Phoenix 2 (SO)

MARCH 30

NY Rangers 0 at Buffalo 1 (Connolly 5:28 2nd) [Enroth]
NY Islanders 2 at New Jersey 3 (Nielsen both Islanders goals)
Montreal 2 at Carolina 6 (Hurricanes scored two goals in each period)
St. Louis 10 at Detroit 3 (Blues led 3–2 after 1st)
Anaheim 4 at Calgary 2 (Perry (ANA) two goals)

MARCH 31

Toronto 4 at Boston 3 (SO)
NY Rangers 2 at NY Islanders 6 (Rangers led 1–0 after 1st)
Atlanta 1 at Philadelphia 0 (Antropov 10:22 3rd) [Mason]
Columbus 3 at Washington 4 (Chimera 2:30 OT)
Pittsburgh 1 at Tampa Bay 2 (Lightning led 2–0 midway through 1st)
Ottawa 4 at Florida 1 (Greening two goals)
Edmonton 2 at Minnesota 4 (Wild led 4–0 midway through 2nd)
Nashville 3 at Colorado 2 (Predators led 3–0 midway through 3rd)
Los Angeles 1 at Vancouver 3 (Kings led 1–0 after 1st)
Dallas 0 at San Jose 6 [Niemi]

APRIL 1

Philadelphia 2 at New Jersey 4 (Flyers led 1–0 after 1st)
Chicago 4 at Columbus 3 (SO)
Calgary 3 at St. Louis 2 (Flames scored only two goals of 3rd)
Colorado 4 at Phoenix 3 (SO)

APRIL 2

Atlanta 2 at Boston 3 (Bruins scored only goal of 3rd)
Tampa Bay 3 at Minnesota 1 (Wild led 1–0 after 1st)
Detroit 4 at Nashville 3 (Cleary 2:58 OT)
Dallas 1 at Los Angeles 3 (Kings scored only two goals of 3rd)
Toronto 4 at Ottawa 2 (Leafs led 2–0 midway through 2nd)
Montreal 3 at New Jersey 1 (Darche two goals)

Carolina 4 at NY Islanders 2 (Islanders led 2–1 after 2nd)
Buffalo 4 at Washington 5 (Ovechkin 3:19 OT)
Pittsburgh 4 at Florida 2 (Panthers led 2–1 after 1st)
Edmonton 4 at Vancouver 1 (Oilers led 3–0 midway through 2nd)
Anaheim 2 at San Jose 4 (Ducks led 2–0 after 1st)

APRIL 3

NY Rangers 3 at Philadelphia 2 (SO)
Buffalo 2 at Carolina 1 (Gragnani 2:56 OT)
Minnesota 2 at Detroit 4 (Red Wings led 2–1 early in 2nd)
St. Louis 6 at Columbus 1 (Blues scored twice in each period)
Tampa Bay 2 at Chicago 0 [M. Smith]
Calgary 2 at Colorado 1 (Flames led 2–0 early in 3rd)
Dallas 4 at Anaheim 3 (game tied 2–2 after 1st)

APRIL 4

Boston 3 at NY Rangers 5 (Rangers scored only three goals of 3rd)
Los Angeles 1 at San Jose 6 (no scoring in 3rd)

APRIL 5

Tampa Bay 2 at Buffalo 4 (game tied 1–1 after 1st)
Washington 3 at Toronto 2 (SO)
New Jersey 2 at Pittsburgh 4 (Dupuis (PIT) two goals)
Chicago 1 at Montreal 2 (OT)
Philadelphia 2 at Ottawa 5 (Flyers led 1–0 early in 1st)
Colorado 1 at St. Louis 3 (game tied 1–1 after 1st)
Atlanta 3 at Nashville 6 (Predators led 4–0 early in 3rd)
Columbus 0 at Dallas 3 [Lehtonen]
Vancouver 0 at Edmonton 2 [Dubnyk]

APRIL 6

NY Islanders 2 at Boston 3 (no scoring in 3rd)
Toronto 2 at New Jersey 4 (Devils led 2–0 early in 3rd)
Florida 2 at Washington 5 (Caps led 3–0 early in 3rd)
Detroit 0 at Carolina 3 [Ward]
St. Louis 3 at Chicago 4 (Toews 3:19 OT)
Edmonton 1 at Calgary 6 (no scoring in 1st)
San Jose 2 at Anaheim 6 (Ducks led 3–0 early in 2nd)
Phoenix 2 at Los Angeles 3 (SO)

APRIL 7

Atlanta 3 at NY Rangers 0 [Pavelec]
Montreal 2 at Ottawa 3 (Kuba 1:16 OT)
Colorado 2 at Dallas 4 (Stars led 3–1 early in 3rd)
Minnesota 0 at Vancouver 5 [Luongo]

APRIL 8

Pittsburgh 4 at NY Islanders 3 (SO)
Chicago 4 at Detroit 2 (Hawks led 3–0 after 1st)
Philadelphia 3 at Buffalo 4 (Vanek 1:16 OT)
Carolina 6 at Atlanta 1 (seven different scorers)
Florida 2 at Tampa Bay 4 (Lecavalier (TB) two goals)
Columbus 1 at Nashville 4 (Hornqvist two goals)
Dallas 3 at Colorado 2 (Stars led 3–1 early in 3rd)
Minnesota 3 at Edmonton 1 (Wild had empty-net goal)
San Jose 3 at Phoenix 4 (Coyotes scored in each period)
Los Angeles 1 at Anaheim 2 (one goal in each period)

APRIL 9

New Jersey 2 at NY Rangers 5 (Rangers scored only three goals of 2nd)
Ottawa 1 at Boston 3 (game tied 1–1 after 1st)
Montreal 4 at Toronto 1 (Gionta two goals)
NY Islanders 4 at Philadelphia 7 (game tied 3–3 after 1st)
Tampa Bay 6 at Carolina 2 (Lightning had two empty-net goals)
Washington 0 at Florida 1 (Thomas 13:55 3rd) [Vokoun]
Buffalo 5 at Columbus 4 (no scoring in 1st)
Nashville 0 at St. Louis 2 [Halak]
Vancouver 3 at Calgary 2 (Ehrhoff 2:41 OT)
Anaheim 3 at Los Angeles 1 (no scoring in 3rd)
Phoenix 1 at San Jose 3 (Sharks led 2–1 early in 3rd)

APRIL 10

Boston 2 at New Jersey 3 (game tied 1–1 after 1st)
Pittsburgh 5 at Atlanta 2 (Penguins scored only four goals of 2nd)
Edmonton 3 at Colorado 4 (Jones 3:57 OT)
Detroit 4 at Chicago 3 (game tied 1–1 midway through 2nd)
Dallas 3 at Minnesota 5 (Wild scored only two goals of 3rd)

2011 NHL ALL-STAR GAME

DRAFT ORDER, JANUARY 28, 2011

TS=Team Staal (captain Eric Staal, assistants Mike Green & Ryan Kesler)
TL=Team Lidstrom (captain Nicklas Lidstrom, assistants Martin St. Louis & Patrick Kane)

Cam Ward (TS)
Steve Stamkos (TL)
Alexander Ovechkin (TS)
Duncan Keith (TL)
Daniel Sedin (TS)
Henrik Sedin (TL)
Zdeno Chara (TS)
Shea Weber (TL)
Rick Nash (TS)
Tim Thomas (TL)
Henrik Lundqvist (TS)
Daniel Briere (TL)
Marc Staal (TS)
Dustin Byfuglien (TL)
Patrick Sharp (TS)
Jonathan Toews (TL)
Dan Boyle (TS)
Marc-Andre Fleury (TL)
Carey Price (TS)
Jonas Hiller (TL)
Jeff Skinner (TS)
Brad Richards (TL)
Kris Letang (TS)
Keith Yandle (TL)
Claude Giroux (TS)
Brent Burns (TL)
Erik Karlsson (TS)
Martin Havlat (TL)
Corey Perry (TS)
Anze Kopitar (TL)
Patrik Elias (TS)
Matt Duchene (TL)
David Backes (TS)
Loui Eriksson (TL)
Paul Stastny (TS)
Phil Kessel (TL)

Rookies

Team Staal—Logan Couture, Tyler Ennis, Michael Grabner, Jamie McBain, Tyler Seguin, P.K. Subban

Team Lidstrom—Evgeni Dadonov, Oliver Ekman-Larsson, Cam Fowler, Taylor Hall, Kevin Shattenkirk, Derek Stepan

GAME SUMMARY

January 30, 2011
RBC Center

First Period

1. Team Staal, Ovechkin (Chara, Green)	0:50
2. Team Staal, Stastny (Sharp, Backes)	2:48
3. Team Staal, Elias (Stastny, Green)	3:20
4. Team Staal, Giroux (Sharp, Backes)	5:41
5. Team Lidstrom, Kopitar (Weber)	10:50
6. Team Lidstrom, Byfuglien (Kane, Keith)	13:17
7. Team Lidstrom, Eriksson (Toews)	16:07
8. Team Lidstrom, Duchene (Lidstrom, Weber)	16:30

Penalties: none

Second Period

9. Team Staal, Sharp (Giroux)	1:18
10. Team Staal, Letang (D. Sedin, Ovechkin)	6:10
11. Team Lidstrom, Kopitar (Eriksson, Havlat)	10:08
12. Team Lidstrom, Stamkos (St. Louis, Richards)	14:11
13. Team Lidstrom, Briere (H. Sedin, Weber)	15:31

Penalties: none

Third Period

14. Team Staal, E. Staal (Perry, Nash)	3:49
15. Team Staal, Letang (Elias, Skinner)	8:46
16. Team Lidstrom, Briere (H. Sedin, Weber)	9:57
17. Team Lidstrom, Toews (Eriksson, Havlat)	10:45
18. Team Lidstrom, St. Louis (Burns)	13:53
19. Team Staal, Nash (Perry, Chara)	15:11
20. Team Lidstrom, Eriksson (Toews, Havlat)	18:49 (en)
21. Team Staal, E. Staal (Boyle, Backes)	19:26

Missed penalty shot: Duchene (Team Staal) 6:13
Penalties: none

GOALIES

Team Lidstrom
   1st period—Marc-Andre Fleury (4 goals)
   2nd period—Jonas Hiller (2 goals)
   3rd period—Tim Thomas (4 goals)

Team Staal
   1st period—Cam Ward (4 goals)
   2nd period—Carey Price (3 goals)
   3rd period—Henrik Lundqvist (3 goals)

SHOTS ON GOAL

Team Staal	14	17	15	**46**
Team Lidstrom	14	16	15	**45**

Referees—Tom Kowal & Kevin Pollock
Linesmen—Don Henderson & Darren Gibbs

MVP—Patrick Sharp

Attendance—18,680

SHOOTOUT LEADERS, 2010–11

SKATERS

Shots

Alex Tanguay (CAL)	16
Kris Letang (PIT)	13
Rick Nash (CBJ)	12
Brad Richards (DAL)	12
Rene Bourque (CAL)	12
Radim Vrbata (PHO)	11
Jonathan Toews (CHI)	11
Mike Santorelli (FLO)	11

Goals

Alex Tanguay (CAL)	10 (16 shots)
Jarret Stoll (LA)	9 (10 shots)
Radim Vrbata (PHO)	7 (11 shots)
Mike Ribeiro (DAL)	6 (10 shots)
Thomas Vanek (BUF)	5 (6 shots)
Frans Nielsen (NYI)	5 (8 shots)
Erik Christensen (NYR)	5 (8 shots)
Brad Boyes (STL/BUF)	5 (8 shots)
Mats Zuccarello (NYR)	5 (9 shots)
Jonathan Toews (CHI)	5 (11 shots)

Shooting Percentage (minimum 5 shots)

Jarret Stoll (LA)	90.00% (9/10)
Thomas Vanek (BUF)	83.33% (5/6)
T.J. Oshie (STL)	80.00% (4/5)
Pierre-Marc Bouchard	66.67% (4/6)
Radim Vrbata (PHO)	63.6% (7/11)
Alex Tanguay (CAL)	62.5% (10/16)
Brad Boyes (STL/BUF)	62.5% (5/8)
Frans Nielsen (NYI)	62.5% (5/8)
Erik Christensen (NYR)	62.5% (5/8)
Mike Ribeiro (DAL)	60.00% (6/10)

Worst Shooting Percentage (minimum 5 shots)

Steve Stamkos (TB)	0.00% (0/7)
Matt Duchene (COL)	0.00% (0/6)
Rich Peverley (ATL/BOS)	0.00% (0/5)
Derek Stepan (NYR)	0.00% (0/5)
Phil Kessel (TOR)	12.5% (1/8)
Niklas Hagman (CAL)	12.5% (1/8)
Jack Johnson (LA)	14.3% (1/7)
Patrick Sharp (CHI)	14.3% (1/7)
Corey Perry (ANA)	16.7% (1/6)
Brian Gionta (MON)	16.7% (1/6)
Matt D'Agostini (STL)	16.7% (1/6)

GOALIES

Wins

Jonathan Quick (LA)	10 (10 SO)
Marc-Andre Fleury (PIT)	8 (10 SO)
Miikka Kiprusoff (CAL)	8 (12 SO)
Henrik Lundqvist (NYR)	7 (10 SO)
Pekka Rinne (NAS)	6 (10 SO)
Cam Ward (CAR)	5 (9 SO)
Jonas Hiller (ANA)	4 (6 SO)
Corey Crawford (CHI)	4 (7 SO)
Ilya Bryzgalov (PHO)	4 (9 SO)
Steve Mason (CBJ)	4 (9 SO)

Save Percentage (minimum 15 shots faced)

Craig Anderson (COL/OTT)	93.3% (14/15)
Jimmy Howard (DET)	88.2% (15/17)
Henrik Lundqvist (NYR)	84.8% (39/46)
Jonas Hiller (ANA)	84.6% (22/26)
Marc-Andre Fleury (PIT)	84.2% (32/38)
Corey Crawford (CHI)	84.2% (16/19)
Jonathan Quick (LA)	81.8% (36/44)
Pekka Rinne (NAS)	79.4% (27/34)
Nikolai Khabibulin (EDM)	77.8% (14/18)
Chris Mason (ATL)	76.5% (13/17)

TEAM RECORDS

Most Shootouts

Team	SO	W	L
Calgary	16	9	7
Pittsburgh	13	10	3
Columbus	13	5	8
Los Angeles	12	10	2
NY Rangers	12	9	3
Tampa Bay	12	6	6
Atlanta	12	5	7
Dallas	12	5	7

Fewest Shootouts

Team	SO	W	L
New Jersey	5	3	2
Buffalo	6	5	1
Anaheim	6	4	2
Montreal	6	3	3
Colorado	7	6	1
Ottawa	7	2	5

NATIONALITY OF ALL PLAYERS, 2010–11

SUMMARY

(figures in parentheses show leaguewide representation as a percentage)

TOTAL	**978**	
CANADA	520	(53.2%)
Alberta	91	
British Columbia	58	
Manitoba	32	
New Brunswick	3	
Newfoundland	7	
Nova Scotia	7	
Ontario	208	
Prince Edward Island	4	
Quebec	65	
Saskatchewan	45	
United States	230	(23.5%)
Sweden	62	(6.3%)
Czech Republic	42	(4.3%)
Russia	32	(3.3%)
Finland	31	(3.2%)
Slovakia	14	(1.4%)
Germany	11	(1.1%)
Denmark	6	(0.6%)
Switzerland	5	(0.5%)
Latvia	4	(0.4%)
Austria	3	(0.3%)
Belarus	3	(0.3%)
Kazakhstan	2	(0.3%)
Norway	2	(0.2%)
Slovenia	2	(0.2%)
Ukraine	2	(0.2%)
Brazil	1	(0.1%)
Brunei	1	(0.1%)
France	1	(0.1%)
Italy	1	(0.1%)
Japan	1	(0.1%)
Lithuania	1	(0.1%)
Poland	1	(0.1%)

NATIONALITY BREAKDOWN

CANADA	**520**	
Alberta	91	
Airdrie	2	Zach Boychuk, Dana Tyrell
Banff	1	Ryan Smyth
Beaverlodge	1	Matt Walker
Blackie	1	Jeremy Colliton
Calgary	19	Cody Almond, Jay Beagle, Mike Brodeur, Braydon Coburn, Joe Colborne, Patrick Eaves, T.J. Galiardi, Mike Green, Taylor Hall, Chad Johnson, Nick Johnson, Nathan Lawson, Mike Moore, Brendon Nash, Chris Phillips, Jeff Schultz, Tyler Sloan, Brent Sopel, Jeff Tambellini
Camrose	1	Josh Green
Caroline	2	Kris Russell, Jim Vandermeer
Cochrane	1	Mason Raymond
Cold Lake	1	Alexander Auld
Coleman	1	Rick Rypien
Daysland	1	Richard Petiot
Edmonton	28	Shawn Belle, Blair Betts, Jay Bouwmeester, Johnny Boychuk, Gilbert Brule, Jason Chimera, Erik Christensen, Mike Comrie, Derek Engelland, Tyler Ennis, Andrew Ference, Vernon Fiddler, Mark Fistric, Matt Frattin, Jarome Iginla, Matt Kassian, Daymond Langkow, Bryan Little, Joffrey Lupul, Derek Morris, Scott Nichol, Dion Phaneuf, Fernando Pisani, Steve Reinprecht, David Schlemko, Jared Spurgeon, Jason Strudwick, Brian Sutherby
Elk Point	1	Mark Letestu
Forestburg	1	Evan Oberg
Fort McMurray	1	Scottie Upshall
Fort Saskatchewan	2	Mike Commodore, Ray Whitney
Halkirk	1	Shane Doan
Hinton	1	Dave Scatchard
Lac La Biche	1	Rene Bourque
Leduc	1	Matt Climie
Lethbridge	3	Rob Klinkhammer, Spencer Machacek, Kris Versteeg
Lloydminster	1	Clarke MacArthur
Medicine Hat	3	Brooks Laich, Stefan Meyer, Zack Smith
Olds	1	Jay Rosehill
Peace River	1	Chris Osgood
Provost	1	Lance Bouma

Red Deer	4	Trent Hunter, Chris Mason, Paul Postma, Colton Sceviour
Rocky Mountain House	1	Brad Stuart
St. Albert	1	Nick Holden
St. Paul	1	Kyle Brodziak
Sherwood Park	1	Cam Ward
Strathmore	1	Keaton Ellerby
Taber	1	Devin Setoguchi
Vermilion	1	Jeff Woywitka
Viking	1	Brett Sutter
Westlock	1	Kyle Chipchura
British Columbia	58	
Abbotsford	3	Ryan Craig, Kyle Cumiskey, David van der Gulik
Burnaby	5	Karl Alzner, Jason LaBarbera, Mark Olver, Patrick Wiercioch, Greg Zanon
Cassiar	1	Rob Niedermayer
Comox	1	Brett McLean
Cranbrook	1	Brad Lukowich
Fernie	1	David LeNeveu
Kamloops	1	Mark Recchi
Kelowna	1	Josh Gorges
Kitimat	1	Rod Pelley
Maple Ridge	1	Andrew Ladd
New Westminster	1	Kyle Turris
North Vancouver	2	Mark Dekanich, Ben Maxwell
Osoyoos	1	Chuck Kobasew
Pitt Meadows	1	Brendan Morrison
Port McNeill	2	Willie Mitchell, Clayton Stoner
Prince George	1	Nicholas Drazenovic
Quesnel	2	Brett Festerling, Aaron Gagnon
Revelstoke	1	Aaron Volpatti
Richmond	5	Scott Hannan, Brandon McMillan, Raymond Sawada, Brent Seabrook, Brandon Segal
Salmon Arm	1	Cody Franson
Sicamous	2	Colin Fraser, Shea Weber
Smithers	1	Dan Hamhuis
Terrace	1	Bradley Mills
Trail	2	Shawn Horcoff, Barret Jackman
Vancouver	11	Troy Brouwer, Tyler Eckford, Zach Hamill, Evander Kane, Milan Lucic, Steve Montador, Shaone Morrisonn, Carey Price, Mike Santorelli, Aaron Voros, Brandon Yip

Vernon	4	Eric Brewer, Andrew Ebbett, Eric Godard, Jerred Smithson
Victoria	2	Jamie Benn, Ryan O'Byrne
White Rock	2	Jason Garrison, Colton Gillies
Manitoba	**32**	
Binscarth	1	Cody McLeod
Brandon	4	Matt Calvert, Carson McMillan, Alex Plante, Ryan White
Churchill	1	Jordin Tootoo
Neepawa	1	Shane Hnidy
Nesbitt	1	Aaron Rome
Oakbank	1	Drew Bagnall
Portage La Prairie	2	Arron Asham, Troy Bodie
Russell	1	Brodie Dupont
Selkirk	1	Andrew Murray
Snowflake	1	Justin Falk
Thompson	1	Jody Shelley
Winkler	2	Eric Fehr, Dustin Penner
Winnipeg	15	Cam Barker, Dustin Boyd, Nigel Dawes, Travis Hamonic, Darren Helm, Duncan Keith, Frazer McLaren, Colton Orr, Ryan Reaves, James Reimer, Alexander Steen, Jonathan Toews, Dale Weise, Ian White, Travis Zajac
Ontario	**208**	
Ajax	1	Brent Burns
Alfred	1	Benoit Pouliot
Almonte	1	Kent Huskins
Amherstburg	1	Kevin Westgarth
Ayr	1	Kyle Clifford
Barrie	1	John Madden
Belleville	5	Matt Cooke, Andrew Raycroft, Brad Richardson, Derek Smith, Ty Wishart
Blyth	1	Justin Peters
Bowmanville	1	Bryan Bickell
Bradford	1	Brandon Mashinter
Bramalea	1	Mike Weaver
Brampton	3	Rick Nash, Kris Newbury, Tyler Seguin
Brantford	1	Adam Henrique
Brights Grove	1	Brad Staubitz
Cambridge	2	Tim Brent, Trevor Gillies

Carp	1	Kurtis Foster
Chatham	2	T.J. Brodie, Ryan Jones
Clinton	1	Ryan O'Reilly
Cobourg	1	Justin Williams
Collingwood	1	Jason Arnott
Courtice	1	Greg Nemisz
Dryden	1	Chris Pronger
Elliot Lake	1	Zack Stortini
Fergus	1	Jamie McGinn
Gloucester	1	Grant Clitsome
Grimsby	1	Kevin Bieksa
Guelph	4	Krys Barch, Logan Couture, David Jones, Rich Peverley
Haliburton	1	Matt Duchene
Hamilton	4	Ray Emery, Adam Mair, Steve Staios, Scott Timmins
Hearst	1	Claude Giroux
Huntsville	1	Ethan Moreau
Kanata	1	Todd White
Kenora	1	Mike Richards
King City	2	Daniel Carcillo, Alex Pietrangelo
Kingston	6	Bryan Allen, Jamie Arniel, John Erskine, Jay McClement, Mike Smith, Andy Sutton
Kitchener	4	Evan Brophey, Kevin Klein, Kyle Quincey, Dennis Wideman
Lively	1	Andrew Desjardins
London	13	Gregory Campbell, Jeff Carter, Drew Doughty, Sam Gagner, Nazem Kadri, Mark Mancari, Cody McCormick, Curtis McElhinney, Brandon Prust, Bryan Rodney, Joe Thornton, Jason Williams, Brian Willsie
Long Sault	1	Jesse Winchester
Markdale	1	Chris Neil
Markham	2	Jeff Skinner, Steve Stamkos
Millgrove	1	Danny Syvret
Mississauga	8	Brad Boyes, Matt Corrente, Tom Kostopoulos, Manny Malhotra, Shawn Matthias, Jason Spezza, Matt Stajan, John Tavares
Newmarket	2	Steve Downie, Brian Elliott
Niagara-on-the-Lake	1	Zenon Konopka
Nobleton	1	Nick Boynton
North Bay	1	Craig Rivet
Oakville	2	Steve Mason, Kyle Wilson
Oshawa	5	Josh Bailey, Michael Haley, Jay Harrison, James Neal, Shawn Thornton

Ottawa	10	Adrian Aucoin, Dan Boyle, Paul Byron, Ben Eager, Mark Fraser, Jon Matsumoto, Marc Methot, Sean O'Donnell, Derek Roy, Marc Savard
Owen Sound	1	Cody Bass
Palmerston	1	Nick Spaling
Paris	1	Zac Dalpe
Peterborough	3	Mike Fisher, Corey Perry, Cory Stillman
Petrolia	1	Michael Leighton
Pickering	1	Sean Avery
Port Elgin	1	Brett MacLean
Port Hope	1	Shane O'Brien
Richmond Hill	4	Mike Cammalleri, Stefan della Rovere, Derek Joslin, Theo Peckham
Sarnia	1	Dustin Jeffrey
Sault Ste. Marie	4	Matt D'Agostini, Tyler Kennedy, Chris Thorburn, Marty Turco
Simcoe	2	Jassen Cullimore, Dwayne Roloson
St. Albert	1	Andre Benoit
St. Catharines	2	Bryan McCabe, John Scott
St. Isidore	1	Francis Wathier
St. Thomas	1	Cory Emmerton
Stittsville	1	Matt Bradley
Stouffville	1	Michael del Zotto
Strathroy	2	Brian Campbell, Andy McDonald
Sudbury	4	Todd Bertuzzi, Andrew Brunette, Cameron Gaunce, Derek MacKenzie
Thornhill	1	Dominic Moore
Thunder Bay	8	Taylor Chorney, Ryan Johnson, Taylor Pyatt, Tom Pyatt, Patrick Sharp, Eric Staal, Jordan Staal, Marc Staal
Timmins	2	Mark Katic, Steve Sullivan
Toronto	36	Mike Blunden, Dave Bolland, Chris Campoli, Luca Caputi, David Clarkson, Andrew Cogliano, Carlo Colaiacovo, Trevor Daley, Justin DiBenedetto, Jamie Doornbosch, Kris Draper, Mike Duco, Adam Foote, Mark Giordano, Matt Halischuk, Cody Hodgson, Chris Kelly, Mike Knuble, Corey Locke, Jamal Mayers, Kenndal McArdle, Matt Moulson, Cal O'Reilly, Brandon Pirri, Chris Porter, Liam Reddox, Wayne Simmonds, Chris Stewart, P.K. Subban, Chris Tanev, Raffi Torres, Michael Vernace, Joel Ward, Stephen Weiss, Daniel Winnick, Mike Zigomanis

Waterloo	1	John Mitchell
Welland	6	Paul Bissonnette, Cal Clutterbuck, Matt Ellis, Daniel Girardi, Nathan Horton, Daniel Paille
Winchester	1	Matt Carkner
Whitby	1	Victor Oreskevich
Windsor	8	Matt Beleskey, Cam Fowler, Ed Jovanovski, David Liffiton, Matt Martin, Eric Wellwood, Kyle Wellwood, Ryan Wilson
Woodbridge	1	Steve Eminger
Woodstock	1	Jake Muzzin
Quebec	65	
Alma	1	Guillaume Desbiens
L'Ancienne-Lorette	1	Patrice Bergeron
Chandler	1	Mathieu Garon
Dorval	1	Jason Demers
Drummondville	1	Mathieu Perreault
Gatineau	2	Daniel Briere, Alexandre Picard (b. Jul '85)
Greenfield Park	1	Jerome Samson
Hull	2	Derick Brassard, P-A Parenteau
Île-Bizard	1	Vincent Lecavalier
Lac-St-Charles	1	Martin Biron
LaSalle	1	Anthony Stewart
Laval	4	Pascal Dupuis, Philippe Dupuis, Martin St. Louis, Jose Theodore
Lemoyne	1	Maxime Talbot
Lévis	1	Pierre-Luc Letourneau-Leblond
Longueuil	1	Bruno Gervais
Montreal	19	Alexandre Bolduc, Martin Brodeur, Corey Crawford, Mathieu Darche, J-P Dumont, J-S Giguere, Marc-Andre Gragnani, Francis Lessard, Kris Letang, Matt Lombardi, Roberto Luongo, Torrey Mitchell, Maxim Noreau, Joel Perrault, Kevin Poulin, Mike Ribeiro, Yann Sauve, Marco Scandella, Marc-Edouard Vlasic
Pointe-Claire	1	Alex Burrows
Quebec City	5	Steve Bernier, David Desharnais, Alexandre Giroux, Marc-Antoine Pouliot, Paul Stastny
Repentigny	2	Pascal Leclaire, Jason Pominville
St-Agapit	1	Antoine Vermette
St-Bonaventure	1	Patrick Lalime
Ste-Cathérine	1	Guillaume Latendresse
Ste-Foy	1	Simon Gagne

St-Georges	1	Mathieu Roy
Ste-Justine	1	Alex Tanguay
St-Léonard	1	Maxim Lapierre
St-Louis-de-France	1	Marc-Andre Bergeron
Sayabec	1	Jordan Caron
Sherbrooke	5	Eric Belanger, Pierre-Marc Bouchard, Olivier Magnan, David Perron, Stephane Robidas
Sorel	2	Francois Beauchemin, Marc-Andre Fleury
Terrebonne	1	J-F Jacques
Trois-Rivières	1	Steve Begin
New Brunswick	3	
Edmundston	1	Cedrick Desjardins
Moncton	1	Patrice Cormier
Quispamsis	1	Randy Jones
Newfoundland	7	
Bonavista	1	Adam Pardy
Carbonear	1	Daniel Cleary
St. John's	5	Luke Adam, Ryane Clowe, Colin Greening, Teddy Purcell, Michael Ryder
Nova Scotia	7	
Halifax	4	Eric Boulton, Sidney Crosby, Andrew Gordon, Brad Marchand
New Glasgow	2	Jon Sim, Colin White
Pictou	1	Joey MacDonald
Prince Edward Island	4	
Charlottetown	1	Adam McQuaid
Murray Harbour	1	Brad Richards
Summerside	2	Darryl Boyce, Steve Ott
Saskatchewan	45	
Aneroid	1	Patrick Marleau
Brock	1	Steve MacIntyre
Carlyle	1	Brenden Morrow
Central Butte	1	Blair Jones
Kamsack	1	Darcy Hordichuk
Kindersley	2	Derek Dorsett, Curtis Glencross
Lanigan	1	Sheldon Brookbank
Lloydminster	2	Colby Armstrong, Braden Holtby
Meadow Lake	3	Blake Comeau, Dwayne King, Dwight King

Melfort	1	Tyson Strachan
Melville	1	Jarret Stoll
Nokomis	1	Jordan Henry
Prince Albert	2	Adam Cracknell, Ryan Parent
Punnichy	1	Nolan Yonkman
Regina	13	Keith Aulie, Tyler Bozak, Brett Carson, Devan Dubnyk, Jordan Eberle, Ryan Getzlaf, Tanner Glass, Scott Hartnell, Chris Kunitz, Brendan Mikkelson, Nathan Oystrick, Peter Schaefer, Jeremy Williams
Saskatoon	9	Wade Belak, Derek Boogaard, Dan Ellis, Warren Peters, Darroll Powe, Cory Sarich, Brayden Schenn, Luke Schenn, James Wright
Stewart Valley	1	Travis Moen
Strasbourg	1	Nick Schultz
Unity	1	Boyd Gordon
Wapella	1	Brett Clark
USA	**209**	
Alaska	7	Matt Carle, Ty Conklin, Joey Crabb, Brandon Dubinsky, Scott Gomez, Nate Thompson, Tim Wallace
California	8	Jonathon Blum, Ryan Hollweg, Ray Macias, Brooks Orpik, Rhett Rakhshani, Garrett Stafford, Brett Sterling, Casey Wellman
Colorado	4	Ben Bishop, Brandon Crombeen, David Hale, Ben Holmstrom
Connecticut	9	Nick Bonino, Chris Clark, Chris Drury, Ron Hainsey, Max Pacioretty, Jonathan Quick, Ryan Shannon, Kevin Shattenkirk, Colin Wilson
Delaware	1	Mark Eaton
Florida	1	Blake Geoffrion
Illinois	13	Craig Anderson, Jarred Boll, Mike Brown, Joe Corvo, Robbie Earl, Brian Fahey, Andrew Hutchinson, Brett Lebda, Al Montoya, John Moore, Tim Stapleton, Lee Sweatt, Tommy Wingels
Indiana	2	Jack Johnson, John-Michael Liles
Iowa	1	Scott Clemmensen
Maryland	1	Jeff Halpern
Massachusetts	19	Keith Aucoin, Brian Boyle, Bobby Butler, Joe Callahan, John Carlson, Rick DiPietro, Benn Ferriero, Hal Gill, Doug Janik, Greg Maudlin, John McCarthy, Mike Mottau, Tom Poti, Pat Rissmiller, Cory Schneider, Brian Strait, Noah Welch, Ryan Whitney, Keith Yandle

Michigan	38	Justin Abdelkader, David Booth, Drayson Bowman, Ian Cole, Sean Collins, Erik Condra, Chris Conner, Nathan Gerbe, Tim Gleason, Andy Greene, Matt Greene, Mike Grier, Adam Hall, T.J. Hensick, Matt Hunwick, Brent Johnson, Steven Kampfer, Ryan Kesler, Chad LaRose, David Legwand, Peter Mannino, Alec Martinez, Ryan Miller, Mike Modano, David Moss, Aaron Palushaj, Scott Parse, Jeff Petry, Kevin Porter, Corey Potter, Brian Rafalski, Brian Rolston, Jim Slater, Chris Summers, Matt Taormina, Tim Thomas, Doug Weight, James Wisniewski
Minnesota	41	Andrew Alberts, David Backes, Keith Ballard, Jason Blake, Justin Braun, Dustin Byfuglien, Ryan Carter, Matt Cullen, Tom Gilbert, Alex Goligoski, Matt Hendricks, Erik Johnson, Jamie Langenbrunner, Nick Leddy, Brian Lee, Jordan Leopold, Mike Lundin, Paul Martin, Jamie McBain, Ryan McDonagh, Philip McRae, Travis Morin, Matt Niskanen, Jim O'Brien, Kyle Okposo, Zach Parise, Mark Parrish, Toby Petersen, Nate Prosser, Mike Sauer, Dan Sexton, Matt Smaby, Alex Stalock, Derek Stepan, Ryan Stoa, Colin Stuart, Mark Stuart, Jeff Taffe, Chris Vande Velde, Blake Wheeler, Clay Wilson
Missouri	4	Chris Butler, Cam Janssen, Mike McKenna, Joe Vitale
Nebraska	1	Jed Ortmeyer
New Hampshire	3	Mark Fayne, Ben Lovejoy, Freddy Meyer
New Jersey	4	Paul Mara, Drew Miller, Bobby Ryan, James van Riemsdyk
New York	35	Zach Bogosian, Francis Bouillon, Dustin Brown, Ryan Callahan, Erik Cole, Tim Connolly, Craig Conroy, Nick Foligno, Matt Gilroy, Brian Gionta, Stephen Gionta, Chris Higgins, Jimmy Howard, Hugh Jessiman, Patrick Kaleta, Patrick Kane, Tim Kennedy, Mike Komisarek, Matt Lashoff, Jay Leach, Todd Marchant, Tom McCollum, Jeremy Morin, Chris Mueller, Eric Nystrom, Kyle Palmieri, Nick Palmieri, Marty Reasoner, Rob Schremp, Rob Scuderi, Tim Sestito, Tom Sestito, Shane Sims, Lee Stempniak, Brandon Sutter
North Carolina	2	Patrick O'Sullivan, Ben Smith
North Dakota	3	Paul Gaustad, Tim Jackman, Ryan Potulny
Ohio	2	Peter Harrold, Mike Rupp

Oregon	1	Jack Hillen
Pennsylvania	14	Matt Bartkowski, Matt Campanale, Colby Cohen, Nate Guenin, Christian Hanson, Chad Kolarik, Ryan Malone, George Parros, Dylan Reese, Eric Tangradi, Bill Thomas, R.J. Umberger, Mike Weber, John Zeiler
Rhode Island	1	Brian Boucher
Texas	1	Tyler Myers
Utah	2	Richard Bachman, Trevor Lewis
Washington	2	Pat Dwyer, T.J. Oshie
Wisconsin	10	Adam Burish, Jake Dowell, Davis Drewiske, Phil Kessel, Joe Pavelski, Jack Skille, Drew Stafford, David Steckel, Ryan Suter, Brad Winchester

INTERNATIONAL

SWEDEN	62	Daniel Alfredsson, Jonas Andersson, Mikael Backlund, Nicklas Backstrom, Niklas Bergfors, Patrik Berglund, Alexander Edler, Oliver Ekman-Larsson, Andreas Engqvist, Jhonas Enroth, Tobias Enstrom, Jonathan Ericsson, Loui Eriksson, Peter Forsberg, Johan Franzen, Nicklas Grossman, Carl Gunnarsson, Erik Gustafsson, Jonas Gustavsson, Johan Harju, Johan Hedberg, Victor Hedman, Niklas Hjalmarsson, Tomas Holmstrom, Patrik Hornqvist, Kristian Huselius, Marcus Johansson, Jacob Josefson, Eric Karlsson, Henrik Karlsson, Linus Klasen, Carl Klingberg, Niklas Kronwall, Marcus Kruger, Robin Lehner, Nicklas Lidstrom, Andreas Lilja, Anders Lindback, Henrik Lundqvist, Jacob Markstrom, Fredrik Modin, Oscar Moller, Doug Murray, John Oduya, Mattias Ohlund, Linus Omark, Magnus Paajarvi, Samuel Pahlsson, Mattias Ritola, Mikael Samuelsson, Daniel Sedin, Henrik Sedin, Fredrik Sjostrom, Viktor Stalberg, Anton Stralman, Henrik Tallinder, Mattias Tedenby, Andreas Thuresson, Alexander Urbom, Niclas Wallin, Tom Wandell, Henrik Zetterberg
CZECH REPUBLIC	42	Radek Dvorak, Patrik Elias, Martin Erat, Tomas Fleischmann, Michael Frolik, Roman Hamrlik, Martin Hanzal, Martin Havlat, Jan Hejda, Milan Hejduk, Ales Hemsky, Jiri Hudler, Tomas Kaberle, Jakub Kindl, Rostislav Klesla, David Koci, Ales Kotalik, David Krejci, Filip Kuba, Tomas Kubalik, Pavel Kubina,

Radek Martinek, Milan Michalek, Zbynek Michalek, Michal Neuvirth, Rostislav Olesz, Ondrej Pavelec, Tomas Plekanec, Roman Polak, Vaclav Prospal, Petr Prucha, Michal Repik, Michal Rozsival, Ladislav Smid, Vladimir Sobotka, Jaroslav Spacek, Jiri Tlusty, Tomas Vincour, Tomas Vokoun, Jakub Voracek, Radim Vrbata, Marek Zidlicky

RUSSIA	32	Artem Anisimov, Anton Babchuk, Sergei Bobrovsky, Ilya Bryzgalov, Alexander Burmistrov, Evgeni Dadonov, Pavel Datsyuk, Nikita Filatov, Alexander Frolov, Sergei Gonchar, Evgeni Grachev, Nikolai Khabibulin, Ilya Kovalchuk, Alexei Kovalev, Nikolai Kulemin, Dmitri Kulikov, Andrei Loktionov, Evgeni Malkin, Andrei Markov, Maxim Mayorov, Nikita Nikitin, Alexander Ovechkin, Sergei Samsonov, Alexander Semin, Sergei Shirokov, Fedor Tyutin, Simeon Varlamov, Alexander Vasyunov, Anton Volchenkov, Vladimir Zharkov, Nikolai Zherdev, Andrei Zubarev
FINLAND	31	Niklas Backstrom, Sean Bergenheim, Valtteri Filppula, Niklas Hagman, Teemu Hartikainen, Jesse Joensuu, Jussi Jokinen, Olli Jokinen, Miikka Kiprusoff, Mikko Koivu, Saku Koivu, Lauri Korpikoski, Mikko Koskinen, Teemu Laakso, Kari Lehtonen, Mikko Lehtonen, Ville Leino, Sami Lepisto, Toni Lydman, Antti Miettinen, Antti Niemi, Antero Niittymaki, Joni Pitkanen, Tuuka Rask, Pekka Rinne, Jarkko Ruutu, Tuomo Ruutu, Anssi Salmela, Sami Salo, Teemu Selanne, Kimmo Timonen
SLOVAKIA	14	Mario Bliznak, Peter Budaj, Zdeno Chara, Marian Gaborik, Jaroslav Halak, Michal Handzus, Marian Hossa, Milan Jurcina, Tomas Kopecky, Andrei Meszaros, Andrej Sekera, Marek Svatos, Tomas Tatar, Lubomir Visnovsky
GERMANY	11	Christian Ehrhoff, Marcel Goc, Mikhail Grabovski, Dany Heatley, Jochen Hecht, Korbinian Holzer, Marcel Mueller, Timo Pielmeier, Dennis Seidenberg, Marco Sturm, Alexander Sulzer

DENMARK	6	Mikkel Boedker, Lars Eller, Jannik Hansen, Philip Larsen, Frans Nielsen, Peter Regin
SWITZERLAND	5	Martin Gerber, Jonas Hiller, Nino Niederreiter, Yannick Weber, Roman Wick
LATVIA	4	Oskars Bartulis, Raitis Ivanins, Arturs Kulda, Karlis Skrastins
AUSTRIA	3	Michael Grabner, Andreas Nodl, Thomas Vanek
BELARUS	3	Andrei Kostitsyn, Sergei Kostitsyn, Ruslan Salei
KAZAKHSTAN	2	Nik Antropov, Antonin Khudobin
NORWAY	2	Jonas Holos, Mats Zuccarello
SLOVENIA	2	Anze Kopitar, Jan Mursak
UKRAINE	2	Ruslan Fedotenko, Alexei Ponikarovsky
BRAZIL	1	Robyn Regehr
BRUNEI	1	Craig Adams
FRANCE	1	Stephane da Costa
ITALY	1	Luca Sbisa
JAPAN	1	Ryan O'Marra
LITHUANIA	1	Dainius Zubrus
POLAND	1	Wojtek Wolski

FIRST GAMES PLAYED, 2010–11

Skater (NAT) Goalie (NAT)	Team (date) Team (date)	G Mins	A GA	P W/L	Pim
Adam, Luke (CAN)	BUF (Oct. 26)	0	0	0	2
Arniel, Jamie (CAN)	BOS (Nov. 28)	0	0	0	0
Aulie, Keith (CAN)	TOR (Nov. 13)	0	0	0	0
Bachman, Richard (USA)	DAL (Dec. 11)	9:35	0	ND	
Bagnall, Drew (CAN)	MIN (Apr. 8)	0	0	0	2
Bartkowski, Matt (USA)	BOS (Jan. 10)	0	0	0	2
Benoit, Andre (CAN)	OTT (Feb. 11)	0	0	0	0
Blum, Jonathon (USA)	NAS (Feb. 22)	0	0	0	0
Bobrovsky, Sergei (RUS)	PHI (Oct. 7)	60:00	2	W	
Bouma, Lance (CAN)	CAL (Feb. 5)	0	0	0	0
Braun, Justin (USA)	SJ (Nov. 26)	0	0	0	0
Brodie, T.J. (CAN)	CAL (Oct. 7)	0	0	0	0
Brophey, Evan (CAN)	CHI (Oct. 23)	0	0	0	0
Burmistrov, Alexander (RUS)	ATL (Oct. 8)	0	0	0	0
Byron, Paul (CAN)	BUF (Jan. 23)	0	1	1	0
Calvert, Matt (CAN)	CBJ (Jan. 7)	0	0	0	2
Campanale, Matt (USA)	NYI (Apr. 6)	0	0	0	2
Caron, Jordan (CAN)	BOS (Oct. 10)	0	0	0	0
Clifford, Kyle (CAN)	LA (Oct. 9)	0	0	0	0
Cohen, Colby (USA)	COL (Nov. 6)	0	0	0	4
Colborne, Joe (CAN)	TOR (Apr. 9)	0	1	1	0
Cole, Ian (USA)	STL (Nov. 6)	0	0	0	2
Condra, Erik (USA)	OTT (Feb. 15)	0	1	1	0
Cormier, Patrice (CAN)	ATL (Dec. 28)	0	0	0	0
Cracknell, Adam (CAN)	STL (Dec. 15)	0	0	0	0
Da Costa, Stephane (FRA)	OTT (Apr. 2)	0	0	0	0
Dalpe, Zac (CAN)	CAR (Oct. 7)	0	1	1	0
Dekanich, Mark (CAN)	NAS (Dec. 18)	49:59	3	ND	
Della Rovere, Stefan (CAN)	STL (Dec. 1)	0	0	0	0
Desjardins, Andrew (CAN)	SJ (Jan. 3)	0	0	0	0
Desjardins, Cedrick (CAN)	TB (Dec. 30)	60:00	1	W	
DiBenedetto, Justin (CAN)	NYI (Mar. 1)	0	0	0	0
Doornbosch, Jamie (CAN)	NYI (Apr. 8)	0	0	0	0
Drazenovic, Nicholas (CAN)	STL (Nov. 11)	0	0	0	0
Dupont, Brodie (CAN)	NYR (Jan. 22)	0	0	0	0
Eberle, Jordan (CAN)	EDM (Oct. 7)	1	1	2	0
Ekman-Larsson, Oliver (SWE)	PHO (Oct. 9)	0	0	0	0

Emmerton, Cory (CAN)	DET (Jan. 22)	1	0	1	0
Engqvist, Andreas (SWE)	MON (Jan. 21)	0	0	0	0
Fahey, Brian (USA)	WAS (Oct. 16)	0	0	0	0
Fayne, Mark (USA)	NJ (Nov. 22)	0	0	0	0
Fowler, Cam (CAN)	ANA (Oct. 8)	0	0	0	0
Frattin, Matt (CAN)	TOR (Apr. 9)	0	0	0	0
Gaunce, Cameron (CAN)	COL (Feb. 12)	0	0	0	0
Geoffrion, Blake (USA)	NAS (Feb. 26)	0	0	0	0
Gionta, Stephen (USA)	NJ (Nov. 5)	0	0	0	0
Grachev, Evgeni (RUS)	NYR (Oct. 29)	0	0	0	0
Greening, Colin (CAN)	OTT (Feb. 1)	0	0	0	0
Gustafsson, Erik (SWE)	PHI (Feb. 26)	0	0	0	4
Hall, Taylor (CAN)	EDM (Oct. 7)	0	0	0	2
Hamonic, Travis (CAN)	NYI (Nov. 24)	0	0	0	2
Harju, Johan (SWE)	TB (Nov. 12)	0	0	0	2
Hartikainen, Teemu (FIN)	EDM (Mar. 17)	0	1	1	0
Henrique, Adam (CAN)	NJ (Apr. 10)	0	0	0	0
Hodgson, Cody (CAN)	VAN (Feb. 1)	0	0	0	0
Holden, Nick (CAN)	CBJ (Oct. 20)	0	0	0	0
Holmstrom, Ben (USA)	PHI (Mar. 3)	0	0	0	0
Holos, Jonas (NOR)	COL (Oct. 16)	0	0	0	0
Holtby, Braden (CAN)	WAS (Nov. 5)	10:09	0	W	
Holzer, Korbinian (GER)	TOR (Nov. 6)	0	0	0	0
Jessiman, Hugh (USA)	FLO (Feb. 27)	0	0	0	0
Johansson, Marcus (SWE)	WAS (Oct. 8)	0	0	0	0
Josefson, Jacob (SWE)	NJ (Oct. 15)	0	0	0	0
Kampfer, Steven (USA)	BOS (Dec. 9)	0	0	0	0
Karlsson, Henrik (SWE)	CAL (Oct. 22)	60:00	2	W	
Kassian, Matt (CAN)	MIN (Nov. 5)	0	0	0	2
Katic, Mark (CAN)	NYI (Feb. 24)	0	1	1	0
King, Dwight (CAN)	LA (Nov. 17)	0	0	0	0
Klasen, Linus (SWE)	NAS (Oct. 30)	0	0	0	0
Klingberg, Carl (SWE)	ATL (Apr. 10)	0	0	0	0
Klinkhammer, Rob (CAN)	CHI (Dec. 8)	0	0	0	0
Koskinen, Mikko (FIN)	NYI (Feb. 8)	58:36	5	L	
Kruger, Marcus (SWE)	CHI (Mar. 23)	0	0	0	2
Kubalik, Tomas (CZE)	CBJ (Mar. 31)	0	2	2	0
Lawson, Nathan (CAN)	NYI (Dec. 18)	64:56	3	OTL	
Leddy, Nick (USA)	CHI (Oct. 7)	0	0	0	0
Lehner, Robin (SWE)	OTT (Oct. 16)	4:42	0	ND	
Lindback, Anders (SWE)	NAS (Oct. 9)	17:22	0	ND	
Macias, Ray (USA)	COL (Apr. 7)	0	0	0	2

MacLean, Brett (CAN)	PHO (Dec. 29)	1	0	1	0
Magnan, Olivier (CAN)	NJ (Oct. 21)	0	0	0	0
Markstrom, Jacob (SWE)	FLO (Jan. 23)	39:49	2	L	
Mashinter, Brandon (CAN)	SJ (Dec. 29)	0	0	0	0
Matsumoto, Jon (CAN)	CAR (Nov. 1)	0	0	0	0
McCollum, Tom (USA)	DET (Mar. 30)	14:37	3	ND	
McDonagh, Ryan (USA)	NYR (Jan. 7)	0	0	0	0
McMillan, Brandon (CAN)	ANA (Nov. 21)	0	0	0	0
McMillan, Carson (CAN)	MIN (Apr. 3)	0	1	1	0
McRae, Philip (USA)	STL (Jan. 12)	0	0	0	2
Mills, Bradley (CAN)	NJ (Oct. 30)	0	0	0	0
Moore, John (USA)	CBJ (Feb. 5)	0	0	0	0
Moore, Mike (CAN)	SJ (Oct. 19)	0	0	0	0
Morin, Jeremy (USA)	CHI (Nov. 6)	0	0	0	0
Morin, Travis (USA)	DAL (Jan. 26)	0	0	0	0
Mueller, Chris (USA)	NAS (Dec. 28)	0	0	0	0
Mueller, Marcel (GER)	TOR (Jan. 15)	0	0	0	0
Mursak, Jan (SLO)	DET (Dec. 27)	0	0	0	2
Muzzin, Jake (CAN)	LA (Oct. 9)	0	0	0	0
Nash, Brendon (CAN)	MON (Feb. 15)	0	0	0	0
Nemisz, Greg (CAN)	CAL (Mar. 23)	0	0	0	0
Niederreiter, Nino (SUI)	NYI (Oct. 9)	0	0	0	0
Nikitin, Nikita (RUS)	STL (Nov. 6)	0	0	0	0
O'Brien, Jim (USA)	OTT (Dec. 31)	0	0	0	0
Olver, Mark (CAN)	COL (Oct. 7)	0	0	0	2
Omark, Linus (SWE)	EDM (Dec. 10)	0	1	1	0
Paajarvi, Magnus (SWE)	EDM (Oct. 7)	0	0	0	2
Palmieri, Kyle (USA)	ANA (Nov. 3)	1	0	1	0
Palushaj, Aaron (USA)	MON (Mar. 17)	0	0	0	0
Petry, Jeff (USA)	EDM (Dec. 28)	0	1	1	0
Pielmeier, Timo (GER)	ANA (Feb. 19)	40:00	5	ND	
Pirri, Brandon (CAN)	CHI (Oct. 9)	0	0	0	0
Postma, Paul (CAN)	ATL (Mar. 9)	0	0	0	0
Poulin, Kevin (CAN)	NYI (Jan. 6)	53:43 0	ND		
Rakhshani, Rhett (USA)	NYI (Dec. 13)	0	0	0	0
Reaves, Ryan (CAN)	STL (Oct. 11)	0	0	0	15
Reimer, James (CAN)	TOR (Dec. 20)	14:09	0	ND	
Sauve, Yann (CAN)	VAN (Feb. 15)	0	0	0	0
Scandella, Marco (CAN)	MIN (Nov. 12)	0	0	0	0
Sceviour, Colton (CAN)	DAL (Feb. 5)	0	0	0	0
Seguin, Tyler (CAN)	BOS (Oct. 9)	0	0	0	0
Shattenkirk, Kevin (USA)	COL (Nov. 4)	0	0	0	2
Sims, Shane (USA)	NYI (Apr. 9)	0	0	0	0

Skinner, Jeff (CAN)	CAR (Oct. 7)	0	0	0	0
Smith, Ben (USA)	CHI (Oct. 29)	0	0	0	0
Spurgeon, Jared (CAN)	MIN (Nov. 29)	0	0	0	0
Stalock, Alex (USA)	SJ (Feb. 1)	29:47	0	W	
Stepan, Derek (USA)	NYR (Oct. 9)	3	0	3	0
Strait, Brian (USA)	PIT (Feb. 21)	0	0	0	0
Summers, Chris (USA)	PHO (Jan. 20)	0	0	0	2
Sweatt, Lee (USA)	VAN (Jan. 26)	1	0	1	0
Tanev, Chris (CAN)	VAN (Jan. 18)	0	0	0	0
Taormina, Matt (USA)	NJ (Oct. 8)	0	0	0	0
Tatar, Tomas (SVK)	DET (Dec. 31)	1	0	1	0
Tedenby, Mattias (SWE)	NJ (Nov. 10)	0	1	1	0
Timmins, Scott (CAN)	FLO (Feb. 1)	0	0	0	2
Tyrell, Dana (CAN)	TB (Oct. 9)	0	0	0	0
Urbom, Alexander (SWE)	NJ (Oct. 8)	0	0	0	0
VandeVelde, Chris (USA)	EDM (Mar. 17)	0	0	0	0
Vasyunov, Alexander (RUS)	NJ (Oct. 23)	0	0	0	0
Vincour, Tomas (CZE)	DAL (Feb. 9)	0	0	0	0
Vitale, Joe (USA)	PIT (Feb. 10)	0	0	0	0
Volpatti, Aaron (CAN)	VAN (Dec. 18)	0	0	0	0
Weise, Dale (CAN)	NYR (Dec. 18)	0	0	0	5
Wellwood, Eric (CAN)	PHI (Nov. 1)	0	0	0	0
Wick, Roman (SUI)	OTT (Feb. 25)	0	0	0	0
Wiercioch, Patrick (CAN)	OTT (Mar. 22)	0	0	0	0
Wingels, Tommy (USA)	SJ (Oct. 8)	0	0	0	0
Zubarev, Andrei (RUS)	ATL (Apr. 5)	0	0	0	0
Zuccarello, Mats (NOR)	NYR (Dec. 23)	0	0	0	0

BY NATION

Canada	71
United States	41
Sweden	17
Russia	6
Germany	3
Czech Republic	2
Finland	2
Norway	2
Switzerland	2
France	1
Slovakia	1
Slovenia	1
TOTAL	149

BY NHL TEAM

Anaheim	4
Atlanta	5
Boston	5
Buffalo	2
Calgary	4
Carolina	3
Chicago	7
Colorado	6
Columbus	4
Dallas	4
Detroit	4
Edmonton	7
Florida	3
Los Angeles	3
Minnesota	5
Montreal	3
Nashville	6
New Jersey	10
NY Islanders	11
NY Rangers	6
Ottawa	8
Philadelphia	4
Phoenix	3
Pittsburgh	2
St. Louis	7
San Jose	6
Tampa Bay	3
Toronto	6
Vancouver	5
Washington	3

PLAYER REGISTER, REGULAR SEASON, 2010–11

Skater YEAR	GP	G	A	P	Pim	

Goalie YEAR	GP	W-L-OTL-T	Mins	GA	SO	GAA

Abdelkader, Justin b. Muskegon, Michigan, February 25, 1987

	GP	G	A	P	Pim
2010–11 DET	74	7	12	19	61
NHL Totals	128	10	15	25	98

Adam, Luke b. St. John's, Newfoundland, June 18, 1990

	GP	G	A	P	Pim
2010–11 BUF	19	3	1	4	12
NHL Totals	19	3	1	4	12

Adams, Craig b. Seria, Brunei, April 26, 1977

	GP	G	A	P	Pim
2010–11 PIT	80	4	11	15	76
NHL Totals	669	41	74	115	531

Alberts, Andrew b. Minneapolis, Minnesota, June 30, 1981

	GP	G	A	P	Pim
2010–11 VAN	42	1	6	7	41
NHL Totals	381	6	45	51	420

Alfredsson, Daniel b. Gothenburg, Sweden, December 11, 1972

	GP	G	A	P	Pim
2010–11 OTT	54	14	17	31	18
NHL Totals	1,056	389	634	1,023	449

Allen, Bryan b. Kingston, Ontario, August 21, 1980

	GP	G	A	P	Pim
2010–11 FLO/CAL	72	4	13	17	82
NHL Totals	519	28	76	104	648

• traded by Florida to Carolina on February 28, 2011, for Sergei Samsonov

Almond, Cody b. Calgary, Alberta, July 24, 1989

	GP	G	A	P	Pim
2010–11 MIN	8	0	0	0	2
NHL Totals	15	1	0	1	11

Alzner, Karl b. Burnaby, British Columbia, September 24, 1988

	GP	G	A	P	Pim
2010–11 WAS	82	2	10	12	24
NHL Totals	133	3	19	22	34

Anderson, Craig **b.** Park Ridge, Illinois, May 21, 1981

2010–11 COL/OTT	51	24–20–4	2,865	135	2	2.83
NHL Totals	231	98–88–22–2	12,917	599	16	2.78

• traded by Colorado to Ottawa on February 18, 2011, for Brian Elliott

Andersson, Jonas **b.** Stockholm, Sweden, February 24, 1981

2010–11 VAN	4	0	0	0	0
NHL Totals	4	0	0	0	0

Anisimov, Artem **b.** Yaroslavl, Soviet Union (Russia), May 24, 1988

2010–11 NYR	82	18	26	44	20
NHL Totals	165	30	42	72	52

Antropov, Nik **b.** Vost, Soviet Union (Kazakhstan), February 18, 1980

2010–11 ATL	76	16	25	41	42
NHL Totals	679	172	240	412	569

Armstrong, Colby **b.** Lloydminster, Saskatchewan, November 23, 1982

2010–11 TOR	50	8	15	23	38
NHL Totals	410	86	115	201	355

Arniel, Jamie **b.** Kingston, Ontario, November 16, 1989

2010–11 BOS	1	0	0	0	0
NHL Totals	1	0	0	0	0

Arnott, Jason **b.** Collingwood, Ontario, October 11, 1974

2010–11 NJ/WAS	73	17	14	31	40
NHL Totals	1,172	400	504	904	1,216

• traded by Nashville to Washington on June 19, 2010, for Matt Halischuk and a 2nd-round draft choice in 2011

Asham, Arron **b.** Portage La Prairie, Manitoba, April 13, 1978

2010–11 PIT	44	5	6	11	46
NHL Totals	692	87	103	190	864

Aucoin, Adrian **b.** Ottawa, Ontario, July 3, 1973

2010–11 PHO	75	3	19	22	52
NHL Totals	1,008	119	267	386	735

Aucoin, Keith **b.** Waltham, Massachusetts, November 6, 1978

2010–11 WAS	1	0	0	0	0
NHL Totals	1	0	0	0	0

Auld, Alexander b. Cold Lake, Alberta, January 7, 1981

2010–11 MON	16	6–2–2	749	33	0	2.64
NHL Totals	223	89–84–30	12,340	570	6	2.77

Aulie, Keith b. Regina, Saskatchewan, June 11, 1989

2010–11 TOR	40	2	0	2	32
NHL Totals	40	2	0	2	32

Avery, Sean b. Pickering, Ontario, April 10, 1980

2010–11 NYR	76	3	21	24	174
NHL Totals	565	87	157	244	1,512

Babchuk, Anton b. Kiev, Soviet Union (Russia), May 6, 1984

2010–11 CAR/CAL	82	11	24	35	32
NHL Totals	250	34	62	96	102

• traded by Carolina to Calgary on November 17, 2010, for Ian White and Brett Sutter

Bachman, Richard b. Salt Lake City, Utah, July 25, 1987

2010–11 DAL	1	0–0–0	10	0	0	0.00
NHL Totals	1	0–0–0	10	0	0	0.00

Backes, David b. Blaine, Minnesota, May 1, 1984

2010–11 STL	82	31	31	62	93
NHL Totals	364	102	116	218	500

Backlund, Mikael b. Vasteras, Sweden, March 17, 1989

2010–11 CAL	73	10	15	25	18
NHL Totals	97	11	24	35	24

Backstrom, Nicklas b. Gavle, Sweden, November 23, 1987

2010–11 WAS	77	18	47	65	40
NHL Totals	323	87	236	323	160

Backstrom, Niklas b. Helsinki, Finland, February 13, 1978

2010–11 MIN	51	22–23–5	2,978	132	3	2.66
NHL Totals	281	141–91–35	16,190	653	22	2.42

Bagnall, Drew b. Oakbank, Manitoba, October 26, 1983

2010–11 MIN	2	0	0	0	4
NHL Totals	2	0	0	0	4

Bailey, Josh b. Oshawa, Ontario, October 2, 1989

2010–11 NYI	70	11	17	28	37
NHL Totals	211	34	54	88	71

Ballard, Keith b. Baudette, Minnesota, November 26, 1982

2010–11 VAN	65	2	5	7	53
NHL Totals	462	35	121	156	456

Barch, Krys b. Guelph, Ontario, March 26, 1980

2010–11 DAL	44	2	1	3	80
NHL Totals	253	10	16	26	555

Barker, Cam b. Winnipeg, Manitoba, April 4, 1986

2010–11 MIN	52	1	4	5	34
NHL Totals	271	19	73	92	263

Bartkowski, Matt b. Pittsburgh, Pennsylvania, June 4, 1988

2010–11 BOS	6	0	0	0	4
NHL Totals	6	0	0	0	4

Bartulis, Oskars b. Ogre, Soviet Union (Latvia), January 21, 1987

2010–11 PHI	13	0	0	0	4
NHL Totals	66	1	8	9	32

Bass, Cody b. Owen Sound, Ontario, January 7, 1987

2010–11 OTT	1	0	0	0	0
NHL Totals	34	2	2	4	34

Beagle, Jay b. Calgary, Alberta, October 16, 1985

2010–11 WAS	31	2	1	3	8
NHL Totals	41	3	2	5	12

Beauchemin, Francois b. Sorel, Quebec, June 4, 1980

2010–11 TOR/ANA	81	5	12	17	32
NHL Totals	409	31	102	133	237

• traded by Toronto to Anaheim on February 9, 2011, for Joffrey Lupul, Jake Gardiner and a 4th-round draft choice in 2013

Begin, Steve b. Trois-Rivières, Quebec, June 14, 1978

2010–11 NAS	2	0	0	0	4
NHL Totals	488	52	48	100	539

Belak, Wade   b. Saskatoon, Saskatchewan, July 3, 1976

2010–11 NAS	15	0	0	0	18
NHL Totals	549	8	25	33	1,263

•retired in July 2011

Belanger, Eric   b. Sherbrooke, Quebec, December 16, 1977

2010–11 PHO	82	13	27	40	36
NHL Totals	716	134	205	339	319

Beleskey, Matt   b. Windsor, Ontario, June 7, 1988

2010–11 ANA	35	3	7	10	36
NHL Totals	97	14	14	28	71

Belle, Shawn   b. Edmonton, Alberta, January 3, 1985

2010–11 EDM/COL	9	0	0	0	2
NHL Totals	20	0	1	1	2

• traded by Edmonton to Colorado on February 28, 2011, for Kevin Montgomery

Benn, Jamie   b. Victoria, British Columbia, July 18, 1989

2010–11 DAL	69	22	34	56	52
NHL Totals	151	44	53	97	97

Benoit, Andre   b. St. Albert, Ontario, January 6, 1984

2010–11 OTT	8	0	1	1	6
NHL Totals	8	0	1	1	6

Bergenheim, Sean   b. Helsinki, Finland, February 8, 1984

2010–11 TB	80	14	15	29	56
NHL Totals	326	54	55	109	251

Bergeron, Marc-Andre   b. St-Louis-de-France, Quebec, October 13, 1980

2010–11 TB	23	2	6	8	8
NHL Totals	422	77	125	202	185

Bergeron, Patrice   b. L'Ancienne-Lorette, Quebec, July 24, 1985

2010–11 BOS	80	22	35	57	26
NHL Totals	456	121	216	337	142

Bergfors, Niclas   b. Sodertalje, Sweden, March 7, 1987

2010–11 ATL/FLO	72	12	24	36	8
NHL Totals	162	34	47	81	18

• traded by Atlanta to Florida on February 28, 2011, with Pat Rissmiller for Radek Dvorak and a 5th-round draft choice in 2011

Berglund, Patrik   b. Vasteras, Sweden, June 2, 1988

2010–11 STL	81	22	30	52	26
NHL Totals	228	56	69	125	58

Bernier, Jonathan   b. Laval, Quebec, August 7, 1988

2010–11 LA	25	11–8–3	1,378	57	3	2.48
NHL Totals	32	15–11–3	1,802	77	4	2.56

Bernier, Steve   b. Quebec City, Quebec, March 31, 1985

2010–11 FLO	68	5	10	15	21
NHL Totals	385	76	83	159	197

Bertuzzi, Todd   b. Sudbury, Ontario, February 2, 1975

2010–11 DET	81	16	29	45	71
NHL Totals	1,022	289	424	713	1,372

Betts, Blair   b. Edmonton, Alberta, February 16, 1980

2010–11 PHI	75	5	7	12	8
NHL Totals	477	41	37	78	118

Bickell, Bryan   b. Bowmanville, Ontario, March 9, 1986

2010–11 CHI	78	17	20	37	40
NHL Totals	101	22	21	43	47

Bieksa, Kevin   b. Grimsby, Ontario, June 16, 1981

2010–11 VAN	66	6	16	22	73
NHL Totals	347	34	113	147	556

Biron, Martin   b. Lac-St-Charles, Quebec, August 15, 1977

2010–11 NYR	17	8–6–0	928	33	0	2.13
NHL Totals	479	216–182–49	26,986	1,175	26	2.61

Bishop, Ben   b. Denver, Colorado, November 21, 1986

2010–11 STL	7	3–4–0	369	17	1	2.76
NHL Totals	13	4–5–1	614	29	1	2.83

Bissonnette, Paul   b. Welland, Ontario, March 11, 1985

2010–11 PHO	48	1	0	1	71
NHL Totals	104	4	3	7	210

Blake, Jason   b. Moorhead, Minnesota, September 2, 1973

2010–11 ANA	76	16	16	32	41
NHL Totals	826	206	268	474	449

Bliznak, Mario   b. Trencin, Czechoslovakia (Czech Republic), March 6, 1987

2010–11 VAN	4	1	0	1	0
NHL Totals	6	1	0	1	0

Blum, Jonathan   b. Long Beach, California, January 30, 1989

2010–11 NAS	23	3	5	8	8
NHL Totals	23	3	5	8	8

Blunden, Mike   b. Toronto, Ontario, December 15, 1986

2010–11 CBJ	1	0	0	0	0
NHL Totals	51	2	2	4	69

Bobrovsky, Sergei   b. Novokuznetsk, Soviet Union (Russia), September 20, 1988

2010–11 PHI	54	28–13–8	3,017	130	0	2.59
NHL Totals	54	28–13–8	3,017	130	0	2.59

Bodie, Troy   b. Portage La Prairie, Manitoba, January 25, 1985

2010–11 ANA/CAR	59	1	3	4	61
NHL Totals	107	6	5	11	141

• claimed off waivers by Carolina from Anaheim on November 16, 2010

Boedker, Mikkel   b. Brondby, Denmark, December 16, 1989

2010–11 PHO	34	4	10	14	8
NHL Totals	126	16	29	45	26

Bogosian, Zach   b. Massena, New York, July 15, 1990

2010–11 ATL	71	5	12	17	29
NHL Totals	199	24	35	59	137

Bolduc, Alexandre   b. Montreal, Quebec, June 26, 1985

2010–11 VAN	24	2	2	4	21
NHL Totals	46	2	3	5	38

Boll, Jarred   b. Crystal Lake, Illinois, May 13, 1986

2010–11 CBJ	73	7	5	12	182
NHL Totals	291	20	23	43	737

Bolland, Dave   b. Toronto, Ontario, June 5, 1986

2010–11 CHI	61	15	22	37	34
NHL Totals	221	44	73	117	142

Bonino, Nick   b. Hartford, Connecticut, April 20, 1988

2010–11 ANA	26	0	0	0	4
NHL Totals	35	1	1	2	10

Boogaard, Derek   b. Saskatoon, Saskatchewan, June 23, 1982

2010–11 NYR	22	1	1	2	45
NHL Totals	277	3	13	16	589

• died May 23, 2011

Booth, David   b. Detroit, Michigan, November 24, 1984

2010–11 FLO	82	23	17	40	26
NHL Totals	303	87	79	166	125

Bouchard, Pierre-Marc   b. Sherbrooke, Quebec, April 27, 1984

2010–11 MIN	59	12	26	38	14
NHL Totals	485	89	216	305	152

Boucher, Brian   b. Woonsocket, Rhode Island, January 2, 1977

2010–11 PHI	34	18–10–4	1,884	76	0	2.42
NHL Totals	314	119–131–44	17,528	785	17	2.69

Bouillon, Francis   b. New York, New York, October 17, 1975

2010–11 NAS	44	1	9	10	27
NHL Totals	610	25	98	123	448

Boulton, Eric   b. Halifax, Nova Scotia, August 17, 1976

2010–11 ATL	69	6	4	10	87
NHL Totals	549	27	46	73	1,150

Bouma, Lance   b. Provost, Alberta, March 25, 1990

2010–11 CAL	16	0	1	1	2
NHL Totals	16	0	1	1	2

Bourque, Rene   b. Lac La Biche, Alberta, December 10, 1981

2010–11 CAL	80	27	23	50	42
NHL Totals	394	108	115	223	336

Bouwmeester, Jay   b. Edmonton, Alberta, September 27, 1983

2010–11 CAL	82	4	20	24	44
NHL Totals	635	60	196	256	421

Bowman, Drayson   b. Grand Rapids, Michigan, March 8, 1989

2010–11 CAR	23	0	1	1	12
NHL Totals	32	2	1	3	16

Boyce, Darryl   b. Summerside, Prince Edward Island, July 7, 1984

2010–11 TOR	46	5	8	13	33
NHL Totals	47	5	8	13	33

Boychuk, Johnny   b. Edmonton, Alberta, January 19, 1984

2010–11 BOS	69	3	13	16	45
NHL Totals	125	8	23	31	88

Boychuk, Zach   b. Airdrie, Alberta, October 4, 1989

2010–11 CAR	23	4	3	7	4
NHL Totals	56	7	9	16	6

Boyd, Dustin   b. Winnipeg, Manitoba, July 16, 1986

2010–11 MON	10	1	0	1	2
NHL Totals	220	32	31	63	41

Boyes, Brad   b. Mississauga, Ontario, April 17, 1982

2010–11 STL/BUF	83	17	38	55	36
NHL Totals	493	150	199	349	169

• traded by St. Louis to Buffalo on February 28, 2011, for a 2nd-round draft choice in 2011

Boyle, Brian   b. Dorchester, Massachusetts, December 18, 1984

2010–11 NYR	82	21	14	35	74
NHL Totals	189	33	18	51	167

Boyle, Dan   b. Ottawa, Ontario, July 12, 1976

2010–11 SJ	76	9	41	50	67
NHL Totals	752	116	341	457	527

Boynton, Nick   b. Nobleton, Ontario, January 14, 1979

2010–11 CHI/PHI	51	1	7	8	40
NHL Totals	605	34	110	144	862

• claimed off waivers by Philadelphia from Chicago on February 26, 2011

Bozak, Tyler   b. Regina, Saskatchewan, March 19, 1986

2010–11 TOR	82	15	17	32	14
NHL Totals	119	23	36	59	20

Bradley, Matt   b. Stittsville, Ontario, June 13, 1978

2010–11 WAS	61	4	7	11	68
NHL Totals	630	56	85	141	531

Brassard, Derick   b. Hull, Quebec, September 22, 1987

2010–11 CBJ	74	17	30	47	55
NHL Totals	201	37	73	110	126

Braun, Justin   b. St. Paul, Minnesota, February 10, 1987

2010–11 SJ	28	2	9	11	2
NHL Totals	28	2	9	11	2

Brent, Tim   b. Cambridge, Ontario, March 10, 1984

2010–11 TOR	79	8	12	20	33
NHL Totals	98	9	12	21	41

Brewer, Eric   b. Vernon, British Columbia, April 17, 1979

2010–11 STL/TB	76	9	7	16	81
NHL Totals	758	65	145	210	618

• traded by St. Louis to Tampa Bay on February 18, 2011, for Brock Beukeboom and a 3rd-round draft choice in 2011

Briere, Daniel   b. Gatineau, Quebec, October 6, 1977

2010–11 PHI	77	34	34	68	87
NHL Totals	743	264	330	594	617

Brodeur, Martin   b. Montreal, Quebec, May 6, 1972

2010–11 NJ	56	23–26–3	3,116	127	6	2.45
NHL Totals	1,132	625–350–137	66,636	2,467	116	2.22

Brodeur, Mike   b. Calgary, Alberta, March 30, 1983

2010–11 OTT	4	0–1–0	97	7	0	4.33
NHL Totals	7	3–1–0	277	10	1	2.17

Brodie, T.J.   b. Chatham, Ontario, June 7, 1990

2010–11 CAL	3	0	0	0	2
NHL Totals	3	0	0	0	2

Brodziak, Kyle   b. St. Paul, Alberta, May 25, 1984

2010–11 MIN	80	16	21	37	56
NHL Totals	337	51	77	128	138

Brookbank, Sheldon   b. Lanigan, Saskatchewan, October 3, 1980

2010–11 ANA	40	0	0	0	63
NHL Totals	197	1	21	22	328

Brophey, Evan   b. Kitchener, Ontario, December 3, 1986

2010–11 CHI	1	0	0	0	0
NHL Totals	1	0	0	0	0

Brouwer, Troy   b. Vancouver, British Columbia, August 17, 1985

2010–11 CHI	79	17	19	36	38
NHL Totals	238	49	54	103	161

Brown, Dustin   b. Ithaca, New York, November 4, 1984

2010–11 LA	82	28	29	57	67
NHL Totals	513	141	164	305	377

Brown, Mike   b. Northbrook, Illinois, June 24, 1985

2010–11 TOR	50	3	5	8	69
NHL Totals	192	12	8	20	375

Brule, Gilbert   b. Edmonton, Alberta, January 1, 1987

2010–11 EDM	41	7	2	9	41
NHL Totals	263	38	43	81	143

Brunette, Andrew   b. Sudbury, Ontario, August 24, 1973

2010–11 MIN	82	18	28	46	16
NHL Totals	1,032	256	450	706	310

Bryzgalov, Ilya   b. Togliatti, Soviet Union (Russia), June 22, 1980

2010–11 PHO	68	36–20–10	4,060	168	7	2.48
NHL Totals	326	156–116–35	18,694	789	23	2.53

Budaj, Peter   b. Banska Bystrica, Czechoslovakia (Slovakia), September 18, 1982

2010–11 COL	45	15–21–4	2,439	130	1	3.20
NHL Totals	242	101–91–27	13,311	627	9	2.83

Burish, Adam   b. Madison, Wisconsin, January 6, 1983

2010–11 DAL	63	8	4	14	91
NHL Totals	232	19	16	35	414

Burmistrov, Alexander   b. Kazan, Soviet Union (Russia), October 21, 1991

2010–11 ATL	74	6	14	20	27
NHL Totals	74	6	14	20	27

Burns, Brent   b. Ajax, Ontario, March 9, 1985

2010–11 MIN	80	17	29	46	98
NHL Totals	453	55	128	183	325

Burrows, Alex   b. Pointe-Claire, Quebec, April 11, 1981

2010–11 VAN	72	26	22	48	77
NHL Totals	442	111	107	218	681

Butler, Bobby   b. Marlborough, Massachusetts, April 26, 1987

2010–11 OTT	36	10	11	21	10
NHL Totals	38	10	11	21	10

Butler, Chris   b. St. Louis, Missouri, October 27, 1986

2010–11 BUF	49	2	7	9	26
NHL Totals	155	5	31	36	66

Byfuglien, Dustin   b. Minneapolis, Minnesota, March 27, 1985

2010–11 ATL	81	20	33	53	93
NHL Totals	341	75	87	162	361

Byron, Paul   b. Ottawa, Ontario, April 27, 1989

2010–11 BUF	8	1	1	2	2
NHL Totals	8	1	1	2	2

Callahan, Joe   b. Brockton, Massachusetts, December 20, 1982

2010–11 FLO	27	0	1	1	12
NHL Totals	46	0	4	4	16

Callahan, Ryan   b. Rochester, New York, March 21, 1985

2010–11 NYR	60	23	25	48	46
NHL Totals	284	76	68	144	179

Calvert, Matt   b. Brandon, Manitoba, December 24, 1989

2010–11 CBJ	42	11	9	20	12
NHL Totals	42	11	9	20	12

Cammalleri, Mike   b. Richmond Hill, Ontario, June 8, 1982

2010–11 MON	67	19	28	47	33
NHL Totals	496	177	207	384	263

Campanale, Matt   b. Chester Springs, Pennsylvania, February 14, 1988

2010–11 NYI	1	0	0	0	2
NHL Totals	1	0	0	0	2

Campbell, Brian   b. Strathroy, Ontario, May 23, 1979

2010–11 CHI	65	5	22	27	6
NHL Totals	626	54	258	312	167

Campbell, Gregory   b. London, Ontario, December 17, 1983

2010–11 BOS	80	13	16	29	93
NHL Totals	443	42	72	114	405

Campoli, Chris   b. North York (Toronto), Ontario, July 9, 1984

2010–11 OTT/CHI	77	4	17	21	36
NHL Totals	397	33	102	135	192

• traded by Ottawa to Chicago on February 28, 2011, with a conditional 7th-round draft choice in 2012 for Ryan Potulny and a 2nd-round draft choice in 2011

Caputi, Luca   b. Toronto, Ontario, October 1, 1988

2010–11 TOR	7	0	0	0	4
NHL Totals	35	3	6	9	20

Carcillo, Daniel   b. King City, Ontario, January 28, 1985

2010–11 PHI	57	4	2	6	127
NHL Totals	282	36	37	73	986

Carkner, Matt   b. Winchester, Ontario, November 3, 1980

2010–11 OTT	50	1	6	7	136
NHL Totals	133	3	16	19	328

Carle, Matt   b. Anchorage, Alaska, September 25, 1984

2010–11 PHI	82	1	39	40	23
NHL Totals	389	28	136	164	131

Carlson, John   b. Natick, Massachusetts, January 10, 1990

2010–11 WAS	82	7	30	37	44
NHL Totals	104	8	35	43	52

Caron, Jordan   b. Sayabec, Quebec, November 2, 1990

2010–11 BOS	23	3	4	7	6
NHL Totals	23	3	4	7	6

Carson, Brett   b. Regina, Saskatchewan, November 29, 1985

2010–11 CAR/CAL	19	0	0	0	4
NHL Totals	78	2	10	12	20

• claimed off waivers by Calgary from Carolina on February 28, 2011

Carter, Jeff   b. London, Ontario, January 1, 1985

2010–11 PHI	80	36	30	66	39
NHL Totals	461	181	162	343	288

Carter, Ryan   b. White Bear Lake, Minnesota, August 3, 1983

2010–11 ANA/CAR/FLO	62	3	6	9	66
NHL Totals	182	14	21	35	185

• traded by Anaheim to Carolina on November 23, 2010, for Stefan Chaput and Matt Kennedy
• traded by Carolina to Florida on February 24, 2011, with a 5th-round draft choice in 2011 for Cory Stillman

Chara, Zdeno   b. Trencin, Czechoslovakia (Slovakia), March 18, 1977

2010–11 BOS	81	14	30	44	88
NHL Totals	928	125	282	407	1,385

Chimera, Jason   b. Edmonton, Alberta, May 2, 1979

2010–11 WAS	81	10	16	26	64
NHL Totals	581	98	117	215	580

Chipchura, Kyle   b. Westlock, Alberta, February 19, 1986

2010–11 ANA	40	0	2	2	32
NHL Totals	163	10	18	28	119

Chorney, Taylor   b. Thunder Bay, Ontario, April 27, 1987

2010–11 EDM	12	1	3	4	4
NHL Totals	56	1	6	7	16

Christensen, Erik   b. Edmonton, Alberta, December 17, 1983

2010–11 NYR	63	11	16	27	18
NHL Totals	338	61	90	151	154

Clark, Brett   b. Wapella, Saskatchewan, December 23, 1976

2010–11 TB	82	9	22	31	14
NHL Totals	599	43	127	170	273

Clark, Chris   b. South Windsor, Connecticut, March 8, 1976

2010–11 CBJ	53	5	10	15	38
NHL Totals	607	103	111	214	700

Clarkson, David   b. Toronto, Ontario, March 31, 1984

2010–11 NJ	82	12	6	16	116
NHL Totals	298	52	48	100	554

Cleary, Daniel   b. Carbonear, Newfoundland, December 18, 1978

2010–11 DET	68	26	20	46	20
NHL Totals	746	139	190	329	385

Clemmensen, Scott   b. Des Moines, Iowa, July 23, 1977

2010–11 FLO	31	8–11–7	1,696	74	1	2.62
NHL Totals	122	50–39–14	6,612	293	6	2.66

Clifford, Kyle   b. Ayr, Ontario, January 13, 1991

2010–11 LA	76	7	7	14	141
NHL Totals	76	7	7	14	141

Climie, Matt   b. Leduc, Alberta, February 11, 1983

2010–11 PHO	1	0–0–0	32	1	0	1.88
NHL Totals	5	2–2–0	277	15	0	3.24

Clitsome, Grant   b. Gloucester, Ontario, April 14, 1985

2010–11 CBJ	31	4	15	19	16
NHL Totals	42	5	17	22	22

Clowe, Ryane   b. St. John's, Newfoundland, September 30, 1982

2010–11 SJ	75	24	38	62	100
NHL Totals	319	84	131	215	391

Clutterbuck, Cal   b. Welland, Ontario, November 18, 1987

2010–11 MIN	76	19	15	34	79
NHL Totals	230	43	30	73	207

Coburn, Braydon   b. Calgary, Alberta, February 27, 1985

2010–11 PHI	82	2	14	16	53
NHL Totals	379	26	85	111	328

Cogliano, Andrew   b. Toronto, Ontario, June 14, 1987

2010–11 EDM	82	11	24	35	64
NHL Totals	328	57	89	146	137

Cohen, Colby b. Villanova, Pennsylvania, April 25, 1989

2010–11 COL	3	0	0	0	4
NHL Totals	3	0	0	0	4

Colaiacovo, Carlo b. Toronto, Ontario, January 27, 1983

2010–11 STL	65	6	20	26	23
NHL Totals	306	28	92	120	169

Colborne, Joe b. Calgary, Alberta, January 30, 1990

2010–11 TOR	1	0	1	1	0
NHL Totals	1	0	1	1	0

Cole, Erik b. Oswego, New York, November 6, 1978

2010–11 CAR	82	26	26	52	49
NHL Totals	620	184	206	390	557

Cole, Ian b. Ann Arbor, Michigan, February 21, 1989

2010–11 STL	26	1	3	4	35
NHL Totals	26	1	3	4	35

Collins, Sean b. Troy, Michigan, October 30, 1983

2010–11 WAS	4	1	0	1	0
NHL Totals	4	1	0	1	0

Colliton, Jeremy b. Blackie, Alberta, January 13, 1985

2010–11 NYI	15	2	1	3	10
NHL Totals	57	3	3	6	26

Comeau, Blake b. Meadow Lake, Saskatchewan, February 18, 1986

2010–11 NYI	77	24	22	46	43
NHL Totals	245	56	65	121	137

Commodore, Mike b. Fort Saskatchewan, Alberta, November 7, 1979

2010–11 CBJ	20	2	4	6	44
NHL Totals	454	23	81	104	645

Comrie, Mike b. Edmonton, Alberta, September 11, 1980

2010–11 PIT	21	1	5	6	18
NHL Totals	589	168	197	365	443

Condra, Eric b. Trenton, Michigan, August 6, 1986

2010–11 OTT	26	6	5	11	12
NHL Totals	26	6	5	11	12

Conklin, Ty   b. Anchorage, Alaska, March 30, 1976

2010–11 STL	25	8–8–4	1,285	69	2	3.22
NHL Totals	200	91–61–20	10,722	472	16	2.64

Conner, Chris   b. Westland, Michigan, December 23, 1983

2010–11 PIT	60	7	8	15	10
NHL Totals	139	16	24	40	30

Connolly, Tim   b. Syracuse, New York, May 7, 1981

2010–11 BUF	68	13	29	42	20
NHL Totals	627	118	277	395	260

Conroy, Craig   b. Potsdam, New York, September 4, 1971

2010–11 CAL	18	2	0	2	8
NHL Totals	1,009	182	360	542	603

• retired early in season

Cooke, Matt   b. Belleville, Ontario, September 7, 1978

2010–11 PIT	67	12	18	30	129
NHL Totals	805	126	175	301	988

Cormier, Patrice   b. Moncton, New Brunswick, June 14, 1990

2010–11 ATL	21	1	1	2	4
NHL Totals	21	1	1	2	4

Corrente, Matt   b. Mississauga, Ontario, March 17, 1988

2010–11 NJ	22	0	6	6	44
NHL Totals	34	0	6	6	68

Corvo, Joe   b. Oak Park, Illinois, June 20, 1977

2010–11 CAR	82	11	29	40	18
NHL Totals	568	79	179	258	204

Couture, Logan   b. Guelph, Ontario, March 28, 1989

2010–11 SJ	79	32	24	56	41
NHL Totals	104	37	28	65	47

Crabb, Joey   b. Anchorage, Alaska, April 3, 1983

2010–11 TOR	48	3	12	15	24
NHL Totals	77	7	17	24	52

Cracknell, Adam   b. Prince Albert, Saskatchewan, July 15, 1985

2010–11 STL	24	3	4	7	8
NHL Totals	24	3	4	7	8

Craig, Ryan   b. Abbotsford, British Columbia, January 6, 1982

2010–11 PIT	6	0	0	0	22
NHL Totals	190	32	31	63	148

Crawford, Corey   b. Montreal, Quebec, December 31, 1984

2010–11 CHI	57	33–18–6	3,337	128	4	2.30
NHL Totals	65	34–21–7	3,706	144	5	2.33

Crombeen, Brandon   b. Denver, Colorado, July 10, 1985

2010–11 STL	80	7	7	14	154
NHL Totals	248	26	27	53	509

Crosby, Sidney   b. Halifax, Nova Scotia, August 7, 1987

2010–11 PIT	41	32	34	66	31
NHL Totals	412	215	357	572	387

Cullen, Matt   b. Virginia, Minnesota, November 2, 1976

2010–11 MIN	78	12	27	39	34
NHL Totals	958	181	319	500	426

Cullimore, Jassen   b. Simcoe, Ontario, December 4, 1972

2010–11 CHI	36	0	8	8	8
NHL Totals	812	26	85	111	704

Cumiskey, Kyle   b. Abbotsford, British Columbia, December 2, 1986

2010–11 COL	18	1	7	8	10
NHL Totals	132	9	26	35	48

Da Costa, Stephane   b. Paris, France, July 11, 1989

2010–11 OTT	4	0	0	0	0
NHL Totals	4	0	0	0	0

Dadonov, Evgeni   b. Chelyabinsk, Soviet Union (Russia), March 12, 1989

2010–11 FLO	36	8	9	17	14
NHL Totals	40	8	9	17	14

D'Agostini, Matt   b. Sault Ste. Marie, Ontario, October 23, 1986

2010–11 STL	82	21	25	46	40
NHL Totals	183	35	36	71	86

Daley, Trevor   b. Toronto, Ontario, October 9, 1983

2010–11 DAL	82	8	19	27	34
NHL Totals	498	34	96	130	381

Dalpe, Zac   b. Paris, Ontario, November 1, 1989

2010–11 CAR	15	3	1	4	0
NHL Totals	15	3	1	4	0

Darche, Mathieu   b. Montreal, Quebec, November 26, 1976

2010–11 MON	59	12	14	26	10
NHL Totals	189	25	35	60	40

Datsyuk, Pavel   b. Sverdlovsk, Soviet Union (Russia), July 20, 1978

2010–11 DET	56	23	36	59	15
NHL Totals	662	221	430	651	172

Dawes, Nigel   b. Winnipeg, Manitoba, February 9, 1985

2010–11 ATL/MON	13	0	1	1	0
NHL Totals	212	39	45	84	43

• traded by Atlanta to Montreal on February 24, 2011, with Brent Sopel for Ben Maxwell and a 4th-round draft choice in 2011

Dekanich, Mark   b. North Vancouver, British Columbia, May 10, 1986

2010–11 NAS	1	0–0–0	50	3	0	3.60
NHL Totals	1	0–0–0	50	3	0	3.60

Della Rovere, Stefan   b. Richmond Hill, Ontario, February 25, 1990

2010–11 STL	7	0	0	0	11
NHL Totals	7	0	0	0	11

Del Zotto, Michael   b. Stouffville, Ontario, June 24, 1990

2010–11 NYR	47	2	9	11	20
NHL Totals	127	11	37	48	52

Demers, Jason   b. Dorval, Quebec, June 9, 1988

2010–11 SJ	75	2	22	24	28
NHL Totals	126	6	39	45	49

Desbiens, Guillaume   b. Alma, Quebec, April 20, 1985

2010–11 VAN	12	0	0	0	10
NHL Totals	13	0	0	0	12

Desharnais, David b. Quebec City, Quebec, September 14, 1986

2010–11 MON	43	8	14	22	12
NHL Totals	49	8	15	23	12

Desjardins, Andrew b. Lively, Ontario, July 27, 1986

2010–11 SJ	17	1	2	3	4
NHL Totals	17	1	2	3	4

Desjardins, Cedrick b. Edmundston, New Brunswick, September 30, 1985

2010–11 TB	2	2–0–0	120	2	0	1.00
NHL Totals	2	2–0–0	120	2	0	1.00

DiBenedetto, Justin b. Etobicoke (Toronto), Ontario, August 25, 1988

2010–11 NYI	8	0	1	1	2
NHL Totals	8	0	1	1	2

DiPietro, Rick b. Winthrop, Massachusetts, September 19, 1981

2010–11 NYI	26	8–14–4	1,533	88	1	3.44
NHL Totals	307	127–131–33	17,669	837	16	2.84

Doan, Shane b. Halkirk, Alberta, October 10, 1976

2010–11 PHO	72	20	40	60	67
NHL Totals	1,119	296	442	738	1,023

Doornbosch, Jamie b. Richmond Hill, Ontario, February 1, 1990

2010–11 NYI	1	0	0	0	0
NHL Totals	1	0	0	0	0

Dorsett, Derek b. Kindersley, Saskatchewan, December 20, 1986

2010–11 CBJ	76	4	13	17	184
NHL Totals	179	12	24	36	439

Doughty, Drew b. London, Ontario, December 8, 1989

2010–11 LA	76	11	29	40	68
NHL Totals	239	33	93	126	178

Dowell, Jake b. Eau Claire, Wisconsin, March 4, 1985

2010–11 CHI	79	6	15	21	63
NHL Totals	102	9	17	26	80

Downie, Steve b. Newmarket, Ontario, April 3, 1987

2010–11 TB	57	10	22	32	171
NHL Totals	197	41	55	96	517

Draper, Kris   b. Toronto, Ontario, May 24, 1971

2010–11 DET	47	6	5	11	12
NHL Totals	1,157	161	203	364	790

•retired at season's end

Drazenovic, Nicholas   b. Prince George, British Columbia, January 14, 1987

2010–11 STL	3	0	0	0	0
NHL Totals	3	0	0	0	0

Drewiske, Davis   b. Hudson, Wisconsin, November 22, 1984

2010–11 LA	38	0	5	5	19
NHL Totals	97	1	15	16	51

Drury, Chris   b. Trumbull, Connecticut, August 20, 1976

2010–11 NYR	24	1	4	5	8
NHL Totals	892	255	360	615	468

•retired in August 2011

Dubinsky, Brandon   b. Anchorage, Alaska, April 29, 1986

2010–11 NYR	77	24	30	54	100
NHL Totals	316	71	108	179	347

Dubnyk, Devan   b. Regina, Saskatchewan, May 4, 1986

2010–11 EDM	35	12–13–8	2,061	93	2	2.71
NHL Totals	54	16–23–10	3,137	157	2	3.00

Duchene, Matt   b. Haliburton, Ontario, January 16, 1991

2010–11 COL	80	27	40	67	33
NHL Totals	161	51	71	122	49

Duco, Mike   b. Toronto, Ontario, July 8, 1987

2010–11 FLO	2	0	0	0	10
NHL Totals	12	0	0	0	60

Dupont, Brodie   b. Russell, Manitoba, February 17, 1987

2010–11 NYR	1	0	0	0	0
NHL Totals	1	0	0	0	0

Dumont, J-P   b. Montreal, Quebec, April 1, 1978

2010–11 NAS	70	10	9	19	16
NHL Totals	822	214	309	523	364

Dupuis, Pascal b. Laval, Quebec, April 7, 1979

2010–11 PIT	81	17	20	37	59
NHL Totals	668	130	147	277	303

Dupuis, Philippe b. Laval, Quebec, April 24, 1985

2010–11 COL	74	6	11	17	40
NHL Totals	86	6	12	18	46

Dvorak, Radek b. Tabor, Czechoslovakia (Czech Republic), March 9, 1977

2010–11 FLO/ATL	66	7	15	22	24
NHL Totals	1,118	215	341	556	394

• traded by Florida to Atlanta on February 28, 2011, with a 5th-round draft choice in 2011 for Niclas Bergfors and Pat Rissmiller

Dwyer, Pat b. Spokane, Washington, June 22, 1983

2010–11 CAR	80	8	10	18	12
NHL Totals	151	16	15	31	18

Eager, Ben b. Ottawa, Ontario, January 22, 1984

2010–11 ATL/SJ	68	7	10	17	120
NHL Totals	323	34	35	69	741

• traded by Atlanta to San Jose on January 18, 2011, for a 5th-round draft choice in 2011

Earl, Robbie b. Chicago, Illinois, June 2, 1985

2010–11 MIN	6	0	0	0	0
NHL Totals	47	6	1	7	6

Eaton, Mark b. Wilmington, Delaware, May 6, 1977

2010–11 NYI	34	0	3	3	8
NHL Totals	565	23	58	81	228

Eaves, Patrick b. Calgary, Alberta, May 1, 1984

2010–11 DET	63	13	7	20	14
NHL Totals	370	70	62	132	139

Ebbett, Andrew b. Vernon, British Columbia, January 2, 1983

2010–11 PHO	33	2	3	5	4
NHL Totals	145	19	33	52	38

Eberle, Jordan b. Regina, Saskatchewan, May 15, 1990

2010–11 EDM	69	18	25	43	22
NHL Totals	69	18	25	43	22

Eckford, Tyler   b. Vancouver, British Columbia, September 8, 1985

2010–11 NJ	4	0	0	0	0
NHL Totals	7	0	1	1	4

Edler, Alexander   b. Stockholm, Sweden, April 21, 1986

2010–11 VAN	51	8	25	33	24
NHL Totals	304	32	103	135	166

Ehrhoff, Christian   b. Moers, West Germany (Germany), July 6, 1982

2010–11 VAN	79	14	36	50	52
NHL Totals	500	53	173	226	338

Ekman-Larsson, Oliver   b. Karlskrona, Sweden, July 17, 1991

2010–11 PHO	48	1	10	11	24
NHL Totals	48	1	10	11	24

Elias, Patrik   b. Trebic, Czechoslovakia (Czech Republic), April 13, 1976

2010–11 NJ	81	21	41	62	16
NHL Totals	961	335	481	816	459

Eller, Lars   b. Herlev, Denmark, May 8, 1989

2010–11 MON	77	7	10	17	48
NHL Totals	84	9	10	19	52

Ellerby, Keaton   b. Strathmore, Alberta, November 5, 1988

2010–11 FLO	54	2	10	12	22
NHL Totals	76	2	10	12	24

Elliott, Brian   b. Newmarket, Ontario, April 9, 1985

2010–11 OTT/COL	55	15–27–9	2,983	166	3	3.44
NHL Totals	142	61–53–16	7,748	374	9	2.90

• traded by Ottawa to Colorado on February 18, 2011, for Craig Anderson

Ellis, Dan   b. Saskatoon, Saskatchewan, June 19, 1980

2010–11 TB/ANA	44	21–10–7	2,408	111	2	2.77
NHL Totals	155	71–52–15	8,377	374	12	2.68

• traded by Tampa Bay to Anaheim on February 24, 2011, for Curtis McElhinney

Ellis, Matt   b. Welland, Ontario, August 31, 1981

2010–11 BUF	14	0	0	0	0
NHL Totals	201	13	20	33	56

Emery, Ray   b. Hamilton, Ontario, September 28, 1982

2010–11 ANA	10	7–2–0	527	20	0	2.28
NHL Totals	173	94–53–15	9,630	429	11	2.67

Eminger, Steve   b. Woodbridge, Ontario, October 31, 1983

2010–11 NYR	65	2	4	6	22
NHL Totals	411	17	74	91	323

Emmerton, Cory   b. St. Thomas, Ontario, June 1, 1988

2010–11 DET	2	1	0	1	0
NHL Totals	2	1	0	1	0

Engelland, Deryk   b. Edmonton, Alberta, April 3, 1982

2010–11 PIT	63	3	7	10	123
NHL Totals	72	3	9	12	140

Engqvist, Andreas   b. Stockholm, Sweden, December 23, 1987

2010–11 MON	3	0	0	0	0
NHL Totals	3	0	0	0	0

Ennis, Tyler   b. Edmonton, Alberta, October 6, 1989

2010–11 BUF	82	20	29	49	30
NHL Totals	92	23	35	58	36

Enroth, Jhonas   b. Stockholm, Sweden, June 25, 1988

2010–11 BUF	14	9–2–2	769	35	1	2.73
NHL Totals	15	9–3–2	828	39	1	2.83

Enstrom, Tobias   b. Nordingra, Sweden, November 5, 1984

2010–11 ATL	72	10	41	51	54
NHL Totals	318	26	145	171	178

Erat, Martin   b. Trebic, Czechoslovakia (Czech Republic), August 28, 1981

2010–11 NAS	64	17	33	50	22
NHL Totals	616	140	262	402	370

Ericsson, Jonathan   b. Karlskrona, Sweden, March 2, 1984

2010–11 DET	74	3	12	15	87
NHL Totals	163	9	24	33	150

Eriksson, Loui   b. Gothenburg, Sweden, July 17, 1985

2010–11 DAL	79	27	46	73	8
NHL Totals	371	112	145	257	94

Erskine, John   b. Kingston, Ontario, June 26, 1980

2010–11 WAS	73	4	7	11	94
NHL Totals	396	11	31	42	724

Fahey, Brian   b. Des Plaines, Illinois, March 2, 1981

2010–11 WAS	7	0	1	1	2
NHL Totals	7	0	1	1	2

Falk, Justin   b. Snowflake, Manitoba, October 11, 1988

2010–11 MIN	22	0	3	3	6
NHL Totals	25	0	3	3	6

Fayne, Mark   b. Nashua, New Hampshire, May 15, 1987

2010–11 NJ	57	4	10	14	27
NHL Totals	57	4	10	14	27

Fedotenko, Ruslan   b. Kiev, Soviet Union (Ukraine), January 18, 1979

2010–11 NYR	66	10	15	25	25
NHL Totals	743	160	173	333	444

Fehr, Eric   b. Winkler, Manitoba, September 7, 1985

2010–11 WAS	52	10	10	20	16
NHL Totals	230	46	47	73	78

Ference, Andrew   b. Edmonton, Alberta, March 17, 1979

2010–11 BOS	70	3	12	15	60
NHL Totals	640	27	129	156	564

Ferriero, Benn   b. Boston, Massachusetts, April 29, 1987

2010–11 SJ	33	5	4	9	9
NHL Totals	57	7	7	14	17

Festerling, Brett   b. Quesnel, British Columbia, March 3, 1986

2010–11 ANA	1	0	0	0	0
NHL Totals	83	0	8	8	33

Fiddler, Vernon   b. Edmonton, Alberta, May 9, 1980

2010–11 PHO	71	6	16	22	46
NHL Totals	452	59	86	145	282

Filatov, Nikita   b. Moscow, Soviet Union (Russia), May 25, 1990

2010–11 CBJ	23	0	7	7	8
NHL Totals	44	6	7	13	16

Filppula, Valtteri   b. Vantaa, Finland, March 20, 1984

2010–11 DET	71	16	23	39	22
NHL Totals	361	68	100	168	138

Fisher, Mike   b. Peterborough, Ontario, June 5, 1980

2010–11 OTT/NAS	82	19	17	36	43
NHL Totals	702	172	188	360	564

• traded by Ottawa to Nashville on February 1, 2011, for a 1st-round draft choice in 2011 and a conditional draft choice in 2012

Fistric, Mark   b. Edmonton, Alberta, June 1, 1986

2010–11 DAL	57	2	3	5	44
NHL Totals	197	3	18	21	179

Fleischmann, Tomas   b. Koprivnice, Czechoslovakia (Czech Republic), May 16, 1984

2010–11 WAS/COL	45	12	19	31	18
NHL Totals	305	68	91	159	92

• traded by Washington to Colorado on November 30, 2010, for Scott Hannan

Fleury, Marc-Andre   b. Sorel, Quebec, November 28, 1984

2010–11 PIT	65	36–20–5	3,695	143	3	2.32
NHL Totals	367	184–126–35	20,860	951	19	2.74

Foligno, Nick   b. Buffalo, New York, October 31, 1987

2010–11 OTT	82	14	20	34	43
NHL Totals	269	46	55	101	175

Foote, Adam   b. Toronto, Ontario, July 10, 1971

2010–11 COL	47	0	8	8	33
NHL Totals	1,154	66	242	308	1,534

• retired midseason

Forsberg, Peter   b. Ornskoldsvik, Sweden, July 20, 1973

2010–11 COL	2	0	0	0	4
NHL Totals	708	249	636	885	690

• retired midseason

Foster, Kurtis   b. Carp, Ontario, November 24, 1981

2010–11 EDM	74	8	14	22	45
NHL Totals	331	37	104	141	248

Fowler, Cam   b. Windsor, Ontario, December 5, 1991

2010–11 ANA	76	10	30	40	20
NHL Totals	76	10	30	40	20

Franson, Cody   b. Salmon Arm, British Columbia, August 8, 1987

2010–11 NAS	80	8	21	29	30
NHL Totals	141	14	36	50	46

Franzen, Johan   b. Landsbro, Sweden, December 23, 1979

2010–11 DET	76	28	27	55	58
NHL Totals	395	121	98	219	248

Fraser, Colin   b. Sicamous, British Columbia, January 28, 1985

2010–11 EDM	67	3	2	5	60
NHL Totals	224	16	25	41	168

Fraser, Mark   b. Ottawa, Ontario, September 29, 1986

2010–11 NJ	26	0	2	2	29
NHL Totals	94	3	5	8	72

Frattin, Matt   b. Edmonton, Alberta, January 3, 1988

2010–11 TOR	1	0	0	0	0
NHL Totals	1	0	0	0	0

Frolik, Michael   b. Kladno, Czechoslovakia (Czech Republic), February 17, 1988

2010–11 FLO/CHI	80	11	27	38	30
NHL Totals	241	53	73	126	95

• traded by Florida to Chicago on February 9, 2011, with Alexander Salak for Jack Skille, Hugh Jessiman and David Pacan

Frolov, Alexander   b. Moscow, Soviet Union (Russia), June 19, 1982

2010–11 NYR	43	7	9	16	8
NHL Totals	579	175	222	397	218

Gaborik, Marian   b. Trencin, Czechoslovakia (Slovakia), February 14, 1982

2010–11 NYR	62	22	26	48	18
NHL Totals	640	283	288	571	356

Gagne, Simon   b. Ste-Foy, Quebec, February 29, 1980

2010–11 TB	63	17	23	40	20
NHL Totals	727	276	288	564	298

Gagner, Sam   b. London, Ontario, August 10, 1989

2010–11 EDM	68	15	27	42	37
NHL Totals	291	59	114	173	144

Gagnon, Aaron   b. Quesnel, British Columbia, April 24, 1986

2010–11 DAL	19	0	2	2	0
NHL Totals	21	0	2	2	0

Galiardi, T.J.   b. Calgary, Alberta, April 22, 1988

2010–11 COL	35	7	8	15	12
NHL Totals	116	25	33	58	46

Garrison, Jason   b. White Rock, British Columbia, November 13, 1984

2010–11 FLO	73	5	13	18	26
NHL Totals	113	7	19	26	49

Garon, Mathieu   b. Chandler, Quebec, January 9, 1978

2010–11 CBJ	36	10–14–6	1,938	88	3	2.72
NHL Totals	275	116–106–25	14,947	703	19	2.82

Gaunce, Cameron   b. Sudbury, Ontario, March 19, 1990

2010–11 COL	11	1	0	1	16
NHL Totals	11	1	0	1	16

Gaustad, Paul   b. Fargo, North Dakota, February 3, 1982

2010–11 BUF	81	12	19	31	101
NHL Totals	423	64	100	164	515

Geoffrion, Blake   b. Plantation, Florida, February 3, 1988

2010–11 NAS	20	6	2	8	7
NHL Totals	20	6	2	8	7

Gerbe, Nathan   b. Oxford, Michigan, July 24, 1987

2010–11 BUF	64	16	15	31	34
NHL Totals	84	18	19	37	42

Gerber, Martin   b. Burgdorf, Switzerland, September 3, 1974

2010–11 EDM	3	3–0–0	185	4	0	1.30
NHL Totals	229	113–78–21	12,920	566	10	2.63

Gervais, Bruno   b. Longueuil, Quebec, October 3, 1984

2010–11 NYI	53	0	6	6	30
NHL Totals	331	9	59	68	164

Getzlaf, Ryan   b. Regina, Saskatchewan, May 10, 1985

2010–11 ANA	67	19	57	76	35
NHL Totals	430	126	289	415	417

Giguere, Jean-Sebastien b. Montreal, Quebec, May 16, 1977

2010–11 TOR	33	11–11–4	1,633	78	0	2.87
NHL Totals	525	231–195–67	29,779	1,258	34	2.53

Gilbert, Tom b. Minneapolis, Minnesota, January 10, 1983

2010–11 EDM	79	6	20	26	32
NHL Totals	337	30	111	141	94

Gill, Hal b. Concord, Massachusetts, April 6, 1975

2010–11 MON	75	2	7	9	43
NHL Totals	994	35	136	171	911

Gillies, Colton b. White Rock, British Columbia, February 12, 1989

2010–11 MIN	7	1	0	1	2
NHL Totals	52	3	5	8	20

Gillies, Trevor b. Cambridge, Ontario, January 30, 1979

2010–11 NYI	39	2	0	2	165
NHL Totals	54	2	1	3	261

Gilroy, Matt b. North Bellmore, New York, July 30, 1984

2010–11 NYR	58	3	8	11	14
NHL Totals	127	7	19	26	37

Gionta, Brian b. Rochester, New York, January 18, 1979

2010–11 MON	82	29	17	46	24
NHL Totals	616	209	195	404	277

Gionta, Stephen b. Rochester, New York, October 9, 1983

2010–11 NJ	12	0	0	0	6
NHL Totals	12	0	0	0	6

Giordano, Mark b. Toronto, Ontario, March 10, 1983

2010–11 CAL	82	8	35	43	67
NHL Totals	277	28	80	108	251

Girardi, Daniel b. Welland, Ontario, April 29, 1984

2010–11 NYR	80	4	27	31	37
NHL Totals	360	24	87	111	165

Giroux, Claude b. Hearst, Ontario, January 12, 1988

2010–11 PHI	82	25	51	76	47
NHL Totals	208	50	100	150	84

Giroux, Alexandre b. Quebec City, Quebec, June 16, 1981

2010–11 EDM	8	1	1	2	2
NHL Totals	39	5	6	11	18

Glass, Tanner b. Regina, Saskatchewan, November 29, 1983

2010–11 VAN	73	3	7	10	72
NHL Totals	184	8	15	23	233

Gleason, Tim b. Southfield, Michigan, January 29, 1983

2010–11 CAR	82	2	14	16	85
NHL Totals	475	14	86	100	470

Glencross, Curtis b. Kindersley, Saskatchewan, December 28, 1982

2010–11 CAL	79	24	19	43	59
NHL Totals	291	68	74	142	214

Goc, Marcel b. Calw, West Germany (Germany), August 24, 1983

2010–11 NAS	51	9	15	24	6
NHL Totals	389	41	67	108	96

Godard, Eric b. Vernon, British Columbia, March 7, 1980

2010–11 PIT	19	0	3	3	105
NHL Totals	335	6	12	18	833

Goligoski, Alex b. Grand Rapids, Minnesota, July 30, 1985

2010–11 PIT/DAL	83	14	32	46	40
NHL Totals	200	28	77	105	80

• traded by Pittsburgh to Dallas on February 21, 2011, for James Neal and Matt Niskanen

Gomez, Scott b. Anchorage, Alaska, December 23, 1979

2010–11 MON	80	7	31	38	48
NHL Totals	864	167	508	675	566

Gonchar, Sergei b. Chelyabinsk, Soviet Union (Russia), April 13, 1974

2010–11 OTT	67	7	20	27	20
NHL Totals	1,058	209	502	711	862

Gordon, Andrew b. Halifax, Nova Scotia, December 13, 1985

2010–11 WAS	9	1	1	2	0
NHL Totals	12	1	1	2	0

Gordon, Boyd   b. Unity, Saskatchewan, October 19, 1983

| 2010–11 WAS | 60 | 3 | 6 | 9 | 16 |
| NHL Totals | 363 | 27 | 58 | 85 | 82 |

Gorges, Josh   b. Kelowna, British Columbia, August 14, 1984

| 2010–11 MON | 36 | 1 | 6 | 7 | 18 |
| NHL Totals | 364 | 9 | 50 | 59 | 183 |

Grabner, Michael   b. Villach, Austria, October 5, 1987

| 2010–11 NYI | 76 | 34 | 18 | 52 | 10 |
| NHL Totals | 96 | 39 | 24 | 63 | 18 |

Grabovski, Mikhail   b. Potsdam, East Germany (Germany), January 31, 1984

| 2010–11 TOR | 81 | 29 | 29 | 58 | 60 |
| NHL Totals | 245 | 62 | 88 | 150 | 170 |

Grachev, Evgeni   b. Khabarovsk, Soviet Union (Russia), February 21, 1990

| 2010–11 NYR | 8 | 0 | 0 | 0 | 0 |
| NHL Totals | 8 | 0 | 0 | 0 | 0 |

Gragnani, Marc-Andre   b. Montreal, Quebec, March 11, 1987

| 2010–11 BUF | 9 | 1 | 2 | 3 | 2 |
| NHL Totals | 15 | 1 | 2 | 3 | 8 |

Green, Josh   b. Camrose, Alberta, November 16, 1977

| 2010–11 ANA | 12 | 0 | 0 | 0 | 6 |
| NHL Totals | 334 | 35 | 39 | 74 | 199 |

Green, Mike   b. Calgary, Alberta, October 12, 1985

| 2010–11 WAS | 49 | 8 | 16 | 24 | 48 |
| NHL Totals | 366 | 79 | 165 | 244 | 286 |

Greene, Andy   b. Trenton, Michigan, October 30, 1982

| 2010–11 NJ | 82 | 4 | 19 | 23 | 22 |
| NHL Totals | 291 | 15 | 70 | 85 | 86 |

Greene, Matt   b. Grand Ledge, Michigan, May 13, 1983

| 2010–11 LA | 71 | 2 | 9 | 11 | 70 |
| NHL Totals | 379 | 7 | 40 | 47 | 469 |

Greening, Colin   b. St. John's, Newfoundland, March 9, 1986

| 2010–11 OTT | 24 | 6 | 7 | 13 | 10 |
| NHL Totals | 24 | 6 | 7 | 13 | 10 |

Grier, Mike   b. Detroit, Michigan, January 5, 1975

2010–11 BUF	73	5	11	16	12
NHL Totals	1,060	162	221	383	510

Grossman, Nicklas   b. Stockholm, Sweden, January 22, 1985

2010–11 DAL	59	1	9	10	35
NHL Totals	281	3	33	36	144

Guenin, Nate   b. Sewickley, Pennsylvania, December 10, 1982

2010–11 CBJ	3	0	0	0	2
NHL Totals	17	0	2	2	8

Gunnarsson, Carl   b. Orebro, Sweden, November 9, 1986

2010–11 TOR	68	4	16	20	14
NHL Totals	111	7	28	35	24

Gustafsson, Erik   b. Kvissleby, Sweden, December 15, 1988

2010–11 PHI	3	0	0	0	4
NHL Totals	3	0	0	0	4

Gustavsson, Jonas   b. Stockholm, Sweden, October 24, 1984

2010–11 TOR	23	6–13–2	1,242	68	0	3.29
NHL Totals	65	22–28–11	3,581	180	1	3.02

Hagman, Niklas   b. Espoo, Finland, December 5, 1979

2010–11 CAL	71	11	16	27	24
NHL Totals	699	138	140	278	206

Hainsey, Ron   b. Bolton, Connecticut, March 24, 1981

2010–11 ATL	82	3	16	19	24
NHL Totals	488	34	135	169	238

Halak, Jaroslav   b. Bratislava, Czechoslovakia (Slovakia), May 13, 1985

2010–11 STL	57	27–21–7	3,294	136	7	2.48
NHL Totals	158	83–55–14	9,051	387	16	2.57

Hale, David   b. Colorado Springs, Colorado, June 18, 1981

2010–11 OTT	25	1	4	5	6
NHL Totals	327	4	25	29	242

Haley, Michael   b. Oshawa, Ontario, March 30, 1986

2010–11 NYI	27	2	1	3	85
NHL Totals	29	2	1	3	94

Halischuk, Matt   b. Toronto, Ontario, June 1, 1988

2010–11 NAS	27	4	8	12	2
NHL Totals	48	5	10	15	4

Hall, Adam   b. Kalamazoo, Michigan, August 14, 1980

2010–11 TB	82	7	11	18	32
NHL Totals	508	63	73	136	219

Hall, Taylor   b. Calgary, Alberta, November 14, 1991

2010–11 EDM	65	22	20	42	27
NHL Totals	65	22	20	42	27

Halpern, Jeff   b. Potomac, Maryland, May 3, 1976

2010–11 MON	72	11	15	26	29
NHL Totals	792	142	200	342	583

Hamhuis, Dan   b. Smithers, British Columbia, December 13, 1982

2010–11 VAN	64	6	17	23	34
NHL Totals	547	38	146	184	409

Hamill, Zach   b. Vancouver, British Columbia, September 23, 1988

2010–11 BOS	3	0	1	1	0
NHL Totals	4	0	2	2	0

Hamonic, Travis   b. Winnipeg, Manitoba, August 16, 1990

2010–11 NYI	62	5	21	26	103
NHL Totals	62	5	21	26	103

Hamrlik, Roman   b. Zlin, Czechoslovakia (Czech Republic), April 12, 1974

2010–11 MON	79	5	29	34	81
NHL Totals	1,311	153	471	624	1,366

Handzus, Michal   b. Banska Bystrica, Czechoslovakia (Slovakia), March 11, 1977

2010–11 LA	82	12	18	30	20
NHL Totals	844	172	263	435	448

Hannan, Scott   b. Richmond, British Columbia, January 23, 1979

2010–11 COL/WAS	78	1	10	11	34
NHL Totals	830	31	154	185	484

• traded by Colorado to Washington on November 30, 2010, for Tomas Fleischmann

Hansen, Jannick b. Herlev, Denmark, March 15, 1986

2010–11 VAN	82	9	20	29	32
NHL Totals	189	24	41	65	89

Hanson, Christian b. Venetia, Pennsylvania, March 10, 1986

2010–11 TOR	6	0	0	0	4
NHL Totals	42	3	6	9	22

Hanzal, Martin b. Pisek, Czechoslovakia (Czech Republic), February 20, 1987

2010–11 PHO	61	16	10	26	54
NHL Totals	288	46	79	125	226

Harju, Johan b. Overtornea, Sweden, May 15, 1986

2010–11 TB	10	1	2	3	2
NHL Totals	10	1	2	3	2

Harrison, Jay b. Oshawa, Ontario, November 3, 1982

2010–11 CAR	72	3	7	10	72
NHL Totals	130	4	14	18	140

Harrold, Peter b. Kirtland Hills, Ohio, June 8, 1983

2010–11 LA	19	1	3	4	4
NHL Totals	164	8	18	26	50

Hartikainen, Teemu b. Kuopio, Finland, May 3, 1990

2010–11 EDM	12	3	2	5	4
NHL Totals	12	3	2	5	4

Hartnell, Scott b. Regina, Saskatchewan, April 18, 1982

2010–11 PHI	82	24	25	49	142
NHL Totals	761	185	222	407	1,143

Havlat, Martin b. Mlada Bolslav, Czechoslovakia (Czech Republic), April 19, 1981

2010–11 MIN	78	22	40	62	52
NHL Totals	621	209	303	512	332

Heatley, Dany b. Freiburg, West Germany (Germany), January 21, 1981

2010–11 SJ	80	26	38	64	56
NHL Totals	669	326	364	689	566

Hecht, Jochen   b. Mannheim, West Germany (Germany), June 21, 1977

2010–11 BUF	67	12	17	29	40
NHL Totals	764	177	264	441	434

Hedberg, Johan   b. Leksand, Sweden, May 3, 1973

2010–11 NJ	34	15–12–2	1,717	68	3	2.38
NHL Totals	327	138–126–31	18,058	867	17	2.88

Hedman, Victor   b. Ornskoldsvik, Sweden, December 18, 1990

2010–11 TB	79	3	23	26	70
NHL Totals	153	7	39	46	149

Hejda, Jan   b. Prague, Czechoslovakia (Czech Republic), June 18, 1978

2010–11 CBJ	77	5	15	20	28
NHL Totals	341	12	64	76	183

Hejduk, Milan   b. Usti-nad-Labem, Czechoslovakia (Czech Republic), February 14, 1976

2010–11 COL	71	22	34	56	18
NHL Totals	910	357	400	757	302

Helm, Darren   b. Winnipeg, Manitoba, January 21, 1987

2010–11 DET	82	12	20	32	16
NHL Totals	180	23	34	57	40

Hemsky, Ales   b. Pardubice, Czechoslovakia (Czech Republic), August 13, 1983

2010–11 EDM	47	14	28	42	18
NHL Totals	490	114	281	395	224

Hendricks, Matt   b. Blaine, Minnesota, June 17, 1981

2010–11 WAS	77	9	16	25	110
NHL Totals	137	18	23	41	197

Hendry, Jordan   b. Nokomis, Saskatchewan, February 23, 1984

2010–11 CHI	37	1	0	1	4
NHL Totals	129	4	9	13	40

Henrique, Adam   b. Brantford, Ontario, February 6, 1990

2010–11 NJ	1	0	0	0	0
NHL Totals	1	0	0	0	0

Hensick, T.J.   b. Lansing, Michigan, December 10, 1985

2010–11 STL	13	1	2	3	2
NHL Totals	112	12	26	38	18

Higgins, Chris   b. Smithtown, New York, June 2, 1983

2010–11 FLO/VAN	62	13	15	28	16
NHL Totals	411	105	91	196	144

• traded by Florida to Vancouver on February 28, 2011, for Evan Oberg and a 3rd-round draft choice in 2013

Hillen, Jack   b. Portland, Oregon, January 24, 1986

2010–11 NYI	64	4	18	22	45
NHL Totals	175	8	42	50	109

Hiller, Jonas   b. Felben Wellhausen, Switzerland, February 12, 1982

2010–11 ANA	49	26–16–3	2,672	114	5	2.56
NHL Totals	177	89–61–9	9,718	407	11	2.51

Hjalmarsson, Niklas   b. Eksjo, Sweden, June 6, 1987

2010–11 CHI	80	3	7	10	39
NHL Totals	191	6	25	31	72

Hnidy, Shane   b. Neepawa, Manitoba, November 8, 1975

2010–11 BOS	3	0	0	0	2
NHL Totals	550	16	55	71	633

Hodgson, Cody   b. Toronto, Ontario, February 18, 1990

2010–11 VAN	8	1	1	2	0
NHL Totals	8	1	1	2	0

Holden, Nick   b. St. Albert, Alberta, May 15, 1987

2010–11 CBJ	5	0	0	0	0
NHL Totals	5	0	0	0	0

Hollweg, Ryan   b. Downey, California, April 23, 1983

2010–11 PHO	3	0	0	0	0
NHL Totals	228	5	9	14	349

Holmstrom, Ben   b. Colorado Springs, Colorado, April 9, 1987

2010–11 PHI	2	0	0	0	5
NHL Totals	2	0	0	0	5

Holmstrom, Tomas   b. Pitea, Sweden, January 23, 1973

2010–11 DET	73	18	19	37	62
NHL Totals	952	232	274	506	729

Holos, Jonas   b. Sarpsborg, Norway, August 27, 1987

2010–11 COL	39	0	6	6	10
NHL Totals	39	0	6	6	10

Holtby, Braden   b. Lloydminster, Saskatchewan, September 16, 1989

2010–11 WAS	14	10–2–2	736	22	2	1.79
NHL Totals	14	10–2–2	736	22	2	1.79

Holzer, Korbinian   b. Munich, West Germany (Germany), February 16, 1988

2010–11 TOR	2	0	0	0	2
NHL Totals	2	0	0	0	2

Horcoff, Shawn   b. Trail, British Columbia, September 17, 1978

2010–11 EDM	47	9	18	27	46
NHL Totals	684	142	259	401	463

Hordichuk, Darcy   b. Kamsack, Saskatchewan, August 10, 1980

2010–11 FLO	64	1	4	5	76
NHL Totals	495	19	19	38	1,074

Hornqvist, Patric   b. Sollentuna, Sweden, January 1, 1987

2010–11 NAS	79	21	27	48	47
NHL Totals	187	53	53	106	103

Horton, Nathan   b. Welland, Ontario, May 29, 1985

2010–11 BOS	80	26	27	53	85
NHL Totals	502	168	180	348	467

Hossa, Marian   b. Stara Lubovna, Czechoslovakia (Slovakia), January 12, 1979

2010–11 CHI	65	25	32	57	32
NHL Totals	897	388	439	827	508

Howard, Jimmy   b. Syracuse, New York, March 26, 1984

2010–11 DET	63	37–17–5	3,615	168	2	2.79
NHL Totals	135	75–37–15	7,811	330	5	2.53

Hudler, Jiri   b. Olomouc, Czechoslovakia (Czech Republic), January 4, 1984

2010–11 DET	73	10	27	37	28
NHL Totals	328	62	102	164	118

Hunter, Trent   b. Red Deer, Alberta, July 5, 1980

2010–11 NYI	17	1	3	4	23
NHL Totals	459	99	130	229	201

Hunwick, Matt   b. Warren, Michigan, May 21, 1985

2010–11 BOS/COL	73	1	12	13	25
NHL Totals	215	13	42	55	92

• traded by Boston to Colorado on November 29, 2010, for Colby Cohen

Huselius, Kristian   b. Osterhaninge, Sweden, November 10, 1978

2010–11 CBJ	39	14	9	23	10
NHL Totals	660	190	261	451	254

Huskins, Kent   b. Almonte, Ontario, May 4, 1979

2010–11 SJ	50	2	8	10	12
NHL Totals	274	11	49	60	159

Hutchinson, Andrew   b. Evanston, Illinois, March 24, 1980

2010–11 PIT	5	0	1	1	6
NHL Totals	140	12	27	39	70

Iginla, Jarome   b. Edmonton, Alberta, July 1, 1977

2010–11 CAL	82	43	43	86	40
NHL Totals	1,106	484	522	1,006	766

Ivanans, Raitis   b. Riga, Soviet Union (Latvia), January 1, 1979

2010–11 CAL	1	0	0	0	5
NHL Totals	281	12	6	18	569

Jackman, Barret   b. Trail, British Columbia, March 5, 1981

2010–11 STL	60	0	13	13	57
NHL Totals	517	19	107	126	786

Jackman, Tim   b. Minot, North Dakota, November 14, 1981

2010–11 CAL	82	10	13	23	86
NHL Totals	273	21	30	51	443

Jacques, Jean-Francois   b. Terrebonne, Quebec, April 29, 1985

2010–11 EDM	51	4	1	5	63
NHL Totals	160	9	8	17	185

Janik, Doug   b. Agawam, Massachusetts, March 26, 1980

2010–11 DET	7	0	0	0	7
NHL Totals	181	3	15	18	148

Janssen, Cam   b. St. Louis, Missouri, April 15, 1984

2010–11 STL	54	1	3	4	131
NHL Totals	260	3	7	10	675

Jeffrey, Dustin   b. Sarnia, Ontario, February 27, 1988

2010–11 PIT	25	7	5	12	4
NHL Totals	40	8	7	15	4

Jessiman, Hugh   b. New York, New York, March 28, 1984

2010–11 FLO	2	0	0	0	5
NHL Totals	2	0	0	0	5

Joensuu, Jesse   b. Pori, Finland, October 5, 1987

2010–11 NYI	42	6	3	9	33
NHL Totals	60	8	5	13	41

Johansson, Marcus   b. Landskrona, Sweden, October 6, 1990

2010–11 WAS	69	13	14	27	10
NHL Totals	69	13	14	27	10

Johnson, Brent   b. Farmington, Michigan, March 12, 1977

2010–11 PIT	23	13–5–3	1,297	47	1	2.17
NHL Totals	293	134–105–29	16,167	702	14	2.61

Johnson, Chad   b. Calgary, Alberta, June 10, 1986

2010–11 NYR	1	0–0–0	20	2	0	6.00
NHL Totals	6	1–2–1	300	13	0	2.59

Johnson, Erik   b. Bloomington, Minnesota, March 21, 1988

2010–11 STL/COL	77	8	21	29	56
NHL Totals	225	23	78	101	163

• traded by St. Louis to Colorado on February 19, 2011, with Jay McClement and a conditional 1st-round draft choice in 2011 or 2012 for Chris Stewart, Kevin Shattenkirk and a conditional 2nd-round draft choice in 2011 or 2012

Johnson, Jack   b. Indianapolis, Indiana, January 13, 1987

2010–11 LA	82	5	37	42	44
NHL Totals	282	22	78	100	232

Johnson, Nick   b. Calgary, Alberta, December 24, 1985

2010–11 PIT	4	1	2	3	5
NHL Totals	10	2	3	5	7

Johnson, Ryan b. Thunder Bay, Ontario, June 14, 1976

2010–11 CHI	34	1	5	6	8
NHL Totals	701	38	84	122	250

Jokinen, Jussi b. Kalajoki, Finland, April1, 1983

2010–11 CAR	70	19	33	52	24
NHL Totals	457	103	186	289	154

Jokinen, Olli b. Kuopio, Finland, December 5, 1978

2010–11 CAL	79	17	37	54	44
NHL Totals	960	269	353	622	913

Jones, Blair b. Central Butte, Saskatchewan, September 27, 1986

2010–11 TB	18	1	2	3	2
NHL Totals	56	2	4	6	14

Jones, David b. Guelph, Ontario, August 10, 1984

2010–11 COL	77	27	18	45	28
NHL Totals	167	47	33	80	46

Jones, Randy b. Quispamsis, New Brunswick, July 23, 1981

2010–11 TB	61	1	12	13	15
NHL Totals	326	19	84	103	177

Jones, Ryan b. Chatham, Ontario, June 14, 1984

2010–11 EDM	81	18	7	25	34
NHL Totals	176	33	21	54	82

Josefson, Jacob b. Stockholm, Sweden, March 2, 1991

2010–11 NJ	28	3	7	10	6
NHL Totals	28	3	7	10	6

Joslin, Derek b. Richmond Hill, Ontario, March 17, 1987

2010–11 SJ/CAR	34	2	7	9	10
NHL Totals	70	2	10	12	28

• traded by San Jose to Carolina on February 18, 2011, for future considerations

Jovanovski, Ed b. Windsor, Ontario, June 26, 1976

2010–11 PHO	50	5	9	14	39
NHL Totals	1,019	133	348	481	1,421

Jurcina, Milan b. Liptovsky Mikulas, Czechoslovakia (Slovakia), June 7, 1983

2010–11 NYI	46	4	13	17	30
NHL Totals	365	19	51	70	250

Kaberle, Tomas b. Rakovnik, Czechoslovakia (Czech Republic), March 2, 1978

2010–11 TOR/BOS	82	4	43	47	18
NHL Totals	902	84	445	529	248

• traded by Toronto to Boston on February 18, 2011, for Joe Colborne, a 1st-round draft choice
  in 2011 and a conditional draft choice in 2012

Kadri, Nazem b. London, Ontario, October 6, 1990

2010–11 TOR	29	3	9	12	8
NHL Totals	30	3	9	12	8

Kaleta, Patrick b. Buffalo, New York, June 8, 1986

2010–11 BUF	51	4	5	9	78
NHL Totals	204	21	19	40	318

Kampfer, Steven b. Ann Arbor, Michigan, September 24, 1988

2010–11 BOS	38	5	5	10	12
NHL Totals	38	5	5	10	12

Kane, Evander b. Vancouver, British Columbia, August 2, 1991

2010–11 ATL	73	19	24	43	68
NHL Totals	139	33	36	69	130

Kane, Patrick b. Buffalo, New York, November 19, 1988

2010–11 CHI	73	27	46	73	28
NHL Totals	317	103	200	303	142

Karlsson, Erik b. Landsbro, Sweden, May 31, 1990

2010–11 OTT	75	13	32	45	50
NHL Totals	135	18	53	71	74

Karlsson, Henrik b. Stockholm, Sweden, November 27, 1983

2010–11 CAL	17	4–5–6	838	36	0	2.58
NHL Totals	17	4–5–6	838	36	0	2.58

Kassian, Matt b. Edmonton, Alberta, October 28, 1986

2010–11 MIN	4	0	0	0	12
NHL Totals	4	0	0	0	12

Katic, Mark   b. Timmins, Ontario, May 9, 1989

2010–11 NYI	11	0	1	1	4
NHL Totals	11	0	1	1	4

Keith, Duncan   b. Winnipeg, Manitoba, July 16, 1983

2010–11 CHI	82	7	38	45	22
NHL Totals	486	52	190	242	344

Kelly, Chris   b. Toronto, Ontario, November 11, 1980

2010–11 OTT/BOS	81	14	14	28	33
NHL Totals	487	77	104	181	255

• traded by Ottawa to Boston on February 15, 2011, for a 2nd-round draft choice in 2011

Kennedy, Tim   b. Buffalo, New York, April 30, 1986

2010–11 FLO	6	0	1	1	0
NHL Totals	85	10	17	27	50

Kennedy, Tyler   b. Sault Ste. Marie, Ontario, July 15, 1986

2010–11 PIT	80	21	24	45	37
NHL Totals	266	59	65	124	133

Kesler, Ryan   b. Detroit, Michigan, August 31, 1984

2010–11 VAN	82	41	32	73	66
NHL Totals	484	131	157	288	445

Kessel, Phil   b. Madison, Wisconsin, October 2, 1987

2010–11 TOR	82	32	32	64	24
NHL Totals	374	128	117	245	101

Khabibulin, Nikolai   b. Sverdlovsk, Soviet Union (Russia), January 13, 1973

2010–11 EDM	47	10–32–4	2,701	153	2	3.40
NHL Totals	743	316–308–88	42,495	1,928	43	2.72

Khudobin, Anton   b. Ust-Kamenogorsk, Soviet Union (Russia), May 7, 1986

2010–11 MIN	4	2–1–0	189	5	1	1.59
NHL Totals	6	4–1–0	258	6	1	1.40

Kindl, Jakub   b. Sumperk, Czechoslovakia (Czech Republic), February 10, 1987

2010–11 DET	48	2	2	4	36
NHL Totals	51	2	2	4	36

King, D.J.   b. Meadow Lake, Saskatchewan, June 27, 1984

2010–11 WAS	16	0	2	2	30	
NHL Totals	117	4	7	11	215	

King, Dwight   b. Meadowlake, Saskatchewan, July 5, 1989

2010–11 LA	6	0	0	0	2	
NHL Totals	6	0	0	0	2	

Kiprusoff, Miikka   b. Turku, Finland, October 26, 1976

2010–11 CAL	71	37–24–6	4,156	182	6	2.63
NHL Totals	529	276–177–58	30,697	1,261	40	2.46

Klasen, Linus   b. Stockholm, Sweden, February 19, 1986

2010–11 NAS	4	0	0	0	0	
NHL Totals	4	0	0	0	0	

Klein, Kevin   b. Kitchener, Ontario, December 13, 1984

2010–11 NAS	81	2	16	18	24	
NHL Totals	243	8	36	44	76	

Klesla, Rostislav   b. Novy Jicin, Czechoslovakia (Czech Republic), March 21, 1982

2010–11 CBJ/PHO	61	4	7	11	38	
NHL Totals	531	42	92	134	520	

• traded by Columbus to Phoenix on February 28, 2011, with Dane Byers for Scottie Upshall and Sami Lepisto

Klingberg, Carl   b. Gothenburg, Sweden, January 28, 1991

2010–11 ATL	1	0	0	0	0	
NHL Totals	1	0	0	0	0	

Klinkhammer, Rob   b. Lethbridge, Alberta, August 12, 1986

2010–11 CHI	1	0	0	0	0	
NHL Totals	1	0	0	0	0	

Knuble, Mike   b. Toronto, Ontario, July 4, 1972

2010–11 WAS	79	24	16	40	36	
NHL Totals	968	268	254	522	589	

Kobasew, Chuck   b. Osoyoos, British Columbia, April 17, 1982

2010–11 MIN	63	9	17	16	19	
NHL Totals	473	96	89	185	307	

Koci, David   b. Prague, Czechoslovakia (Czech Republic), May 12, 1981

2010–11 COL	35	1	0	1	80
NHL Totals	142	3	1	4	461

Koivu, Mikko   b. Turku, Finland, March 12, 1983

2010–11 MIN	71	17	45	62	50
NHL Totals	433	96	221	317	306

Koivu, Saku   b. Turku, Finland, November 23, 1974

2010–11 ANA	75	15	30	45	36
NHL Totals	938	225	513	738	695

Kolarik, Chad   b. Abington, Pennsylvania, January 26, 1986

2010–11 NYR	4	0	1	1	2
NHL Totals	6	0	1	1	2

Komisarek, Mike   b. Islip Terrace, New York, January 19, 1982

2010–11 TOR	75	1	9	10	86
NHL Totals	470	13	59	72	622

Konopka, Zenon   b. Niagara-on-the-Lake, Ontario, January 2, 1981

2010–11 NYI	82	2	7	9	307
NHL Totals	195	8	14	22	684

Kopecky, Tomas   b. Ilava, Czechoslovakia (Slovakia), February 5, 1982

2010–11 CHI	81	15	27	42	60
NHL Totals	338	37	58	95	201

Kopitar, Anze   b. Jesenice, Yugoslavia (Slovenia), August 24, 1987

2010–11 LA	75	25	48	73	20
NHL Totals	393	138	220	358	114

Korpikoski, Lauri   b. Turku, Finland, July 28, 1986

2010–11 PHO	79	19	21	40	20
NHL Totals	218	30	35	65	50

Koskinen, Mikko   b. Vantaa, Finland, July 18, 1988

2010–11 NYI	4	2–1–0	218	15	0	4.33
NHL Totals	4	2–1–0	218	15	0	4.33

Kostitsyn, Andrei   b. Novopolotsk, Soviet Union (Belarus), February 3, 1985

2010–11 MON	81	20	25	45	36
NHL Totals	326	87	99	186	155

Kostitsyn, Sergei   b. Novopolotsk, Soviet Union (Belarus), March 20, 1987

2010–11 NAS	77	23	27	50	20
NHL Totals	232	47	71	118	143

Kostopoulos, Tom   b. Mississauga, Ontario, January 24, 1979

2010–11 CAR/CAL	76	8	10	18	74
NHL Totals	534	56	88	144	648

• traded by Carolina to Calgary on November 17, 2010, with Anton Babchuk for Ian White and
  Brett Sutter

Kotalik, Ales   b. Jindrichuv Hradec, Czechoslovakia (Czech Republic), December 23, 1978

2010–11 CAL	26	4	2	6	8
NHL Totals	542	136	148	284	348

Kovalchuk, Ilya   b. Tver, Soviet Union (Russia), April 15, 1983

2010–11 NJ	81	31	29	60	28
NHL Totals	702	369	333	702	465

Kovalev, Alexei   b. Togliatti, Soviet Union (Russia), February 24, 1973

2010–11 OTT/PIT	74	16	18	34	44
NHL Totals	1,302	428	596	1,024	1,298

• traded by Ottawa to Pittsburgh on February 24, 2011, for a conditional 7th-round draft choice in 2011

Krejci, David   b. Sternberk, Czechoslovakia (Czech Republic), April 28, 1986

2010–11 BOS	75	13	49	62	28
NHL Totals	298	58	156	214	102

Kronwall, Niklas   b. Stockholm, Sweden, January 12, 1981

2010–11 DET	77	11	26	37	36
NHL Totals	385	34	147	181	260

Kruger, Marcus   b. Stockholm, Sweden, May 27, 1990

2010–11 CHI	7	0	0	0	4
NHL Totals	7	0	0	0	4

Kuba, Filip   b. Ostrava, Czechoslovakia (Czech Republic), December 29, 1976

2010–11 OTT	64	2	14	16	16
NHL Totals	719	63	228	291	311

Kubalik, Tomas   b. Plzen, Czechoslovakia (Czech Republic), May 1, 1990

2010–11 CBJ	4	0	2	2	0
NHL Totals	4	0	2	2	0

Kubina, Pavel b. Celadna, Czechoslovakia (Czech Republic), April 15, 1977

2010–11 TB	79	4	19	23	62
NHL Totals	901	107	264	371	1,049

Kulda, Arturs b. Riga, Soviet Union (Latvia), July 25, 1988

2010–11 ATL	2	0	0	0	2
NHL Totals	6	0	2	2	4

Kulemin, Nikolai b. Magnitogorsk, Soviet Union (Russia), July 14, 1986

2010–11 TOR	82	30	27	57	26
NHL Totals	233	61	63	124	60

Kulikov, Dmitri b. Lipetsk, Soviet Union (Russia), October 29, 1990

2010–11 FLO	72	6	20	26	45
NHL Totals	140	9	33	42	77

Kunitz, Chris b. Regina, Saskatchewan, September 26, 1979

2010–11 PIT	66	23	25	48	47
NHL Totals	451	124	166	290	401

Laakso, Teemu b. Tuusula, Finland, August 27, 1987

2010–11 NAS	1	0	0	0	0
NHL Totals	8	0	0	0	2

LaBarbera, Jason b. Burnaby, British Columbia, January 18, 1980

2010–11 PHO	17	7–6–3	883	48	2	3.26
NHL Totals	141	52–55–14	7,318	354	6	2.90

Ladd, Andrew b. Maple Ridge, British Columbia, December 12, 1985

2010–11 ATL	81	29	30	59	39
NHL Totals	402	92	116	208	219

Laich, Brooks b. Medicine Hat, Alberta, June 23, 1983

2010–11 WAS	82	16	32	48	46
NHL Totals	475	100	137	237	203

Lalime, Patrick b. St-Bonaventure, Quebec, July 7, 1974

2010–11 BUF	7	0–5–0	365	18	0	2.96
NHL Totals	444	200–174–48	25,240	1,085	35	2.58

Langenbrunner, Jamie   b. Duluth, Minnesota, July 24, 1975

2010–11 NJ/DAL	70	9	23	32	45
NHL Totals	1,035	237	401	638	805

• traded by New Jersey to Dallas on January 7, 2011, for a conditional 3rd-round draft choice in 2011

Langkow, Daymond   b. Edmonton, Alberta, September 27, 1976

2010–11 CAL	4	0	1	1	0
NHL Totals	1,017	259	383	642	533

Lapierre, Maxim   b. St–Léonard, Quebec, March 29, 1985

2010–11 MON/ANA/VAN	78	6	6	12	80
NHL Totals	333	41	43	84	301

• traded by Montreal to Anaheim on December 31, 2010, for Brett Festerling and a 5th-round draft choice in 2012
• traded by Anaheim to Vancouver on February 28, 2011, with MacGregor Sharp for Joel Perrault and a 3rd-round draft choice in 2012

LaRose, Chad   b. Fraser, Michigan, March 27, 1982

2010–11 CAR	82	16	15	31	59
NHL Totals	406	64	80	144	209

Larsen, Philip   b. Esbjerg, Denmark, December 7, 1989

2010–11 DAL	6	0	2	2	0
NHL Totals	8	0	3	3	0

Lashoff, Matt   b. East Greenbush, New York, September 29, 1986

2010–11 TOR	11	0	1	1	6
NHL Totals	74	1	15	16	59

Latendresse, Guillaume   b. Ste-Cathérine, Quebec, May 24, 1987

2010–11 MIN	11	3	3	6	8
NHL Totals	298	76	52	128	157

Lawson, Nathan   b. Calgary, Alberta, September 29, 1983

2010–11 NYI	10	1–4–2	384	26	0	4.06
NHL Totals	10	1–4–2	384	26	0	4.06

Leach, Jay   b. Syracuse, New York, September 2, 1979

2010–11 NJ	7	0	0	0	7
NHL Totals	70	1	2	3	60

Lebda, Brett b. Buffalo Grove, Illinois, January 15, 1982

2010–11 TOR	41	1	3	4	14
NHL Totals	367	19	53	72	215

Lecavalier, Vincent b. Île-Bizard, Quebec, April 21, 1980

2010–11 TB	65	25	29	54	43
NHL Totals	934	351	442	793	667

Leclaire, Pascal b. Repentigny, Quebec, November 7, 1982

2010–11 OTT	14	4–7–1	763	36	0	2.83
NHL Totals	173	61–76–15	9,406	453	10	2.89

Leddy, Nick b. Eden Prairie, Minnesota, March 20, 1991

2010–11 CHI	46	4	3	7	4
NHL Totals	46	4	3	7	4

Lee, Brian b. Moorhead, Minnesota, March 26, 1987

2010–11 OTT	50	0	3	3	24
NHL Totals	132	4	16	20	73

Legwand, David b. Detroit, Michigan, August 17, 1980

2010–11 NAS	64	17	24	41	24
NHL Totals	768	169	279	448	398

Lehner, Robin b. Gothenburg, Sweden, July 24, 1991

2010–11 OTT	8	1–4–0	341	20	0	3.52
NHL Totals	8	1–4–0	341	20	0	3.52

Lehtonen, Kari b. Helsinki, Finland, November 16, 1983

2010–11 DAL	69	34–24–11	4,119	175	3	2.55
NHL Totals	285	134–111–28	16,452	765	17	2.79

Leighton, Michael b. Petrolia, Ontario, May 19, 1981

2010–11 PHI	1	1–0–0	60	4	0	4.00
NHL Totals	104	35–40–4	5,694	280	4	2.95

Leino, Ville b. Savonlinna, Finland, October 6, 1983

2010–11 PHI	81	19	34	53	22
NHL Totals	149	30	43	73	38

LeNeveu, David b. Fernie, British Columbia, May 23, 1983

2010–11 CBJ	1	0–0–0	20	2	0	6.00
NHL Totals	22	5–9–2	1,067	61	0	3.43

Leopold, Jordan   b. Golden Valley, Minnesota, August 3, 1980

2010–11 BUF	71	13	22	35	36
NHL Totals	503	53	117	170	226

Lepisto, Sami   b. Espoo, Finland, October 17, 1984

2010–11 PHO/CBJ	70	4	12	16	55
NHL Totals	150	5	27	32	133

• traded by Phoenix to Columbus on February 28, 2011, with Scottie Upshall for Rostislav Klesla and Dane Byers

Lessard, Francis   b. Montreal, Quebec, May 30, 1979

2010–11 OTT	24	0	0	0	78
NHL Totals	115	1	3	4	346

Letang, Kris   b. Montreal, Quebec, April 24, 1987

2010–11 PIT	82	8	42	50	101
NHL Totals	299	29	100	129	203

Letestu, Mark   b. Elk Point, Alberta, February 4, 1985

2010–11 PIT	64	14	13	27	13
NHL Totals	74	15	13	28	15

Letourneau-Leblond, Pierre-Luc   b. Lévis, Quebec, June 4, 1985

2010–11 NJ	2	0	0	0	21
NHL Totals	37	0	3	3	91

Lewis, Trevor   b. Salt Lake City, Utah, January 8, 1987

2010–11 LA	72	3	10	13	6
NHL Totals	83	4	12	16	6

Lidstrom, Nicklas   b. Vasteras, Sweden, April 28, 1970

2010–11 DET	82	16	46	62	20
NHL Totals	1,494	253	855	1,108	486

Liffiton, David   b. Windsor, Ontario, October 18, 1984

2010–11 COL	4	1	0	1	17
NHL Totals	7	1	0	1	26

Liles, John-Michael   b. Zionsville, Indiana, November 25, 1980

2010–11 COL	76	6	40	46	35
NHL Totals	523	68	207	275	218

Lilja, Andreas b. Helsingborg, Sweden, July 13, 1975

2010–11 ANA	52	1	6	7	28
NHL Totals	530	16	65	81	529

Lindback, Anders b. Gavle, Sweden, May 3, 1988

2010–11 NAS	22	11–5–2	1,131	49	2	2.60
NHL Totals	22	11–5–2	1,131	49	2	2.60

Little, Bryan b. Edmonton, Alberta, November 12, 1987

2010–11 ATL	76	18	30	48	33
NHL Totals	282	68	81	149	95

Locke, Corey b. Toronto, Ontario, May 8, 1984

2010–11 OTT	5	0	1	1	0
NHL Totals	9	0	1	1	0

Loktionov, Andrei b. Voskresensk, Soviet Union (Russia), May 30, 1990

2010–11 LA	19	4	3	7	2
NHL Totals	20	4	3	7	2

Lombardi, Matt b. Montreal, Quebec, March 18, 1982

2010–11 NAS	2	0	0	0	0
NHL Totals	446	89	147	236	275

Lovejoy, Ben b. Concord, New Hampshire, February 20, 1984

2010–11 PIT	47	3	15	18	48
NHL Totals	61	3	17	20	50

Lucic, Milan b. Vancouver, British Columbia, June 7, 1988

2010–11 BOS	79	30	32	62	121
NHL Totals	278	64	87	151	390

Lukowich, Brad b. Cranbrook, British Columbia, August 12, 1976

2010–11 DAL	5	0	0	0	0
NHL Totals	658	23	90	113	369

Lundin, Mike b. Burnsville, Minnesota, September 24, 1984

2010–11 TB	69	1	11	12	12
NHL Totals	224	4	29	33	50

Lundqvist, Henrik b. Are, Sweden, March 2, 1982

2010–11 NYR	68	36–27–5	4,007	152	11	2.28
NHL Totals	406	213–137–49	23,888	923	35	2.32

Luongo, Roberto b. Montreal, Quebec, April 4, 1979

2010–11 VAN	60	38–15–7	3,590	126	4	2.11
NHL Totals	672	308–269–75	38,526	1,622	55	2.53

Lupul, Joffrey b. Edmonton, Alberta, September 23, 1983

2010–11 ANA/TOR	54	14	17	31	33
NHL Totals	449	126	130	256	265

• traded by Anaheim to Toronto on February 9, 2011, with Jake Gardiner and a conditional 4th-round draft choice in 2013 for Francois Beauchemin

Lydman, Toni b. Lahti, Finland, September 25, 1977

2010–11 ANA	78	3	22	25	42
NHL Totals	738	36	187	223	493

MacArthur, Clarke b. Lloydminster, Alberta, April 6, 1985

2010–11 TOR	82	21	42	62	37
NHL Totals	290	65	85	150	166

MacDonald, Andrew b. Judique, Nova Scotia, September 7, 1986

2010–11 NYI	60	4	23	27	37
NHL Totals	109	5	29	34	59

MacDonald, Joey b. Pictou, Nova Scotia, February 7, 1980

2010–11 DET	15	5–5–3	721	31	1	2.58
NHL Totals	87	23–43–12	4,778	254	2	3.19

Machacek, Spencer b. Lethbridge, Alberta, October 14, 1988

2010–11 ATL	10	0	0	0	0
NHL Totals	12	0	0	0	0

Macias, Ray b. Long Beach, California, September 18, 1986

2010–11 COL	2	0	0	0	2
NHL Totals	8	0	1	1	2

MacIntyre, Steve b. Brock, Saskatchewan, August 8, 1980

2010–11 EDM	34	0	1	1	93
NHL Totals	78	2	2	4	157

MacKenzie, Derek b. Sudbury, Ontario, June 11, 1981

2010–11 CBJ	63	9	14	23	22
NHL Totals	127	12	19	31	52

MacLean, Brett b. Port Elgin, Ontario, December 24, 1988

2010–11 PHO	13	2	1	3	2
NHL Totals	13	2	1	3	2

Madden, John b. Barrie, Ontario, May 4, 1973

2010–11 MIN	76	12	13	25	10
NHL Totals	867	162	183	345	215

Magnan, Olivier b. Sherbrooke, Quebec, May 1, 1986

2010–11 NJ	18	0	0	0	4
NHL Totals	18	0	0	0	4

Mair, Adam b. Hamilton, Ontario, February 15, 1979

2010–11 NJ	65	1	3	4	45
NHL Totals	615	38	76	114	829

Malhotra, Manny b. Mississauga, Ontario, May 18, 1980

2010–11 VAN	72	11	19	30	22
NHL Totals	777	101	159	260	407

Malkin, Evgeni b. Magnitogorsk, Soviet Union (Russia), July 31, 1986

2010–11 PIT	43	15	22	37	18
NHL Totals	352	158	260	418	356

Malone, Ryan b. Pittsburgh, Pennsylvania, December 1, 1979

2010–11 TB	54	14	24	38	51
NHL Totals	492	148	151	299	518

Mancari, Mark b. London, Ontario, July 11, 1985

2010–11 BUF	20	1	7	8	12
NHL Totals	36	3	10	13	22

Mannino, Peter b. Farmington Hills, Michigan, February 17, 1984

2010–11 ATL	2	0–0–0	73	5	0	4.11
NHL Totals	5	1–1–0	205	15	0	4.37

Mara, Paul b. Ridgewood, New Jersey, September 7, 1979

2010–11 ANA/MON	53	1	5	6	88
NHL Totals	734	64	189	253	776

• traded by Anaheim to Montreal on February 17, 2011, for a 5th-round draft choice in 2012

Marchand, Brad   b. Halifax, Nova Scotia, May 11, 1988

2010–11 BOS	77	21	20	41	51
NHL Totals	97	21	21	42	71

Marchant, Todd   b. Buffalo, New York, August 12, 1973

2010–11 ANA	79	1	7	8	26
NHL Totals	1,195	186	312	498	774

Markov, Andrei   b. Voskresensk, Soviet Union (Russia), December 20, 1978

2010–11 MON	7	1	2	3	4
NHL Totals	623	81	285	366	361

Markstrom, Jakob   b. Gavle, Sweden, January 31, 1990

2010–11 FLO	1	0–1–0	40	2	0	3.00
NHL Totals	1	0–1–0	40	2	0	3.00

Marleau, Patrick   b. Aneroid, Saskatchewan, September 15, 1979

2010–11 SJ	82	37	36	73	16
NHL Totals	1,035	357	409	766	341

Martin, Matt   b. Windsor, Ontario, May 8, 1989

2010–11 NYI	68	5	9	14	147
NHL Totals	73	5	11	16	173

Martin, Paul   b. Minneapolis, Minnesota, March 5, 1981

2010–11 PIT	77	3	21	24	16
NHL Totals	477	29	158	187	130

Martinek, Radek   b. Havlickuv Brod, Czechoslovakia (Czech Republic), August 31, 1976

2010–11 NYI	64	3	13	16	35
NHL Totals	453	21	82	103	272

Martinez, Alec   b. Rochester Hills, Michigan, July 26, 1987

2010–11 LA	60	5	11	16	18
NHL Totals	64	5	11	16	20

Mashinter, Brandon   b. Bradford, Ontario, September 20, 1988

2010–11 SJ	13	0	0	0	17
NHL Totals	13	0	0	0	17

Mason, Chris   b. Red Deer, Alberta, April 20, 1976

2010–11 ATL	33	13–13–3	1,682	95	1	3.39
NHL Totals	286	128–99–30	15,540	682	21	2.63

Mason, Steve   b. Oakville, Ontario, May 29, 1988

2010–11 CBJ	54	24–21–7	3,027	153	3	3.03
NHL Totals	173	77–67–23	9,891	456	18	2.77

Matsumoto, Jon   b. Ottawa, Ontario, October 13, 1986

2010–11 CAR	13	2	0	2	4
NHL Totals	13	2	0	2	4

Matthias, Shawn   b. Mississauga, Ontario, February 19, 1988

2010–11 FLO	51	6	10	16	16
NHL Totals	126	15	21	36	30

Maudlin, Greg   b. Boston, Massachusetts, June 10, 1982

2010–11 COL	29	5	5	10	8
NHL Totals	36	5	5	10	12

Maxwell, Ben   b. North Vancouver, British Columbia, March 30, 1988

2010–11 ATL	12	1	1	2	9
NHL Totals	32	1	1	2	17

Mayers, Jamal   b. Toronto, Ontario, October 24, 1974

2010–11 SJ	78	3	11	14	124
NHL Totals	815	84	118	202	1,093

Mayorov, Maxim   b. Andizhan, Soviet Union (Russia), March 26, 1989

2010–11 CBJ	5	1	0	1	0
NHL Totals	12	1	0	1	0

McArdle, Kenndal   b. Toronto, Ontario, January 4, 1987

2010–11 FLO	11	0	0	0	16
NHL Totals	33	1	2	3	47

McBain, Jamie   b. Edina, Minnesota, February 25, 1988

2010–11 CAR	76	7	23	30	32
NHL Totals	90	10	30	40	32

McCabe, Bryan   b. St. Catharines, Ontario, June 8, 1975

2010–11 FLO/NYR	67	7	21	28	34
NHL Totals	1,135	145	383	528	1,732

• traded by Florida to the Rangers on February 26, 2011, for Tim Kennedy and a 3rd-round draft choice in 2011

McCarthy, John b. Boston, Massachusetts, August 9, 1986

2010–11 SJ	37	2	2	4	8
NHL Totals	41	2	2	4	8

McClement, Jay b. Kingston, Ontario, March 2, 1983

2010–11 STL/COL	80	7	13	20	30
NHL Totals	473	53	107	160	192

• traded by St. Louis to Colorado on February 19, 2011, with Erik Johnson and a conditional 1st-round draft choice in 2011 or 2012 for Kevin Shattenkirk, Chris Stewart and a conditional 2nd-round draft choice in 2011 or 2012

McCollum, Tom b. Amherst, New York, December 7, 1989

2010–11 DET	1	0–0–0	15	3	0	12.00
NHL Totals	1	0–0–0	15	3	0	12.00

McCormick, Cody b. London, Ontario, April 18, 1983

2010–11 BUF	81	8	12	20	142
NHL Totals	271	17	33	50	392

McDonagh, Ryan b. St. Paul, Minnesota, June 13, 1989

2010–11 NYR	40	1	8	9	14
NHL Totals	40	1	8	9	14

McDonald, Andy b. Strathroy, Ontario, August 25, 1977

2010–11 STL	58	20	30	50	26
NHL Totals	623	165	281	446	262

McElhinney, Curtis b. London, Ontario, May 23, 1983

2010–11 ANA/OTT	28	9–13–1	1,395	74	2	3.18
NHL Totals	67	18–26–4	3,086	161	2	3.13

• claimed off waivers by Ottawa from Anaheim on February 28, 2011

McGinn, Jamie b. Fergus, Ontario, August 5, 1988

2010–11 SJ	49	1	5	6	33
NHL Totals	143	15	10	25	73

McKenna, Mike b. St. Louis, Missouri, April 11, 1983

2010–11 NJ	2	0–1–0	118	6	0	3.05
NHL Totals	17	4–9–1	893	52	1	3.49

McLaren, Frazer b. Winnipeg, Manitoba, October 29, 1987

2010–11 SJ	9	0	0	0	22
NHL Totals	32	1	5	6	76

McLeod, Cody b. Binscarth, Manitoba, June 26, 1984

2010–11 COL	71	5	3	8	189
NHL Totals	273	31	24	55	609

McMillan, Brandon b. Richmond, British Columbia, March 22, 1990

2010–11 ANA	60	11	10	21	18
NHL Totals	60	11	10	21	18

McMillan, Carson b. Brandon, Manitoba, September 10, 1988

2010–11 MIN	4	1	1	2	0
NHL Totals	4	1	1	2	0

McQuaid, Adam b. Charlottetown, Prince Edward Island, October 12, 1986

2010–11 BOS	67	3	12	15	96
NHL Totals	86	4	12	16	117

McRae, Philip b. Minneapolis, Minnesota, March 15, 1990

2010–11 STL	15	1	2	3	2
NHL Totals	15	1	2	3	2

Meszaros, Andrei b. Povazska Bystrica, Czechoslovakia (Slovakia), October 13, 1985

2010–11 PHI	81	8	24	32	42
NHL Totals	460	42	133	175	341

Methot, Marc b. Ottawa, Ontario, June 21, 1985

2010–11 CBJ	74	0	15	15	58
NHL Totals	229	6	38	44	184

Meyer, Freddy b. Sanbornville, New Hampshire, January 4, 1981

2010–11 ATL	15	1	1	2	8
NHL Totals	281	20	53	73	155

Meyer, Stefan b. Medicine Hat, Alberta, July 20, 1985

2010–11 CAL	16	0	2	2	17
NHL Totals	20	0	2	2	17

Michalek, Milan b. Jindrichuv Hradec, Czechoslovakia (Czech Republic), December 7, 1984

2010–11 OTT	66	18	15	33	49
NHL Totals	449	131	150	281	251

Michalek, Zbynek   b. Jindrichuv Hradec, Czechoslovakia (Czech Republic), December 23, 1982

2010–11 PIT	73	5	14	19	30
NHL Totals	488	32	102	134	222

Miettinen, Antti   b. Hameenlinna, Finland, July 3, 1980

2010–11 MIN	73	16	19	35	38
NHL Totals	472	89	123	212	232

Mikkelson, Brendan   b. Regina, Saskatchewan, June 22, 1987

2010–11 ANA/CAL	24	0	2	2	9
NHL Totals	86	0	6	6	40

• claimed off waivers by Calgary from Anaheim on October 19, 2010

Miller, Drew   b. Dover, New Jersey, February 17, 1984

2010–11 DET	67	10	8	18	13
NHL Totals	200	26	26	52	48

Miller, Ryan   b. East Lansing, Michigan, July 17, 1980

2010–11 BUF	66	34–22–8	3,829	165	5	2.59
NHL Totals	399	221–126–42	23,438	1,004	22	2.57

Mills, Brad   b. Terrace, British Columbia, May 3, 1983

2010–11 NJ	4	1	0	1	5
NHL Totals	4	1	0	1	5

Mitchell, John   b. Waterloo, Ontario, January 22, 1985

2010–11 TOR	23	2	1	3	12
NHL Totals	159	20	35	55	76

Mitchell, Torrey   b. Montreal, Quebec, January 30, 1985

2010–11 SJ	66	9	14	23	46
NHL Totals	204	21	33	54	123

Mitchell, Willie   b. Port McNeill, British Columbia, April 23, 1977

2010–11 LA	57	5	5	10	21
NHL Totals	643	24	105	129	642

Modano, Mike   b. Livonia, Michigan, June 7, 1970

2010–11 DET	40	4	11	15	8
NHL Totals	1,499	561	813	1,374	930

Modin, Fredrik   b. Sundsvall, Sweden, October 8, 1974

2010–11 ATL/CAL	40	7	3	10	14
NHL Totals	898	232	230	462	453

• traded by Atlanta to Calgary on February 28, 2011, for a 7th-round draft choice in 2011
• retired at season's end

Moen, Travis   b. Stewart Valley, Saskatchewan, April 6, 1982

2010–11 MON	79	6	10	16	96
NHL Totals	522	43	48	91	640

Moller, Oscar   b. Stockholm, Sweden, January 22, 1989

2010–11 LA	13	1	3	4	2
NHL Totals	87	12	14	26	22

Montador, Steve   b. Vancouver, British Columbia, December 21, 1979

2010–11 BUF	73	5	21	26	83
NHL Totals	519	28	89	117	762

Montoya, Al   b. Chicago, Illinois, February 13, 1985

2010–11 NYI	21	9–5–5	1,154	46	1	2.39
NHL Totals	26	12–6–5	1,413	55	2	2.34

Moore, Dominic   b. Thornhill, Ontario, August 3, 1980

2010–11 TB	77	18	14	32	52
NHL Totals	451	63	97	160	295

Moore, John   b. Winnetka, Illinois, November 19, 1990

2010–11 CBJ	2	0	0	0	0
NHL Totals	2	0	0	0	0

Moore, Mike   b. Calgary, Alberta, December 12, 1984

2010–11 SJ	6	1	0	1	7
NHL Totals	6	1	0	1	7

Moreau, Ethan   b. Huntsville, Ontario, September 22, 1975

2010–11 CBJ	37	1	5	6	24
NHL Totals	900	146	137	283	1,090

Morin, Jeremy   b. Auburn, New York, April 16, 1991

2010–11 CHI	9	2	1	3	9
NHL Totals	9	2	1	3	9

Morin, Travis   b. Minneapolis, Minnesota, January 9, 1984

2010–11 DAL	3	0	0	0	0
NHL Totals	3	0	0	0	0

Morris, Derek   b. Edmonton, Alberta, August 24, 1978

2010–11 PHO	77	5	11	16	58
NHL Totals	946	85	300	385	889

Morrison, Brendan   b. Pitt Meadows, British Columbia, August 15, 1975

2010–11 CAL	66	9	34	43	16
NHL Totals	895	196	394	590	440

Morrisonn, Shaone   b. Vancouver, British Columbia, December 23, 1982

2010–11 BUF	62	1	4	5	32
NHL Totals	480	11	64	75	455

Morrow, Brenden   b. Carlyle, Saskatchewan, January 16, 1979

2010–11 DAL	82	33	23	56	76
NHL Totals	749	226	265	491	1,088

Moss, David   b. Dearborn, Michigan, December 28, 1981

2010–11 CAL	58	17	13	30	18
NHL Totals	285	59	56	115	82

Mottau, Mike   b. Quincy, Massachusetts, March 19, 1978

2010–11 NYI	20	0	3	3	8
NHL Totals	278	7	49	56	145

Moulson, Matt   b. North York (Toronto), Ontario, November 1, 1983

2010–11 NYI	82	31	22	53	24
NHL Totals	193	67	44	111	46

Mueller, Chris   b. West Seneca, New York, March 6, 1986

2010–11 NAS	15	0	3	3	2
NHL Totals	15	0	3	3	2

Mueller, Marcel   b. Berlin, East Germany (Germany), July 10, 1988

2010–11 TOR	3	0	0	0	2
NHL Totals	3	0	0	0	2

Murray, Andrew   b. Selkirk, Manitoba, November 6, 1981

2010–11 CBJ	29	4	4	8	4
NHL Totals	181	23	13	36	32

Murray, Doug   b. Bromma, Sweden, March 12, 1980

2010–11 SJ	73	1	13	14	44
NHL Totals	362	6	46	52	304

Mursak, Jan   b. Maribor, Yugoslavia (Slovenia), January 20, 1988

2010–11 DET	19	1	0	1	4
NHL Totals	19	1	0	1	4

Muzzin, Jake   b. Woodstock, Ontario, February 21, 1989

2010–11 LA	11	0	1	1	0
NHL Totals	11	0	1	1	0

Myers, Tyler   b. Houston, Texas, February 1, 190

2010–11 BUF	80	10	27	37	40
NHL Totals	162	21	64	85	72

Nash, Brendon   b. Calgary, Alberta, March 31, 1987

2010–11 MON	2	0	0	0	0
NHL Totals	2	0	0	0	0

Nash, Rick   b. Brampton, Ontario, June 16, 1984

2010–11 CBJ	75	32	34	66	34
NHL Totals	592	259	229	488	528

Neal, James   b. Oshawa, Ontario, September 3, 1987

2010–11 DAL/PIT	79	22	23	45	66
NHL Totals	234	73	64	137	181

• traded by Dallas to Pittsburgh on February 21, 2011, with Matt Niskanen for Alex Goligoski

Neil, Chris   b. Markdale, Ontario, June 18, 1979

2010–11 OTT	80	6	10	16	210
NHL Totals	659	77	95	172	1,683

Nemisz, Greg   b. Courtice, Ontario, June 5, 1990

2010–11 CAL	6	0	1	1	0
NHL Totals	6	0	1	1	0

Neuvirth, Michal   b. Usti nad Labem, Czechoslovakia (Czech Republic), March 23, 1988

2010–11 WAS	48	27–12–4	2,689	110	4	2.45
NHL Totals	70	38–17–4	3,781	161	4	2.55

Newbury, Kris   b. Brampton, Ontario, February 19, 1982

2010–11 NYR	11	0	1	1	35
NHL Totals	59	4	4	8	99

Nichol, Scott   b. Edmonton, Alberta, December 31, 1974

2010–11 SJ	56	4	3	7	50
NHL Totals	552	52	66	118	808

Niedermayer, Rob   b. Cassiar, British Columbia, December 28, 1974

2010–11 BUF	71	5	14	19	22
NHL Totals	1,153	186	283	469	904

Niederreiter, Nino   b. Chur, Switzerland, September 8, 1992

2010–11 NYI	9	1	1	2	8
NHL Totals	9	1	1	2	8

Nielsen, Frans   b. Herning, Denmark, April 24, 1984

2010–11 NYI	71	13	31	44	38
NHL Totals	237	37	83	120	62

Niemi, Antti   b. Vantaa, Finland, August 29, 1983

2010–11 SJ	60	35–18–6	3,524	140	6	2.38
NHL Totals	102	62–26–11	5,855	230	13	2.36

Niittymaki, Antero   b. Turku, Finland, June 18, 1980

2010–11 SJ	24	12–7–3	1,414	64	0	2.72
NHL Totals	234	95–86–31	13,113	645	5	2.95

Nikitin, Nikita   b. Omsk, Soviet Union (Russia), June 16, 1986

2010–11 STL	41	1	8	9	10
NHL Totals	41	1	8	9	10

Niskanen, Matt   b. Virginia, Minnesota, December 6, 1986

2010–11 DAL/PIT	63	1	9	10	50
NHL Totals	295	17	69	86	156

• traded by Dallas to Pittsburgh on February 21, 2011, with James Neal for Alex Goligoski

Nodl, Andreas   b. Vienna, Austria, February 28, 1987

2010–11 PHI	67	11	11	22	16
NHL Totals	115	12	15	27	18

Noreau, Maxim   b. Montreal, Quebec, May 14, 1987

2010–11 MIN	5	0	0	0	0
NHL Totals	6	0	0	0	0

Nystrom, Eric   b. Syosset, New York, February 14, 1983

2010–11 MIN	82	4	8	12	30
NHL Totals	286	23	28	51	221

Oberg, Evan   b. Forestburg, Alberta, February 16, 1988

2010–11 VAN	2	0	0	0	0
NHL Totals	4	0	0	0	0

O'Brien, Jim   b. Maplewood, Minnesota, January 29, 1989

2010–11 OTT	6	0	0	0	2
NHL Totals	6	0	0	0	2

O'Brien, Shane   b. Port Hope, Ontario, August 9, 1983

2010–11 NAS	80	2	7	9	83
NHL Totals	379	10	54	64	688

O'Byrne, Ryan   b. Victoria, British Columbia, July 19, 1984

2010–11 MON/COL	67	0	10	10	75
NHL Totals	192	2	24	26	252

• traded by Montreal to Colorado on November 11, 2010, for Michael Bournival

O'Donnell, Sean   b. Ottawa, Ontario, October 13, 1971

2010–11 PHI	81	1	17	18	87
NHL Totals	1,173	31	191	222	1,786

Oduya, John   b. Stockholm, Sweden, October 1, 1981

2010–11 ATL	82	2	15	17	22
NHL Totals	382	20	76	96	189

Ohlund, Mattias   b. Pitea, Sweden, September 9, 1976

2010–11 TB	72	0	5	5	70
NHL Totals	909	93	250	343	885

Okposo, Kyle   b. St. Paul, Minnesota, April 16, 1988

2010–11 NYI	38	5	15	20	40
NHL Totals	192	44	72	116	112

Olesz, Rostislav   b. Bilovec, Czechoslovakia (Czech Republic), October 10, 1985

2010–11 FLO	44	6	11	17	8
NHL Totals	349	57	75	132	112

Olver, Mark   b. Burnaby, British Columbia, January 1, 1988

2010–11 COL	18	2	7	9	18
NHL Totals	18	2	7	9	18

Omark, Linus   b. Overtornea, Sweden, February 5, 1987

2010–11 EDM	51	5	22	27	26
NHL Totals	51	5	22	27	26

O'Marra, Ryan   b. Tokyo, Japan, June 9, 1987

2010–11 EDM	21	1	4	5	13
NHL Totals	24	1	5	6	13

O'Reilly, Cal   b. Toronto, Ontario, September 30, 1986

2010–11 NAS	38	6	12	18	2
NHL Totals	80	11	23	34	8

O'Reilly, Ryan   b. Clinton, Ontario, February 7, 1991

2010–11 COL	74	13	13	26	16
NHL Totals	155	21	31	52	34

Oreskovich, Victor   b. Whitby, Ontario, August 15, 1986

2010–11 VAN	16	0	3	3	8
NHL Totals	66	2	7	9	34

Orpik, Brooks   b. San Francisco, California, September 26, 1980

2010–11 PIT	63	1	12	13	66
NHL Totals	512	9	84	93	595

Orr, Colton   b. Winnipeg, Manitoba, March 3, 1982

2010–11 TOR	46	2	0	2	128
NHL Totals	373	10	9	19	916

Ortmeyer, Jed   b. Omaha, Nebraska, September 3, 1978

2010–11 MIN	4	0	0	0	2
NHL Totals	310	21	30	51	147

Osgood, Chris   b. Peace River, Alberta, November 26, 1972

2010–11 DET	11	5–3–2	629	29	0	2.77
NHL Totals	744	401–216–95	42,563	1,768	50	2.49

•retired in July 2011

Oshie, T.J.   b. Mt. Vernon, Washington, December 23, 1986

2010–11 STL	49	12	22	34	15
NHL Totals	182	44	77	121	81

O'Sullivan, Patrick   b. Winston-Salem, North Carolina, February 1, 1985

2010–11 CAR/MIN	31	2	6	8	4
NHL Totals	311	56	101	157	114

• claimed off waivers by Minnesota from Carolina on November 23, 2010

Ott, Steve   b. Summerside, Prince Edward Island, August 19, 1982

2010–11 DAL	82	12	20	32	183
NHL Totals	492	74	107	181	1,014

Ovechkin, Alexander   b. Moscow, Soviet Union (Russia), September 17, 1985

2010–11 WAS	79	32	53	85	41
NHL Totals	475	301	313	614	346

Oystrick, Nathan   b. Regina, Saskatchewan, December 17, 1982

2010–11 STL	9	1	2	3	9
NHL Totals	65	5	10	15	61

Paajarvi, Magnus   b. Norrkoping, Sweden, April 12, 1991

2010–11 EDM	80	15	19	34	16
NHL Totals	80	15	19	34	16

Pacioretty, Max   b. New Canaan, Connecticut, November 20, 1988

2010–11 MON	37	14	10	24	39
NHL Totals	123	20	29	49	86

Pahlsson, Samuel   b. Ornskoldsvik, Sweden, December 17, 1977

2010–11 CBJ	82	7	13	20	30
NHL Totals	718	64	118	182	322

Paille, Daniel   b. Welland, Ontario, April 15, 1984

2010–11 BOS	43	6	7	13	28
NHL Totals	312	51	58	109	94

Palmieri, Kyle   b. Smithtown, New York, February 1, 1991

2010–11 ANA	10	1	0	1	0
NHL Totals	10	1	0	1	0

Palmieri, Nick   b. Utica, New York, July 12, 1989

2010–11 NJ	43	9	8	17	6
NHL Totals	49	9	9	18	6

Palushaj, Aaron   b. Livonia, Michigan, September 7, 1989

2010–11 MON	3	0	0	0	2
NHL Totals	3	0	0	0	2

Pardy, Adam   b. Bonavista, Newfoundland, March 29, 1984

2010–11 CAL	30	1	6	7	24
NHL Totals	147	4	22	26	141

Parent, Ryan   b. Prince Albert, Saskatchewan, March 17, 1987

2010–11 VAN	4	0	0	0	0
NHL Totals	106	1	6	7	36

Parenteau, P-A   b. Hull, Quebec, March 24, 1983

2010–11 NYI	81	20	33	53	46
NHL Totals	108	23	39	62	52

Parise, Zach   b. Minneapolis, Minnesota, July 28, 1984

2010–11 NJ	13	3	3	6	6
NHL Totals	420	163	178	341	145

Parrish, Mark   b. Edina, Minnesota, February 2, 1977

2010–11 BUF	2	0	0	0	0
NHL Totals	722	216	171	387	246

Parros, George   b. Washington, Pennsylvania, December 29, 1979

2010–11 ANA	78	3	1	4	171
NHL Totals	367	16	13	29	865

Parse, Scott   b. Portage, Michigan, September 5, 1984

2010–11 LA	5	1	3	4	0
NHL Totals	64	12	16	28	22

Pavelec, Ondrej   b. Kladno, Czechoslovakia (Czech Republic), August 31, 1987

2010–11 ATL	58	21–23–9	3,225	147	4	2.73
NHL Totals	119	41–51–16	6,489	328	6	3.03

Pavelski, Joe   b. Plover, Wisconsin, July 11, 1984

2010–11 SJ	74	20	46	66	24
NHL Totals	349	103	141	244	142

Peckham, Theo   b. Richmond Hill, Ontario, November 10, 1987

2010–11 EDM	71	3	10	13	198
NHL Totals	102	3	11	14	302

Pelley, Rod   b. Kitimat, British Columbia, September 1, 1984

2010–11 NJ	74	3	7	10	27
NHL Totals	204	7	19	26	86

Penner, Dustin   b. Winkler, Manitoba, September 28, 1982

2010–11 EDM/LA	81	23	22	45	47
NHL Totals	424	128	116	244	263

• traded by Edmonton to Los Angeles on February 28, 2011, for Colton Teubert, a 1st-round draft choice in 2011 and a conditional 2nd-round draft choice in 2012

Perrault, Joel   b. Montreal, Quebec, April 6, 1983

2010–11 VAN	7	0	0	0	0
NHL Totals	96	12	14	26	68

Perreault, Mathieu   b. Drummondville, Quebec, January 5, 1988

2010–11 WAS	35	7	7	14	20
NHL Totals	56	11	12	23	26

Perron, David   b. Sherbrooke, Quebec, May 28, 1988

2010–11 STL	10	5	2	7	12
NHL Totals	235	53	78	131	160

Perry, Corey   b. Peterborough, Ontario, May 16, 1985

2010–11 ANA	82	50	48	98	104
NHL Totals	450	168	201	369	537

Peters, Justin   b. Blyth, Ontario, August 30, 1986

2010–11 CAR	12	3–5–1	648	43	0	3.98
NHL Totals	21	9–8–1	1,136	66	0	3.49

Peters, Warren b. Saskatoon, Saskatchewan, July 10, 1982

2010–11 MIN	11	1	0	1	4
NHL Totals	38	3	0	3	18

Petersen, Toby b. Minneapolis, Minnesota, October 27, 1978

2010–11 DAL	60	2	4	6	8
NHL Totals	358	31	45	76	44

Petiot, Richard b. Daysland, Alberta, August 20, 1982

2010–11 EDM	2	0	0	0	2
NHL Totals	15	0	3	3	25

Petry, Jeff b. Ann Arbor, Michigan, December 9, 1987

2010–11 EDM	35	1	4	5	10
NHL Totals	35	1	4	5	10

Peverley, Rich b. Guelph, Ontario, July 8, 1982

2010–11 ATL/BOS	82	18	21	41	37
NHL Totals	276	60	91	151	114

• traded by Atlanta to Boston on February 18, 2011, with Boris Valabik for Blake Wheeler and Mark Stuart

Phaneuf, Dion b. Edmonton, Alberta, April 10, 1985

2010–11 TOR	66	8	22	30	88
NHL Totals	470	85	183	268	644

Phillips, Chris b. Calgary, Alberta, March 9, 1978

2010–11 OTT	82	1	8	9	32
NHL Totals	945	60	177	237	655

Picard, Alexandre b. Gatineau, Quebec, July 5, 1985

2010–11 MON	43	3	5	8	17
NHL Totals	236	19	46	65	82

Pielmeier, Timo b. Deggendorf, West Germany (Germany), July 7, 1989

2010–11 ANA	1	0–0–0	40	5	0	7.50
NHL Totals	1	0–0–0	40	5	0	7.50

Pietrangelo, Alex b. King City, Ontario, January 18, 1990

2010–11 STL	79	11	32	43	19
NHL Totals	96	12	34	46	27

Pirri, Brandon b. Toronto, Ontario, April 10, 1991

| 2010–11 CHI | 1 | 0 | 0 | 0 | 0 |
| NHL Totals | 1 | 0 | 0 | 0 | 0 |

Pisani, Fernando b. Edmonton, Alberta, December 27, 1976

| 2010–11 CHI | 60 | 7 | 9 | 16 | 10 |
| NHL Totals | 462 | 87 | 82 | 169 | 200 |

Pitkanen, Joni b. Oulu, Finland, September 19, 1983

| 2010–11 CAR | 72 | 5 | 30 | 35 | 60 |
| NHL Totals | 483 | 51 | 205 | 256 | 456 |

Plante, Alex b. Brandon, Manitoba, May 9, 1989

| 2010–11 EDM | 3 | 0 | 0 | 0 | 11 |
| NHL Totals | 7 | 0 | 1 | 1 | 13 |

Plekanec, Tomas b. Kladno, Czechoslovakia (Czech Republic), October 31, 1982

| 2010–11 MON | 77 | 22 | 35 | 57 | 60 |
| NHL Totals | 470 | 125 | 186 | 311 | 274 |

Polak, Roman b. Ostrava, Czechoslovakia (Czech Republic), April 28, 1986

| 2010–11 STL | 55 | 3 | 9 | 12 | 33 |
| NHL Totals | 227 | 8 | 41 | 49 | 143 |

Pominville, Jason b. Repentigny, Quebec, November 30, 1982

| 2010–11 BUF | 73 | 22 | 30 | 52 | 15 |
| NHL Totals | 459 | 145 | 213 | 358 | 127 |

Ponikarovsky, Alexei b. Kiev, Soviet Union (Ukraine), April 9, 1980

| 2010–11 LA | 61 | 5 | 10 | 15 | 36 |
| NHL Totals | 554 | 121 | 160 | 281 | 371 |

Porter, Chris b. Toronto, Ontario, May 29, 1984

| 2010–11 STL | 45 | 3 | 4 | 7 | 16 |
| NHL Totals | 51 | 4 | 5 | 9 | 16 |

Porter, Kevin b. Detroit, Michigan, March 12, 1986

| 2010–11 COL | 74 | 14 | 11 | 25 | 27 |
| NHL Totals | 128 | 21 | 17 | 38 | 31 |

Postma, Paul b. Red Deer, Alberta, February 22, 1989

| 2010–11 ATL | 1 | 0 | 0 | 0 | 0 |
| NHL Totals | 1 | 0 | 0 | 0 | 0 |

Poti, Tom   b. Worcester, Massachusetts, March 22, 1977

2010–11 WAS	21	2	5	7	8
NHL Totals	808	69	256	325	586

Potter, Corey   b. Lansing, Michigan, January 5, 1984

2010–11 PIT	1	0	0	0	0
NHL Totals	9	1	1	2	2

Potulny, Ryan   b. Grand Forks, North Dakota, September 5, 1984

2010–11 CHI/OTT	10	0	0	0	0
NHL Totals	126	22	27	49	54

• traded by Chicago to Ottawa on February 28, 2011, with a 2nd-round draft choice in 2011
  for Chris Campoli and a 7th-round draft choice in 2012

Poulin, Kevin   b. Montreal, Quebec, April 12, 1990

2010–11 NYI	10	4–2–1	491	20	0	2.44
NHL Totals	10	4–2–1	491	20	0	2.44

Pouliot, Benoit   b. Alfred, Ontario, September 29, 1986

2010–11 MON	79	13	17	30	87
NHL Totals	183	37	35	72	148

Pouliot, Marc-Antoine   b. Quebec City, Quebec, May 22, 1985

2010–11 TB	3	0	0	0	0
NHL Totals	179	21	32	53	74

Powe, Darroll   b. Saskatoon, Saskatchewan, June 22, 1985

2010–11 PHI	81	7	10	17	41
NHL Totals	204	22	21	43	130

Price, Carey   b. Vancouver, British Columbia, August 16, 1987

2010–11 MON	72	38–28–6	4,206	165	8	2.35
NHL Totals	206	98–76–24	12,013	520	12	2.60

Pronger, Chris   b. Dryden, Ontario, October 10, 1974

2010–11 PHI	50	4	21	25	44
NHL Totals	1,154	156	530	686	1,580

Prospal, Vaclav   b. Ceske Budejovice, Czechoslovakia (Czech Republic), February 17, 1975

2010–11 NYR	29	9	14	23	8
NHL Totals	978	227	453	680	513

Prosser, Nate b. Elk River, Minnesota, May 7, 1986

2010–11 MIN	2	0	0	0	0
NHL Totals	5	0	1	1	8

Prucha, Petr b. Chrudim, Czechoslovakia (Czech Republic), September 14, 1982

2010–11 PHO	11	0	1	1	4
NHL Totals	346	78	68	146	133

Prust, Brandon b. London, Ontario, March 16, 1984

2010–11 NYR	82	13	16	29	160
NHL Totals	197	19	27	46	456

Purcell, Teddy b. St. John's, Newfoundland, September 8, 1985

2010–11 TB	81	17	34	51	10
NHL Totals	191	28	57	85	24

Pyatt, Taylor b. Thunder Bay, Ontario, August 19, 1981

2010–11 PHO	76	18	13	31	27
NHL Totals	682	121	124	245	381

Pyatt, Tom b. Thunder Bay, Ontario, February 14, 1987

2010–11 MON	61	2	5	7	9
NHL Totals	101	4	8	12	19

Quick, Jonathan b. Milford, Connecticut, January 21, 1986

2010–11 LA	61	35–22–3	3,591	134	6	2.24
NHL Totals	180	96–66–12	10,484	426	14	2.44

Quincey, Kyle b. Kitchener, Ontario, August 12, 1985

2010–11 COL	21	0	1	1	18
NHL Totals	185	11	58	69	161

Rafalski, Brian b. Dearborn, Michigan, September 28, 1973

2010–11 DET	63	4	44	48	22
NHL Totals	833	79	436	515	282

•retired at season's end

Rakhshani, Rhett b. Orange, California, March 6, 1988

2010–11 NYR	2	0	0	0	0
NHL Totals	2	0	0	0	0

Rask, Tuukka b. Savonlinna, Finland, March 10, 1987

2010–11 BOS	29	11–14–2	1,594	71	2	2.67
NHL Totals	79	36–27–8	4,400	165	8	2.25

Raycroft, Andrew b. Belleville, Ontario, May 4, 1980

2010–11 DAL	19	8–5–0	847	40	2	2.83
NHL Totals	270	111–106–17	14,662	701	9	2.87

Raymond, Mason b. Cochrane, Alberta, September 17, 1985

2010–11 VAN	70	15	24	39	10
NHL Totals	273	60	76	136	84

Reasoner, Marty b. Honeoye Falls, New York, February 26, 1977

2010–11 FLO	82	14	18	32	22
NHL Totals	706	96	159	255	341

Reaves, Ryan b. Winnipeg, Manitoba, January 20, 1987

2010–11 STL	28	2	2	4	78
NHL Totals	28	2	2	4	78

Recchi, Mark b. Kamloops, British Columbia, February 1, 1968

2010–11 BOS	81	14	34	48	35
NHL Totals	1,652	577	956	1,533	1,033

• retired at season's end

Reddox, Liam b. East York (Toronto), Ontario, January 27, 1986

2010–11 EDM	44	1	9	10	20
NHL Totals	100	6	18	24	34

Reese, Dylan b. Pittsburgh, Pennsylvania, August 29, 1984

2010–11 NYI	27	0	6	6	15
NHL Totals	46	2	8	10	29

Regehr, Robyn b. Recife, Brazil, April 19, 1980

2010–11 CAL	79	2	15	17	58
NHL Totals	826	29	134	163	802

Regin, Peter b. Herning, Denmark, April 16, 1986

2010–11 OTT	55	3	14	17	12
NHL Totals	141	17	31	48	34

Reimer, James b. Winnipeg, Manitoba, March 15, 1988

2010–11 TOR	37	20–10–5	2,080	90	3	2.60
NHL Totals	37	20–10–5	2,080	90	3	2.60

Reinprecht, Steve   b. Edmonton, Alberta, May 7, 1976

2010–11 FLO	29	4	6	10	6	
NHL Totals	663	140	242	382	186	

Repik, Michal   b. Vlasim, Czechoslovakia (Czech Republic), December 31, 1988

2010–11 FLO	31	2	6	8	22	
NHL Totals	55	7	8	15	30	

Ribeiro, Mike   b. Montreal, Quebec, February 10, 1980

2010–11 DAL	82	19	52	71	28	
NHL Totals	663	155	342	497	278	

Richards, Brad   b. Murray Harbour, Prince Edward Island, May 2, 1980

2010–11 DAL	72	28	49	77	24	
NHL Totals	772	220	496	716	177	

Richards, Mike   b. Kenora, Ontario, February 11, 1985

2010–11 PHI	81	23	43	66	62	
NHL Totals	453	133	216	349	397	

Richardson, Brad   b. Belleville, Ontario, February 4, 1985

2010–11 LA	68	7	12	19	47	
NHL Totals	316	37	54	91	143	

Rinne, Pekka   b. Kempele, Finland, November 3, 1982

2010–11 NAS	64	33–22–9	3,789	134	6	2.12
NHL Totals	177	95–54–18	10,126	394	20	2.33

Rissmiller, Pat   b. Belmont, Massachusetts, October 26, 1978

2010–11 ATL/FLO	10	0	1	1	0	
NHL Totals	192	18	28	46	60	

• traded by Atlanta to Florida on February 28, 2011, with Niclas Bergfors for Radek Dvorak and a 5th-round draft choice in 2011

Ritola, Mattias   b. Borlange, Sweden, March 14, 1987

2010–11 TB	31	4	4	8	11	
NHL Totals	38	4	5	9	11	

Rivet, Craig   b. North Bay, Ontario, September 13, 1974

2010–11 BUF/CBJ	37	2	2	4	35	
NHL Totals	923	50	187	237	1,171	

• claimed off re-entry waivers by Columbus from Buffalo on February 26, 2011

Robidas, Stephane   b. Sherbrooke, Quebec, March 3, 1977

2010–11 DAL	81	5	25	30	67
NHL Totals	724	45	161	206	555

Rodney, Bryan   b. London, Ontario, April 22, 1984

2010–11 CAR	3	0	0	0	2
NHL Totals	33	1	12	13	12

Roloson, Dwayne   b. Simcoe, Ontario, October 12, 1969

2010–11 NYI/TB	54	24–25–5	3,199	138	4	2.59
NHL Totals	566	214–241–42–37	32,198	1,424	28	2.65

• traded by the Islanders to Tampa Bay on January 1, 2011, for Ty Wishart

Rolston, Brian   b. Flint, Michigan, February 21, 1973

2010–11 NJ	65	14	20	34	34
NHL Totals	1,186	335	402	737	458

Rome, Aaron   b. Nesbitt, Manitoba, September 27, 1983

2010–11 VAN	56	1	4	5	53
NHL Totals	131	2	10	12	110

Rosehill, Jay   b. Olds, Alberta, July 16, 1985

2010–11 TOR	26	1	2	3	71
NHL Totals	41	2	3	5	138

Roy, Derek   b. Ottawa, Ontario, May 4, 1983

2010–11 BUF	35	10	25	35	16
NHL Totals	469	144	239	383	277

Roy, Mathieu   b. St-Georges, Quebec, August 10, 1983

2010–11 TB	4	0	0	0	2
NHL Totals	65	2	11	13	76

Rozsival, Michal   b. Vlasim, Czechoslovakia (Czech Republic), September 3, 1978

2010–11 NYR/PHO	65	6	15	21	42
NHL Totals	702	63	184	247	555

• traded by the Rangers to Phoenix on January 10, 2011, for Wojtek Wolski

Rupp, Mike   b. Cleveland, Ohio, January 13, 1980

2010–11 PIT	81	9	8	17	124
NHL Totals	497	49	40	89	656

Russell, Kris   b. Caroline, Alberta, May 2, 1987

2010–11 CBJ	73	5	18	23	37
NHL Totals	276	16	60	76	111

Ruutu, Jarkko   b. Vantaa, Finland, August 23, 1975

2010–11 OTT/ANA	73	3	9	12	97
NHL Totals	652	58	84	142	1,078

• traded by Ottawa to Anaheim on February 17, 2011, for a 6th-round draft choice in 2011

Ruutu, Tuomo   b. Vantaa, Finland, February 16, 1983

2010–11 CAR	82	19	38	57	54
NHL Totals	460	111	154	265	458

Ryan, Bobby   b. Cherry Hill, New Jersey, March 17, 1987

2010–11 ANA	82	34	37	71	61
NHL Totals	250	105	97	202	181

Ryder, Michael   b. St. John's, Newfoundland, March 31, 1980

2010–11 BOS	79	18	23	41	26
NHL Totals	549	162	172	334	243

Rypien, Rick   b. Coleman, Alberta, May 16, 1984

2010–11 VAN	9	0	1	1	31
NHL Totals	119	9	7	16	226

•died August 15, 2011

Salei, Ruslan   b. Minsk, Soviet Union (Belarus), November 2, 1974

2010–11 DET	75	2	8	10	48
NHL Totals	917	45	159	204	1,065

Salmela, Anssi   b. Tampere, Finland, August 13, 1984

2010–11 NJ	48	1	6	7	14
NHL Totals	112	4	17	21	44

Salo, Sami   b. Turku, Finland, September 2, 1974

2010–11 VAN	27	3	4	7	14
NHL Totals	692	84	196	280	242

Samson, Jerome   b. Greenfield Park, Quebec, September 4, 1987

2010–11 CAR	23	0	2	2	0
NHL Totals	30	0	4	4	10

Samsonov, Sergei   b. Moscow, Soviet Union (Russia), October 27, 1978

2010–11 CAR/FLO	78	13	27	40	14
NHL Totals	888	235	336	571	209

• traded by Carolina to Florida on February 28, 2011, for Bryan Allen

Samuelsson, Mikael   b. Mariefred, Sweden, December 23, 1976

2010–11 VAN	75	18	32	50	36
NHL Totals	615	134	177	311	344

Santorelli, Mike   b. Vancouver, British Columbia, December 14, 1985

2010–11 FLO	82	20	21	41	20
NHL Totals	114	22	22	44	30

Sarich, Cory   b. Saskatoon, Saskatchewan, August 16, 1978

2010–11 CAL	76	4	13	17	75
NHL Totals	825	19	120	139	969

Sauer, Mike   b. St. Cloud, Minnesota, August 7, 1987

2010–11 NYR	76	3	12	15	75
NHL Totals	79	3	12	15	75

Sauve, Yann   b. Montreal, Quebec, February 18, 1990

2010–11 VAN	5	0	0	0	0
NHL Totals	5	0	0	0	0

Savard, Marc   b. Ottawa, Ontario, July 17, 1977

2010–11 BOS	25	2	8	10	29
NHL Totals	807	207	499	706	737

Sawada, Raymond   b. Richmond, British Columbia, February 19, 1985

2010–11 DAL	1	0	0	0	0
NHL Totals	11	1	0	1	0

Sbisa, Luca   b. Ozieri, Italy, January 30, 1990

2010–11 ANA	68	2	9	11	43
NHL Totals	115	2	16	18	85

Scandella, Marco   b. Montreal, Quebec, February 23, 1990

2010–11 MIN	20	0	2	2	2
NHL Totals	20	0	2	2	2

Scatchard, Dave b. Hinton, Alberta, February 20, 1976

2010–11 STL	8	0	1	1	6
NHL Totals	659	128	141	269	1,040

Sceviour, Colton b. Red Deer, Alberta, April 20, 1989

2010–11 DAL	1	0	0	0	0
NHL Totals	1	0	0	0	0

Schaefer, Peter b. Regina, Saskatchewan, July 12, 1977

2010–11 VAN	16	1	1	2	2
NHL Totals	572	99	162	261	200

Schenn, Brayden b. Saskatoon, Saskatchewan, August 22, 1991

2010–11 LA	8	0	2	2	0
NHL Totals	9	0	2	2	0

Schenn, Luke b. Saskatoon, Saskatchewan, November 2, 1989

2010–11 TOR	82	5	17	22	34
NHL Totals	231	12	41	53	155

Schlemko, David b. Edmonton, Alberta, May 7, 1987

2010–11 PHO	43	4	10	14	24
NHL Totals	63	5	15	20	32

Schneider, Cory b. Marblehead, Massachusetts, March 18, 1986

2010–11 VAN	25	16–4–2	1,372	51	1	2.23
NHL Totals	35	18–9–3	1,805	76	1	2.52

Schremp, Rob b. Syracuse, New York, July 1, 1986

2010–11 NYI/ATL	63	13	13	26	16
NHL Totals	114	20	34	54	26

• claimed off waivers by Atlanta from the Islanders on February 28, 2011

Schultz, Jeff b. Calgary, Alberta, February 25, 1986

2010–11 WAS	72	1	9	10	12
NHL Totals	319	10	56	66	109

Schultz, Nick b. Strasbourg, Saskatchewan, August 25, 1982

2010–11 MIN	74	3	14	17	38
NHL Totals	681	25	100	125	292

Scott, John b. St. Catharines, Ontario, September 26, 1982

2010–11 CHI	40	0	1	1	72
NHL Totals	111	1	3	4	183

Scuderi, Rob b. Syosset, New York, December 30, 1978

2010–11 LA	82	2	13	15	16
NHL Totals	455	5	60	65	149

Seabrook, Brent b. Richmond, British Columbia, April 20, 1985

2010–11 CHI	82	9	39	48	47
NHL Totals	474	39	153	192	422

Sedin, Daniel b. Ornskoldsvik, Sweden, September 26, 1980

2010–11 VAN	82	41	63	104	32
NHL Totals	787	249	402	651	324

Sedin, Henrik b. Ornskoldsvik, Sweden, September 26, 1980

2010–11 VAN	82	19	75	94	40
NHL Totals	810	157	509	666	458

Segal, Brandon b. Richmond, British Columbia, July 12, 1983

2010–11 DAL	46	5	5	10	41
NHL Totals	92	11	11	22	79

Seguin, Tyler b. Brampton, Ontario, January 31, 1992

2010–11 BOS	74	11	11	22	18
NHL Totals	74	11	11	22	18

Seidenberg, Dennis b. Schwenningen, West Germany (Germany), July 18, 1981

2010–11 BOS	81	7	25	32	41
NHL Totals	455	25	123	148	193

Sekera, Andrej b. Bojnice, Czechoslovakia (Slovakia), June 8, 1986

2010–11 BUF	76	3	26	29	34
NHL Totals	233	12	55	67	80

Selanne, Teemu b. Helsinki, Finland, July 3, 1970

2010–11 ANA	73	31	49	80	49
NHL Totals	1,259	637	703	1,340	570

Semin, Alexander b. Krasjonarsk, Soviet Union (Russia), March 3, 1984

2010–11 WAS	65	28	26	54	71
NHL Totals	392	176	178	354	394

Sestito, Tim   b. Rome, New York, August 28, 1984

2010–11 NJ	36	0	2	2	9
NHL Totals	46	0	3	3	11

Sestito, Tom   b. Rome, New York, September 28, 1987

2010–11 CBJ	9	2	2	4	40
NHL Totals	13	2	2	4	64

Setoguchi, Devin   b. Taber, Alberta, January 1, 1987

2010–11 SJ	72	22	19	41	37
NHL Totals	267	84	75	159	89

Sexton, Dan   b. Apple Valley, Minnesota, April 29, 1987

2010–11 ANA	47	4	9	13	4
NHL Totals	88	13	19	32	20

Shannon, Ryan   b. Darien, Connecticut, March 2, 1983

2010–11 OTT	79	11	16	27	26
NHL Totals	260	31	56	87	80

Sharp, Patrick   b. Thunder Bay, Ontario, December 27, 1981

2010–11 CHI	74	34	37	71	38
NHL Totals	493	160	156	316	339

Shattenkirk, Kevin   b. Greenwich, Connecticut, January 29, 1989

2010–11 COL/STL	72	9	34	43	36
NHL Totals	72	9	34	43	36

• traded by Colorado to St. Louis on February 19, 2011, with Chris Stewart and a conditional 2nd-round draft choice in 2011 or 2012 for Erik Johnson, Jay McClement and a conditional 1st-round draft choice in 2011 or 2012

Shelley, Jody   b. Thompson, Manitoba, February 7, 1976

2010–11 PHI	58	2	2	4	127
NHL Totals	596	18	35	53	1,474

Shirokov, Sergei   b. Ozery, Soviet Union (Russia), March 10, 1986

2010–11 VAN	2	1	0	1	0
NHL Totals	8	1	0	1	2

Sim, Jon   b. New Glasgow, Nova Scotia, September 29, 1977

2010–11 NYI	34	1	3	4	22
NHL Totals	469	75	64	139	314

Simmonds, Wayne   b. Scarborough (Toronto), Ontario, August 26, 1988

2010–11 LA	80	14	16	30	75
NHL Totals	240	39	54	93	264

Sims, Shane   b. East Amherst, New York, April 30, 1988

2010–11 NYI	1	0	0	0	0
NHL Totals	1	0	0	0	0

Sjostrom, Fredrik   b. Fargelanda, Sweden, May 6, 1983

2010–11 TOR	66	2	3	5	14
NHL Totals	489	46	58	104	190

Skille, Jack   b. Madison, Wisconsin, May 19, 1987

2010–11 CHI/FLO	62	8	11	19	29
NHL Totals	92	13	14	27	34

• traded by Chicago to Florida on February 9, 2011, with Hugh Jessiman and David Pacan for Alexander Salak and Michael Frolik

Skinner, Jeff   b. Markham, Ontario, May 16, 1992

2010–11 CAR	82	31	32	63	46
NHL Totals	82	31	32	63	46

Skrastins, Karlis   b. Riga, Soviet Union (Latvia), July 9, 1974

2010–11 DAL	74	3	5	8	38
NHL Totals	832	32	104	136	375

Slater, Jim   b. Petoskey, Michigan, December 9, 1982

2010–11 ATL	36	5	7	12	19
NHL Totals	371	47	53	100	280

Sloan, Tyler   b. Calgary, Alberta, March 15, 1981

2010–11 WAS	33	1	5	6	14
NHL Totals	99	4	13	17	50

Smaby, Matt   b. Minneapolis, Minnesota, October 14, 1984

2010–11 TB	32	0	0	0	17
NHL Totals	122	0	6	6	106

Smid, Ladislav   b. Frydlant, Czechoslovakia (Czech Republic), February 1, 1986

2010–11 EDM	78	0	10	10	85
NHL Totals	331	4	40	44	276

Smith, Ben   b. Winston-Salem, North Carolina, July 11, 1988

2010–11 CHI	6	1	0	1	0
NHL Totals	6	1	0	1	0

Smith, Derek   b. Belleville, Ontario, October 13, 1984

2010–11 OTT	9	0	1	1	0
NHL Totals	11	0	1	1	0

Smith, Mike   b. Kingston, Ontario, March 22, 1982

2010–11 TB	22	13–6–1	1,202	58	1	2.90
NHL Totals	162	67–66–19	9,105	412	11	2.71

Smith, Zack   b. Medicine Hat, Alberta, April 5, 1988

2010–11 OTT	55	4	5	9	120
NHL Totals	71	6	6	12	134

Smithson, Jerred   b. Vernon, British Columbia, February 4, 1979

2010–11 NAS	82	5	8	13	34
NHL Totals	474	35	49	84	308

Smyth, Ryan   b. Banff, Alberta, February 21, 1976

2010–11 LA	82	23	24	47	35
NHL Totals	1,069	355	405	760	810

Sobotka, Vladimir   b. Trebic, Czechoslovakia (Czech Republic), July 2, 1987

2010–11 STL	65	7	22	29	69
NHL Totals	199	13	38	51	133

Sopel, Brent   b. Calgary, Alberta, January 7, 1977

2010–11 ATL/MON	71	2	5	7	16
NHL Totals	659	44	174	218	309

• traded by Atlanta to Montreal on February 24, 2011, with Nigel Dawes for Ben Maxwell and a 4th-round draft choice in 2011

Spacek, Jaroslav   b. Rokycany, Czechoslovakia (Czech Republic), February 11, 1974

2010–11 MON	59	1	15	16	45
NHL Totals	834	77	263	340	610

Spaling, Nick   b. Palmerston, Ontario, September 19, 1988

2010–11 NAS	74	8	6	14	20
NHL Totals	102	8	9	17	20

Spezza, Jason b. Mississauga, Ontario, June 13, 1983

2010–11 OTT	62	21	36	57	28
NHL Totals	526	192	340	532	350

Spurgeon, Jared b. Edmonton, Alberta, November 29, 1989

2010–11 MIN	53	4	8	12	2
NHL Totals	53	4	8	12	2

Staal, Eric b. Thunder Bay, Ontario, October 29, 1984

2010–11 CAR	81	33	43	76	72
NHL Totals	560	226	278	504	429

Staal, Jordan b. Thunder Bay, Ontario, September 10, 1988

2010–11 PIT	42	11	19	30	24
NHL Totals	369	95	103	198	197

Staal, Marc b. Thunder Bay, Ontario, January 13, 1987

2010–11 NYR	77	7	22	29	50
NHL Totals	321	20	61	81	200

Stafford, Drew b. Milwaukee, Wisconsin, October 30, 1985

2010–11 BUF	62	31	21	52	34
NHL Totals	317	94	102	196	182

Stafford, Garrett b. Los Angeles, California, January 28, 1980

2010–11 PHO	2	0	0	0	0
NHL Totals	7	0	2	2	0

Staios, Steve b. Hamilton, Ontario, July 28, 1973

2010–11 CAL	39	3	7	10	24
NHL Totals	936	56	156	212	1,269

Stajan, Matt b. Mississauga, Ontario, December 19, 1983

2010–11 CAL	76	6	25	31	32
NHL Totals	548	96	174	270	281

Stalberg, Viktor b. Stockholm, Sweden, January 17, 1986

2010–11 CHI	77	12	12	24	43
NHL Totals	117	21	17	38	73

Stalock, Alex b. St. Paul, Minnesota, July 28, 1987

2010–11 SJ	1	1–0–0	30	0	0	0.00
NHL Totals	1	1–0–0	30	0	0	0.00

Stamkos, Steve   b. Markham, Ontario, February 7, 1960

2010–11 TB	82	45	46	91	74
NHL Totals	243	119	113	232	151

Stapleton, Tim   b. LaGrange, Illinois, July 9, 1982

2010–11 ATL	45	5	2	7	12
NHL Totals	55	8	2	10	14

Stastny, Paul   b. Quebec City, Quebec, December 27, 1985

2010–11 COL	74	22	35	57	56
NHL Totals	348	105	216	321	194

Staubitz, Brad   b. Brights Grove, Ontario, July 28, 1984

2010–11 MIN	71	4	5	9	173
NHL Totals	153	8	10	18	359

Steckel, David   b. Milwaukee, Wisconsin, March 15, 1982

2010–11 WAS/NJ	7	56	6	12	26
NHL Totals	309	24	35	59	115

• traded by Washington to New Jersey on February 28, 2011, with a 2nd-round draft choice in 2012 for Jason Arnott

Steen, Alexander   b. Winnipeg, Manitoba, March 1, 1984

2010–11 STL	72	20	31	51	26
NHL Totals	454	100	148	248	186

Stempniak, Lee   b. Buffalo, New York, February 4, 1983

2010–11 PHO	82	19	19	38	19
NHL Totals	456	115	132	247	173

Stepan, Derek   b. Hastings, Minnesota, June 18, 1990

2010–11 NYR	82	21	24	45	20
NHL Totals	82	21	24	45	20

Sterling, Brett   b. Los Angeles, California, April 24, 1984

2010–11 PIT	7	3	2	5	16
NHL Totals	26	5	4	9	32

Stewart, Anthony   b. LaSalle, Quebec, January 5, 1985

2010–11 ATL	80	14	25	39	55
NHL Totals	185	18	33	51	93

Stewart, Chris   b. Toronto, Ontario, October 30, 1987

| 2010–11 COL/STL | 62 | 28 | 25 | 53 | 53 |
| NHL Totals | 192 | 67 | 69 | 136 | 180 |

• traded by Colorado to St. Louis on February 19, 2011, with Kevin Shattenkirk and a conditional 2nd-round draft choice in 2011 or 2012 for Jay McClement, Erik Johnson and a conditional 1st-round draft choice in 2011 or 2012

Stillman, Cory   b. Peterborough, Ontario, December 20, 1973

| 2010–11 FLO/CAR | 65 | 12 | 27 | 39 | 24 |
| NHL Totals | 1,025 | 278 | 449 | 727 | 489 |

• traded by Florida to Carolina on February 24, 2011, for Ryan Carter and a 5th-round draft choice in 2011

St. Louis, Martin   b. Laval, Quebec, June 18, 1975

| 2010–11 TB | 82 | 31 | 68 | 99 | 12 |
| NHL Totals | 854 | 298 | 480 | 778 | 250 |

Stoa, Ryan   b. Bloomington, Minnesota, April 13, 1987

| 2010–11 COL | 25 | 2 | 2 | 4 | 20 |
| NHL Totals | 37 | 4 | 3 | 7 | 20 |

Stoll, Jarret   b. Melville, Saskatchewan, June 25, 1982

| 2010–11 LA | 82 | 20 | 23 | 43 | 42 |
| NHL Totals | 515 | 113 | 183 | 296 | 388 |

Stoner, Clayton   b. Port McNeill, British Columbia, February 19, 1985

| 2010–11 MIN | 57 | 2 | 7 | 9 | 96 |
| NHL Totals | 65 | 2 | 9 | 11 | 108 |

Stortini, Zack   b. Elliot Lake, Ontario, September 11, 1985

| 2010–11 EDM | 32 | 0 | 4 | 4 | 76 |
| NHL Totals | 256 | 14 | 27 | 41 | 718 |

Strachan, Tyson   b. Melfort, Saskatchewan, October 30, 1984

| 2010–11 STL | 29 | 0 | 1 | 1 | 39 |
| NHL Totals | 67 | 0 | 6 | 6 | 82 |

Strait, Brian   b. Boston, Massachusetts, January 4, 1988

| 2010–11 PIT | 3 | 0 | 0 | 0 | 0 |
| NHL Totals | 3 | 0 | 0 | 0 | 0 |

Stralman, Anton   b. Tibro, Sweden, August 1, 1986

2010–11 CBJ	51	1	17	18	22
NHL Totals	212	11	63	74	97

Strudwick, Jason   b. Edmonton, Alberta, July 17, 1975

2010–11 EDM	43	0	2	2	23
NHL Totals	674	13	42	55	811

Stuart, Brad   b. Rocky Mountain House, Alberta, November 6, 1979

2010–11 DET	67	3	17	20	40
NHL Totals	795	68	216	284	460

Stuart, Colin   b. Rochester, Minnesota, July 8, 1982

2010–11 BUF	3	0	0	0	2
NHL Totals	54	8	5	13	26

Stuart, Mark   b. Rochester, Minnesota, April 27, 1984

2010–11 BOS/ATL	54	2	4	6	47
NHL Totals	306	14	27	41	308

• traded by Boston to Atlanta on February 18, 2011, with Blake Wheeler for Rich Peverley and Boris Valabik

Sturm, Marco   b. Dingolfing, West Germany (Germany), September 8, 1978

2010–11 LA/WAS	35	5	11	16	23
NHL Totals	890	239	243	482	421

• claimed off waivers by Washington from Los Angeles on February 26, 2011

Subban, P.K.   b. Toronto, Ontario, May 13, 1989

2010–11 MON	77	14	24	38	124
NHL Totals	79	14	26	40	126

Sullivan, Steve   b. Timmins, Ontario, July 6, 1974

2010–11 NAS	44	10	12	22	28
NHL Totals	890	266	416	682	543

Sulzer, Alexander   b. Kaufbeuren, West Germany (Germany), May 30, 1984

2010–11 NAS/FLO	40	1	4	5	14
NHL Totals	62	1	6	7	18

• traded by Nashville to Florida on February 25, 2011, for a conditional 7th-round draft choice in 2012

Summers, Chris   b. Ann Arbor, Michigan, February 5, 1988

2010–11 PHO	2	0	0	0	4
NHL Totals	2	0	0	0	4

Suter, Ryan   b. Madison, Wisconsin, January 21, 1985

2010–11 NAS	70	4	35	39	54
NHL Totals	463	31	161	192	366

Sutherby, Brian   b. Edmonton, Alberta, March 1, 1982

2010–11 DAL	51	2	2	4	58
NHL Totals	460	41	49	90	533

Sutter, Brandon   b. Huntington, New York, February 14, 1989

2010–11 CAR	82	14	15	29	25
NHL Totals	204	36	39	75	43

Sutter, Brett   b. Viking, Alberta, June 2, 1987

2010–11 CAL/CAR	5	0	1	1	5
NHL Totals	19	1	1	2	12

• traded by Calgary to Carolina on November 17, 2010, with Ian White for Anton Babchuk and Tom Kostopoulos

Sutton, Andy   b. Kingston, Ontario, March 10, 1975

2010–11 ANA	39	0	4	4	87
NHL Totals	624	35	105	140	1,105

Svatos, Marek   b. Kosice, Czechoslovakia (Slovakia), July 17, 1982

2010–11 NAS/OTT	28	4	4	8	10
NHL Totals	344	100	72	172	217

• claimed off waivers by Ottawa from Nashville on February 24, 2011

Sweatt, Lee   b. Elburn, Illinois, August 13, 1985

2010–11 VAN	3	1	1	2	2
NHL Totals	3	1	1	2	2

Syvret, Danny   b. Millgrove, Ontario, June 13, 1985

2010–11 ANA/PHI	10	1	1	2	6
NHL Totals	59	3	4	7	30

• traded by Anaheim to Philadelphia on November 21, 2010, with Rob Bordson for Patrick Maroon and David Laliberte

Taffe, Jeff   b. Hastings, Minnesota, February 19, 1981

2010–11 CHI	1	0	0	0	0
NHL Totals	175	21	23	44	40

Talbot, Maxime   b. Lemoyne, Quebec, February 11, 1984

2010–11 PIT	82	8	13	21	66
NHL Totals	388	52	56	108	324

Tallinder, Henrik   b. Stockholm, Sweden, January 10, 1979

2010–11 NJ	82	5	11	16	40
NHL Totals	550	25	99	124	318

Tambellini, Jeff   b. Calgary, Alberta, April 13, 1984

2010–11 VAN	62	9	8	17	18
NHL Totals	242	27	36	63	88

Tanev, Chris   b. Toronto, Ontario, December 20, 1989

2010–11 VAN	29	0	1	1	0
NHL Totals	29	0	1	1	0

Tangradi, Eric   b. Philadelphia, Pennsylvania, February 10, 1989

2010–11 PIT	15	1	2	3	10
NHL Totals	16	1	2	3	10

Tanguay, Alex   b. Ste-Justine, Quebec, November 21, 1979

2010–11 CAL	79	22	47	69	24
NHL Totals	818	225	461	686	401

Taormina, Matt   b. Washington Township, Michigan, October 20, 1986

2010–11 NJ	17	3	2	5	2
NHL Totals	17	3	2	5	2

Tatar, Tomas   b. Ilava, Czechoslovakia (Slovakia), December 1, 1990

2010–11 DET	9	1	0	1	0
NHL Totals	9	1	0	1	0

Tavares, John   b. Mississauga, Ontario, September 20, 1990

2010–11 NYI	79	29	38	67	53
NHL Totals	161	53	68	121	75

Tedenby, Mattias   b. Vetlanda, Sweden, February 21, 1990

2010–11 NJ	58	8	14	22	14
NHL Totals	58	8	14	22	14

Theodore, Jose   b. Laval, Quebec, September 13, 1976

2010–11 MIN	32	15–11–3	1,793	81	1	2.71
NHL Totals	580	260–232–55	32,790	1,468	30	2.69

Thomas, Bill   b. Pittsburgh, Pennsylvania, June 20, 1983

2010–11 FLO	24	4	3	7	6	
NHL Totals	80	15	12	27	18	

Thomas, Tim   b. Flint, Michigan, April 15, 1974

2010–11 BOS	57	35–11–9	3,364	112	9	2.00
NHL Totals	319	161–102–44	18,432	767	26	2.50

Thompson, Nate   b. Anchorage, Alaska, October 5, 1984

2010–11 TB	79	10	15	25	29	
NHL Totals	197	14	25	39	134	

Thorburn, Chris   b. Sault Ste. Marie, Ontario, June 3, 1983

2010–11 ATL	82	9	10	19	77	
NHL Totals	354	28	43	71	438	

Thornton, Joe   b. London, Ontario, July 2, 1979

2010–11 SJ	80	21	49	70	47	
NHL Totals	995	306	695	1,001	932	

Thornton, Shawn   b. Oshawa, Ontario, July 23, 1977

2010–11 BOS	79	10	10	20	122	
NHL Totals	369	25	35	60	618	

Thuresson, Andreas   b. Kristianstad, Sweden, November 18, 1987

2010–11 NAS	3	0	0	0	2	
NHL Totals	25	1	2	3	6	

Timmins, Scott   b. Hamilton, Ontario, September 11, 1989

2010–11 FLO	19	1	0	1	8	
NHL Totals	19	1	0	1	8	

Timonen, Kimmo   b. Kuopio, Finland, March 18, 1975

2010–11 PHI	82	6	31	37	36	
NHL Totals	894	102	362	464	538	

Tlusty, Jiri   b. Slany, Czechoslovakia (Czech Republic), March 16, 1988

2010–11 CAR	57	6	6	12	14	
NHL Totals	149	17	21	38	34	

Toews, Jonathan   b. Winnipeg, Manitoba, April 29, 1988

2010–11 CHI	80	32	44	76	26	
NHL Totals	302	115	152	267	168	

Tootoo, Jordin b. Churchill, Manitoba, February 2, 1983

2010–11 NAS	54	8	10	18	61	
NHL Totals	409	40	55	95	633	

Torres, Raffi b. Toronto, Ontario, October 8, 1981

2010–11 VAN	80	14	15	29	78	
NHL Totals	512	112	99	211	390	

Turco, Marty b. Sault Ste. Marie, Ontario, August 13, 1975

2010–11 CHI	29	11–11–3	1,631	82	1	3.02
NHL Totals	538	273–165–66	30,695	1,200	41	2.35

Turris, Kyle b. New Westminster, British Columbia, August 14, 1989

2010–11 PHO	65	11	14	25	16	
NHL Totals	131	19	27	46	39	

Tyrell, Dana b. Airdrie, Alberta, April 23, 1989

2010–11 TB	78	6	9	15	12	
NHL Totals	78	6	9	15	12	

Tyutin, Fedor b. Izhevsk, Soviet Union (Russia), July 19, 1983

2010–11 CBJ	80	7	20	27	32	
NHL Totals	492	37	122	159	321	

Umberger, R.J. b. Pittsburgh, Pennsylvania, May 3, 1982

2010–11 CBJ	82	25	32	57	38	
NHL Totals	474	123	151	274	209	

Upshall, Scottie b. Fort McMurray, Alberta, October 7, 1983

2010–11 PHO/CBJ	82	22	12	34	52	
NHL Totals	361	86	86	172	325	

• traded by Phoenix to Columbus on February 28, 2011, with Sami Lepisto for Dane Byers and Rostislav Klesla

Urbom, Alexander b. Stockholm, Sweden, December 20, 1990

2010–11 NJ	8	1	0	1	0	
NHL Totals	8	1	0	1	0	

Van der Gulik, David b. Abbotsford, British Columbia, April 20, 1983

2010–11 COL	6	1	2	3	2	
NHL Totals	12	1	4	5	2	

Vandermeer, Jim   b. Caroline, Alberta, February 21, 1980

2010–11 EDM	62	2	12	14	74
NHL Totals	436	24	77	101	631

VandeVelde, Chris   b. Moorhead, Minnesota, March 15, 1987

2010–11 EDM	12	0	2	2	12
NHL Totals	12	0	2	2	12

Vanek, Thomas   b. Vienna, Austria, January 19, 1984

2010–11 BUF	80	32	41	73	24
NHL Totals	469	204	182	386	286

van Riemsdyk, James   b. Middletown, New Jersey, May 4, 1989

2010–11 PHI	75	21	19	40	35
NHL Totals	153	36	39	75	65

Varlamov, Semyon   b. Kuybyshev, Soviet Union (Russia), April 27, 1988

2010–11 WAS	27	11–9–5	1,560	58	2	2.23
NHL Totals	59	30–13–12	3,416	136	4	2.39

Vasyunov, Alexander   b. Yaroslavl, Soviet Union (Russia), April 22, 1988

2010–11 NJ	18	1	4	5	0
NHL Totals	18	1	4	5	0

Vermette, Antoine   b. St-Agapit, Quebec, July 20, 1982

2010–11 CBJ	82	19	28	47	60
NHL Totals	540	133	159	292	305

Vernace, Michael   b. Toronto, Ontario, May 26, 1986

2010–11 TB	10	0	1	1	2
NHL Totals	22	0	1	1	10

Versteeg, Kris   b. Lethbridge, Alberta, May 13, 1986

2010–11 TOR/PHI	80	21	25	46	53
NHL Totals	250	65	82	147	149

• traded by Toronto to Philadelphia on February 14, 2011, for a 1st- and 3rd-round draft choice in 2011

Vincour, Tomas   b. Brno, Czechoslovakia (Czech Republic), November 19, 1990

2010–11 DAL	24	1	1	2	4
NHL Totals	24	1	1	2	4

Visnovsky, Lubomir b. Topolcany, Czechoslovakia (Slovakia), August 11, 1976

2010–11 ANA	81	18	50	68	24
NHL Totals	703	111	312	423	288

Vitale, Joe b. St. Louis, Missouri, August 20, 1985

2010–11 PIT	9	1	1	2	13
NHL Totals	9	1	1	2	13

Vlasic, Marc-Edouard b. Montreal, Quebec, March 30, 1987

2010–11 SJ	80	4	14	18	18
NHL Totals	389	18	92	110	135

Vokoun, Tomas b. Karlovy Vary, Czechoslovakia (Czech Republic), July 2, 1976

2010–11 FLO	57	22–28–5	3,224	137	6	2.55
NHL Totals	632	262–267–76	36,082	1,538	44	2.56

Volchenkov, Anton b. Moscow, Soviet Union (Russia), February 25, 1982

2010–11 NJ	57	0	8	8	36
NHL Totals	485	16	86	102	333

Volpatti, Aaron b. Revelstoke, British Columbia, May 30, 1985

2010–11 VAN	15	1	1	2	16
NHL Totals	15	1	1	2	16

Voracek, Jakub b. Kladno, Czechoslovakia (Czech Republic), August 15, 1989

2010–11 CBJ	80	14	32	46	26
NHL Totals	241	39	95	134	96

Voros, Aaron b. Vancouver, British Columbia, July 2, 1981

2010–11 ANA	12	0	0	0	43
NHL Totals	162	18	19	37	395

Vrbata, Radim b. Mlada Boleslav, Czechoslovakia (Czech Republic), June 13, 1981

2010–11 PHO	79	19	29	48	20
NHL Totals	601	148	175	323	170

Walker, Matt b. Beaverlodge, Alberta, April 7, 1980

2010–11 PHI	4	0	0	0	4
NHL Totals	310	4	26	30	448

Wallace, Tim b. Anchorage, Alaska, August 6, 1984

2010–11 PIT	7	0	0	0	5
NHL Totals	24	0	2	2	12

Wallin, Niclas b. Boden, Sweden, February 20, 1975

2010–11 SJ	74	3	5	8	46
NHL Totals	614	21	58	79	460

Wandell, Tom b. Sodertalje, Sweden, January 29, 1987

2010–11 DAL	75	7	2	9	14
NHL Totals	139	13	14	27	32

Ward, Cam b. Sherwood Park, Alberta, February 29, 1984

2010–11 CAR	74	37–26–10	4,318	184	4	2.56
NHL Totals	346	175–126–33	19,732	901	16	2.74

Ward, Joel b. Toronto, Ontario, December 2, 1980

2010–11 NAS	80	10	19	29	42
NHL Totals	241	40	59	99	89

Wathier, Francis b. St. Isidore, Ontario, December 7, 1984

2010–11 DAL	3	0	0	0	0
NHL Totals	8	0	0	0	5

Weaver, Mike b. Bramalea, Ontario, May 2, 1978

2010–11 FLO	82	2	11	13	34
NHL Totals	421	6	49	55	168

Weber, Mike b. Pittsburgh, Pennsylvania, December 16, 1987

2010–11 BUF	58	4	13	17	69
NHL Totals	81	4	16	20	102

Weber, Shea b. Sicamous, British Columbia, August 14, 1985

2010–11 NAS	82	16	32	48	56
NHL Totals	402	80	134	214	323

Weber, Yannick b. Morges, Switzerland, September 23, 1988

2010–11 MON	41	1	10	11	14
NHL Totals	49	1	11	12	20

Weight, Doug b. Warren, Michigan, January 21, 1971

2010–11 NYI	18	2	7	9	10
NHL Totals	1,238	278	755	1,033	970

• retired at season's end

Weise, Dale b. Winnipeg, Manitoba, August 5, 1988

2010–11 NYR	10	0	0	0	19
NHL Totals	10	0	0	0	19

Weiss, Stephen b. Toronto, Ontario, April 3, 1983

2010–11 FLO	76	21	28	49	49
NHL Totals	557	124	209	333	228

Welch, Noah b. Brighton, Massachusetts, August 26, 1982

2010–11 ATL	2	0	0	0	0
NHL Totals	75	4	5	9	58

Wellman, Casey b. Brentwood, California, October 18, 1987

2010–11 MIN	15	1	1	2	4
NHL Totals	27	2	4	6	4

Wellwood, Eric b. Windsor, Ontario, March 6, 1990

2010–11 PHI	3	0	1	1	2
NHL Totals	3	0	1	1	2

Wellwood, Kyle b. Windsor, Ontario, May 16, 1983

2010–11 SJ	35	5	8	13	0
NHL Totals	373	68	105	173	30

Westgarth, Kevin b. Amherstburg, Ontario, February 7, 1984

2010–11 LA	56	0	3	3	105
NHL Totals	65	0	3	3	114

Wheeler, Blake b. Robbinsdale, Minnesota, August 31, 1986

2010–11 BOS/ATL	81	18	26	44	46
NHL Totals	244	57	70	127	145

• traded by Boston to Atlanta on February 18, 2011, with Mark Stuart for Rich Peverley and Boris Valabik

White, Colin b. New Glasgow, Nova Scotia, December 12, 1977

2010–11 NJ	69	0	6	6	48
NHL Totals	743	20	105	125	848

White, Ian b. Winnipeg, Manitoba, June 4, 1984

2010–11 CAL/CAR/SJ	78	4	22	26	26
NHL Totals	401	36	107	143	228

• traded by Calgary to Carolina on November 17, 2010, with Brett Sutter for Anton Babchuk and Tom Kostopoulos
• traded by Carolina to San Jose on February 18, 2011, for a 2nd-round draft choice in 2012

White, Ryan   b. Brandon, Manitoba, March 17, 1988

2010–11 MON	27	2	3	5	38
NHL Totals	43	2	5	7	54

White, Todd   b. Kanata, Ontario, May 21, 1975

2010–11 NYR	18	1	1	2	2
NHL Totals	653	141	240	381	228

Whitney, Ray   b. Fort Saskatchewan, Alberta, May 8, 1972

2010–11 PHO	75	17	40	57	24
NHL Totals	1,147	341	585	926	419

Whitney, Ryan   b. Boston, Massachusetts, February 19, 1983

2010–11 EDM	35	2	25	27	33
NHL Totals	389	43	183	226	338

Wick, Roman   b. Kloten, Switzerland, December 30, 1985

2010–11 OTT	7	0	0	0	0
NHL Totals	7	0	0	0	0

Wideman, Dennis   b. Kitchener, Ontario, March 20, 1983

2010–11 FLO/WAS	75	10	30	40	39
NHL Totals	453	56	149	205	331

• traded by Florida to Washington on February 28, 2011, for Jake Hauswirth and a 3rd-round draft choice in 2011

Wiercioch, Patrick   b. Burnaby, British Columbia, September 12, 1990

2010–11 OTT	8	0	2	2	4
NHL Totals	8	0	2	2	4

Williams, Jason   b. London, Ontario, August 11, 1980

2010–11 DAL	27	2	3	5	6
NHL Totals	447	93	132	225	153

Williams, Jeremy   b. Regina, Saskatchewan, January 26, 1984

2010–11 NYR	1	0	0	0	0
NHL Totals	32	9	2	11	6

Williams, Justin   b. Cobourg, Ontario, October 4, 1981

2010–11 LA	73	22	35	57	59
NHL Totals	625	157	249	406	431

Willsie, Brian   b. London, Ontario, March 16, 1978

2010–11 WAS	1	0	1	1	0
NHL Totals	381	52	57	109	217

Wilson, Clay   b. Sturgeon Lake, Minnesota, April 5, 1983

2010–11 FLO	15	3	2	5	6
NHL Totals	31	4	4	8	8

Wilson, Colin   b. Greenwich, Connecticut, October 20, 1989

2010–11 NAS	82	16	18	34	17
NHL Totals	117	24	25	49	24

Wilson, Kyle   b. Oakville, Ontario, December 15, 1984

2010–11 CBJ	32	4	7	11	12
NHL Totals	34	4	9	13	12

Wilson, Ryan   b. Windsor, Ontario, February 3, 1987

2010–11 COL	67	3	13	16	68
NHL Totals	128	6	31	37	104

Winchester, Brad   b. Madison, Wisconsin, March 1, 1981

2010–11 STL/ANA	76	10	6	16	114
NHL Totals	323	31	27	58	464

• traded by St. Louis to Anaheim on February 28, 2011, for a 3rd-round draft choice in 2012

Winchester, Jesse   b. Long Sault, Ontario, October 4, 1983

2010–11 OTT	72	4	9	13	42
NHL Totals	201	9	35	44	99

Wingels, Tommy   b. Evanston, Illinois, April 12, 1988

2010–11 SJ	5	0	0	0	0
NHL Totals	5	0	0	0	0

Winnik, Daniel   b. Toronto, Ontario, March 6, 1985

2010–11 COL	80	11	15	26	35
NHL Totals	282	29	49	78	135

Wishart, Ty   b. Belleville, Ontario, May 19, 1988

2010–11 NYI	20	1	4	5	10
NHL Totals	25	1	5	6	10

Wisniewski, James   b. Canton, Michigan, February 21, 1984

2010–11 NYI/MON	75	10	41	51	38
NHL Totals	329	27	121	148	302

• traded by the Islanders to Montreal on December 28, 2011, for a 2nd-round draft choice in 2011 and a conditional 5th-round draft choice in 2012

Wolski, Wojtek   b. Zabrze, Poland, February 24, 1986

2010–11 PHO/NYR	73	12	23	35	18
NHL Totals	393	91	155	246	105

• traded by Phoenix to the Rangers on January 10, 2011, for Michal Rozsival

Woywitka, Jeff   b. Vermilion, Alberta, September 1, 1983

2010–11 DAL	63	2	9	11	24
NHL Totals	251	8	41	49	141

Wright, James   b. Saskatoon, Saskatchewan, March 24, 1990

2010–11 TB	1	0	0	0	0
NHL Totals	49	2	3	5	18

Yandle, Keith   b. Boston, Massachusetts, September 9, 1986

2010–11 PHO	82	11	48	59	68
NHL Totals	283	32	112	144	172

Yip, Brandon   b. Vancouver, British Columbia, April 25, 1985

2010–11 COL	71	12	10	22	54
NHL Totals	103	23	18	41	76

Yonkman, Nolan   b. Punnichy, Saskatchewan, April 1, 1981

2010–11 PHO	16	0	1	1	39
NHL Totals	66	1	8	9	129

Zajac, Travis   b. Winnipeg, Manitoba, May 13, 1985

2010–11 NJ	82	13	31	44	24
NHL Totals	408	89	160	249	124

Zanon, Greg   b. Burnaby, British Columbia, June 5, 1980

2010–11 MIN	82	0	7	7	48
NHL Totals	393	9	39	48	184

Zeiler, John   b. Jefferson Hills, Pennsylvania, November 21, 1982

2010–11 LA	4	0	0	0	0
NHL Totals	90	1	4	5	87

Zetterberg, Henrik   b. Njurunda, Sweden, October 9, 1980

2010–11 DET	80	24	56	80	40
NHL Totals	586	230	325	555	224

Zharkov, Vladimir   b. Elektrostal, Soviet Union (Russia), January 10, 1988

2010–11 NJ	38	2	2	4	2
NHL Totals	78	2	12	14	10

Zherdev, Nikolai   b. Kiev, Soviet Union (Russia), November 5, 1984

2010–11 PHI	56	16	6	22	22
NHL Totals	421	115	146	261	225

Zidlicky, Marek   b. Most, Czechoslovakia (Czech Republic), February 3, 1977

2010–11 MIN	46	7	17	24	30
NHL Totals	507	60	224	284	472

Zigomanis, Mike   b. Toronto, Ontario, January 17, 1981

2010–11 TOR	8	0	1	1	4
NHL Totals	197	21	19	40	89

Zubarev, Andrei   b. Ufa, Soviet Union (Russia), March 3, 1987

2010–11 ATL	4	0	1	1	4
NHL Totals	4	0	1	1	4

Zubrus, Dainius   b. Eelektrenai, Soviet Union (Lithuania), June 16, 1978

2010–11 NJ	79	13	17	30	53
NHL Totals	983	189	306	495	637

Zuccarello, Mats   b. Oslo, Norway, September 1, 1987

2010–11 NYR	42	6	17	23	4
NHL Totals	42	6	17	23	4

COACHES' REGISTER, 2010–11

(OTL are listed in ties column)

	Games	W	L	T
Arniel, Scott b. Kingston, Ontario, September 17, 1962				
2010-11 CBJ	82	34	35	13
NHL Totals	82	34	35	13
• hired June 8, 2010				
Babcock, Mike b. Manitouwadge, Ontario, April 29, 1963				
2010-11 DET	82	47	25	10
NHL Totals	656	373	188	95
• hired July 14, 2005				
Boucher, Guy b. Notre-Dame-du-Lac, Quebec, August 3, 1971				
2010-11 TB	82	46	25	11
NHL Totals	82	46	25	11
• hired June 10, 2010				
Boudreau, Bruce b. Toronto, Ontario, January 9, 1955				
2010–11 WAS	82	48	23	11
NHL Totals	307	189	79	39
• hired November 22, 2007				
Bylsma, Dan b. Grand Haven, Michigan, September 19, 1970				
2010–11 PIT	82	49	25	8
NHL Totals	189	114	56	19
• hired February 15, 2009				
Capuano, Jack b. Cranston, Rhode Island, July 7, 1966				
2010-11 NYI	65	26	29	10
NHL Totals	65	26	29	10
• hired November 15, 2010				
Carlyle, Randy b. Sudbury, Ontario, April 19, 1956				
2010–11 ANA	82	47	30	5
NHL Totals	492	266	169	57
• hired August 1, 2005				

Clouston, Cory   b. Viking, Alberta, September 19, 1969

2010–11 OTT	82	32	40	10
NHL Totals	198	95	83	20

• hired February 2, 2009; fired April 9, 2011

Crawford, Marc   b. Belleville, Ontario, February 13, 1961

2010–11 DAL	82	42	28	11
NHL Totals	1,151	549	420	181

• hired June 11, 2009; fired April 12, 2011

DeBoer, Peter   b. Dunnville, Ontario, June 13, 1968

2010–11 FLO	82	30	40	12
NHL Totals	246	103	107	36

• hired June 13, 2008; fired April 10, 2011
• hired by New Jersey on July 19, 2011

Dineen, Kevin   b. Quebec City, Quebec, October 28, 1963

• hired by Florida on June 1, 2011

Gordon, Scott   b. Easton, Massachusetts, February 6, 1963

2010–11 NYI	17	4	10	3
NHL Totals	164	60	84	20

• hired August 12, 2008; fired November 15, 2010

Gulutzan, Glen   b. The Pas, Manitoba, August 12, 1971

• hired by Dallas on June 17, 2011

Julien, Claude   b. Orleans, Ontario, April 23, 1960

2010–11 BOS	82	46	25	11
NHL Totals	566	298	189	79

• hired June 21, 2007

Laviolette, Peter   b. Norwood, Massachusetts, December 7, 1964

2010–11 PHI	82	47	23	12
NHL Totals	626	319	231	76

• hired December 4, 2009

Lemaire, Jacques   b. LaSalle, Quebec, September 7, 1945

2010–11 NJ	49	29	17	3
NHL Totals	1,262	617	458	187

• hired December 23, 2010; resigned April 10, 2011

MacLean, John   b. Oshawa, Ontario, November 20, 1964

2010-11 NJ	33	9	22	2
NHL Totals	33	9	22	2

• hired June 17, 2010; fired December 23, 2010

MacLean, Paul   b. Grostenquin, France, March 9, 1958
• hired by Ottawa on June 13, 2011

Martin, Jacques   b. St. Pascal, Ontario, October 1, 1952

2010–11 MON	82	44	30	8
NHL Totals	1,262	600	469	193

• hired June 1, 2009

Maurice, Paul   b. Sault Ste. Marie, Ontario, January 30, 1967

2010–11 CAR	82	40	31	11
NHL Totals	1,059	452	444	163

• hired December 3, 2008

McLellan, Todd   b. Melville, Saskatchewan, October 3, 1967

2010–11 SJ	82	48	25	9
NHL Totals	246	152	63	31

• hired June 12, 2008

Murray, Terry   b. Shawville, Quebec, July 20, 1950

2010–11 LA	82	46	30	6
NHL Totals	983	486	371	126

• hired July 17, 2008

Noel, Claude   b. Kirkland Lake, Ontario, October 31, 1955

NHL Totals	24	10	8	6

• hired by Winnipeg on June 24, 2011

Payne, Davis   b. King City, Ontario, October 24, 1970

2010–11 STL	82	38	33	11
NHL Totals	124	61	48	5

• hired January 2, 2010

Quenneville, Joel   b. Windsor, Ontario, September 15, 1958

2010–11 CHI	82	44	29	9
NHL Totals	1,081	579	356	146

• hired October 16, 2008

Ramsay, Craig   b. March 17, 1951, Weston (Toronto), Ontario
| 2010–11 ATL | 82 | 34 | 36 | 12 |
| NHL Totals | 131 | 50 | 63 | 8 |

• hired June 24, 2010; fired June 20, 2011, after franchise relocated to Winnipeg

Renney, Tom   b. Cranbrook, British Columbia, March 1, 1955
| 2010-11 EDM | 82 | 25 | 45 | 12 |
| NHL Totals | 510 | 228 | 215 | 66 |

• hired June 22, 2010

Richards, Todd   b. Crystal, Minnesota, October 20, 1966
| 2010–11 MIN | 82 | 39 | 35 | 8 |
| NHL Totals | 164 | 77 | 71 | 16 |

• hired June 16, 2009; fired April 11, 2011

Ruff, Lindy   b. Warburg, Alberta, February 17, 1960
| 2010–11 BUF | 82 | 43 | 29 | 10 |
| NHL Totals | 1,066 | 526 | 390 | 150 |

• hired July 21, 1997

Sacco, Joe   b. Medford, Massachusetts, February 4, 1969
| 2010–11 COL | 82 | 30 | 44 | 8 |
| NHL Totals | 164 | 73 | 74 | 17 |

• hired June 4, 2009

Sutter, Brent   b. Viking, Alberta, June 10, 1962
| 2010–11 CAL | 82 | 41 | 29 | 12 |
| NHL Totals | 328 | 178 | 117 | 33 |

• hired June 23, 2009

Tippett, Dave   b. Moosomin, Saskatchewan, August 25, 1961
| 2010–11 PHO | 82 | 43 | 26 | 13 |
| NHL Totals | 656 | 364 | 207 | 85 |

• hired September 24, 2009

Tortorella, John   b. Boston, Massachusetts, June 24, 1958
| 2010–11 NYR | 82 | 44 | 33 | 5 |
| NHL Totals | 724 | 333 | 298 | 93 |

• hired February 23, 2009

Trotz, Barry   b. Winnipeg, Manitoba, July 15, 1962

2010–11 NAS	82	44	27	11
NHL Totals	984	455	398	131

• hired August 6, 1997, a year before the Predators played their first NHL game

Vigneault, Alain   b. Quebec City, Quebec, May 14, 1961

2010–11 VAN	82	54	19	9
NHL Totals	676	345	251	80

• hired June 20, 2006

Wilson, Ron   b. Windsor, Ontario, May 28, 1955

2010–11 TOR	82	37	34	11
NHL Totals	1,337	619	533	185

• hired June 10, 2008

Yeo, Mike   b. North Bay, Ontario, July 31, 1973
• hired by Minnesota on June 17, 2011

2011 NHL ENTRY DRAFT

St. Paul, Minnesota, June 24–25, 2011

First Round

1. Edmonton—Ryan Nugent-Hopkins (CAN)
2. Colorado—Gabriel Landeskog (SWE)
3. Florida—Jonathan Huberdeau (CAN)
4. New Jersey—Adam Larsson (SWE)
5. NY Islanders—Ryan Strome (CAN)
6. Ottawa—Mika Zibanejad (SWE)
7. Winnipeg—Mark Scheifele (CAN)
8. Philadelphia—Sean Couturier (CAN/USA)
9. Boston—Doug Hamilton (CAN)
10. Minnesota—Jonas Brodin (SWE)
11. Colorado—Duncan Siemens (CAN)
12. Carolina—Ryan Murphy (CAN)
13. Calgary—Sven Bartschi (SUI)
14. Dallas—Jamieson Oleksiak (CAN)
15. NY Rangers—Jonathan Miller (USA)
16. Buffalo—Joel Armia (FIN)
17. Montreal—Nathan Beaulieu (CAN)
18. Chicago—Mark McNeill (CAN)
19. Edmonton—Oscar Klefbom (SWE)
20. Phoenix—Connor Murphy (USA)
21. Ottawa—Stefan Noesen (USA)
22. Toronto—Tyler Biggs (USA)
23. Pittsburgh—Joseph Morrow (CAN)
24. Ottawa—Matt Puempel (CAN)
25. Toronto—Stuart Percy (CAN)
26. Chicago—Phillip Danault (CAN)
27. Tampa Bay—Vladislav Namestnikov (RUS)
28. Minnesota—Zack Phillips (CAN)
29. Vancouver—Nicklas Jensen (DEN)
30. Anaheim—Rickard Rakell (SWE)

Second Round

31. Edmonton—David Musil (CAN)
32. St. Louis—Ty Rattie (CAN)
33. Florida—Rocco Grimaldi (USA)
34. NY Islanders—Scott Mayfield (USA)
35. Detroit—Tomas Jurco (SVK)

36.   Chicago—Adam Clendening (USA)
37.   Columbus—Boone Jenner (CAN)
38.   Nashville—Magnus Hellberg (SWE)
39.   Anaheim—John Gibson (USA)
40.   Boston—Alexander Khokhlachev (RUS)
41.   St. Louis—Dmitri Yaskin (RUS)
42.   Carolina—Victor Rask (SWE)
43.   Chicago—Brandon Saad (USA)
44.   Dallas—Brett Ritchie (CAN)
45.   Calgary—Markus Granlund (FIN)
46.   St. Louis—Joel Edmundson (CAN)
47.   San Jose—Matthew Nieto (USA)
48.   Detroit—Xavier Oullet (FRA)
49.   Los Angeles—Christopher Gibson (FIN)
50.   NY Islanders—Johan Sundstrom (SWE)
51.   Phoenix—Alexander Ruutu (USA)
52.   Nashville—Miikka Salomaki (FIN)
53.   Anaheim—William Karlsson (SWE)
54.   Pittsburgh—Scott Harrington (CAN)
55.   Detroit—Ryan Sproul (CAN)
56.   Phoenix—Lucas Lessio (CAN)
57.   Calgary—Tyler Wotherspoon (CAN)
58.   Tampa Bay—Nikita Kucherov (RUS)
59.   Florida—Rasmus Bengtsson (SWE)
60.   Minnesota—Mario Lucia (USA)
61.   Ottawa—Shane Prince (USA)

Third Round
62.   Edmonton—Samu Perhonen (FIN)
63.   NY Islanders—Andrei Pedan (LTU)
64.   Florida—Vincent Trocheck (USA)
65.   Anaheim—Joseph Cramarossa (CAN)
66.   Columbus—Thomas Tynan (USA)
67.   Winnipeg—Adam Lowry (USA)
68.   Philadelphia—Nick Cousins (CAN)
69.   *New Jersey—pick forfeited*
70.   Chicago—Michael Paliotta (USA)
71.   Vancouver—David Honzik (CZE)
72.   NY Rangers—Steven Fogarty (USA)
73.   Carolina—Keegan Lowe (USA)
74.   Edmonton—Travis Ewanyk (CAN)
75.   New Jersey—Blake Coleman (USA)

76. Florida—Logan Shaw (CAN)
77. Buffalo—Daniel Catenacci (CAN)
78. Winnipeg—Brennan Serville (CAN)
79. Chicago—Klas Dahlbeck (SWE)
80. Los Angeles—Andy Andreoff (CAN)
81. Boston—Anthony Camara (CAN)
82. Los Angeles—Nicholas Shore (USA)
83. Anaheim—Andy Welinski (USA)
84. Phoenix—Harrison Ruopp (CAN)
85. Detroit—Alan Quine (CAN)
86. Toronto—Josh Leivo (CAN)
87. Florida—Jonathan Racine (CAN)
88. St. Louis—Jordan Binnington (CAN)
89. San Jose—Justin Sefton (CAN)
90. Vancouver—Alexandre Grenier (CAN)
91. Florida—Kyle Rau (USA)

Fourth Round
92. Edmonton—Dillon Simpson (CAN)
93. Colorado—Joachim Nermark (SWE)
94. Nashville—Josh Shalla (CAN)
95. NY Islanders—Robbie Russo (USA)
96. Ottawa—Jean-Gabriel Pageau (CAN)
97. Montreal—Josiah Didier (USA)
98. Columbus—Mike Reilly (USA)
99. New Jersey—Reid Boucher (USA)
100. Toronto—Tom Nilsson (SWE)
101. Vancouver—Joseph Labate (USA)
102. St. Louis—Yannick Veilleux (CAN)
103. Carolina—Gregory Hofmann (SUI)
104. Calgary—John Gaudreau (USA)
105. Dallas—Emil Molin (SWE)
106. NY Rangers—Michael St. Croix (CAN)
107. Buffalo—Colin Jacobs (USA)
108. Montreal—Olivier Archambault (CAN)
109. Chicago—Maxim Shalunov (RUS)
110. Los Angeles—Michael Mersch (USA)
111. Phoenix—Kale Kessy (CAN)
112. Nashville—Garrett Noonan (USA)
113. Montreal—Magnus Nygren (SWE)
114. Edmonton—Tobias Reider (GER)
115. Detroit—Marek Tvrdon (SVK)

116. Philadelphia—Colin Suellentrop (USA)
117. Washington—Steffen Soberg (NOR)
118. Philadelphia—Marcel Noebels (GER)
119. Winnipeg—Zachary Yuen (CAN)
120. Vancouver—Ludwig Blomstrand (SWE)
121. Boston—Brian Ferlin (USA)

Fifth Round

122. Edmonton—Martin Gernat (SVK)
123. Colorado—Garrett Meurs (CAN)
124. Florida—Jaroslav Kosov (RUS)
125. NY Islanders—John Persson (SWE)
126. Ottawa—Fredrik Claesson (SWE)
127. NY Islanders—Brenden Kichton (CAN)
128. Columbus—Seth Ambroz (USA)
129. New Jersey—Blake Pietila (USA)
130. Toronto—Tony Cameranesi (USA)
131. Minnesota—Nick Seeler (USA)
132. St. Louis—Niklas Lundstrom (SWE)
133. San Jose—Sean Kuraly (USA)
134. NY Rangers—Shane McColgan (USA)
135. Dallas—Troy Vance (USA)
136. NY Rangers—Samuel Noreau (CAN)
137. Buffalo—Alex Lepkowski (USA)
138. Montreal—Darren Dietz (CAN)
139. Chicago—Andrew Shaw (CAN)
140. Los Angeles—Joel Lowry (USA)
141. Phoenix—Darian Dziurzynski (CAN)
142. Nashville—Simon Karlsson (SWE)
143. Anaheim—Max Friberg (SWE)
144. Pittsburgh—Dominik Uher (CZE)
145. Detroit—Philippe Hudon (CAN)
146. Detroit—Mattias Backman (SWE)
147. Washington—Patrick Koudys (CAN)
148. Tampa Bay—Nikita Nesterov (RUS)
149. Winnipeg—Austen Brassard (CAN)
150. Vancouver—Frank Corrado (CAN)
151. Boston—Rob O'Gara (USA)

Sixth Round

152. Toronto—David Broll (CAN)
153. Colorado—Gabriel Beaupre (CAN)

154.   Florida—Edward Wittchow (USA)
155.   Phoenix—Andrew Fritsch (CAN)
156.   Ottawa—Darren Kramer (CAN)
157.   Winnipeg—Jason Kasdorf (CAN)
158.   Columbus—Lukas Sedlak (CZE)
159.   New Jersey—Reece Scarlett (CAN)
160.   Anaheim—Josh Manson (CAN)
161.   Minnesota—Stephen Michalek (USA)
162.   St. Louis—Ryan Tesink (USA)
163.   Carolina—Matt Mahalak (USA)
164.   Calgary—Laurent Brossoit (CAN)
165.   Dallas—Matej Stransky (CZE)
166.   San Jose—Daniil Sobchenko (UKR)
167.   Buffalo—Nathan Lieuwen (CAN)
168.   Montreal—Daniel Pribyl (CZE)
169.   Chicago—Sam Jardine (CAN)
170.   Nashville—Chasen Balisy (USA)
171.   Ottawa—Max McCormick (USA)
172.   NY Rangers—Peter Ceresnak (SVK)
173.   Toronto—Dennis Robertson (CAN)
174.   Pittsburgh—Josh Archibald (CAN)
175.   Detroit—Richard Ledomlel (CZE)
176.   Philadelphia—Petr Placek (CZE)
177.   Washington—Travis Boyd (USA)
178.   Tampa Bay—Adam Wilcox (USA)
179.   San Jose—Dylan Demelo (CAN)
180.   Vancouver—Pathrik Westerholm (SWE)
181.   Boston—Lars Volden (NOR)

Seventh Round
182.   Edmonton—Frans Tuohimaa (FIN)
183.   Colorado—Dillon Donnelly (USA)
184.   Florida—Iiro Pakarinen (FIN)
185.   NY Islanders—Mitchell Theoret (CAN)
186.   Ottawa—Jordan Fransoo (CAN)
187.   Winnipeg—Aaron Harstad (USA)
188.   Columbus—Anton Forsberg (SWE)
189.   New Jersey—Patrick Daly (USA)
190.   Toronto—Garret Sparks (USA)
191.   Minnesota—Tyler Graovac (CAN)
192.   St. Louis—Teemu Eronen (FIN)
193.   Carolina—Brody Sutter (CAN)

194. San Jose—Colin Blackwell (USA)
195. Dallas—Jyrki Jokipakka (FIN)
196. Phoenix—Zac Larraza (USA)
197. Buffalo—Brad Navin (USA)
198. Montreal—Colin Sullivan (USA)
199. Chicago—Alexander Broadhurst (USA)
200. Los Angeles—Michael Schumacher (SWE)
201. Tampa Bay—Matthew Peca (CAN)
202. Nashville—Brent Andrews (CAN)
203. Toronto—Max Everson (USA)
204. Ottawa—Ryan Dzingel (USA)
205. Detroit—Alexei Marchenko (RUS)
206. Philadelphia—Derek Mathers (CAN)
207. Washington—Garrett Haar (USA)
208. Tampa Bay—Ondrej Palat (CZE)
209. Pittsburgh—Scott Wilson (CAN)
210. Vancouver—Henrik Tommernes (SWE)
211. Chicago—Johan Mattsson (SWE)

FATHERS & SONS
• Connor Murphy (20th) is the son of former NHLer Gord
• Tyler Biggs (22nd) is the son of former NHLer Don
• Vladislav Namestnikov (27th) is the son of former NHLer Evgeni
• David Musil (31st) is the son of former NHLer Frantisek
• Alexander Ruuttu (51st) is the son of former NHLer Christian
• Keegan Lowe (73rd) is the son of former NHLer Kevin
• Dillon Simpson (91st) is the son of former NHLer Craig
• Tyler Garovac (191st) is the son of former Team Canada junior Tom
• Brody Sutter (103rd) is the son of former NHLer Duane

MODERN OUTDOOR GAMES

Date	Game Promoted As	League	Host City	Venue	Attendance	Score
March 5, 1957	none	IIHF WM	Moscow	Lenin Stadium	55,000	Soviet Union 4, Sweden 4
November 8, 1962	none	SEL	Gothenburg	Ullevi Stadium	23,192	Frolunda 3, Djurgarden 2
September 28, 1991	none	NHL	Las Vegas	Caesars Palace	13,000	Los Angeles 5, NY Rangers 2
October 6, 2001	The Cold War	NCAA	East Lansing, Mich.	Spartan Stadium	74,554	Michigan State 3, Michigan 3
November 22, 2003	Heritage Classic	NHL	Edmonton	Commonwealth Stadium	57,167	Montreal 4, Edmonton 3
February 11, 2006	Frozen Tundra Classic	NCAA	Green Bay, Wisc.	Lambeau Field	40,890	Ohio State 2, Wisconsin 4
January 14, 2007	Tatzen Derby	SUI	Bern	Stade de Suisse	30,076	Langnau 2, Bern 5
January 1, 2008	Winter Classic 1	NHL	Buffalo	Ralph Wilson Stadium	71,217	Pittsburgh 2, Buffalo 1 (SO)
January 10, 2008	All-Star Game	KHL	Moscow	Red Square	3,000	Team Jagr 7, Team Yashin 6
January 1, 2009	Winter Classic 2	NHL	Chicago	Wrigley Field	40,818	Detroit 6, Chicago 4
December 28, 2009	none	SEL	Gothenburg	Ullevi Stadium	31,144	Frolunda 4, Farjestad 1
January 1, 2010	Winter Classic 3	NHL	Boston	Fenway Park	38,112	Boston 2, Philadelphia 1
January 8, 2010	Frozen Fenway	NCAA	Boston	Fenway Park	6,889	New Hampshire 5, Northeastern 3 (women)
January 8, 2010	Frozen Fenway	NCAA	Boston	Fenway Park	38,472	Boston University 3, Boston College 2
January 9, 2010	none	AUT	Klagenfurt	Sportpark	30,500	Klagenfurt 1, Villach 3

February 6, 2010	Camp Randall Hockey Classic	NCAA	Madison, Wisc.	Camp Randall Stadium	8,263	Wisconsin 6, Bemidji State 1 (women)
February 6, 2010	Camp Randall Hockey Classic	NCAA	Madison, Wisc.	Camp Randall Stadium	55,031	Wisconsin 3, Michigan 2
February 20, 2010	Mirabito Outdoor Classic	AHL	Syracuse, N.Y.	New York State Fairgrounds	21,502	Syracuse 2, Binghamton 1
April 8, 2010	Frozen Four Semifinals 1	NCAA	Detroit	Ford Field	34,954	Wisconsin 8, Rochester 1
April 8, 2010	Frozen Four Semifinals 2	NCAA	Detroit	Ford Field	34,954	Boston College 7, Miami (Ohio) 1
April 10, 2010	Frozen Four Final	NCAA	Detroit	Ford Field	37,592	Boston College 5, Wisconsin 0
May 7, 2010	none	IIHF WM	Gelsenkirchen	Veltins Arena	77,803	Germany 2, United States 1 (OT)
December 11, 2010	The Big Chill at the Big House	NCAA	Ann Arbor, Mich.	Michigan Stadium	104,173	Michigan 5, Michigan State 0
December 26, 2010	none	SEL	Karlstad	Lofbergs Lila Utomhusarena	15,274	Farjestad 5, Frolunda 2
January 1, 2011	Winter Classic 4	NHL	Pittsburgh	Heinz Field	68,111	Washington 3, Pittsburgh 1
February 5, 2011	Talviklassikko	FIN	Helsinki	Olympic Stadium	36,644	HIFK 4, Jokerit 3
February 20, 2011	Heritage Classic 2	NHL	Calgary	McMahon Stadium	41,022	Calgary 4, Montreal 0

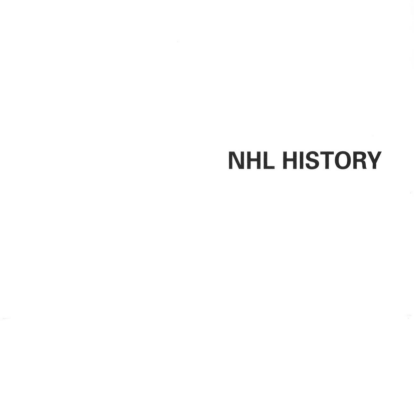

NHL HISTORY

ALL-TIME LEADERS

MOST GAMES

1,767	Gordie Howe
1,756	Mark Messier
1,731	Ron Francis
1,651	Chris Chelios
1,639	Dave Andreychuk

MOST POINTS, REGULAR SEASON

2,857	Wayne Gretzky
1,887	Mark Messier
1,850	Gordie Howe
1,798	Ron Francis
1,771	Marcel Dionne

MOST GOALS, REGULAR SEASON

894	Wayne Gretzky
801	Gordie Howe
741	Brett Hull
731	Marcel Dionne
717	Phil Esposito

MOST ASSISTS, REGULAR SEASON

1,963	Wayne Gretzky
1,249	Ron Francis
1,193	Mark Messier
1,169	Ray Bourque
1,135	Paul Coffey

MOST PENALTY MINUTES, REGULAR SEASON

3,966	Dave "Tiger" Williams
3,565	Dale Hunter
3,515	Tie Domi
3,381	Marty McSorley
3,300	Bob Probert

MOST GAMES, GOALIE, REGULAR SEASON

1,076	Martin Brodeur*
1,029	Patrick Roy
971	Terry Sawchuk
963	Ed Belfour
943	Curtis Joseph

MOST WINS, GOALIE, REGULAR SEASON

602	Martin Brodeur*
551	Patrick Roy
484	Ed Belfour
454	Curtis Joseph
447	Terry Sawchuk

MOST SHUTOUTS, GOALIE, REGULAR SEASON

110	Martin Brodeur*
103	Terry Sawchuk
94	George Hainsworth
84	Glenn Hall
82	Jacques Plante

* active player

YEAR-BY-YEAR STANDINGS AND
STANLEY CUP FINALS RESULTS

After playoff scores, goalies who have registered a shutout will appear in square brackets (i.e., [Broda] means Turk Broda registered a shutout). All overtime goals are also recorded.

1917–18

First Half

	GP	W	L	GF	GA	PTS
Canadiens	14	10	4	81	47	20
Arenas	14	8	6	71	75	16
Ottawa	14	5	9	67	79	10
Wanderers⁺	6	1	5	17	35	2

Second Half

	GP	W	L	GF	GA	PTS
Arenas	8	5	3	37	34	10
Ottawa	8	4	4	35	35	8
Canadiens	8	3	5	34	37	6

⁺ Wanderers' rink burned down on January 2, 1918, and team withdrew from league. Arenas and Canadiens each counted a win for defaulted games with the Wanderers.

* winner of first half played winner of second half in a two-game total-goals series for a place in the Stanley Cup finals against the winner of the Pacific Coast Hockey Association and the Western Canada Hockey League. If one team won both halves, it went to the best-of-five Stanley Cup finals automatically.

* from 1917–21 games were played until a winner decided

NHL Finals

March 11   Canadiens 3 at Arenas 7
March 13   Arenas 3 at Canadiens 4
Arenas won two-game total-goals series 10–7

Stanley Cup Finals

March 20   Vancouver 3 at Toronto 5
March 23   Vancouver 6 at Toronto 4
March 26   Vancouver 3 at Toronto 6
March 28   Vancouver 8 at Toronto 1
March 30   Vancouver 1 at Toronto 2
Toronto won best-of-five finals 3–2

1918–19

First Half

	GP	W	L	GF	GA	PTS
Canadiens	10	7	3	57	50	14
Ottawa	10	5	5	39	39	10
Arenas	10	3	7	42	49	6

Second Half

	GP	W	L	GF	GA	PTS
Ottawa	8	7	1	32	14	14
Canadiens	8	3	5	31	28	6
Arenas	8	2	6	22	43	4

* Spanish influenza epidemic caused the cancellation of the Stanley Cup finals
* the 1918–19 season was supposed to be, like the ones before and after it, a 24–game schedule. However, when Canadiens and Ottawa clinched first place in both halves early, Arenas manager Charlie Querrie refused to play the remaining games, fearing a lack of fan interest. The league almost sued the Arenas, but instead Canadiens and Ottawa played a best-of-seven, rather than a two-game total-goals series, to create extra home dates for the clubs.

NHL Finals

February 22	Ottawa 4 at Canadiens 8
February 27	Canadiens 5 at Ottawa 3
March 1	Ottawa 3 at Canadiens 6
March 3	Canadiens 3 at Ottawa 6
March 6	Ottawa 2 at Canadiens 4

Canadiens won best-of-seven series 4–1

Stanley Cup Finals

March 19	Canadiens 0 at Seattle 7 [Holmes]
March 22	Canadiens 4 at Seattle 2
March 24	Canadiens 2 at Seattle 7
March 26	Canadiens 0 at Seattle 0 (20:00 OT) [Vezina/Holmes]
March 30	Canadiens 4 at Seattle 3 (Odie Cleghorn 15:57 OT)

Finals cancelled after five games because of Spanish influenza and the death of Canadiens player Joe Hall

1919–20

First Half

	GP	W	L	GP	GA	PTS
Ottawa	12	9	3	59	23	18
Canadiens	12	8	4	62	51	16
St. Pats	12	5	7	52	62	10
Bulldogs	12	2	10	44	81	4

Second Half

	GP	W	L	GP	GA	PTS
Ottawa	12	10	2	62	41	20
St. Pats	12	7	5	67	44	14
Canadiens	12	5	7	67	62	10
Bulldogs	12	2	10	47	96	4

No NHL finals because Ottawa won both halves

Stanley Cup Finals

March 22	Seattle 2 at Ottawa 3
March 24	Seattle 0 at Ottawa 3 [Benedict]
March 27	Seattle 3 at Ottawa 1
March 30	Seattle 5 Ottawa 2*
April 1	Ottawa 6 Seattle 1*

Ottawa won best-of-five finals 3–2

* played in Toronto because of poor ice conditions in Ottawa

1920–21

First Half

	GP	W	L	GP	GA	PTS
Ottawa	10	8	2	49	23	16
St. Pats	10	5	5	39	47	10
Canadiens	10	4	6	37	51	8
Hamilton	10	3	7	34	38	6

Second Half

	GP	W	L	GP	GA	PTS
St. Pats	14	10	4	66	53	20
Canadiens	14	9	5	75	48	18
Ottawa	14	6	8	48	52	12
Hamilton	14	3	11	58	94	6

NHL Finals

    March 10   St. Pats 0 at Ottawa 5 [Benedict]
    March 15   Ottawa 2 at St. Pats 0 [Benedict]
    Ottawa won two-game total-goals series 7–0

Stanley Cup Finals

    March 21   Ottawa 1 at Vancouver 3
    March 24   Ottawa 4 at Vancouver 3
    March 28   Ottawa 3 at Vancouver 2
    March 31   Ottawa 2 at Vancouver 3
    April 4   Ottawa 2 at Vancouver 1
    Ottawa won best-of-five finals 3–2

1921–22

	GP	W	L	T	GF	GA	PTS
Ottawa	24	14	8	2	106	84	30
St. Pats	24	13	10	1	98	97	27
Canadiens	24	12	11	1	88	94	25
Hamilton	24	7	17	0	88	105	14

* overtime limited to 20 minutes (not sudden-death); minor penalties reduced from three to two minutes
* top two teams advance to playoffs; winner met the Pacific Coast Hockey Association–Western Canadian Hockey League Champion for the Stanley Cup

NHL Finals

    March 11   Ottawa 4 at St. Pats 5
    March 13   St. Pats 0 at Ottawa 0 [Roach/Benedict]
    St. Pats won two-game total-goals series 5–4

Stanley Cup Finals

    March 17   Vancouver 4 at St. Pats 3
    March 21   Vancouver 1 at St. Pats 2 (Dye 4:50 OT)
    March 23   Vancouver 3 at St. Pats 0 [Lehman]
    March 25   Vancouver 0 at St. Pats 6 [Roach]
    March 28   Vancouver 1 at St. Pats 5
    St. Pats won best-of-five finals 3–2

1922–23

	GP	W	L	T	GF	GA	PTS
Ottawa	24	14	9	1	77	54	29
Canadiens	24	13	9	2	73	61	28
St. Pats	24	13	10	1	82	88	27
Hamilton	24	6	18	0	81	110	12

NHL Finals
March 7   Ottawa 2 at Canadiens 0 [Benedict]
March 9   Canadiens 2 at Ottawa 1
Ottawa won two-game total-goals series 3–2

Stanley Cup Playoffs
March 16   Ottawa 1 at Vancouver 0 [Benedict]
March 19   Ottawa 1 at Vancouver 4
March 23   Ottawa 3 at Vancouver 2
March 26   Ottawa 5 at Vancouver 1
Ottawa won best-of-five semifinals 3–1

Stanley Cup Finals
March 29   Ottawa 2 Edmonton 1 (Cy Denneny 2:08 OT)*
March 31   Ottawa 1 Edmonton 0 [Benedict]*
Ottawa won best-of-three finals 2–0
* games played at Vancouver

1923–24

	GP	W	L	T	GF	GA	PTS
Ottawa	24	16	8	0	74	54	32
Canadiens	24	13	11	0	59	48	26
St. Pats	24	10	14	0	59	85	20
Hamilton	24	9	15	0	63	68	18

NHL Finals
March 8   Ottawa 0 at Canadiens 1 [Vezina]
March 11   Canadiens 4 at Ottawa 2
Canadiens won two-game total-goals series 5–2

Stanley Cup Playoffs
March 18   Vancouver 2 at Canadiens 3
March 20   Vancouver 1 at Canadiens 2
Canadiens won best-of-three semifinals 2–0

Stanley Cup Finals
    March 22   Calgary 1 at Canadiens 6
    March 25   Canadiens 3 Calgary 0 [Vezina]*
Canadiens won best-of-three finals 2–0

* played at Ottawa

1924–25

	GP	W	L	T	GF	GA	PTS
Hamilton	30	19	10	1	90	60	39
St. Pats	30	19	11	0	90	84	38
Canadiens	30	17	11	2	93	56	36
Ottawa	30	17	12	1	83	66	35
Maroons	30	9	19	2	45	65	20
Boston	30	6	24	0	49	119	12

* the top two teams (Hamilton and Toronto) were supposed to compete for the NHL championship
and the right to advance to the Stanley Cup Finals against the WCHL winners. However, the Tigers'
players demanded more money for these extra games and the NHL simply disqualified the team.
Thus, the St. Pats played the Canadiens.

NHL Finals
    March 13   Canadiens 2 at St. Pats 0
    March 19   St. Pats 2 at Canadiens 3
Canadiens won two-game total-goals series 5–2

Stanley Cup Finals
    March 21   Canadiens 2 at Victoria 5
    March 23   Canadiens 1 at Victoria 3*
    March 27   Canadiens 4 at Victoria 2
    March 30   Canadiens 1 at Victoria 6
Victoria won best-of-five finals 3–1

* played at Vancouver

1925–26

	GP	W	L	T	GF	GA	PTS
Ottawa	36	24	8	4	77	42	52
Maroons	36	20	11	5	91	73	45
Pirates	36	19	16	1	82	70	39
Boston	36	17	15	4	92	85	38
Americans	36	12	20	4	68	89	28
St. Pats	36	12	21	3	92	114	27
Canadiens	36	11	24	1	79	108	23

NHL Finals
March 25   Ottawa 1 at Maroons 1
March 27   Maroons 1 at Ottawa 0 [Benedict]
Maroons win two-game total-goals finals 2–1

Stanley Cup Finals
March 30   Victoria 0 at Maroons 3 [Benedict]
April 1   Victoria 0 at Maroons 3 [Benedict]
April 3   Victoria 3 at Maroons 2
April 6   Victoria 0 at Maroons 2 [Benedict]
Maroons won best-of-five finals 3–1

1926–27

Canadian Division

	GP	W	L	T	GF	GA	PTS
Ottawa	44	30	10	4	86	69	64
Canadiens	44	28	14	2	99	67	58
Maroons	44	20	20	4	71	68	44
Americans	44	17	25	2	82	91	36
Toronto*	44	15	24	5	79	94	35

American Division

	GP	W	L	T	GF	GA	PTS
Rangers	44	25	13	6	95	72	56
Boston	44	21	20	3	97	89	45
Chicago	44	19	22	3	115	116	41
Pirates	44	15	26	3	79	108	33
Cougars	44	12	28	4	76	105	28

* on February 14, 1927, the St. Pats changed their name to Maple Leafs

Stanley Cup Finals
April 7   Ottawa 0 at Boston 0* [Connell/Winkler]
April 9   Ottawa 3 at Boston 1
April 11   Boston 1 at Ottawa 1**
April 13   Boston 1 at Ottawa 3
Ottawa won best-of-five finals 2–0–2

* two 10-minute overtime periods
** one 20-minute overtime period

1927–28

Canadian Division

	GP	W	L	T	GF	GA	PTS
Canadiens	44	26	11	7	116	48	59
Maroons	44	24	14	6	96	77	54
Ottawa	44	20	14	10	78	57	50
Toronto	44	18	18	8	89	88	44
Americans	44	11	27	6	63	128	28

American Division

	GP	W	L	T	GF	GA	PTS
Boston	44	20	13	11	77	70	51
Rangers	44	19	16	9	94	79	47
Pirates	44	19	17	8	67	76	46
Cougars	44	19	19	6	88	79	44
Chicago	44	7	34	3	68	134	17

* overtime limited to 10 minutes of sudden-death; forward passing now allowed in defending zone

Stanley Cup Finals

April 5	Rangers 0 at Maroons 2 [Benedict]
April 7	Rangers 2 at Maroons 1 (Frank Boucher 7:05 OT)
April 10	Rangers 0 at Maroons 2 [Benedict]
April 12	Rangers 1 at Maroons 0 [Miller]
April 14	Rangers 2 at Maroons 1

Rangers won best-of-five finals 3–2

1928–29

Canadian Division

	GP	W	L	T	GF	GA	PTS
Canadiens	44	22	7	15	71	43	59
Americans	44	19	13	12	53	53	50
Toronto	44	21	18	5	85	69	47
Ottawa	44	14	17	13	54	67	41
Maroons	44	15	20	9	67	65	39

American Division

Boston	44	26	13	5	89	52	57
Rangers	44	21	13	10	72	65	52
Cougars	44	19	16	9	72	63	47
Pirates	44	9	27	8	46	80	26
Chicago	44	7	29	8	33	85	22

* overtime set at 10 minutes without sudden-death; passing allowed into, but not within, the offensive zone
* the two division winners played a best-of-five and the two second place teams and third-place teams played two-game total-goals series. Those two winners then played to see who would play the winner of the two division champions' series.

Stanley Cup Finals

March 28   Rangers 0 at Boston 2 [Thompson]
March 29   Boston 2 at Rangers 1
Boston won best-of-three finals 2–0

1929–30

Canadian Division

	GP	W	L	T	GF	GA	PTS
Maroons	44	23	16	5	141	114	51
Canadiens	44	21	14	9	142	114	51
Ottawa	44	21	15	8	138	118	50
Toronto	44	17	21	6	116	124	40
Americans	44	14	25	5	113	161	33

American Division

Boston	44	38	5	1	179	98	77
Chicago	44	21	18	5	117	111	47
Rangers	44	17	17	10	136	143	44
Falcons	44	14	24	6	117	133	34
Pirates	44	5	36	3	102	185	13

* forward passing allowed in all three zones, producing twice the number of goals this season over last

Stanley Cup Finals

April 1   Canadiens 3 at Boston 0 [Hainsworth]
April 3   Boston 3 at Canadiens 4
Canadiens won best-of-three finals 2–0

1930–31

Canadian Division

	GP	W	L	T	GF	GA	PTS
Canadiens	44	26	10	8	129	89	60
Toronto	44	22	13	9	118	99	53
Maroons	44	20	18	6	105	106	46
Americans	44	18	16	10	76	74	46
Ottawa	44	10	30	4	91	142	24

American Division

	GP	W	L	T	GF	GA	PTS
Boston	44	28	10	6	143	90	62
Chicago	44	24	17	3	108	78	51
Rangers	44	19	16	9	106	87	47
Falcons	44	16	21	7	102	105	39
Quakers	44	4	36	4	76	184	12

Stanley Cup Finals

April 3	Canadiens 2 at Chicago 1
April 5	Canadiens 1 at Chicago 2 (24:50 OT)
April 9	Chicago 3 at Canadiens 2 (53:50 OT)
April 11	Chicago 2 at Canadiens 4
April 14	Chicago 0 at Canadiens 2 [Hainsworth]

Canadiens won best-of-five finals 3–2

1931–32

Canadian Division

	GP	W	L	T	GF	GA	PTS
Canadiens	48	25	16	7	128	111	57
Toronto	48	23	18	7	155	127	53
Maroons	48	19	22	7	142	139	45
Americans	48	16	24	8	95	142	40

American Division

	GP	W	L	T	GF	GA	PTS
Rangers	48	23	17	8	134	112	54
Chicago	48	18	19	11	86	101	47
Falcons	48	18	20	10	95	108	46
Boston	48	15	21	12	122	117	42

Stanley Cup Finals

April 5	Toronto 6 at Rangers 4
April 7	Toronto 6 at Rangers 2*
April 9	Rangers 4 at Toronto 6

Toronto won best-of-five finals 3–0

* played at Boston because Madison Square Garden unavailable April 7 because of circus. Because of the scores in the finals (6–4, 6–2, 6–4) this series has long been dubbed the "Tennis Series"
* all members of this Toronto team were given gold coins by Conn Smythe as lifetime passes to the Gardens

1932–33

Canadian Division

	GP	W	L	T	GF	GA	PTS
Toronto	48	24	18	6	119	111	54
Maroons	48	22	20	6	135	119	50
Canadiens	48	18	25	5	92	115	41
Americans	48	15	22	11	91	118	41
Ottawa	48	11	27	10	88	131	32

American Division

Boston	48	25	15	8	124	88	58
Detroit	48	25	15	8	111	93	58
Rangers	48	23	17	8	135	107	54
Chicago	48	16	20	12	88	101	44

Stanley Cup Finals

April 4	Toronto 1 at Rangers 5
April 8	Rangers 3 at Toronto 1
April 11	Rangers 2 at Toronto 3
April 13	Rangers 1 at Toronto 0 (Bill Cook 7:33 OT) [Aitkenhead]

Rangers won best-of-five finals 3–1

1933–34

Canadian Division

	GP	W	L	T	GF	GA	PTS
Toronto	48	26	13	9	174	119	61
Canadiens	48	22	20	6	99	101	50
Maroons	48	19	18	11	117	122	49
Americans	48	15	23	10	104	132	40
Ottawa	48	13	29	6	115	143	32

American Division

Detroit	48	24	14	10	113	98	58
Chicago	48	20	17	11	88	83	51
Rangers	48	21	19	8	120	113	50
Boston	48	18	25	5	111	130	41

Stanley Cup Finals

April 3	Chicago 2 at Detroit 1 (Paul Thompson 21:10 OT)
April 5	Chicago 4 at Detroit 1
April 8	Detroit 5 at Chicago 2
April 10	Detroit 0 at Chicago 1 (Mush March 30:05 OT) [Gardiner]

Chicago won best-of-five finals 3–1

1934–35

Canadian Division

	GP	W	L	T	GF	GA	PTS
Toronto	48	30	14	4	157	111	64
Maroons	48	24	19	5	123	92	53
Canadiens	48	19	23	6	110	145	44
Americans	48	12	27	9	100	142	33
Eagles	48	11	31	6	86	144	28

American Division

Boston	48	26	16	6	129	112	58
Chicago	48	26	17	5	118	88	57
Rangers	48	22	20	6	137	139	50
Detroit	48	19	22	7	127	114	45

Stanley Cup Finals

April 4	Maroons 3 at Toronto 2 (Dave Trottier 5:28 OT)
April 6	Maroons 3 at Toronto 1
April 9	Toronto 1 at Maroons 4

Maroons won best-of-five finals 3–0

1935–36

Canadian Division

	GP	W	L	T	GF	GA	PTS
Maroons	48	22	16	10	114	106	54
Toronto	48	23	19	6	126	106	52
Americans	48	16	25	7	109	122	39
Canadiens	48	11	26	11	82	123	33

American Division

	GP	W	L	T	GF	GA	PTS
Detroit	48	24	16	8	124	103	56
Boston	48	22	20	6	92	83	50
Chicago	48	21	19	8	93	92	50
Rangers	48	19	17	12	91	96	50

Stanley Cup Finals

April 5	Toronto 1 at Detroit 3
April 7	Toronto 4 at Detroit 9
April 9	Detroit 3 at Toronto 4 (Buzz Boll 0:31 OT)
April 11	Detroit 3 at Toronto 2

Detroit won best-of-five finals 3–1

1936–37

Canadian Division

	GP	W	L	T	GF	GA	PTS
Canadiens	48	24	18	6	115	111	54
Maroons	48	22	17	9	126	110	53
Toronto	48	22	21	5	119	115	49
Americans	48	15	29	4	122	161	34

American Division

	GP	W	L	T	GF	GA	PTS
Detroit	48	25	14	9	128	102	59
Boston	48	23	18	7	120	110	53
Rangers	48	19	20	9	117	106	47
Chicago	48	14	27	7	99	131	35

Stanley Cup Finals

April 6	Detroit 1 at Rangers 5
April 8	Rangers 2 at Detroit 4
April 11	Rangers 1 at Detroit 0 [Kerr]

April 13   Rangers 0 at Detroit 1 [Robertson]
April 15   Rangers 0 at Detroit 3 [Robertson]
Detroit won best-of-five finals 3–2

1937–38

Canadian Division

	GP	W	L	T	GF	GA	PTS
Toronto	48	24	15	9	151	127	57
Americans	48	19	18	11	110	111	49
Canadiens	48	18	17	13	123	128	49
Maroons	48	12	30	6	101	149	30

American Division

	GP	W	L	T	GF	GA	PTS
Boston	48	30	11	7	142	89	67
Rangers	48	27	15	6	149	96	60
Chicago	48	14	25	9	97	139	37
Detroit	48	12	25	11	99	133	35

Stanley Cup Finals

April 5   Chicago 3 at Toronto 1
April 7   Chicago 1 at Toronto 5
April 10   Toronto 1 at Chicago 2
April 12   Toronto 1 at Chicago 4
Chicago won best-of-five finals 3–1

1938–39

	GP	W	L	T	GF	GA	PTS
Boston	48	36	10	2	156	76	74
Rangers	48	26	16	6	149	105	58
Toronto	48	19	20	9	114	107	47
Americans	48	17	21	10	119	157	44
Detroit	48	18	24	6	107	128	42
Canadiens	48	15	24	9	115	146	39
Chicago	48	12	28	8	91	132	32

* only the last-place team did not qualify for the playoffs under the new one-division, 7–team format. The first- and second-place team played a best-of-seven to advance to the finals. The second played third and fourth played fifth in best-of-three, the two winners playing another best-of-three to advance to the finals.

Stanley Cup Finals

April 6	Toronto 1 at Boston 2
April 9	Toronto 3 at Boston 2 (Doc Romnes 10:38 OT)
April 11	Boston 3 at Toronto 1
April 13	Boston 2 at Toronto 0 [Brimsek]
April 16	Toronto 1 at Boston 3

Boston won best-of-seven finals 4–1

1939–40

	GP	W	L	T	GF	GA	PTS
Boston	48	31	12	5	170	98	67
Rangers	48	27	11	10	136	77	64
Toronto	48	25	17	6	134	110	56
Chicago	48	23	19	6	112	120	52
Detroit	48	16	26	6	90	126	38
Americans	48	15	29	4	106	140	34
Canadiens	48	10	33	5	90	167	25

Stanley Cup Finals

April 2	Toronto 1 at Rangers 2 (Alf Pike 15:30 OT)
April 3	Toronto 2 at Rangers 6
April 6	Rangers 1 at Toronto 2
April 9	Rangers 0 at Toronto 3 [Broda]
April 11	Rangers 2 at Toronto 1 (Muzz Patrick 31:43 OT)*
April 13	Rangers 3 at Toronto 2 (Bryan Hextall 2:07 OT)

Rangers won best-of-seven finals 4–2

* game could not be played at Madison Square Garden as it was previously booked for the circus

1940–41

	GP	W	L	T	GF	GA	PTS
Boston	48	27	8	13	168	102	67
Toronto	48	28	14	6	145	99	62
Detroit	48	21	16	11	112	102	53
Rangers	48	21	19	8	143	125	50
Chicago	48	16	25	7	112	139	39
Canadiens	48	16	26	6	121	147	38
Americans	48	8	29	11	99	186	27

Stanley Cup Finals

April 6	Detroit 2 at Boston 3
April 8	Detroit 1 at Boston 2
April 10	Boston 4 at Detroit 2
April 12	Boston 3 at Detroit 1

Boston won best-of-seven finals 4–0

1941–42

	GP	W	L	T	GF	GA	PTS
Rangers	48	29	17	2	177	143	60
Toronto	48	27	18	3	158	136	57
Boston	48	25	17	6	160	118	56
Chicago	48	22	23	3	145	155	47
Detroit	48	19	25	4	140	147	42
Canadiens	48	18	27	3	134	173	39
Brooklyn	48	16	29	3	133	175	35

Stanley Cup Finals

April 4	Detroit 3 at Toronto 2
April 7	Detroit 4 at Toronto 2
April 9	Toronto 2 at Detroit 5
April 12	Toronto 4 at Detroit 3
April 14	Detroit 3 at Toronto 9
April 16	Toronto 3 at Detroit 0 [Broda]
April 18	Detroit 1 at Toronto 3

Toronto won best-of-seven finals 4–3

* only time in NHL history that a team has trailed 3–0 in the finals and won the Stanley Cup

1942–43

	GP	W	L	T	GF	GA	PTS
Detroit	50	25	14	11	169	124	61
Boston	50	24	17	9	195	176	57
Toronto	50	22	19	9	198	159	53
Canadiens	50	19	19	12	181	191	50
Chicago	50	17	18	15	179	180	49
Rangers	50	11	31	8	161	253	30

* because of wartime restrictions on train schedules overtime was eliminated as of November 21, 1942
* the top four teams qualified for the playoffs in the six-team league, and both rounds were best-of-seven

Stanley Cup Finals

April 1	Boston 2 at Detroit 6
April 4	Boston 3 at Detroit 4
April 7	Detroit 4 at Boston 0 [Mowers]
April 8	Detroit 2 at Boston 0 [Mowers]

Detroit won best-of-seven finals 4–0

1943–44

	GP	W	L	T	GF	GA	PTS
Canadiens	50	38	5	7	234	109	83
Detroit	50	26	18	6	214	177	58
Toronto	50	23	23	4	214	174	50
Chicago	50	22	23	5	178	187	49
Boston	50	19	26	5	223	268	43
Rangers	50	6	39	5	162	310	17

Stanley Cup Finals

April 4	Chicago 1 at Canadiens 5
April 6	Canadiens 3 at Chicago 1
April 9	Canadiens 3 at Chicago 2
April 13	Chicago 4 at Canadiens 5 (Toe Blake 9:12 OT)

Canadiens won best-of-seven finals 4–0

1944–45

	GP	W	L	T	GF	GA	PTS
Canadiens	50	38	8	4	228	121	80
Detroit	50	31	14	5	218	161	67
Toronto	50	24	22	4	183	161	52
Boston	50	16	30	4	179	219	36
Chicago	50	13	30	7	141	194	33
Rangers	50	11	29	10	154	247	32

Stanley Cup Finals

April 6	Toronto 1 at Detroit 0 [McCool]
April 8	Toronto 2 at Detroit 0 [McCool]
April 12	Detroit 0 at Toronto 1 [McCool]
April 14	Detroit 5 at Toronto 3
April 19	Toronto 0 at Detroit 2 [Lumley]
April 21	Detroit 1 at Toronto 0 (Ed Bruneteau 14:16 OT)[Lumley]
April 22	Toronto 2 at Detroit 1

Toronto won best-of-seven finals 4–3

1945–46

	GP	W	L	T	GF	GA	PTS
Canadiens	50	28	17	5	172	134	61
Boston	50	24	18	8	167	156	56
Chicago	50	23	20	7	200	178	53
Detroit	50	20	20	10	146	159	50
Toronto	50	19	24	7	174	185	45
Rangers	50	13	28	9	144	191	35

Stanley Cup Finals

March 30   Boston 3 at Canadiens 4 (Maurice Richard 9:08 OT)
April 2   Boston 2 at Canadiens 3 (Jimmy Peters 16:55 OT)
April 4   Canadiens 4 at Boston 2
April 7   Canadiens 2 at Boston 3 (Terry Reardon 15:13 OT)
April 9   Boston 3 at Canadiens 6
Canadiens won best-of-seven finals 4–1

1946–47

	GP	W	L	T	GF	GA	PTS
Canadiens	60	34	16	10	189	138	78
Toronto	60	31	19	10	209	172	72
Boston	60	26	23	11	190	175	63
Detroit	60	22	27	11	190	193	55
Rangers	60	22	32	6	167	186	50
Chicago	60	19	37	4	193	274	42

Stanley Cup Finals

April 8   Toronto 0 at Canadiens 6 [Durnan]
April 10   Toronto 4 at Canadiens 0 [Broda]
April 12   Canadiens 2 at Toronto 4
April 15   Canadiens 1 at Toronto 2 (Syl Apps 16:36 OT)
April 17   Toronto 1 at Canadiens 3
April 19   Canadiens 1 at Toronto 2
Toronto won best-of-seven finals 4–2

1947–48

	GP	W	L	T	GF	GA	PTS
Toronto	60	32	15	13	182	143	77
Detroit	60	30	18	12	187	148	72
Boston	60	23	24	13	167	168	59
Rangers	60	21	26	13	176	201	55
Canadiens	60	20	29	11	147	169	51
Chicago	60	20	34	6	195	225	46

Stanley Cup Finals

April 7   Detroit 3 at Toronto 5
April 10   Detroit 2 at Toronto 4
April 11   Toronto 2 at Detroit 0 [Broda]
April 14   Toronto 7 at Detroit 2
Toronto won best-of-seven finals 4–0

1948–49

	GP	W	L	T	GF	GA	PTS
Detroit	60	34	19	7	195	145	75
Boston	60	29	23	8	178	163	66
Canadiens	60	28	23	9	152	126	65
Toronto	60	22	25	13	147	161	57
Chicago	60	21	31	8	173	211	50
Rangers	60	18	31	11	133	172	47

Stanley Cup Finals

April 8   Toronto 3 at Detroit 2 (Joe Klukay 17:31 OT)
April 10   Toronto 3 at Detroit 1
April 13   Detroit 1 at Toronto 3
April 16   Detroit 1 at Toronto 3
Toronto won best-of-seven finals 4–0

1949–50

	GP	W	L	T	GF	GA	PTS
Detroit	70	37	19	14	229	164	88
Canadiens	70	29	22	19	172	150	77
Toronto	70	31	27	12	176	173	74
Rangers	70	28	31	11	170	189	67
Boston	70	22	32	16	198	228	60
Chicago	70	22	38	10	203	244	54

Stanley Cup Finals

April 11	Rangers 1 at Detroit 4
April 13	Detroit 1 Rangers 3*
April 15	Detroit 4 Rangers 0*[Lumley]
April 18	Rangers 4 at Detroit 3 (Don Raleigh 8:34 OT)
April 20	Rangers 2 at Detroit 1 (Don Raleigh 1:38 OT)
April 22	Rangers 4 at Detroit 5
April 23	Rangers 3 at Detroit 4 (Pete Babando 28:31 OT)**

Detroit won best-of-seven finals 4–3

* played at Toronto because Madison Square Garden was previously booked for the circus. Games 6 and 7 played in Detroit because league by-laws stipulated a Stanley Cup-winning game cannot be played on neutral ice.

** first time in history the Cup was won on an OT goal in game 7

1950–51

	GP	W	L	T	GF	GA	PTS
Detroit	70	44	13	13	236	139	101
Toronto	70	41	16	13	212	138	95
Canadiens	70	25	30	15	173	184	65
Boston	70	22	30	18	178	197	62
Rangers	70	20	29	21	169	201	61
Chicago	70	13	47	10	171	280	36

Stanley Cup Finals

April 11	Canadiens 2 at Toronto 3 (Sid Smith 5:51 OT)
April 14	Canadiens 3 at Toronto 2(Maurice Richard 2:55 OT)
April 17	Toronto 2 at Canadiens 1 (Ted Kennedy 4:47 OT)
April 19	Toronto 3 at Canadiens 2 (Harry Watson 5:15 OT)
April 21	Canadiens 2 at Toronto 3 (Bill Barilko 2:53 OT)

Toronto won best-of-seven finals 4–1

1951–52

	GP	W	L	T	GF	GA	PTS
Detroit	70	44	14	12	215	133	100
Canadiens	70	34	26	10	195	164	78
Toronto	70	29	25	16	168	157	74
Boston	70	25	29	16	162	176	66
Rangers	70	23	34	13	192	219	59
Chicago	70	17	44	9	158	241	43

Stanley Cup Finals

April 10	Detroit 3 at Canadiens 1
April 12	Detroit 2 at Canadiens 1
April 13	Canadiens 0 at Detroit 3 [Sawchuk]
April 15	Canadiens 0 at Detroit 3 [Sawchuk]

Detroit won best-of-seven finals 4–0

1952–53

	GP	W	L	T	GF	GA	PTS
Detroit	70	36	16	18	222	133	90
Canadiens	70	28	23	19	155	148	75
Boston	70	28	29	13	152	172	69
Chicago	70	27	28	15	169	175	69
Toronto	70	27	30	13	156	167	67
Rangers	70	17	37	16	152	211	50

Stanley Cup Finals

April 9	Boston 2 at Canadiens 4
April 11	Boston 4 at Canadiens 1
April 12	Canadiens 3 at Boston 0 [McNeil]
April 14	Canadiens 7 at Boston 3
April 16	Boston 0 at Canadiens 1 (Elmer Lach 1:22 OT) [McNeil]

Canadiens won best-of-seven finals 4–1

1953–54

	GP	W	L	T	GF	GA	PTS
Detroit	70	37	19	14	191	132	88
Canadiens	70	35	24	11	195	141	81
Toronto	70	32	24	14	152	131	78
Boston	70	32	28	10	177	181	74
Rangers	70	29	31	10	161	182	68
Chicago	70	12	51	7	133	242	31

Stanley Cup Finals

April 4	Canadiens 1 at Detroit 3
April 6	Canadiens 3 at Detroit 1
April 8	Detroit 5 at Canadiens 2
April 10	Detroit 2 at Canadiens 0 [Sawchuk]
April 11	Canadiens 1 at Detroit 0 (Ken Mosdell 5:45 OT) [McNeil]
April 13	Detroit 1 at Canadiens 4
April 16	Canadiens 1 at Detroit 2 (Tony Leswick 4:29 OT)

Detroit won best-of-seven finals 4–3

1954–55

	GP	W	L	T	GF	GA	PTS
Detroit	70	42	17	11	204	134	95
Canadiens	70	41	18	11	228	157	93
Toronto	70	24	24	22	147	135	70
Boston	70	23	26	21	169	188	67
Rangers	70	17	35	18	150	210	52
Chicago	70	13	40	17	161	235	43

Stanley Cup Finals

April 3	Canadiens 2 at Detroit 4
April 5	Canadiens 1 at Detroit 7
April 7	Detroit 2 at Canadiens 4
April 9	Detroit 3 at Canadiens 5
April 10	Canadiens 1 at Detroit 5
April 12	Detroit 3 at Canadiens 6
April 14	Canadiens 1 at Detroit 3

Detroit won best-of-seven finals 4–3

1955–56

	GP	W	L	T	GF	GA	PTS
Canadiens	70	45	15	10	222	131	100
Detroit	70	30	24	16	183	148	76
Rangers	70	32	28	10	204	203	74
Toronto	70	24	33	13	153	181	61
Boston	70	23	34	13	147	185	59
Chicago	70	19	39	12	155	216	50

Stanley Cup Finals

March 31	Detroit 4 at Canadiens 6
April 3	Detroit 1 at Canadiens 5
April 5	Canadiens 1 at Detroit 3
April 8	Canadiens 3 at Detroit 0 [Plante]
April 10	Detroit 1 at Canadiens 3

Canadiens won best-of-seven finals 4–1

1956–57

	GP	W	L	T	GF	GA	PTS
Detroit	70	38	20	12	198	157	88
Canadiens	70	35	23	12	210	155	82
Boston	70	34	24	12	195	174	80
Rangers	70	26	30	14	184	227	66
Toronto	70	21	34	15	174	192	57
Chicago	70	16	39	15	169	225	47

* penalized player allowed to return to the ice after a power-play goal has been scored by the opposition

Stanley Cup Finals

April 6   Boston 1 at Canadiens 5
April 9   Boston 0 at Canadiens 1 [Plante]
April 11   Canadiens 4 at Boston 2
April 14   Canadiens 0 at Boston 2 [Simmons]
April 16   Boston 1 at Canadiens 5
Canadiens won best-of-seven finals 4–1

1957–58

	GP	W	L	T	GF	GA	PTS
Canadiens	70	43	17	10	250	158	96
Rangers	70	32	25	13	195	188	77
Detroit	70	29	29	12	176	207	70
Boston	70	27	28	15	199	194	69
Chicago	70	24	39	7	163	202	55
Toronto	70	21	38	11	192	226	53

Stanley Cup Finals

April 8   Boston 1 at Canadiens 2
April 10   Boston 5 at Canadiens 2
April 13   Canadiens 3 at Boston 0 [Plante]
April 15   Canadiens 1 at Boston 3
April 17   Boston 2 at Canadiens 3 (Maurice Richard 5:45 OT)
April 20   Canadiens 5 at Boston 3
Canadiens won best-of-seven finals 4–2

1958–59

	GP	W	L	T	GF	GA	PTS
Canadiens	70	39	18	13	258	158	91
Boston	70	32	29	9	205	215	73
Chicago	70	28	29	13	197	208	69
Toronto	70	27	32	11	189	201	65
Rangers	70	26	32	12	201	217	64
Detroit	70	25	37	8	167	218	58

Stanley Cup Finals

April 9   Toronto 3 at Canadiens 5
April 11   Toronto 1 at Canadiens 3
April 14   Canadiens 2 at Toronto 3 (Dick Duff 10:06 OT)
April 16   Canadiens 3 at Toronto 2
April 18   Toronto 3 at Canadiens 5
Canadiens won best-of-seven finals 4–1

1959–60

	GP	W	L	T	GF	GA	PTS
Canadiens	70	40	18	12	255	178	92
Toronto	70	35	26	9	199	195	79
Chicago	70	28	29	13	191	180	69
Detroit	70	26	29	15	186	197	67
Boston	70	28	34	8	220	241	64
Rangers	70	17	38	15	187	247	49

Stanley Cup Finals

April 7   Toronto 2 at Canadiens 4
April 9   Toronto 1 at Canadiens 2
April 12   Canadiens 5 at Toronto 2
April 14   Canadiens 4 at Toronto 0 [Plante]
Canadiens won best-of-seven finals 4–0

1960–61

	GP	W	L	T	GF	GA	PTS
Canadiens	70	41	19	10	254	188	92
Toronto	70	39	19	12	234	176	90
Chicago	70	29	24	17	198	180	75
Detroit	70	25	29	16	195	215	66
Rangers	70	22	38	10	204	248	54
Boston	70	15	42	13	176	254	43

Stanley Cup Finals

April 6	Detroit 2 at Chicago 3
April 8	Chicago 1 at Detroit 3
April 10	Detroit 1 at Chicago 3
April 12	Chicago 1 at Detroit 2
April 14	Detroit 3 at Chicago 6
April 16	Chicago 5 at Detroit 1

Chicago won best-of-seven finals 4–2

1961–62

	GP	W	L	T	GF	GA	PTS
Canadiens	70	42	14	14	259	166	98
Toronto	70	37	22	11	232	180	85
Chicago	70	31	26	13	217	186	75
Rangers	70	26	32	12	195	207	64
Detroit	70	23	33	14	184	219	60
Boston	70	15	47	8	177	306	38

Stanley Cup Finals

April 10	Chicago 1 at Toronto 4
April 12	Chicago 2 at Toronto 3
April 15	Toronto 0 at Chicago 3 [Hall]
April 17	Toronto 1 at Chicago 4
April 19	Chicago 4 at Toronto 8
April 22	Toronto 2 at Chicago 1

Toronto won best-of-seven finals 4–2

1962–63

	GP	W	L	T	GF	GA	PTS
Toronto	70	35	23	12	221	180	82
Chicago	70	32	21	17	194	178	81
Canadiens	70	28	19	23	225	183	79
Detroit	70	32	25	13	200	194	77
Rangers	70	22	36	12	211	233	56
Boston	70	14	39	17	198	281	45

Stanley Cup Finals

April 9	Detroit 2 at Toronto 4
April 11	Detroit 2 at Toronto 4
April 14	Toronto 2 at Detroit 3
April 16	Toronto 4 at Detroit 2
April 18	Detroit 1 at Toronto 3

Toronto won best-of-seven finals 4–1

1963–64

	GP	W	L	T	GF	GA	PTS
Canadiens	70	36	21	13	209	167	85
Chicago	70	36	22	12	218	169	84
Toronto	70	33	25	12	192	172	78
Detroit	70	30	29	11	191	204	71
Rangers	70	22	38	10	186	242	54
Boston	70	18	40	12	170	212	48

Stanley Cup Finals

April 11	Detroit 2 at Toronto 3
April 14	Detroit 4 at Toronto 3 (Larry Jeffrey 7:52 OT)
April 16	Toronto 3 at Detroit 4
April 18	Toronto 4 at Detroit 2
April 21	Detroit 2 at Toronto 1
April 23	Toronto 4 at Detroit 3 (Bobby Baun 1:43 OT)
April 25	Detroit 0 at Toronto 4 [Bower]

Toronto won best-of-seven finals 4–3

1964–65

	GP	W	L	T	GF	GA	PTS
Detroit	70	40	23	7	224	175	87
Canadiens	70	36	23	11	211	185	83
Chicago	70	34	28	8	224	176	76
Toronto	70	30	26	14	204	173	74
Rangers	70	20	38	12	179	246	52
Boston	70	21	43	6	166	253	48

Stanley Cup Finals

April 17	Chicago 2 at Canadiens 3
April 20	Chicago 0 at Canadiens 2 [Worsley]
April 22	Canadiens 1 at Chicago 3
April 25	Canadiens 1 at Chicago 5
April 27	Chicago 0 at Canadiens 6 [Hodge]
April 29	Canadiens 1 at Chicago 2
May 1	Chicago 0 at Canadiens 4 [Worsley]

Canadiens won best-of-seven finals 4–3

1965–66

	GP	W	L	T	GF	GA	PTS
Canadiens	70	41	21	8	239	173	90
Chicago	70	37	25	8	240	187	82
Toronto	70	34	25	11	208	187	79
Detroit	70	31	27	12	221	194	74
Boston	70	21	43	6	174	275	48
Rangers	70	18	41	11	195	261	47

Stanley Cup Finals

April 24	Detroit 3 at Canadiens 2
April 26	Detroit 5 at Canadiens 2
April 28	Canadiens 4 at Detroit 2
May 1	Canadiens 2 at Detroit 1
May 3	Detroit 1 at Canadiens 5
May 5	Canadiens 3 at Detroit 2 (Henri Richard 2:20 OT)

Canadiens won best-of-seven finals 4–2

1966–67

	GP	W	L	T	GF	GA	PTS
Chicago	70	41	17	12	264	170	94
Canadiens	70	32	25	13	202	188	77
Toronto	70	32	27	11	204	211	75
Rangers	70	30	28	12	188	189	72
Detroit	70	27	39	4	212	241	58
Boston	70	17	43	10	182	253	44

Stanley Cup Finals

April 20	Toronto 2 at Canadiens 6
April 22	Toronto 3 at Canadiens 0 [Bower]
April 25	Canadiens 2 at Toronto 3 (Bob Pulford 28:26 OT)
April 27	Canadiens 6 at Toronto 2
April 29	Toronto 4 at Canadiens 1
May 2	Canadiens 1 at Toronto 3

Toronto won best-of-seven finals 4–2

1967–68

East Division

	GP	W	L	T	GF	GA	PTS
Canadiens	74	42	22	10	236	167	94
Rangers	74	39	23	12	226	183	90
Boston	74	37	27	10	259	216	84
Chicago	74	32	26	16	212	222	80
Toronto	74	33	31	10	209	176	76
Detroit	74	27	35	12	245	257	66

West Division

	GP	W	L	T	GF	GA	PTS
Philadelphia	74	31	32	11	173	179	73
Los Angeles	74	31	33	10	200	224	72
St. Louis	74	27	31	16	177	191	70
North Stars	74	27	32	15	191	226	69
Pittsburgh	74	27	34	13	195	216	67
Oakland	74	15	42	17	153	219	47

* top four teams in each division qualified for the playoffs

Stanley Cup Finals

| May 5 | Canadiens 3 at St. Louis 2 (Jacques Lemaire 1:41 OT) |
| May 7 | Canadiens 1 at St. Louis 0 [Worsley] |

May 9   St. Louis 3 at Canadiens 4 (Bobby Rousseau 1:13 OT)
May 11   St. Louis 2 at Canadiens 3
Canadiens won best-of-seven finals 4–0

1968–69

East Division

	GP	W	L	T	GF	GA	PTS
Canadiens	76	46	19	11	271	202	103
Boston	76	42	18	16	303	221	100
Rangers	76	41	26	9	231	196	91
Toronto	76	35	26	15	234	217	85
Detroit	76	33	31	12	239	221	78
Chicago	76	34	33	9	280	246	77

West Division

	GP	W	L	T	GF	GA	PTS
St. Louis	76	37	25	14	204	157	88
Oakland	76	29	36	11	219	251	69
Philadelphia	76	20	35	21	174	225	61
Los Angeles	76	24	42	10	185	260	58
Pittsburgh	76	20	45	11	189	252	51
North Stars	76	18	43	15	189	270	51

Stanley Cup Finals

April 27   St. Louis 1 at Canadiens 3
April 29   St. Louis 1 at Canadiens 3
May 1   Canadiens 4 at St. Louis 0 [Vachon]
May 4   Canadiens 2 at St. Louis 1
Canadiens won best-of-seven finals 4–0

1969–70

East Division

	GP	W	L	T	GF	GA	PTS
Chicago	76	45	22	9	250	170	99
Boston	76	40	17	19	277	216	99
Detroit	76	40	21	15	246	199	95
Rangers	76	38	22	16	246	189	92
Canadiens	76	38	22	16	244	201	92
Toronto	76	29	34	13	222	242	71

West Division

St. Louis	76	37	27	12	224	179	86
Pittsburgh	76	26	38	12	182	238	64
North Stars	76	19	35	22	224	257	60
Oakland	76	22	40	14	169	243	58
Philadelphia	76	17	35	24	197	225	58
Los Angeles	76	14	52	10	168	290	38

Stanley Cup Finals

May 3	Boston 6 at St. Louis 1
May 5	Boston 6 at St. Louis 2
May 7	St. Louis 1 at Boston 4
May 10	St. Louis 3 at Boston 4 (Bobby Orr 0:40 OT)

Boston won best-of-seven finals 4–0

1970–71

East Division

	GP	W	L	T	GF	GA	PTS
Boston	78	57	14	7	399	207	121
Rangers	78	49	18	11	259	177	109
Canadiens	78	42	23	13	291	216	97
Toronto	78	37	33	8	248	211	82
Buffalo	78	24	39	15	217	291	63
Vancouver	78	24	46	8	229	296	56
Detroit	78	22	45	11	209	308	55

West Division

Chicago	78	49	20	9	277	184	107
St. Louis	78	34	25	19	223	208	87
Philadelphia	78	28	33	17	207	225	73
North Stars	78	28	34	16	191	223	72
Los Angeles	78	25	40	13	239	303	63
Pittsburgh	78	21	37	20	221	240	62
California	78	20	53	5	199	320	45

Stanley Cup Finals

May 4	Canadiens 1 at Chicago 2 (Jim Pappin 21:11 OT)
May 6	Canadiens 3 at Chicago 5
May 9	Chicago 2 at Canadiens 4
May 11	Chicago 2 at Canadiens 5
May 13	Canadiens 0 at Chicago 2 [Esposito]

May 16   Chicago 3 at Canadiens 4
May 18   Canadiens 3 at Chicago 2
Canadiens won best-of-seven finals 4–3

1971–72

East Division

	GP	W	L	T	GF	GA	PTS
Boston	78	54	13	11	330	204	119
Rangers	78	48	17	13	317	192	109
Canadiens	78	46	16	16	307	205	108
Toronto	78	33	31	14	209	208	80
Detroit	78	33	35	10	261	262	76
Buffalo	78	16	43	19	203	289	51
Vancouver	78	20	50	8	203	297	48

West Division

	GP	W	L	T	GF	GA	PTS
Chicago	78	46	17	15	256	166	107
North Stars	78	37	29	12	212	191	86
St. Louis	78	28	39	11	208	247	67
Pittsburgh	78	26	38	14	220	258	66
Philadelphia	78	26	38	14	200	236	66
California	78	21	39	18	216	288	60
Los Angeles	78	20	49	9	206	305	49

Stanley Cup Finals

April 30   Rangers 5 at Boston 6
May 2   Rangers 1 at Boston 2
May 4   Boston 2 at Rangers 5
May 7   Boston 3 at Rangers 2
May 9   Rangers 3 at Boston 2
May 11   Boston 3 at Rangers 0 [Johnston]
Boston won best-of-seven finals 4–2

1972–73

East Division

	GP	W	L	T	GF	GA	PIM	PTS
Canadiens	78	52	10	16	329	184	783	120
Boston	78	51	22	5	330	235	1097	107
Rangers	78	47	23	8	297	208	765	102
Buffalo	78	37	27	14	257	219	940	88
Detroit	78	37	29	12	265	243	893	86
Toronto	78	27	41	10	247	279	716	64
Vancouver	78	22	47	9	233	339	943	53
Islanders	78	12	60	6	170	347	881	30

West Division

	GP	W	L	T	GF	GA	PIM	PTS
Chicago	78	42	27	9	284	225	864	93
Philadelphia	78	37	30	11	296	256	1756	85
North Stars	78	37	30	11	254	230	881	85
St. Louis	78	32	34	12	233	251	1195	76
Pittsburgh	78	32	37	9	257	265	866	73
Los Angeles	78	31	36	11	232	245	888	73
Flames	78	25	38	15	191	239	852	65
California	78	16	46	16	213	323	840	48

Stanley Cup Finals

April 29	Chicago 3 at Canadiens 8
May 1	Chicago 1 at Canadiens 4
May 3	Canadiens 4 at Chicago 7
May 6	Canadiens 4 at Chicago 0 [Dryden]
May 8	Chicago 8 at Canadiens 7
May 10	Canadiens 6 at Chicago 4

Canadiens won best-of-seven finals 4–2

1973–74

East Division

	GP	W	L	T	GF	GA	PTS
Boston	78	52	17	9	349	221	113
Canadiens	78	45	24	9	293	240	99
Rangers	78	40	24	14	300	251	94
Toronto	78	35	27	16	274	230	86
Buffalo	78	32	34	12	242	250	76
Detroit	78	29	39	10	255	319	68
Vancouver	78	24	43	11	224	296	59
Islanders	78	19	41	18	182	247	56

West Division

	GP	W	L	T	GF	GA	PTS
Philadelphia	78	50	16	12	273	164	112
Chicago	78	41	14	23	272	164	105
Los Angeles	78	33	33	12	233	231	78
Flames	78	30	34	14	214	238	74
Pittsburgh	78	28	41	9	242	273	65
St. Louis	78	26	40	12	206	248	64
North Stars	78	23	38	17	235	275	63
California	78	13	55	10	195	342	36

Stanley Cup Finals

May 7	Philadelphia 2 at Boston 3
May 9	Philadelphia 3 at Boston 2 (Bobby Clarke 12:01 OT)
May 12	Boston 1 at Philadelphia 4
May 14	Boston 2 at Philadelphia 4
May 16	Philadelphia 1 at Boston 5
May 19	Boston 0 at Philadelphia 1 [Parent]

Philadelphia won best-of-seven finals 4–2

1974–75

PRINCE OF WALES CONFERENCE
Adams Division

	GP	W	L	T	GF	GA	PTS
Buffalo	80	49	16	15	354	240	113
Boston	80	40	26	14	345	245	94
Toronto	80	31	33	16	280	309	78
California	80	19	48	13	212	316	51

Norris Division

	GP	W	L	T	GF	GA	PTS
Canadiens	80	47	14	19	374	225	113
Los Angeles	80	42	17	21	269	185	105
Pittsburgh	80	37	28	15	326	289	89
Detroit	80	23	45	12	259	335	58
Washington	80	8	67	5	181	446	21

CLARENCE CAMPBELL CONFERENCE
Patrick Division

	GP	W	L	T	GF	GA	PTS
Philadelphia	80	51	18	11	293	181	113
Rangers	80	37	29	14	319	276	88
Islanders	80	33	25	22	264	221	88
Flames	80	34	31	15	243	233	83

Smythe Division

	GP	W	L	T	GF	GA	PTS
Vancouver	80	38	32	10	271	254	86
St. Louis	80	35	31	14	269	267	84
Chicago	80	37	35	8	268	241	82
North Stars	80	23	50	7	221	341	53
Kansas City	80	15	54	11	184	328	41

* the top three teams in each division qualified for the playoffs. The four division champions received byes to the second round and all second- and third-place clubs were seeded 1–8 by points, #1 playing # 8, #2 and #7, etc. The first round was best-of-three, the subsequent rounds best-of-seven.

Stanley Cup Finals
May 15	Buffalo 1 at Philadelphia 4
May 18	Buffalo 1 at Philadelphia 2
May 20	Philadelphia 4 at Buffalo 5 (Rene Robert 18:29 OT)
May 22	Philadelphia 2 at Buffalo 4
May 25	Buffalo 1 at Philadelphia 5
May 27	Philadelphia 2 at Buffalo 0 [Parent]

Philadelphia won best-of-seven finals 4–2

1975–76

PRINCE OF WALES CONFERENCE
Adams Division

	GP	W	L	T	GF	GA	PTS
Boston	80	48	15	17	313	237	113
Buffalo	80	46	21	13	339	240	105
Toronto	80	34	31	15	294	276	83
California	80	27	42	11	250	278	65

Norris Division

	GP	W	L	T	GF	GA	PTS
Canadiens	80	58	11	11	337	174	127
Los Angeles	80	38	33	9	263	265	85
Pittsburgh	80	35	33	12	339	303	82
Detroit	80	26	44	10	226	300	62
Washington	80	11	59	10	224	394	32

CLARENCE CAMPBELL CONFERENCE
Patrick Division

	GP	W	L	T	GF	GA	PTS
Philadelphia	80	51	13	16	348	209	118
Islanders	80	42	21	17	297	190	101
Flames	80	35	33	12	262	237	82
Rangers	80	29	42	9	262	333	67

Smythe Division

	GP	W	L	T	GF	GA	PTS
Chicago	80	32	30	18	254	261	82
Vancouver	80	33	32	15	271	272	81
St. Louis	80	29	37	14	249	290	72
North Stars	80	20	53	7	195	303	47
Kansas City	80	12	56	12	190	351	36

Stanley Cup Finals
May 9	Philadelphia 3 at Canadiens 4
May 11	Philadelphia 1 at Canadiens 2
May 13	Canadiens 3 at Philadelphia 2
May 16	Canadiens 5 at Philadelphia 3

Canadiens won best-of-seven finals 4–0

1976–77

PRINCE OF WALES CONFERENCE

Adams Division

	GP	W	L	T	GF	GA	PTS
Boston	80	49	23	8	312	240	106
Buffalo	80	48	24	8	301	220	104
Toronto	80	33	32	15	301	285	81
Cleveland	80	25	42	13	240	292	63

Norris Division

	GP	W	L	T	GF	GA	PTS
Canadiens	80	60	8	12	387	171	132
Los Angeles	80	34	31	15	271	241	83
Pittsburgh	80	34	33	13	240	252	81
Washington	80	24	42	14	221	307	62
Detroit	80	16	55	9	183	309	41

CLARENCE CAMPBELL CONFERENCE

Patrick Division

	GP	W	L	T	GF	GA	PTS
Philadelphia	80	48	16	16	323	213	112
Islanders	80	47	21	12	288	193	106
Flames	80	34	34	12	264	265	80
Rangers	80	29	37	14	272	310	64

Smythe Division

	GP	W	L	T	GF	GA	PTS
St. Louis	80	32	39	9	239	276	73
North Stars	80	23	39	18	240	310	64
Chicago	80	26	43	11	240	298	63
Vancouver	80	25	42	13	235	294	63
Rockies	80	20	46	14	226	307	54

Stanley Cup Finals

May 7	Boston 3 at Canadiens 7
May 10	Boston 0 at Canadiens 3 [Dryden]
May 12	Canadiens 4 at Boston 2
May 14	Canadiens 2 at Boston 1

Canadiens won best-of-seven finals 4–0

1977–78

PRINCE OF WALES CONFERENCE
Adams Division

	GP	W	L	T	GF	GA	PTS
Boston	80	51	18	11	333	218	113
Buffalo	80	44	19	17	288	215	105
Toronto	80	41	29	10	271	237	92
Cleveland	80	22	45	13	230	325	57

Norris Division

Canadiens	80	59	10	11	359	183	129
Detroit	80	32	34	14	252	266	78
Los Angeles	80	31	34	15	243	245	77
Pittsburgh	80	25	37	18	254	321	68
Washington	80	17	49	14	195	321	48

CLARENCE CAMPBELL CONFERENCE
Patrick Division

Islanders	80	48	17	15	334	210	111
Philadelphia	80	45	20	15	296	200	105
Flames	80	34	27	19	274	252	87
Rangers	80	30	37	13	279	280	73

Smythe Division

Chicago	80	32	29	19	230	220	83
Rockies	80	19	40	21	257	305	59
Vancouver	80	20	43	17	239	320	57
St. Louis	80	20	47	13	195	304	53
North Stars	80	18	53	9	218	325	45

* all 1st- and 2nd-place teams qualified for playoffs and the next best four regardless of division also qualified

Stanley Cup Finals
May 13	Boston 1 at Canadiens 4
May 16	Boston 2 at Canadiens 3 (Guy Lafleur 13:09 OT)
May 18	Canadiens 0 at Boston 4 [Cheevers]
May 21	Canadiens 3 at Boston 4 (Bobby Schmautz 6:22 OT)
May 23	Boston 1 at Canadiens 4
May 25	Canadiens 4 at Boston 1

Canadiens won best-of-seven finals 4–2

1978–79

PRINCE OF WALES CONFERENCE

Adams Division

	GP	W	L	T	GF	GA	PTS
Boston	80	43	23	14	316	270	100
Buffalo	80	36	28	16	280	263	88
Toronto	80	34	33	13	267	252	81
North Stars	80	28	40	12	257	289	68

Norris Division

	GP	W	L	T	GF	GA	PTS
Canadiens	80	52	17	11	337	204	115
Pittsburgh	80	36	31	13	281	279	85
Los Angeles	80	34	34	12	292	286	80
Washington	80	24	41	15	273	338	63
Detroit	80	23	41	16	252	295	62

CLARENCE CAMPBELL CONFERENCE

Patrick Division

	GP	W	L	T	GF	GA	PTS
Islanders	80	51	15	14	358	214	116
Philadelphia	80	40	25	15	281	248	95
Rangers	80	40	29	11	316	292	91
Flames	80	41	31	8	327	280	90

Smythe Division

	GP	W	L	T	GF	GA	PTS
Chicago	80	29	36	15	244	277	73
Vancouver	80	25	42	13	217	291	63
St. Louis	80	18	50	12	249	348	48
Rockies	80	15	53	12	210	331	42

Stanley Cup Finals

May 13	Rangers 4 at Canadiens 1
May 15	Rangers 2 at Canadiens 6
May 17	Canadiens 4 at Rangers 1
May 19	Canadiens 4 at Rangers 3 (Serge Savard 7:25 OT)
May 21	Rangers 1 at Canadiens 4

Canadiens won best-of-seven finals 4–1

1979–80

PRINCE OF WALES CONFERENCE
Adams Division

	GP	W	L	T	GF	GA	PTS
Buffalo	80	47	17	16	318	201	110
Boston	80	46	21	13	310	234	105
North Stars	80	36	28	16	311	253	88
Toronto	80	35	40	5	304	327	75
Quebec	80	25	44	11	248	313	61

Norris Division

	GP	W	L	T	GF	GA	PTS
Canadiens	80	47	20	13	328	240	107
Los Angeles	80	30	36	14	290	313	74
Pittsburgh	80	30	37	13	251	303	73
Hartford	80	27	34	19	303	312	73
Detroit	80	26	43	11	268	306	63

CLARENCE CAMPBELL CONFERENCE
Patrick Division

	GP	W	L	T	GF	GA	PTS
Philadelphia	80	48	12	20	327	254	116
Islanders	80	39	28	13	281	247	91
Rangers	80	38	32	10	308	284	86
Flames	80	35	32	13	282	269	83
Washington	80	27	40	13	261	293	67

Smythe Division

	GP	W	L	T	GF	GA	PTS
Chicago	80	34	27	19	241	250	87
St. Louis	80	34	34	12	266	278	80
Vancouver	80	27	37	16	256	281	70
Edmonton	80	28	39	13	301	322	69
Winnipeg	80	20	49	11	214	314	51
Rockies	80	19	48	13	234	308	51

* top four teams in each division qualified for the playoffs

Stanley Cup Finals

May 13	Islanders 4 at Philadelphia 3 (Denis Potvin 4:07 OT)
May 15	Islanders 3 at Philadelphia 8
May 17	Philadelphia 2 at Islanders 6
May 19	Philadelphia 2 at Islanders 5
May 22	Islanders 3 at Philadelphia 6
May 24	Philadelphia 4 at Islanders 5 (Bob Nystrom 7:11 OT)

Islanders won best-of-seven finals 4–2

1980–81

PRINCE OF WALES CONFERENCE

Adams Division

	GP	W	L	T	GF	GA	PTS
Buffalo	80	39	20	21	327	250	99
Boston	80	37	30	13	316	272	87
North Stars	80	35	28	17	291	263	87
Quebec	80	30	32	18	314	318	78
Toronto	80	28	37	15	322	367	71

Norris Division

	GP	W	L	T	GF	GA	PTS
Canadiens	80	45	22	13	332	232	103
Los Angeles	80	43	24	13	337	290	99
Pittsburgh	80	30	37	13	302	345	73
Hartford	80	21	41	18	292	372	60
Detroit	80	19	43	18	252	339	56

CLARENCE CAMPBELL CONFERENCE

Patrick Division

	GP	W	L	T	GF	GA	PTS
Islanders	80	48	18	14	355	260	110
Philadelphia	80	41	24	15	313	249	97
Calgary	80	39	27	14	329	298	92
Rangers	80	30	36	14	312	317	74
Washington	80	26	36	18	286	317	70

Smythe Division

	GP	W	L	T	GF	GA	PTS
St. Louis	80	45	18	17	352	281	107
Chicago	80	31	33	16	304	315	78
Vancouver	80	28	32	20	289	301	76
Edmonton	80	29	35	16	328	327	74
Rockies	80	22	45	13	258	344	57
Winnipeg	80	9	57	14	246	400	32

Stanley Cup Finals

May 12	North Stars 3 at Islanders 6
May 14	North Stars 3 at Islanders 6
May 17	Islanders 7 at North Stars 5
May 19	Islanders 2 at North Stars 4
May 21	North Stars 1 at Islanders 5

Islanders won best-of-seven finals 4–1

1981–82

CLARENCE CAMPBELL CONFERENCE
Norris Division

	GP	W	L	T	GF	GA	PTS
North Stars	80	37	23	20	346	288	94
Winnipeg	80	33	33	14	319	332	80
St. Louis	80	32	40	8	315	349	72
Chicago	80	30	38	12	332	363	72
Toronto	80	20	44	16	298	380	56
Detroit	80	21	47	12	270	351	54

Smythe Division

Edmonton	80	48	17	15	417	295	111
Vancouver	80	30	33	17	290	286	77
Calgary	80	29	34	17	334	345	75
Los Angeles	80	24	41	15	314	369	63
Rockies	80	18	49	13	241	362	49

PRINCE OF WALES CONFERENCE
Adams Division

Canadiens	80	46	17	17	360	223	109
Boston	80	43	27	10	323	285	96
Buffalo	80	39	26	15	307	273	93
Quebec	80	33	31	16	356	345	82
Hartford	80	21	41	18	264	351	60

Patrick Division

Islanders	80	54	16	10	385	250	118
Rangers	80	39	27	14	316	306	92
Philadelphia	80	38	31	11	325	313	87
Pittsburgh	80	31	36	13	310	337	75
Washington	80	26	41	13	319	338	65

Stanley Cup Finals

May 8	Vancouver 5 at Islanders 6 (Mike Bossy 19:58 OT)
May 11	Vancouver 4 at Islanders 6
May 13	Islanders 3 at Vancouver 0 [Smith]
May 16	Islanders 3 at Vancouver 1

Islanders won best-of-seven finals 4–0

1982–83

CLARENCE CAMPBELL CONFERENCE
Norris Division

	GP	W	L	T	GF	GA	PTS
Chicago	80	47	23	10	338	268	104
North Stars	80	40	24	16	321	290	96
Toronto	80	28	40	12	293	330	68
St. Louis	80	25	40	15	285	316	65
Detroit	80	21	44	15	263	344	57

Smythe Division

	GP	W	L	T	GF	GA	PTS
Edmonton	80	47	21	12	424	315	106
Calgary	80	32	34	14	321	317	78
Vancouver	80	30	35	15	303	309	75
Winnipeg	80	33	39	8	311	333	74
Los Angeles	80	27	41	12	308	365	66

PRINCE OF WALES CONFERENCE
Adams Division

	GP	W	L	T	GF	GA	PTS
Boston	80	50	20	10	327	228	110
Canadiens	80	42	24	14	350	286	98
Buffalo	80	38	29	13	318	285	89
Quebec	80	34	34	12	343	336	80
Hartford	80	19	54	7	261	403	45

Patrick Division

	GP	W	L	T	GF	GA	PTS
Philadelphia	80	49	23	8	326	240	106
Islanders	80	42	26	12	302	226	96
Washington	80	39	25	16	306	283	94
Rangers	80	35	35	10	306	287	80
New Jersey	80	17	49	14	230	338	48
Pittsburgh	80	18	53	9	257	394	45

Stanley Cup Finals

May 10	Islanders 2 at Edmonton 0 [Smith]
May 12	Islanders 6 at Edmonton 3
May 14	Edmonton 1 at Islanders 5
May 17	Edmonton 2 at Islanders 4

Islanders won best-of-seven finals 4–0

1983–84

CLARENCE CAMPBELL CONFERENCE

Norris Division

	GP	W	L	T	GF	GA	PTS
North Stars	80	39	31	10	345	344	88
St. Louis	80	32	41	7	293	316	71
Detroit	80	31	42	7	298	323	69
Chicago	80	30	42	8	277	311	68
Toronto	80	26	45	9	303	387	61

Smythe Division

	GP	W	L	T	GF	GA	PTS
Edmonton	80	57	18	5	446	314	119
Calgary	80	34	32	14	311	314	82
Vancouver	80	32	39	9	306	328	73
Winnipeg	80	31	38	11	340	374	73
Los Angeles	80	23	44	13	309	376	59

PRINCE OF WALES CONFERENCE

Adams Division

	GP	W	L	T	GF	GA	PTS
Boston	80	49	25	6	336	261	104
Buffalo	80	48	25	7	315	257	103
Quebec	80	42	28	10	360	278	94
Canadiens	80	35	40	5	286	295	75
Hartford	80	28	42	10	288	320	66

Patrick Division

	GP	W	L	T	GF	GA	PTS
Islanders	80	50	26	4	357	269	104
Washington	80	48	27	5	308	226	101
Philadelphia	80	44	26	10	350	290	98
Rangers	80	42	29	9	314	304	93
New Jersey	80	17	56	7	231	350	41
Pittsburgh	80	16	58	6	254	390	38

* five-minute sudden-death overtime introduced for regular-season games

Stanley Cup Finals

May 10	Edmonton 1 at Islanders 0 [Fuhr]
May 12	Edmonton 1 at Islanders 6
May 15	Islanders 2 at Edmonton 7
May 17	Islanders 2 at Edmonton 7
May 19	Islanders 2 at Edmonton 5

Edmonton won best-of-seven finals 4–1

1984–85

CLARENCE CAMPBELL CONFERENCE

Norris Division

	GP	W	L	T	GF	GA	PTS
St. Louis	80	37	31	12	299	288	86
Chicago	80	38	35	7	309	299	83
Detroit	80	27	41	12	313	357	66
North Stars	80	25	43	12	268	321	62
Toronto	80	20	52	8	253	358	48

Smythe Division

	GP	W	L	T	GF	GA	PTS
Edmonton	80	49	20	11	401	298	109
Winnipeg	80	43	27	10	358	332	96
Calgary	80	41	27	12	363	302	94
Los Angeles	80	34	32	14	339	326	82
Vancouver	80	25	46	9	284	401	59

PRINCE OF WALES CONFERENCE

Adams Division

	GP	W	L	T	GF	GA	PTS
Canadiens	80	41	27	12	309	262	94
Quebec	80	41	30	9	323	275	91
Buffalo	80	38	28	14	290	237	90
Boston	80	36	34	10	303	287	82
Hartford	80	30	41	9	268	318	69

Patrick Division

	GP	W	L	T	GF	GA	PTS
Philadelphia	80	53	20	7	348	241	113
Washington	80	46	25	9	322	240	101
Islanders	80	40	34	6	345	312	86
Rangers	80	26	44	10	295	345	62
New Jersey	80	22	48	10	264	346	54
Pittsburgh	80	24	51	5	276	385	53

Stanley Cup Finals

May 21	Edmonton 1 at Philadelphia 4
May 23	Edmonton 3 at Philadelphia 1
May 25	Philadelphia 3 at Edmonton 4
May 28	Philadelphia 3 at Edmonton 5
May 30	Philadelphia 3 at Edmonton 8

Edmonton won best-of-seven finals 4–1

1985–86

CLARENCE CAMPBELL CONFERENCE
Norris Division

	GP	W	L	T	GF	GA	PTS
Chicago	80	39	33	8	351	349	86
North Stars	80	38	33	9	327	305	85
St. Louis	80	37	34	9	302	291	83
Toronto	80	25	48	7	311	386	57
Detroit	80	17	57	6	266	415	40

Smythe Division

	GP	W	L	T	GF	GA	PTS
Edmonton	80	56	17	7	426	310	119
Calgary	80	40	31	9	354	315	89
Winnipeg	80	26	47	7	295	372	59
Vancouver	80	23	44	13	282	333	59
Los Angeles	80	23	49	8	284	389	54

PRINCE OF WALES CONFERENCE
Adams Division

	GP	W	L	T	GF	GA	PTS
Quebec	80	43	31	6	330	289	92
Canadiens	80	40	33	7	330	280	87
Boston	80	37	31	12	311	288	86
Hartford	80	40	36	4	332	302	84
Buffalo	80	37	37	6	296	291	80

Patrick Division

	GP	W	L	T	GF	GA	PTS
Philadelphia	80	53	23	4	335	241	110
Washington	80	50	23	7	315	272	107
Islanders	80	39	29	12	327	284	90
Rangers	80	36	38	6	280	276	78
Pittsburgh	80	34	38	8	313	305	76
New Jersey	80	28	49	3	300	374	59

Stanley Cup Finals

May 16	Canadiens 2 at Calgary 5
May 18	Canadiens 3 at Calgary 2 (Brian Skrudland 0:09 OT)
May 20	Calgary 3 at Canadiens 5
May 22	Calgary 0 at Canadiens 1 [Roy]
May 24	Canadiens 4 at Calgary 3

Canadiens won best-of-seven finals 4–1

1986–87

CLARENCE CAMPBELL CONFERENCE

Norris Division

	GP	W	L	T	GF	G	PTS
St. Louis	80	32	33	15	281	293	79
Detroit	80	34	36	10	260	274	78
Chicago*	80	29	37	14	290	310	72
Toronto	80	32	42	6	286	319	70
North Stars	80	30	40	10	296	314	70

Smythe Division

Edmonton	80	50	24	6	372	284	106
Calgary	80	46	31	3	318	289	95
Winnipeg	80	40	32	8	279	271	88
Los Angeles	80	31	41	8	318	341	70
Vancouver	80	29	43	8	282	314	66

PRINCE OF WALES CONFERENCE

Adams Division

Hartford	80	43	30	7	287	270	93
Canadiens	80	41	29	10	277	241	92
Boston	80	39	34	7	301	276	85
Quebec	80	31	39	10	267	276	72
Buffalo	80	28	44	8	280	308	64

Patrick Division

Philadelphia	80	46	26	8	310	245	100
Washington	80	38	32	10	285	278	86
Islanders	80	35	33	12	279	281	82
Rangers	80	34	38	8	307	323	76
Pittsburgh	80	30	38	12	297	290	72
New Jersey	80	29	45	6	293	368	64

* Chicago changed spelling of nickname from Black Hawks to Blackhawks at start of season

Stanley Cup Finals

May 17	Philadelphia 2 at Edmonton 4
May 20	Philadelphia 2 at Edmonton 3 (Jari Kurri 6:50 OT)
May 22	Edmonton 3 at Philadelphia 5
May 24	Edmonton 4 at Philadelphia 1
May 26	Philadelphia 4 at Edmonton 3
May 28	Edmonton 2 at Philadelphia 3
May 31	Philadelphia 1 at Edmonton 3

Edmonton won best-of-seven finals 4–3

1987–88

CLARENCE CAMPBELL CONFERENCE

Norris Division

	GP	W	L	T	GF	GA	PTS
Detroit	80	41	28	11	322	269	93
St. Louis	80	34	38	8	278	294	76
Chicago	80	30	41	9	284	326	69
Toronto	80	21	49	10	273	345	52
North Stars	80	19	48	13	242	349	51

Smythe Division

	GP	W	L	T	GF	GA	PTS
Calgary	80	48	23	9	397	305	105
Edmonton	80	44	25	11	363	288	99
Winnipeg	80	33	36	11	292	310	77
Los Angeles	80	30	42	8	318	359	68
Vancouver	80	25	46	9	272	320	59

PRINCE OF WALES CONFERENCE

Adams Division

	GP	W	L	T	GF	GA	PTS
Canadiens	80	45	22	13	298	238	103
Boston	80	44	30	6	300	251	94
Buffalo	80	37	32	11	283	305	85
Hartford	80	35	38	7	249	267	77
Quebec	80	32	43	5	271	306	69

Patrick Division

	GP	W	L	T	GF	GA	PTS
Islanders	80	39	31	10	308	267	88
Washington	80	38	33	9	281	249	85
Philadelphia	80	38	33	9	292	282	85
New Jersey	80	38	36	6	295	296	82
Rangers	80	36	34	10	300	283	82
Pittsburgh	80	36	35	9	319	316	81

Stanley Cup Finals

May 18	Boston 1 at Edmonton 2
May 20	Boston 2 at Edmonton 4
May 22	Edmonton 6 at Boston 3
May 24	Edmonton 3 at Boston 3*
May 26	Boston 3 at Edmonton 6

Edmonton won best-of-seven finals 4–0

* game suspended because of power failure but statistics counted (if necessary, this game would have been made up at the end of the series)

1988–89

CLARENCE CAMPBELL CONFERENCE

Norris Division

	GP	W	L	T	GF	GA	PTS
Detroit	80	34	34	12	313	316	80
St. Louis	80	33	35	12	275	285	78
North Stars	80	27	37	16	258	278	70
Chicago	80	27	41	12	297	335	66
Toronto	80	28	46	6	259	342	62

Smythe Division

	GP	W	L	T	GF	GA	PTS
Calgary	80	54	17	9	354	226	117
Los Angeles	80	42	31	7	376	335	91
Edmonton	80	38	34	8	325	306	84
Vancouver	80	33	39	8	251	253	74
Winnipeg	80	26	42	12	300	355	64

PRINCE OF WALES CONFERENCE

Adams Division

	GP	W	L	T	GF	GA	PTS
Canadiens	80	53	18	9	315	218	115
Boston	80	37	29	14	289	256	88
Buffalo	80	38	35	7	291	299	83
Hartford	80	37	38	5	299	290	79
Quebec	80	27	46	7	269	342	61

Patrick Division

	GP	W	L	T	GF	GA	PTS
Washington	80	41	29	10	305	259	92
Pittsburgh	80	40	33	7	347	349	87
Rangers	80	37	35	8	310	307	82
Philadelphia	80	36	36	8	307	285	80
New Jersey	80	27	41	12	281	325	66
Islanders	80	28	47	5	265	325	61

Stanley Cup Finals

May 14	Canadiens 2 at Calgary 3
May 17	Canadiens 4 at Calgary 2
May 19	Calgary 3 at Canadiens 4 (Ryan Walter 38:08 OT)
May 21	Calgary 4 at Canadiens 2
May 23	Canadiens 2 at Calgary 3
May 25	Calgary 4 at Canadiens 2

Calgary won best-of-seven finals 4–2

1989–90

CLARENCE CAMPBELL CONFERENCE

Norris Division

	GP	W	L	T	GF	GA	PTS
Chicago	80	41	33	6	316	294	88
St. Louis	80	37	34	9	295	279	83
Toronto	80	38	38	4	337	358	80
North Stars	80	36	40	4	284	291	76
Detroit	80	28	38	14	288	323	70

Smythe Division

	GP	W	L	T	GF	GA	PTS
Calgary	80	42	23	15	348	265	99
Edmonton	80	38	28	14	315	283	90
Winnipeg	80	37	32	11	298	290	85
Los Angeles	80	34	39	7	338	337	75
Vancouver	80	25	41	14	245	306	64

PRINCE OF WALES CONFERENCE

Adams Division

	GP	W	L	T	GF	GA	PTS
Boston	80	46	25	9	289	232	101
Buffalo	80	45	27	8	286	248	98
Canadiens	80	41	28	11	288	234	93
Hartford	80	38	33	9	275	268	85
Quebec	80	12	61	7	240	407	31

Patrick Division

	GP	W	L	T	GF	GA	PTS
Rangers	80	36	31	13	279	267	85
New Jersey	80	37	34	9	295	288	83
Washington	80	36	38	6	284	275	78
Islanders	80	31	38	11	281	288	73
Pittsburgh	80	32	40	8	318	359	72
Philadelphia	80	30	39	11	290	297	71

Stanley Cup Finals

May 15	Edmonton 3 at Boston 2 (Petr Klima 55:13 OT)
May 18	Edmonton 7 at Boston 2
May 20	Boston 2 at Edmonton 1
May 22	Boston 1 at Edmonton 5
May 24	Edmonton 4 at Boston 1

Edmonton won best-of-seven finals 4–1

1990–91

CLARENCE CAMPBELL CONFERENCE

Norris Division

	GP	W	L	T	GF	GA	PTS
Chicago	80	49	23	8	284	211	106
St. Louis	80	47	22	11	310	250	105
Detroit	80	34	38	8	273	298	76
North Stars	80	27	39	14	256	266	68
Toronto	80	23	46	11	241	318	57

Smythe Division

	GP	W	L	T	GF	GA	PTS
Los Angeles	80	46	24	10	340	254	102
Calgary	80	46	26	8	344	263	100
Edmonton	80	37	37	6	272	272	80
Vancouver	80	28	43	9	243	315	65
Winnipeg	80	26	43	11	260	288	63

PRINCE OF WALES CONFERENCE

Adams Division

	GP	W	L	T	GF	GA	PTS
Boston	80	44	24	12	299	264	100
Canadiens	80	39	30	11	273	249	89
Buffalo	80	31	30	19	292	278	81
Hartford	80	31	38	11	238	276	73
Quebec	80	16	50	14	236	354	46

Patrick Division

	GP	W	L	T	GF	GA	PTS
Pittsburgh	80	41	33	6	342	305	88
Rangers	80	36	31	13	297	265	85
Washington	80	37	36	7	258	258	81
New Jersey	80	32	33	15	272	264	79
Philadelphia	80	33	37	10	252	267	76
Islanders	80	25	45	10	223	290	60

Stanley Cup Finals

May 15	Minnesota 5 at Pittsburgh 4
May 17	Minnesota 1 at Pittsburgh 4
May 19	Pittsburgh 1 at Minnesota 3
May 21	Pittsburgh 5 at Minnesota 3
May 23	Minnesota 4 at Pittsburgh 6
May 25	Pittsburgh 8 at Minnesota 0 [Barrasso]

Pittsburgh won best-of-seven finals 4–2

1991–92

CLARENCE CAMPBELL CONFERENCE
Norris Division

	GP	W	L	T	GF	GA	PTS
Detroit	80	43	25	12	320	256	98
Chicago	80	36	29	15	257	236	87
St. Louis	80	36	33	11	279	266	83
North Stars	80	32	42	6	246	278	70
Toronto	80	30	43	7	234	294	67

Smythe Division

	GP	W	L	T	GF	GA	PTS
Vancouver	80	42	26	12	285	250	96
Los Angeles	80	35	31	14	287	296	84
Edmonton	80	36	34	10	295	297	82
Winnipeg	80	33	32	15	251	244	81
Calgary	80	31	37	12	296	305	74
San Jose	80	17	58	5	219	359	39

PRINCE OF WALES CONFERENCE
Adams Division

	GP	W	L	T	GF	GA	PTS
Canadiens	80	41	28	11	267	207	93
Boston	80	36	32	12	270	275	84
Buffalo	80	31	37	12	289	299	74
Hartford	80	26	41	13	247	283	65
Quebec	80	20	48	12	255	318	52

Patrick Division

	GP	W	L	T	GF	GA	PTS
Rangers	80	50	25	5	321	246	105
Washington	80	45	27	8	330	275	98
Pittsburgh	80	39	32	9	343	308	87
New Jersey	80	38	31	11	289	259	87
Islanders	80	34	35	11	291	299	79
Philadelphia	80	32	37	11	252	273	75

Stanley Cup Finals

May 26	Chicago 4 at Pittsburgh 5
May 28	Chicago 1 at Pittsburgh 3
May 30	Pittsburgh 1 at Chicago 0 [Barrasso]
June 1	Pittsburgh 6 at Chicago 5

Pittsburgh won best-of-seven finals 4–0

1992–93

CLARENCE CAMPBELL CONFERENCE

Norris Division

	GP	W	L	T	GF	GA	PTS
Chicago	84	47	25	12	279	230	106
Detroit	84	47	28	9	369	280	103
Toronto	84	44	29	11	288	241	99
St. Louis	84	37	36	11	282	278	85
North Stars	84	36	38	10	272	293	82
Tampa Bay	84	23	54	7	245	332	53

Smythe Division

	GP	W	L	T	GF	GA	PTS
Vancouver	84	46	29	9	346	278	101
Calgary	84	43	30	11	322	282	97
Los Angeles	84	39	35	10	338	340	88
Winnipeg	84	40	37	7	322	320	87
Edmonton	84	26	50	8	242	337	60
San Jose	84	11	71	2	218	414	24

PRINCE OF WALES CONFERENCE

Adams Division

	GP	W	L	T	GF	GA	PTS
Boston	84	51	26	7	332	268	109
Quebec	84	47	27	10	351	300	104
Canadiens	84	48	30	6	326	280	102
Buffalo	84	38	36	10	335	297	86
Hartford	84	26	52	6	284	369	58
Ottawa	84	10	70	4	202	395	24

Patrick Division

	GP	W	L	T	GF	GA	PTS
Pittsburgh	84	56	21	7	367	268	119
Washington	84	43	34	7	325	286	93
Islanders	84	40	37	7	335	297	87
New Jersey	84	40	37	7	308	299	87
Philadelphia	84	36	37	11	319	319	83
Rangers	84	34	39	11	304	308	79

Stanley Cup Finals

June 1	Los Angeles 4 at Canadiens 1
June 3	Los Angeles 2 at Canadiens 3 (Eric Desjardins 0:51 OT)
June 5	Canadiens 4 at Los Angeles 3 (John LeClair 0:34 OT)
June 7	Canadiens 3 at Los Angeles 2 (John LeClair 14:37 OT)
June 9	Los Angeles 1 at Canadiens 4

Canadiens won best-of-seven finals 4–1

1993–94

WESTERN CONFERENCE
Central Division

	GP	W	L	T	GF	GA	PTS
Detroit	84	46	30	8	356	275	100
Toronto	84	43	29	12	280	243	98
Dallas	84	42	29	13	286	265	97
St. Louis	84	40	33	11	270	283	91
Chicago	84	39	36	9	254	240	87
Winnipeg	84	24	51	9	245	344	57

Pacific Division

	GP	W	L	T	GF	GA	PTS
Calgary	84	42	29	13	302	256	97
Vancouver	84	41	40	3	279	276	85
San Jose	84	33	35	16	252	265	82
Anaheim	84	33	46	5	229	251	71
Los Angeles	84	27	45	12	294	322	66
Edmonton	84	25	45	14	261	305	64

EASTERN CONFERENCE
Northeast Division

	GP	W	L	T	GF	GA	PTS
Pittsburgh	84	44	27	13	299	285	101
Boston	84	42	29	13	289	252	97
Canadiens	84	41	29	14	283	248	96
Buffalo	84	43	32	9	282	218	95
Quebec	84	34	42	8	277	292	76
Hartford	84	27	48	9	227	288	63
Ottawa	84	14	61	9	201	397	37

Atlantic Division

	GP	W	L	T	GF	GA	PTS
Rangers	84	52	24	8	299	231	112
New Jersey	84	47	25	12	306	220	106
Washington	84	39	35	10	277	263	88
Islanders	84	36	36	12	282	264	84
Florida	84	33	34	17	233	233	83
Philadelphia	84	35	39	10	294	314	80
Tampa Bay	84	30	43	11	224	251	71

* the top eight teams in each conference qualified for the playoffs

Stanley Cup Finals

May 31	Vancouver 3 at Rangers 2 (Greg Adams 19:26 OT)
June 2	Vancouver 1 at Rangers 3
June 4	Rangers 5 at Vancouver 1
June 7	Rangers 4 at Vancouver 2
June 9	Vancouver 6 at Rangers 3
June 11	Rangers 1 at Vancouver 4
June 14	Vancouver 2 at Rangers 3

Rangers won best-of-seven finals 4–3

1994–95

WESTERN CONFERENCE

Central Division

	GP	W	L	T	GF	GA	PTS
Detroit	48	33	11	4	180	117	70
St. Louis	48	28	15	5	178	135	61
Chicago	48	24	19	5	156	115	53
Toronto	48	21	19	8	135	146	50
Dallas	48	17	23	8	136	135	42
Winnipeg	48	16	25	7	157	177	39

Pacific Division

	GP	W	L	T	GF	GA	PTS
Calgary	48	24	17	7	163	135	55
Vancouver	48	18	18	12	153	148	48
San Jose	48	19	25	4	129	161	42
Los Angeles	48	16	23	9	142	174	41
Edmonton	48	17	27	4	136	183	38
Anaheim	48	16	27	5	125	164	37

EASTERN CONFERENCE

Northeast Division

Quebec	48	30	13	5	185	134	65
Pittsburgh	48	29	16	3	181	158	61
Boston	48	27	18	3	150	127	57
Buffalo	48	22	19	7	130	119	51
Hartford	48	19	24	5	127	141	43
Canadiens	48	18	23	7	125	148	43
Ottawa	48	9	34	5	116	174	23

Atlantic Division

Philadelphia	48	28	16	4	150	132	60
New Jersey	48	22	18	8	136	121	52
Washington	48	22	18	8	136	120	52
Rangers	48	22	23	3	139	134	47
Florida	48	20	22	6	115	127	46
Tampa Bay	48	17	28	3	120	144	37
Islanders	48	15	28	5	126	158	35

Stanley Cup Finals

June 17	New Jersey 2 at Detroit 1
June 20	New Jersey 4 at Detroit 2
June 22	Detroit 2 at New Jersey 5
June 24	Detroit 2 at New Jersey 5

New Jersey won best-of-seven finals 4–0

1995–96

WESTERN CONFERENCE

Central Division

	GP	W	L	T	GF	GA	PTS
Detroit	82	62	13	7	325	181	131
Chicago	82	40	28	14	273	220	94
Toronto	82	34	36	12	247	252	80
St. Louis	82	32	34	16	219	248	80
Winnipeg	82	36	40	6	275	291	78
Dallas	82	26	42	14	227	280	66

Pacific Division

Colorado	82	47	25	10	326	240	104
Calgary	82	34	37	11	241	240	79
Vancouver	82	32	35	15	278	278	79
Anaheim	82	35	39	8	234	247	78
Edmonton	82	30	44	8	240	304	68
Los Angeles	82	24	40	18	256	302	66
San Jose	82	20	55	7	252	357	47

EASTERN CONFERENCE

Northeast Division

Pittsburgh	82	49	29	4	362	284	102
Boston	82	40	31	11	282	269	91
Canadiens	82	40	32	10	265	248	90
Hartford	82	34	39	9	237	259	77
Buffalo	82	33	42	7	247	262	73
Ottawa	82	18	59	5	191	291	41

Atlantic Division

Philadelphia	82	45	24	13	282	208	103
Rangers	82	41	27	14	272	237	96
Florida	82	41	31	10	254	234	92
Washington	82	39	32	11	234	204	89
Tampa Bay	82	38	32	12	238	248	88
New Jersey	82	37	33	12	215	202	86
Islanders	82	22	50	10	229	315	54

Stanley Cup Finals

June 4	Florida 1 at Colorado 3
June 6	Florida 1 at Colorado 8
June 8	Colorado 3 at Florida 2
June 10	Colorado 1 at Florida 0 (Uwe Krupp 44:31 OT) [Roy]

Colorado won best-of seven finals 4–0

1996–97

WESTERN CONFERENCE

Central Division

	GP	W	L	T	GF	GA	PTS
Dallas	82	48	26	8	252	198	104
Detroit	82	38	26	18	253	197	94
Phoenix	82	38	37	7	240	243	83
St. Louis	82	36	35	11	236	239	83
Chicago	82	34	35	13	223	210	81
Toronto	82	30	44	8	230	273	68

Pacific Division

	GP	W	L	T	GF	GA	PTS
Colorado	82	49	24	9	277	205	107
Anaheim	82	36	33	13	245	233	85
Edmonton	82	36	37	9	252	247	81
Vancouver	82	35	40	7	257	273	77
Calgary	82	32	41	9	214	239	73
Los Angeles	82	28	43	11	214	268	67
San Jose	82	27	47	8	211	278	62

EASTERN CONFERENCE

Northeast Division

	GP	W	L	T	GF	GA	PTS
Buffalo	82	40	30	12	237	208	92
Pittsburgh	82	38	36	8	285	280	84
Ottawa	82	31	36	15	226	234	77
Canadiens	82	31	36	15	249	276	77
Hartford	82	32	39	11	226	256	75
Boston	82	26	47	9	234	300	61

Atlantic Division

	GP	W	L	T	GF	GA	PTS
New Jersey	82	45	23	14	231	182	104
Philadelphia	82	45	24	13	274	217	103
Florida	82	35	28	19	221	201	89
Rangers	82	38	34	10	258	231	86
Washington	82	33	40	9	214	231	75
Tampa Bay	82	32	40	10	217	247	74
Islanders	82	29	41	12	240	250	70

Stanley Cup Finals

May 31	Detroit 4 at Philadelphia 2
June 3	Detroit 4 at Philadelphia 2
June 5	Philadelphia 1 at Detroit 6
June 7	Philadelphia 1 at Detroit 2

Detroit won best-of-seven finals 4–0

1997–98

WESTERN CONFERENCE

Central Division

	GP	W	L	T	GF	GA	PTS
Dallas	82	49	22	11	242	167	109
Detroit	82	44	23	15	250	196	103
St. Louis	82	45	29	8	256	204	98
Phoenix	82	35	35	12	224	227	82
Chicago	82	30	39	13	192	199	73
Toronto	82	30	43	9	194	237	69

Pacific Division

	GP	W	L	T	GF	GA	PTS
Colorado	82	39	26	17	231	205	95
Los Angeles	82	38	33	11	227	225	87
Edmonton	82	35	37	10	215	224	80
San Jose	82	34	38	10	210	216	78
Calgary	82	26	41	15	217	252	67
Anaheim	82	26	43	13	205	261	65
Vancouver	82	25	43	14	224	273	64

EASTERN CONFERENCE

Northeast Division

	GP	W	L	T	GF	GA	PTS
Pittsburgh	82	40	24	18	228	188	98
Boston	82	39	30	13	221	194	91
Buffalo	82	36	29	17	211	187	89
Canadiens	82	37	32	13	235	208	87
Ottawa	82	34	33	15	193	20	83
Carolina	82	33	41	8	200	219	74

Atlantic Division

New Jersey	82	48	23	11	225	166	107
Philadelphia	82	42	29	11	242	193	95
Washington	82	40	30	12	219	202	92
Islanders	82	30	41	11	212	225	71
Rangers	82	25	39	18	197	231	68
Florida	82	24	43	15	203	256	63
Tampa Bay	82	17	55	10	151	269	44

Stanley Cup Finals

June 9	Washington 1 at Detroit 2
June 11	Washington 4 at Detroit 5 (Kris Draper 15:24 OT)
June 13	Detroit 2 at Washington 1
June 16	Detroit 4 at Washington 1

Detroit won best-of-seven finals 4–0

1998–99

EASTERN CONFERENCE

Northeast Division

	GP	W	L	T	GF	GA	PTS
Ottawa	82	44	23	15	239	179	103
Toronto	82	45	30	7	268	231	97
Boston	82	39	30	13	214	181	91
Buffalo	82	37	28	17	207	175	91
Canadiens	82	32	39	11	184	209	75

Atlantic Division

New Jersey	82	47	24	11	248	196	105
Philadelphia	82	37	26	19	231	196	93
Pittsburgh	82	38	30	14	242	225	90
Rangers	82	33	38	11	217	227	77
Islanders	82	24	48	10	194	244	58

Southeast Division

Carolina	82	34	30	18	210	202	86
Florida	82	30	34	18	210	228	78
Washington	82	31	45	6	200	218	68
Tampa Bay	82	19	54	9	179	292	47

WESTERN CONFERENCE

Central Division

Detroit	82	43	32	7	245	202	93
St. Louis	82	37	32	13	237	209	87
Chicago	82	29	41	12	202	248	70
Nashville	82	28	47	7	190	261	63

Pacific Division

Dallas	82	51	19	12	236	168	114
Phoenix	82	39	31	12	205	197	90
Anaheim	82	35	34	13	215	206	83
San Jose	82	31	33	18	196	191	80
Los Angeles	82	32	45	5	189	222	69

Northwest Division

Colorado	82	44	28	10	239	205	98
Edmonton	82	33	37	12	230	226	78
Calgary	82	30	40	12	211	234	72
Vancouver	82	23	47	12	192	258	58

Stanley Cup Finals

June 8	Buffalo 3 at Dallas 2 (Jason Woolley 15:30 OT)
June 10	Buffalo 2 at Dallas 4
June 12	Dallas 2 at Buffalo 1
June 15	Dallas 1 at Buffalo 2
June 17	Buffalo 0 at Dallas 2 [Belfour]
June 19	Dallas 2 at Buffalo 1 (Brett Hull 54:51 OT)

Dallas won best-of-seven finals 4–2

1999–2000

EASTERN CONFERENCE

Northeast Division

	GP	W	L	T	OTL	GF	GA	PTS
Toronto	82	45	30	7	3	246	222	100
Ottawa	82	41	30	11	2	244	210	95
Buffalo	82	35	36	11	4	213	204	85
Canadiens	82	35	38	9	4	196	194	83
Boston	82	24	39	19	6	210	248	73

Atlantic Division

Philadelphia	82	45	25	12	3	237	179	105
New Jersey	82	45	29	8	5	251	203	103
Pittsburgh	82	37	37	8	6	241	236	88
Rangers	82	29	42	12	3	218	246	73
Islanders	82	24	49	9	1	194	275	58

Southeast Division

Washington	82	44	26	12	2	227	194	102
Florida	82	43	33	6	6	244	209	98
Carolina	82	37	35	10	0	217	216	84
Tampa Bay	82	19	54	9	7	204	309	54
Atlanta	82	14	61	7	4	170	313	39

WESTERN CONFERENCE

Central Division

St. Louis	82	51	20	11	1	248	165	114
Detroit	82	48	24	10	2	278	210	108
Chicago	82	33	39	10	2	242	245	78
Nashville	82	28	47	7	7	199	240	70

Northwest Division

Colorado	82	42	29	11	1	233	201	96
Edmonton	82	32	34	16	8	226	212	88
Vancouver	82	30	37	15	8	227	237	83
Calgary	82	31	41	10	5	211	256	77

Pacific Division

Dallas	82	43	29	10	6	211	184	102
Los Angeles	82	39	31	12	4	245	228	94
Phoenix	82	39	35	8	4	232	228	90
San Jose	82	35	37	10	7	225	214	87
Anaheim	82	34	36	12	3	217	227	83

Stanley Cup Finals

May 30	Dallas 3 at New Jersey 7
June 1	Dallas 2 at New Jersey 1
June 3	New Jersey 2 at Dallas 1
June 5	New Jersey 3 at Dallas 1
June 8	Dallas 1 at New Jersey 0 (Mike Modano 46:21 OT) [Belfour]
June 10	New Jersey 2 at Dallas 1 (Jason Arnott 28:20 OT)

New Jersey won best-of-seven finals 4–2

2000–01

EASTERN CONFERENCE
Northeast Division

	GP	W	L	T	OTL	GF	GA	PTS
Ottawa	82	48	21	9	4	274	205	109
Buffalo	82	46	30	5	1	218	184	98
Toronto	82	37	29	11	5	232	207	90
Boston	82	36	30	8	8	227	249	88
Montreal	82	28	40	8	6	206	232	70

Atlantic Division

New Jersey	82	48	19	12	3	295	195	111
Philadelphia	82	43	25	11	3	240	207	100
Pittsburgh	82	42	28	9	3	281	256	96
Rangers	82	33	43	5	1	250	290	72
Islanders	82	21	51	7	3	185	268	52

Southeast Division

Washington	82	41	27	10	4	233	211	96
Carolina	82	38	32	9	3	212	225	88
Florida	82	22	38	13	9	200	246	66
Atlanta	82	23	45	12	2	211	289	60
Tampa Bay	82	24	47	6	5	201	280	59

WESTERN CONFERENCE
Central Division

Detroit	82	49	20	9	4	253	202	111
St. Louis	82	43	22	12	5	249	195	103
Nashville	82	34	36	9	3	186	200	80
Chicago	82	29	40	8	5	210	246	71
Columbus	82	28	39	9	6	190	233	71

Northwest Division

Colorado	82	52	16	10	4	270	192	118
Edmonton	82	39	28	12	3	243	222	93
Vancouver	82	36	28	11	7	239	238	90
Calgary	82	27	36	15	4	197	236	73
Minnesota	82	25	39	13	5	168	210	68

Pacific Division

Dallas	82	48	24	8	2	241	187	106
San Jose	82	40	27	12	3	217	192	95
Los Angeles	82	38	28	13	3	252	228	92
Phoenix	82	35	27	17	3	214	212	90
Anaheim	82	25	41	11	5	188	245	66

Stanley Cup Finals

May 26	New Jersey 0 at Colorado 5 [Roy]
May 29	New Jersey 2 at Colorado 1
May 31	Colorado 3 at New Jersey 1
June 2	Colorado 2 at New Jersey 3
June 4	New Jersey 4 at Colorado 1
June 7	Colorado 4 at New Jersey 0 [Roy]
June 9	New Jersey 1 at Colorado 3

Colorado won best-of-seven finals 4–3

2001–02

EASTERN CONFERENCE

Northeast Division

	GP	W	L	T	OTL	GF	GA	PTS
Boston	82	43	24	6	9	236	201	101
Toronto	82	43	25	10	4	249	207	100
Ottawa	82	39	27	9	7	243	208	94
Montreal	82	36	31	12	3	207	209	87
Buffalo	82	35	35	11	1	213	200	82

Atlantic Division

Philadelphia	82	42	27	10	3	234	192	97
Islanders	82	42	28	8	4	239	220	96
New Jersey	82	41	28	9	4	205	187	95
Rangers	82	36	38	4	4	227	258	80
Pittsburgh	82	28	41	8	5	198	249	69

Southeast Division

Carolina	82	35	26	16	5	217	217	91
Washington	82	36	33	11	2	228	240	85
Tampa Bay	82	27	40	11	4	178	219	69
Florida	82	22	44	10	6	180	250	60
Atlanta	82	19	47	11	5	187	288	54

WESTERN CONFERENCE
Central Division

Detroit	82	51	17	10	4	251	187	116
St. Louis	82	43	27	8	4	227	188	98
Chicago	82	41	27	13	1	216	207	96
Nashville	82	28	41	13	0	196	230	69
Columbus	82	22	47	8	5	164	255	57

Pacific Division

San Jose	82	44	27	8	3	248	199	99
Phoenix	82	40	27	9	6	228	210	95
Los Angeles	82	40	27	11	4	214	190	95
Dallas	82	36	28	13	5	215	213	90
Anaheim	82	29	42	8	3	175	198	69

Northwest Division

Colorado	82	42	28	8	1	212	169	99
Vancouver	82	42	30	7	3	254	211	94
Edmonton	82	38	28	12	4	205	182	92
Calgary	82	32	35	12	3	201	220	79
Minnesota	82	26	35	12	9	195	238	73

Stanley Cup Finals

June 4	Carolina 3 at Detroit 2
June 6	Carolina 1 at Detroit 3
June 8	Detroit 3 at Carolina 2
June 10	Detroit 3 at Carolina 0
June 13	Carolina 1 at Detroit 3

Detroit won best-of-seven finals 4–1

2002–03

EASTERN CONFERENCE
Northeast Division

	GP	W	L	T	OTL	GF	GA	PTS
Ottawa	82	52	21	8	1	263	182	113
Toronto	82	44	28	7	3	236	208	98
Boston	82	36	31	11	4	245	237	87
Montreal	82	30	35	8	9	206	234	77
Buffalo	82	27	37	10	8	190	219	72

Atlantic Division

New Jersey	82	46	20	10	6	216	166	108
Philadelphia	82	45	20	13	4	211	166	107
Islanders	82	35	34	11	2	224	231	83
Rangers	82	32	36	10	4	210	231	78
Pittsburgh	82	27	44	6	5	189	255	65

Southeast Division

Tampa Bay	82	36	25	16	5	219	210	93
Washington	82	39	29	8	6	224	220	92
Atlanta	82	31	39	7	5	226	284	74
Florida	82	24	36	13	9	176	237	70
Carolina	82	22	43	11	6	171	240	61

Western Conference

Central Division

Detroit	82	48	20	10	4	269	203	110
St. Louis	82	41	24	11	6	253	222	99
Chicago	82	30	33	13	6	207	226	79
Nashville	82	27	35	13	7	183	206	74
Columbus	82	29	42	8	3	213	263	69

Pacific Division

Dallas	82	46	17	15	4	245	169	111
Anaheim	82	40	27	9	6	203	193	95
Los Angeles	82	33	37	6	6	203	221	78
Phoenix	82	31	35	11	5	204	230	78
San Jose	82	28	37	9	8	214	239	73

Northwest Division

Colorado	82	42	19	13	8	251	194	105
Vancouver	82	45	23	13	1	264	208	104
Minnesota	82	42	29	10	1	198	178	95
Edmonton	82	36	26	11	9	231	230	92
Calgary	82	29	36	13	4	186	228	75

Stanley Cup Finals

May 27	Anaheim 0 at New Jersey 3 [Brodeur]
May 29	Anaheim 0 at New Jersey 3 [Brodeur]
May 31	New Jersey 2 at Anaheim 3 (Ruslan Salei 6:59 OT)
June 2	New Jersey 0 at Anaheim 1 (Steve Thomas 0:39 OT) [Giguere]
June 5	Anaheim 3 at New Jersey 6
June 7	New Jersey 2 at Anaheim 5
June 9	Anaheim 0 at New Jersey 3 [Brodeur]

New Jersey won best-of-seven finals 4–3

2003–04

EASTERN CONFERENCE

Atlantic Division

	GP	W	L	T	OTL	PTS	GF	GA
Philadelphia	82	40	21	15	6	101	229	186
New Jersey	82	43	25	12	2	100	213	164
Islanders	82	38	29	11	4	91	237	210
Rangers	82	27	40	7	8	69	206	250
Pittsburgh	82	23	47	8	4	58	190	303

Northeast Division

	GP	W	L	T	OTL	PTS	GF	GA
Boston	82	41	19	15	7	104	209	188
Toronto	82	45	24	10	3	103	242	204
Ottawa	82	43	23	10	6	102	262	189
Montreal	82	41	30	7	4	93	208	192
Buffalo	82	37	34	7	4	85	220	221

Southeast Division

	GP	W	L	T	OTL	PTS	GF	GA
Tampa Bay	82	46	22	8	6	106	245	192
Atlanta	82	33	37	8	4	78	214	243
Carolina	82	28	34	14	6	76	172	209
Florida	82	28	35	15	4	75	188	221
Washington	82	23	46	10	3	59	186	253

WESTERN CONFERENCE

Central Division

Detroit	82	48	21	11	2	109	255	189
St. Louis	82	39	30	11	2	91	191	198
Nashville	82	38	29	11	4	91	216	217
Columbus	82	25	45	8	4	62	177	238
Chicago	82	20	43	11	8	59	188	259

Northwest Division

Vancouver	82	43	24	10	5	101	235	194
Colorado	82	40	22	13	7	100	236	198
Calgary	82	42	30	7	3	94	200	176
Edmonton	82	36	29	12	5	89	221	208
Minnesota	82	30	29	20	3	83	188	183

Pacific Division

San Jose	82	43	21	12	6	104	219	183
Dallas	82	41	26	13	2	97	194	175
Los Angeles	82	28	29	16	9	81	205	217
Anaheim	82	29	35	10	8	76	184	213
Phoenix	82	22	36	18	6	68	188	245

Note: overtime losses (OTL) are worth one point in the standings and are not included in the loss column (L)

Stanley Cup Finals

May 25	Calgary 4 at Tampa Bay 1
May 27	Calgary 1 at Tampa Bay 4
May 29	Tampa Bay 0 at Calgary 3 [Kiprusoff]
May 31	Tampa Bay 1 at Calgary 0 (Richards 2:48 1st) [Khabibulin]
June 3	Calgary 3 at Tampa Bay 2 (Saprykin 14:40 OT)
June 5	Tampa Bay 3 at Calgary 2 (St. Louis 20:33 OT)
June 7	Calgary 1 at Tampa Bay 2

Tampa Bay won best-of-seven finals 4–3

Note: 2004–05 no season

2005–06

EASTERN CONFERENCE
Northeast Division

	GP	W	L	OTL	SOL	GF	GA	P
Ottawa	82	52	21	3	6	314	211	113
Buffalo	82	52	24	1	5	281	239	110
Canadiens	82	42	31	6	3	243	247	93
Toronto	82	41	33	1	7	257	270	90
Boston	82	29	37	8	8	230	266	74

Atlantic Division

	GP	W	L	OTL	SOL	GF	GA	P
New Jersey	82	46	27	5	4	242	229	101
Philadelphia	82	45	26	5	6	267	259	101
Rangers	82	44	26	8	4	257	215	100
Islanders	82	36	40	3	3	230	278	78
Pittsburgh	82	22	46	8	6	244	316	58

Southeast Division

	GP	W	L	OTL	SOL	GF	GA	P
Carolina	82	52	22	6	2	294	260	112
Tampa Bay	82	43	33	2	4	252	260	92
Atlanta	82	41	33	3	5	281	275	90
Florida	82	37	34	6	5	240	257	85
Washington	82	29	41	6	6	237	306	70

WESTERN CONFERENCE
Central Division

	GP	W	L	OTL	SOL	GF	GA	P
Detroit	82	58	16	5	3	305	209	124
Nashville	82	49	25	5	3	259	227	106
Columbus	82	35	43	1	3	223	279	74
Chicago	82	26	43	7	6	211	285	65
St. Louis	82	21	46	6	9	197	292	57

Northwest Division

	GP	W	L	OTL	SOL	GF	GA	P
Calgary	82	46	25	4	7	218	200	103
Colorado	82	43	30	3	6	283	257	95
Edmonton	82	41	28	4	9	256	251	95
Vancouver	82	42	32	4	4	256	255	92
Minnesota	82	38	36	5	3	231	215	84

Pacific Division

Dallas	82	53	23	5	1	265	218	112
San Jose	82	44	27	4	7	266	242	99
Anaheim	82	43	27	5	7	254	229	98
Los Angeles	82	42	35	4	1	249	270	89
Phoenix	82	38	39	2	3	246	271	81

Stanley Cup Finals

June 5	Edmonton 4 at Carolina 5
June 7	Edmonton 0 at Carolina 5 [Ward]
June 10	Carolina 1 at Edmonton 2
June 12	Carolina 2 at Edmonton 1
June 14	Edmonton 4 at Carolina 3 (Pisani 3:31 OT)]
June 17	Carolina 0 at Edmonton 4 [Ward]
June 19	Edmonton 1 at Carolina 3

Carolina won best-of-seven finals 4–3

2006–07

EASTERN CONFERENCE

Atlantic Division

	GP	W	L	OT	GF	GA	P
New Jersey	82	49	24	9	216	201	107
Pittsburgh	82	47	24	11	277	246	105
Rangers	82	42	30	10	242	216	94
Islanders	82	40	30	12	248	240	92
Philadelphia	82	22	48	12	214	303	56

Northeast Division

Buffalo	82	53	22	7	308	242	113
Ottawa	82	48	25	9	288	222	105
Toronto	82	40	31	11	258	269	91
Canadiens	82	42	34	6	245	256	90
Boston	82	35	41	6	219	289	76

Southeast Division

Atlanta	82	43	28	11	246	245	97
Tampa Bay	82	44	33	5	253	261	93
Carolina	82	40	34	8	241	253	88
Florida	82	35	31	16	247	257	86
Washington	82	28	40	14	235	286	70

WESTERN CONFERENCE
Central Division

Detroit	82	50	19	13	254	199	113
Nashville	82	51	23	8	272	212	110
St. Louis	82	34	35	13	214	254	81
Columbus	82	33	42	7	201	249	73
Chicago	82	31	42	9	201	258	71

Northwest Division

Vancouver	82	49	26	7	222	201	105
Minnesota	82	48	26	8	235	191	104
Calgary	82	43	29	10	258	226	96
Colorado	82	44	31	7	272	251	95
Edmonton	82	32	43	7	195	248	71

Pacific Division

Anaheim	82	48	20	14	258	208	110
San Jose	82	51	26	5	258	199	107
Dallas	82	50	25	7	226	197	107
Los Angeles	82	27	41	14	227	283	68
Phoenix	82	31	46	5	216	284	67

Stanley Cup Finals

May 28	Ottawa 2 at Anaheim 3
May 30	Ottawa 0 at Anaheim 1 (Pahlsson 14:15 3rd) [Giguere]
June 2	Anaheim 3 at Ottawa 5
June 4	Anaheim 3 at Ottawa 2
June 6	Ottawa 2 at Anaheim 6

Anaheim won best-of-seven 4–1

2007–08

EASTERN CONFERENCE
Northeast Division

	GP	W	L	OT	GF	GA	P
Canadiens	82	47	25	10	262	222	104
Ottawa	82	43	31	8	261	247	94
Boston	82	41	29	12	212	222	94
Buffalo	82	39	31	12	255	242	90
Toronto	82	36	35	11	231	260	83

Atlantic Division

Pittsburgh	82	47	27	8	247	216	102
New Jersey	82	46	29	7	206	197	99
Rangers	82	42	27	13	213	199	97
Philadelphia	82	42	29	11	248	233	95
Islanders	82	35	38	9	194	243	79

Southeast Division

Washington	82	43	31	8	242	231	94
Carolina	82	43	33	6	252	249	92
Florida	82	38	35	9	216	226	85
Atlanta	82	34	40	8	216	272	76
Tampa Bay	82	31	42	9	223	267	71

WESTERN CONFERENCE

Central Division

Detroit	82	54	21	7	257	184	115
Nashville	82	41	32	9	230	229	91
Chicago	82	40	34	8	239	235	88
Columbus	82	34	36	12	193	218	80
St. Louis	82	33	36	13	205	237	79

Northwest Division

Minnesota	82	44	28	10	223	218	98
Colorado	82	44	31	7	231	219	95
Calgary	82	42	30	10	229	227	94
Edmonton	82	41	35	6	235	251	88
Vancouver	82	39	33	10	213	215	88

Pacific Division

San Jose	82	49	23	10	222	193	108
Anaheim	82	47	27	8	205	191	102
Dallas	82	45	30	7	242	207	97
Phoenix	82	38	37	7	214	231	83
Los Angeles	82	32	43	7	231	266	71

Stanley Cup Finals

May 24	Pittsburgh 0 at Detroit 4 [Osgood]
May 26	Pittsburgh 0 at Detroit 3 [Osgood]
May 28	Detroit 2 at Pittsburgh 3
May 31	Detroit 2 at Pittsburgh 1

| June 2 | Pittsburgh 4 at Detroit 3 (Sykora 49:57 OT) |
| June 4 | Detroit 3 at Pittsburgh 2 |

Detroit won best of seven 4–2

2008–09

EASTERN CONFERENCE

Northeast Division

	GP	W	L	OT	GF	GA	Pts
Boston	82	53	19	10	274	196	116
Montreal	82	41	30	11	249	247	93
Buffalo	82	41	32	9	250	234	91
Ottawa	82	36	35	11	217	237	83
Toronto	82	34	35	13	250	293	81

Southeast Division

Washington	82	50	24	8	272	245	108
Carolina	82	45	30	7	239	226	97
Florida	82	41	30	11	234	231	93
Atlanta	82	35	41	6	257	280	76
Tampa Bay	82	24	40	18	210	279	66

Atlantic Division

New Jersey	82	51	27	4	244	209	106
Pittsburgh	82	45	28	9	264	239	99
Philadelphia	82	44	27	11	264	238	99
NY Rangers	82	43	30	9	210	218	95
NY Islanders	82	26	47	9	201	279	61

WESTERN CONFERENCE

Central Division

Detroit	82	51	21	10	295	244	112
Chicago	82	46	24	12	264	216	104
St. Louis	82	41	31	10	233	233	92
Columbus	82	41	31	10	226	230	92
Nashville	82	40	34	8	213	233	88

Northwest Division

Vancouver	82	45	27	10	246	220	100
Calgary	82	46	30	6	254	248	98
Minnesota	82	40	33	9	219	200	89
Edmonton	82	38	35	9	234	248	85
Colorado	82	32	45	5	199	257	69

Pacific Division

San Jose	82	53	18	11	257	204	117
Anaheim	82	42	33	7	245	238	91
Dallas	82	36	35	11	230	257	83
Phoenix	82	36	39	7	208	252	79
Los Angeles	82	34	37	11	207	234	79

Stanley Cup Finals

May 30	Pittsburgh 1 at Detroit 3
May 31	Pittsburgh 1 at Detroit 3
June 2	Detroit 2 at Pittsburgh 4
June 4	Detroit 2 at Pittsburgh 4
June 6	Pittsburgh 0 at Detroit 5 [Osgood]
June 9	Detroit 1 at Pittsburgh 2
June 12	Pittsburgh 2 at Detroit 1

Pittsburgh won best-of-seven finals 4–3

2009–10

EASTERN CONFERENCE
Northeast Division

	GP	W	L	OT	GF	GA	Pts
Buffalo	82	45	27	10	235	207	100
Ottawa	82	44	32	6	225	238	94
Boston	82	39	30	13	206	200	91
Montreal	82	39	33	10	217	223	88
Toronto	82	30	38	14	214	267	74

Southeast Division

Washington	82	54	15	13	318	233	121
Atlanta	82	35	34	13	234	256	83
Carolina	82	35	37	10	230	256	80
Tampa Bay	82	34	36	12	217	260	80
Florida	82	32	37	13	208	244	77

Atlantic Division

New Jersey	82	48	27	7	222	191	103
Pittsburgh	82	47	28	7	257	237	101
Philadelphia	82	41	35	6	236	225	88
NY Rangers	82	38	33	11	222	218	87
NY Islanders	82	34	37	11	222	264	79

WESTERN CONFERENCE
Central Division

Chicago	82	52	22	8	271	209	112
Detroit	82	44	24	14	229	216	102
Nashville	82	47	29	6	225	225	100
St. Louis	82	40	32	10	225	223	90
Columbus	82	32	35	15	216	259	79

Northwest Division

Vancouver	82	49	28	5	272	222	103
Colorado	82	43	30	9	244	233	95
Calgary	82	40	32	10	204	210	90
Minnesota	82	38	36	8	219	246	84
Edmonton	82	27	47	8	214	284	62

Pacific Division

San Jose	82	51	20	11	264	215	113
Phoenix	82	50	25	7	225	202	107
Los Angeles	82	46	27	9	241	219	101
Anaheim	82	39	32	11	238	251	89
Dallas	82	37	31	14	237	254	88

Stanley Cup Finals

May 29	Philadelphia 5 at Chicago 6
May 31	Philadelphia 1 at Chicago 2
June 2	Chicago 3 at Philadelphia 4 [Claude Giroux 5:59 OT]
June 4	Chicago 3 at Philadelphia 5
June 6	Philadelphia 4 at Chicago 7
June 9	Chicago 4 at Philadelphia 3 [Patrick Kane 4:06 OT]

Chicago won best-of-seven finals 4–2

STANLEY CUP CHAMPIONS

1892–93	Montreal AAA
1893–94	Montreal AAA
1894–95	Montreal Victorias
1895–96	Winnipeg Victorias, Montreal Victorias
1896–97	Montreal Victorias
1897–98	Montreal Victorias
1898–99	Montreal Victorias, Montreal Shamrocks
1899–00	Montreal Shamrocks
1900–01	Winnipeg Victorias
1901–02	Montreal AAA, Winnipeg Victorias
1902–03	Montreal AAA, Ottawa Silver Seven
1903–04	Ottawa Silver Seven
1904–05	Ottawa Silver Seven
1905–06	Ottawa Silver Seven, Montreal Wanderers
1906–07	Kenora Thistles, Montreal Wanderers
1907–08	Montreal Wanderers
1908–09	Ottawa Senators
1909–10	Ottawa Senators, Montreal Wanderers
1910–11	Ottawa Senators
1911–12	Quebec Bulldogs
1912–13	Quebec Bulldogs
1913–14	Toronto Blueshirts
1914–15	Vancouver Millionaires
1915–16	Montreal Canadiens
1916–17	Seattle Metropolitans
1917–18	Toronto Arenas
1918–19	*No winner—flu pandemic*
1919–20	Ottawa Senators
1920–21	Ottawa Senators
1921–22	Toronto St. Pats
1922–23	Ottawa Senators
1923–24	Montreal Canadiens
1924–25	Victoria Cougars
1925–26	Montreal Maroons
1926–27	Ottawa Senators
1927–28	New York Rangers
1928–29	Boston Bruins
1929–30	Montreal Canadiens
1930–31	Montreal Canadiens
1931–32	Toronto Maple Leafs

1932–33	New York Rangers
1933–34	Chicago Black Hawks
1934–35	Montreal Maroons
1935–36	Detroit Red Wings
1936–37	Detroit Red Wings
1937–38	Chicago Black Hawks
1938–39	Boston Bruins
1939–40	New York Rangers
1940–41	Boston Bruins
1941–42	Toronto Maple Leafs
1942–43	Detroit Red Wings
1943–44	Montreal Canadiens
1944–45	Toronto Maple Leafs
1945–46	Montreal Canadiens
1946–47	Toronto Maple Leafs
1947–48	Toronto Maple Leafs
1948–49	Toronto Maple Leafs
1949–50	Detroit Red Wings
1950–51	Toronto Maple Leafs
1951–52	Detroit Red Wings
1952–53	Montreal Canadiens
1953–54	Detroit Red Wings
1954–55	Detroit Red Wings
1955–56	Montreal Canadiens
1956–57	Montreal Canadiens
1957–58	Montreal Canadiens
1958–59	Montreal Canadiens
1959–60	Montreal Canadiens
1960–61	Chicago Black Hawks
1961–62	Toronto Maple Leafs
1962–63	Toronto Maple Leafs
1963–64	Toronto Maple Leafs
1964–65	Montreal Canadiens
1965–66	Montreal Canadiens
1966–67	Toronto Maple Leafs
1967–68	Montreal Canadiens
1968–69	Montreal Canadiens
1969–70	Boston Bruins
1970–71	Montreal Canadiens
1971–72	Boston Bruins
1972–73	Montreal Canadiens
1973–74	Philadelphia Flyers

1974–75	Philadelphia Flyers
1975–76	Montreal Canadiens
1976–77	Montreal Canadiens
1977–78	Montreal Canadiens
1978–79	Montreal Canadiens
1979–80	New York Islanders
1980–81	New York Islanders
1981–82	New York Islanders
1982–83	New York Islanders
1983–84	Edmonton Oilers
1984–85	Edmonton Oilers
1985–86	Montreal Canadiens
1986–87	Edmonton Oilers
1987–88	Edmonton Oilers
1988–89	Calgary Flames
1989–90	Edmonton Oilers
1990–91	Pittsburgh Penguins
1991–92	Pittsburgh Penguins
1992–93	Montreal Canadiens
1993–94	New York Rangers
1994–95	New Jersey Devils
1995–96	Colorado Avalanche
1996–97	Detroit Red Wings
1997–98	Detroit Red Wings
1998–99	Dallas Stars
1999–00	New Jersey Devils
2000–01	Detroit Red Wings
2001–02	Colorado Avalanche
2002–03	New Jersey Devils
2003–04	Tampa Bay Lightning
2004–05	*No winner—lockout*
2005–06	Carolina Hurricanes
2006–07	Anaheim Ducks
2007–08	Detroit Red Wings
2008–09	Pittsburgh Penguins
2009–10	Chicago Blackhawks
2010–11	Boston Bruins

NHL AWARDS

ART ROSS TROPHY

Awarded to the player with the most points (goals plus assists) in the regular season

1917–18	Joe Malone	Montreal Canadiens (48 points)
1918–19	Newsy Lalonde	Montreal Canadiens (32 points)
1919–20	Joe Malone	Quebec Bulldogs (49 points)
1920–21	Newsy Lalonde	Montreal Canadiens (43 points)
1921–22	Punch Broadbent	Ottawa Senators (46 points)
1922–23	Babe Dye	Toronto St. Pats (37 points)
1923–24	Cy Denneny	Ottawa Senators (24 points)
1924–25	Babe Dye	Toronto St. Pats (46 points)
1925–26	Nels Stewart	Montreal Maroons (42 points)
1926–27	Bill Cook	New York Rangers (37 points)
1927–28	Howie Morenz	Montreal Canadiens (51 points)
1928–29	Ace Bailey	Toronto Maple Leafs (32 points)
1929–30	Cooney Weiland	Boston Bruins (73 points)
1930–31	Howie Morenz	Montreal Canadiens (51 points)
1931–32	Busher Jackson	Toronto Maple Leafs (53 points)
1932–33	Bill Cook	New York Rangers (50 points)
1933–34	Charlie Conacher	Toronto Maple Leafs (52 points)
1934–35	Charlie Conacher	Toronto Maple Leafs (57 points)
1935–36	Sweeney Schriner	New York Americans (45 points)
1936–37	Sweeney Schriner	New York Americans (46 points)
1937–38	Gordie Drillon	Toronto Maple Leafs (52 points)
1938–39	Toe Blake	Montreal Canadiens (47 points)
1939–40	Milt Schmidt	Boston Bruins (52 points)
1940–41	Bill Cowley	Boston Bruins (62 points)
1941–42	Bryan Hextall	New York Rangers (56 points)
1942–43	Doug Bentley	Chicago Black Hawks (73 points)
1943–44	Herb Cain	Boston Bruins (82 points)
1944–45	Elmer Lach	Montreal Canadiens (80 points)
1945–46	Max Bentley	Chicago Black Hawks (61 points)
1947–48	Elmer Lach	Montreal Canadiens (61 points)
1948–49	Roy Conacher	Chicago Black Hawks (68 points)
1949–50	Ted Lindsay	Detroit Red Wings (78 points)
1950–51	Gordie Howe	Detroit Red Wings (86 points)
1951–52	Gordie Howe	Detroit Red Wings (86 points)
1952–53	Gordie Howe	Detroit Red Wings (95 points)
1953–54	Gordie Howe	Detroit Red Wings (81 points)
1954–55	Bernie Geoffrion	Montreal Canadiens (75 points)

1955–56	Jean Beliveau	Montreal Canadiens (88 points)
1956–57	Gordie Howe	Detroit Red Wings (89 points)
1957–58	Dickie Moore	Montreal Canadiens (84 points)
1958–59	Dickie Moore	Montreal Canadiens (96 points)
1959–60	Bobby Hull	Chicago Black Hawks (81 points)
1960–61	Bernie Geoffrion	Montreal Canadiens (95 points)
1961–62	Bobby Hull	Chicago Black Hawks (84 points)
1962–63	Gordie Howe	Detroit Red Wings (86 points)
1963–64	Stan Mikita	Chicago Black Hawks (89 points)
1964–65	Stan Mikita	Chicago Black Hawks (87 points)
1965–66	Bobby Hull	Chicago Black Hawks (97 points)
1966–67	Stan Mikita	Chicago Black Hawks (97 points)
1967–68	Stan Mikita	Chicago Black Hawks (87 points)
1968–69	Phil Esposito	Boston Bruins (126 points)
1969–70	Bobby Orr	Boston Bruins (120 points)
1970–71	Phil Esposito	Boston Bruins (152 points)
1971–72	Phil Esposito	Boston Bruins (133 points)
1972–73	Phil Esposito	Boston Bruins (130 points)
1973–74	Phil Esposito	Boston Bruins (145 points)
1974–75	Bobby Orr	Boston Bruins (135 points)
1975–76	Guy Lafleur	Montreal Canadiens (125 points)
1976–77	Guy Lafleur	Montreal Canadiens (136 points)
1977–78	Guy Lafleur	Montreal Canadiens (132 points)
1978–79	Bryan Trottier	New York Islanders (134 points)
1979–80	Marcel Dionne	Los Angeles Kings (137 points)
1980–81	Wayne Gretzky	Edmonton Oilers (164 points)
1981–82	Wayne Gretzky	Edmonton Oilers (212 points)
1982–83	Wayne Gretzky	Edmonton Oilers (196 points)
1983–84	Wayne Gretzky	Edmonton Oilers (205 points)
1984–85	Wayne Gretzky	Edmonton Oilers (208 points)
1985–86	Wayne Gretzky	Edmonton Oilers (215 points)
1986–87	Wayne Gretzky	Edmonton Oilers (183 points)
1987–88	Mario Lemieux	Pittsburgh Penguins (168 points)
1988–89	Mario Lemieux	Pittsburgh Penguins (199 points)
1989–90	Wayne Gretzky	Los Angeles Kings (142 points)
1990–91	Wayne Gretzky	Los Angeles Kings (163 points)
1991–92	Mario Lemieux	Pittsburgh Penguins (131 points)
1992–93	Mario Lemieux	Pittsburgh Penguins (160 points)
1993–94	Wayne Gretzky	Los Angeles Kings (130 points)
1994–95	Jaromir Jagr	Pittsburgh Penguins (70 points)
1995–96	Mario Lemieux	Pittsburgh Penguins (161 points)
1996–97	Mario Lemieux	Pittsburgh Penguins (122 points)

1997–98	Jaromir Jagr	Pittsburgh Penguins (102 points)
1998–99	Jaromir Jagr	Pittsburgh Penguins (127 points)
1999–00	Jaromir Jagr	Pittsburgh Penguins (96 points)
2000–01	Jaromir Jagr	Pittsburgh Penguins (121 points)
2001–02	Jarome Iginla	Calgary Flames (96 points)
2002–03	Peter Forsberg	Colorado Avalanche (106 points)
2003–04	Martin St. Louis	Tampa Bay Lightning (94 points)
2004–05	no winner	
2005–06	Joe Thornton	Boston Bruins/San Jose Sharks (125 points)
2006–07	Sidney Crosby	Pittsburgh Penguins (120 points)
2007–08	Alexander Ovechkin	Washington Capitals (112 points)
2008–09	Evgeni Malkin	Pittsburgh Penguins (113 points)
2009–10	Henrik Sedin	Vancouver Canucks (112 points)
2010–11	Daniel Sedin	Vancouver Canucks (104 points)

HART TROPHY

Awarded to the league's most valuable player as voted by members of the Professional Hockey Writers' Association

1923–24	Frank Nighbor	Ottawa Senators
1924–25	Billy Burch	Hamilton Tigers
1925–26	Nels Stewart	Montreal Maroons
1926–27	Herb Gardiner	Montreal Canadiens
1927–28	Howie Morenz	Montreal Canadiens
1928–29	Roy Worters	New York Americans
1929–30	Nels Stewart	Montreal Maroons
1930–31	Howie Morenz	Montreal Canadiens
1931–32	Howie Morenz	Montreal Canadiens
1932–33	Eddie Shore	Boston Bruins
1933–34	Aurel Joliat	Montreal Canadiens
1934–35	Eddie Shore	Boston Bruins
1935–36	Eddie Shore	Boston Bruins
1936–37	Babe Siebert	Montreal Canadiens
1937–38	Eddie Shore	Boston Bruins
1938–39	Toe Blake	Montreal Canadiens
1939–40	Ebbie Goodfellow	Detroit Red Wings
1940–41	Bill Cowley	Boston Bruins
1941–42	Tom Anderson	Brooklyn Americans
1942–43	Bill Cowley	Boston Bruins
1943–44	Babe Pratt	Toronto Maple Leafs
1944–45	Elmer Lach	Montreal Canadiens
1945–46	Max Bentley	Chicago Black Hawks

1946–47	Maurice Richard	Montreal Canadiens
1947–48	Buddy O'Connor	New York Rangers
1948–49	Sid Abel	Detroit Red Wings
1949–50	Chuck Rayner	New York Rangers
1950–51	Milt Schmidt	Boston Bruins
1951–52	Gordie Howe	Detroit Red Wings
1952–53	Gordie Howe	Detroit Red Wings
1953–54	Al Rollins	Chicago Black Hawks
1954–55	Ted Kennedy	Toronto Maple Leafs
1955–56	Jean Beliveau	Montreal Canadiens
1956–57	Gordie Howe	Detroit Red Wings
1957–58	Gordie Howe	Detroit Red Wings
1958–59	Andy Bathgate	New York Rangers
1959–60	Gordie Howe	Detroit Red Wings
1960–61	Bernie Geoffrion	Montreal Canadiens
1961–62	Jacques Plante	Montreal Canadiens
1962–63	Gordie Howe	Detroit Red Wings
1963–64	Jean Beliveau	Montreal Canadiens
1964–65	Bobby Hull	Chicago Black Hawks
1965–66	Bobby Hull	Chicago Black Hawks
1966–67	Stan Mikita	Chicago Black Hawks
1967–68	Stan Mikita	Chicago Black Hawks
1968–69	Phil Esposito	Boston Bruins
1969–70	Bobby Orr	Boston Bruins
1970–71	Bobby Orr	Boston Bruins
1971–72	Bobby Orr	Boston Bruins
1972–73	Bobby Clarke	Philadelphia Flyers
1973–74	Phil Esposito	Boston Bruins
1974–75	Bobby Clarke	Philadelphia Flyers
1975–76	Bobby Clarke	Philadelphia Flyers
1976–77	Guy Lafleur	Montreal Canadiens
1977–78	Guy Lafleur	Montreal Canadiens
1978–79	Bryan Trottier	New York Islanders
1979–80	Wayne Gretzky	Edmonton Oilers
1980–81	Wayne Gretzky	Edmonton Oilers
1981–82	Wayne Gretzky	Edmonton Oilers
1982–83	Wayne Gretzky	Edmonton Oilers
1983–84	Wayne Gretzky	Edmonton Oilers
1984–85	Wayne Gretzky	Edmonton Oilers
1985–86	Wayne Gretzky	Edmonton Oilers
1986–87	Wayne Gretzky	Edmonton Oilers
1987–88	Mario Lemieux	Pittsburgh Penguins

1988–89	Wayne Gretzky	Edmonton Oilers
1989–90	Mark Messier	Edmonton Oilers
1990–91	Brett Hull	St. Louis Blues
1991–92	Mark Messier	New York Rangers
1992–93	Mario Lemieux	Pittsburgh Penguins
1993–94	Sergei Fedorov	Detroit Red Wings
1994–95	Eric Lindros	Philadelphia Flyers
1995–96	Mario Lemieux	Pittsburgh Penguins
1996–97	Dominik Hasek	Buffalo Sabres
1997–98	Dominik Hasek	Buffalo Sabres
1998–99	Jaromir Jagr	Pittsburgh Penguins
1999–00	Chris Pronger	St. Louis Blues
2000–01	Joe Sakic	Colorado Avalanche
2001–02	Jose Theodore	Montreal Canadiens
2002–03	Peter Forsberg	Colorado Avalanche
2003–04	Martin St. Louis	Tampa Bay Lightning
2004–05	no winner	
2005–06	Joe Thornton	Boston Bruins/San Jose Sharks
2006–07	Sidney Crosby	Pittsburgh Penguins
2007–08	Alexander Ovechkin	Washington Capitals
2008–09	Alexander Ovechkin	Washington Capitals
2009–10	Henrik Sedin	Vancouver Canucks
2010–11	Corey Perry	Anaheim Ducks

LADY BYNG TROPHY

Awarded to the player who best displays gentlemanly play

1924–25	Frank Nighbor	Ottawa Senators
1925–26	Frank Nighbor	Ottawa Senators
1926–27	Billy Burch	New York Americans
1927–28	Frank Boucher	New York Rangers
1928–29	Frank Boucher	New York Rangers
1929–30	Frank Boucher	New York Rangers
1930–31	Frank Boucher	New York Rangers
1931–32	Joe Primeau	Toronto Maple Leafs
1932–33	Frank Boucher	New York Rangers
1933–34	Frank Boucher	New York Rangers
1934–35	Frank Boucher	New York Rangers
1935–36	Doc Romnes	Chicago Black Hawks
1936–37	Marty Barry	Detroit Red Wings
1937–38	Gordie Drillon	Toronto Maple Leafs
1938–39	Clint Smith	New York Rangers

1939–40	Bobby Bauer	Boston Bruins
1940–41	Bobby Bauer	Boston Bruins
1941–42	Syl Apps	Toronto Maple Leafs
1942–43	Max Bentley	Chicago Black Hawks
1943–44	Clint Smith	Chicago Black Hawks
1944–45	Bill Mosienko	Chicago Black Hawks
1945–46	Toe Blake	Montreal Canadiens
1946–47	Bobby Bauer	Boston Bruins
1947–48	Buddy O'Connor	New York Rangers
1948–49	Bill Quackenbush	Detroit Red Wings
1949–50	Edgar Laprade	New York Rangers
1950–51	Red Kelly	Detroit Red Wings
1951–52	Sid Smith	Toronto Maple Leafs
1952–53	Red Kelly	Detroit Red Wings
1953–54	Red Kelly	Detroit Red Wings
1954–55	Sid Smith	Toronto Maple Leafs
1955–56	Dutch Reibel	Detroit Red Wings
1956–57	Andy Hebenton	New York Rangers
1957–58	Camille Henry	New York Rangers
1958–59	Alex Delvecchio	Detroit Red Wings
1959–60	Don McKenney	Boston Bruins
1960–61	Red Kelly	Toronto Maple Leafs
1961–62	Dave Keon	Toronto Maple Leafs
1962–63	Dave Keon	Toronto Maple Leafs
1963–64	Kenny Wharram	Chicago Black Hawks
1964–65	Bobby Hull	Chicago Black Hawks
1965–66	Alex Delvecchio	Detroit Red Wings
1966–67	Stan Mikita	Chicago Black Hawks
1967–68	Stan Mikita	Chicago Black Hawks
1968–69	Alex Delvecchio	Detroit Red Wings
1969–70	Phil Goyette	St. Louis Blues
1970–71	John Bucyk	Boston Bruins
1971–72	Jean Ratelle	New York Rangers
1972–73	Gilbert Perreault	Buffalo Sabres
1973–74	John Bucyk	Boston Bruins
1974–75	Marcel Dionne	Detroit Red Wings
1975–76	Jean Ratelle	New York Rangers/Boston Bruins
1976–77	Marcel Dionne	Los Angeles Kings
1977–78	Butch Goring	Los Angeles Kings
1978–79	Bob MacMillan	Atlanta Flames
1979–80	Wayne Gretzky	Edmonton Oilers
1980–81	Rick Kehoe	Pittsburgh Penguins

1981–82	Rick Middleton	Boston Bruins
1982–83	Mike Bossy	New York Islanders
1983–84	Mike Bossy	New York Islanders
1984–85	Jari Kurri	Edmonton Oilers
1985–86	Mike Bossy	New York Islanders
1986–87	Joe Mullen	Calgary Flames
1987–88	Mats Naslund	Montreal Canadiens
1988–89	Joe Mullen	Calgary Flames
1989–90	Brett Hull	St. Louis Blues
1990–91	Wayne Gretzky	Los Angeles Kings
1991–92	Wayne Gretzky	Los Angeles Kings
1992–93	Pierre Turgeon	New York Islanders
1993–94	Wayne Gretzky	Los Angeles Kings
1994–95	Ron Francis	Pittsburgh Penguins
1995–96	Paul Kariya	Mighty Ducks of Anaheim
1996–97	Paul Kariya	Mighty Ducks of Anaheim
1997–98	Ron Francis	Pittsburgh Penguins
1998–99	Wayne Gretzky	New York Rangers
1999–00	Pavol Demitra	St. Louis Blues
2000–01	Joe Sakic	Colorado Avalanche
2001–02	Ron Francis	Carolina Hurricanes
2002–03	Alexander Mogilny	Toronto Maple Leafs
2003–04	Brad Richards	Tampa Bay Lightning
2004–05	no winner	
2005–06	Pavel Datsyuk	Detroit Red Wings
2006–07	Pavel Datsyuk	Detroit Red Wings
2007–08	Pavel Datsyuk	Detroit Red Wings
2008–09	Pavel Datsyuk	Detroit Red Wings
2009–10	Martin St. Louis	Tampa Bay Lightning
2010–11	Martin St. Louis	Tampa Bay Lightning

VEZINA TROPHY

Awarded to the best goalie as voted on by the league's 30 general managers

1926–27	George Hainsworth	Montreal Canadiens (1.47 GAA)
1927–28	George Hainsworth	Montreal Canadiens (1.05 GAA)
1928–29	George Hainsworth	Montreal Canadiens (0.92 GAA)
1929–30	Tiny Thompson	Boston Bruins (2.19 GAA)
1930–31	Roy Worters	New York Americans (1.61 GAA)
1931–32	Charlie Gardiner	Chicago Black Hawks (1.85 GAA)
1932–33	Tiny Thompson	Boston Bruins (1.76 GAA)
1933–34	Charlie Gardiner	Chicago Black Hawks (1.63 GAA)

1934–35	Lorne Chabot	Chicago Black Hawks (1.80 GAA)
1935–36	Tiny Thompson	Boston Bruins (1.68 GAA)
1936–37	Normie Smith	Detroit Red Wings (2.05 GAA)
1937–38	Tiny Thompson	Boston Bruins (1.80 GAA)
1938–39	Frank Brimsek	Boston Bruins (1.56 GAA)
1939–40	Dave Kerr	New York Rangers (1.54 GAA)
1940–41	Turk Broda	Toronto Maple Leafs (2.00 GAA)
1941–42	Frank Brimsek	Boston Bruins (2.35 GAA)
1942–43	Johnny Mowers	Detroit Red Wings (2.47 GAA)
1943–44	Bill Durnan	Montreal Canadiens (2.18 GAA)
1944–45	Bill Durnan	Montreal Canadiens (2.42 GAA)
1945–46	Bill Durnan	Montreal Canadiens (2.60 GAA)
1946–47	Bill Durnan	Montreal Canadiens (2.30 GAA)
1947–48	Turk Broda	Toronto Maple Leafs (2.38 GAA)
1948–49	Bill Durnan	Montreal Canadiens (2.10 GAA)
1949–50	Bill Durnan	Montreal Canadiens (2.20 GAA)
1950–51	Al Rollins	Toronto Maple Leafs (1.77 GAA)
1951–52	Terry Sawchuk	Detroit Red Wings (1.90 GAA)
1952–53	Terry Sawchuk	Detroit Red Wings (1.90 GAA)
1953–54	Harry Lumley	Toronto Maple Leafs (1.86 GAA)
1954–55	Terry Sawchuk	Detroit Red Wings (1.96 GAA)
1955–56	Jacques Plante	Montreal Canadiens (1.86 GAA)
1956–57	Jacques Plante	Montreal Canadiens (2.00 GAA)
1957–58	Jacques Plante	Montreal Canadiens (2.11 GAA)
1958–59	Jacques Plante	Montreal Canadiens (2.16 GAA)
1959–60	Jacques Plante	Montreal Canadiens (2.54 GAA)
1960–61	Johnny Bower	Toronto Maple Leafs (2.50 GAA)
1961–62	Jacques Plante	Montreal Canadiens (2.37 GAA)
1962–63	Glenn Hall	Chicago Black Hawks (2.47 GAA)
1963–64	Charlie Hodge	Montreal Canadiens (2.26 GAA)
1964–65	Terry Sawchuk	Toronto Maple Leafs (2.56 GAA)
	Johnny Bower	Toronto Maple Leafs (2.38 GAA)
1965–66	Gump Worsley	Montreal Canadiens (2.36 GAA)
	Charlie Hodge	Montreal Canadiens (2.58 GAA)
1966–67	Glenn Hall	Chicago Black Hawks (2.38 GAA)
	Denis DeJordy	Chicago Black Hawks (2.46 GAA)
1967–68	Gump Worsley	Montreal Canadiens (1.98 GAA)
	Rogie Vachon	Montreal Canadiens (2.48 GAA)
1968–69	Jacques Plante	St. Louis Blues (1.96 GAA)
	Glenn Hall	St. Louis Blues (2.17 GAA)
1969–70	Tony Esposito	Chicago Black Hawks (2.17 GAA)

1970–71	Ed Giacomin	New York Rangers (2.16 GAA)
	Gilles Villemure	New York Rangers (2.30 GAA)
1971–72	Tony Esposito	Chicago Black Hawks (1.77 GAA)
	Gary Smith	Chicago Black Hawks (2.42 GAA)
1972–73	Ken Dryden	Montreal Canadiens (2.26 GAA)
1973–74	Bernie Parent	Philadelphia Flyers (1.89 GAA)
	Tony Esposito	Chicago Black Hawks (2.04 GAA)
1974–75	Bernie Parent	Philadelphia Flyers (2.03 GAA)
1975–76	Ken Dryden	Montreal Canadiens (2.03 GAA)
1976–77	Ken Dryden	Montreal Canadiens (2.14 GAA)
	Michel Larocque	Montreal Canadiens (2.09 GAA)
1977–78	Ken Dryden	Montreal Canadiens (2.05 GAA)
	Michel Larocque	Montreal Canadiens (2.67 GAA)
1978–79	Ken Dryden	Montreal Canadiens (2.30 GAA)
	Michel Larocque	Montreal Canadiens (2.84 GAA)
1979–80	Bob Sauve	Buffalo Sabres (2.36 GAA)
	Don Edwards	Buffalo Sabres (2.57 GAA)
1980–81	Richard Sevigny	Montreal Canadiens (2.40 GAA)
	Denis Herron	Montreal Canadiens (3.50 GAA)
	Michel Larocque	Montreal Canadiens (3.03 GAA)
1981–82	Billy Smith	New York Islanders (2.97 GAA)
1982–83	Pete Peeters	Boston Bruins (2.36 GAA)
1983–84	Tom Barrasso	Buffalo Sabres (2.84 GAA)
1984–85	Pelle Lindbergh	Philadelphia Flyers (3.02 GAA)
1985–86	John Vanbiesbrouck	New York Rangers (3.32 GAA)
1986–87	Ron Hextall	Philadelphia Flyers (3.00 GAA)
1987–88	Grant Fuhr	Edmonton Oilers (3.43 GAA)
1988–89	Patrick Roy	Montreal Canadiens (2.47 GAA)
1989–90	Patrick Roy	Montreal Canadiens (2.53 GAA)
1990–91	Ed Belfour	Chicago Blackhawks (2.47 GAA)
1991–92	Patrick Roy	Montreal Canadiens (2.36 GAA)
1992–93	Ed Belfour	Chicago Blackhawks (2.59 GAA)
1993–94	Dominik Hasek	Buffalo Sabres (1.95 GAA)
1994–95	Dominik Hasek	Buffalo Sabres (2.11 GAA)
1995–96	Jim Carey	Washington Capitals (2.26 GAA)
1996–97	Dominik Hasek	Buffalo Sabres (2.27 GAA)
1997–98	Dominik Hasek	Buffalo Sabres (2.09 GAA)
1998–99	Dominik Hasek	Buffalo Sabres (1.87 GAA)
1999–00	Olaf Kolzig	Washington Capitals (2.24 GAA)
2000–01	Dominik Hasek	Buffalo Sabres (2.11 GAA)
2001–02	Jose Theodore	Montreal Canadiens (2.11 GAA)
2002–03	Martin Brodeur	New Jersey Devils (2.02 GAA)

2003–04	Martin Brodeur	New Jersey Devils (2.62 GAA)
2004–05	no winner	
2005–06	Miikka Kiprusoff	Calgary Flames (2.07 GAA)
2006–07	Martin Brodeur	New Jersey Devils (2.18 GAA)
2007–08	Martin Brodeur	New Jersey Devils (2.17 GAA)
2008–09	Tim Thomas	Boston Bruins (2.10 GAA)
2009–10	Ryan Miller	Buffalo Sabres (2.22 GAA)
2010–11	Tim Thomas	Boston Bruins (2.00 GAA)

CALDER MEMORIAL TROPHY

Awarded to the best rookie in the league

1932–33	Carl Voss	Detroit Red Wings
1933–34	Russ Blinco	Montreal Maroons
1934–35	Sweeney Schriner	New York Americans
1935–36	Mike Karakas	Chicago Black Hawks
1936–37	Syl Apps	Toronto Maple Leafs
1937–38	Cully Dahlstrom	Chicago Black Hawks
1938–39	Frank Brimsek	Boston Bruins
1939–40	Kilby MacDonald	New York Rangers
1940–41	John Quilty	Montreal Canadiens
1941–42	Grant Warwick	New York Rangers
1942–43	Gaye Stewart	Toronto Maple Leafs
1943–44	Gus Bodnar	Toronto Maple Leafs
1944–45	Frank McCool	Toronto Maple Leafs
1945–46	Edgar Laprade	New York Rangers
1946–47	Howie Meeker	Toronto Maple Leafs
1947–48	Jim McFadden	Detroit Red Wings
1948–49	Pentti Lund	New York Rangers
1949–50	Jack Gelineau	Boston Bruins
1950–51	Terry Sawchuk	Detroit Red Wings
1951–52	Bernie Geoffrion	Montreal Canadiens
1952–53	Gump Worsley	New York Rangers
1953–54	Camille Henry	New York Rangers
1954–55	Ed Litzenberger	Chicago Black Hawks
1955–56	Glenn Hall	Detroit Red Wings
1956–57	Larry Regan	Boston Bruins
1957–58	Frank Mahovlich	Toronto Maple Leafs
1958–59	Ralph Backstrom	Montreal Canadiens
1959–60	Bill Hay	Chicago Black Hawks
1960–61	Dave Keon	Toronto Maple Leafs
1961–62	Bobby Rousseau	Montreal Canadiens

1962–63	Kent Douglas	Toronto Maple Leafs
1963–64	Jacques Laperriere	Montreal Canadiens
1964–65	Roger Crozier	Detroit Red Wings
1965–66	Brit Selby	Toronto Maple Leafs
1966–67	Bobby Orr	Boston Bruins
1967–68	Derek Sanderson	Boston Bruins
1968–69	Danny Grant	Minnesota North Stars
1969–70	Tony Esposito	Chicago Black Hawks
1970–71	Gilbert Perreault	Buffalo Sabres
1971–72	Ken Dryden	Montreal Canadiens
1972–73	Steve Vickers	New York Rangers
1973–74	Denis Potvin	New York Islanders
1974–75	Eric Vail	Atlanta Flames
1975–76	Bryan Trottier	New York Islanders
1976–77	Willi Plett	Atlanta Flames
1977–78	Mike Bossy	New York Islanders
1978–79	Bobby Smith	Minnesota North Stars
1979–80	Raymond Bourque	Boston Bruins
1980–81	Peter Stastny	Quebec Nordiques
1981–82	Dale Hawerchuk	Winnipeg Jets
1982–83	Steve Larmer	Chicago Black Hawks
1983–84	Tom Barrasso	Buffalo Sabres
1984–85	Mario Lemieux	Pittsburgh Penguins
1985–86	Gary Suter	Calgary Flames
1986–87	Luc Robitaille	Los Angeles Kings
1987–88	Joe Nieuwendyk	Calgary Flames
1988–89	Brian Leetch	New York Rangers
1989–90	Sergei Makarov	Calgary Flames
1990–91	Ed Belfour	Chicago Blackhawks
1991–92	Pavel Bure	Vancouver Canucks
1992–93	Teemu Selanne	Winnipeg Jets
1993–94	Martin Brodeur	New Jersey Devils
1994–95	Peter Forsberg	Quebec Nordiques
1995–96	Daniel Alfredsson	Ottawa Senators
1996–97	Bryan Berard	New York Islanders
1997–98	Sergei Samsonov	Boston Bruins
1998–99	Chris Drury	Colorado Avalanche
1999–00	Scott Gomez	New Jersey Devils
2000–01	Evgeni Nabokov	San Jose Sharks
2001–02	Danny Heatley	Atlanta Thrashers
2002–03	Barret Jackman	St. Louis Blues
2003–04	Andrew Raycroft	Boston Bruins
2004–05	no winner	

2005–06	Alexander Ovechkin	Washington Capitals
2006–07	Evgeni Malkin	Pittsburgh Penguins
2007–08	Patrick Kane	Chicago Blackhawks
2008–09	Steve Mason	Columbus Blue Jackets
2009–10	Tyler Myers	Buffalo Sabres
2010–11	Jeff Skinner	Carolina Hurricanes

JAMES NORRIS TROPHY

Awarded to the best defenceman during the regular season

1953–54	Red Kelly	Detroit Red Wings
1954–55	Doug Harvey	Montreal Canadiens
1955–56	Doug Harvey	Montreal Canadiens
1956–57	Doug Harvey	Montreal Canadiens
1957–58	Doug Harvey	Montreal Canadiens
1958–59	Tom Johnson	Montreal Canadiens
1959–60	Doug Harvey	Montreal Canadiens
1960–61	Doug Harvey	Montreal Canadiens
1961–62	Doug Harvey	Montreal Canadiens
1962–63	Pierre Pilote	Chicago Black Hawks
1963–64	Pierre Pilote	Chicago Black Hawks
1964–65	Pierre Pilote	Chicago Black Hawks
1965–66	Jacques Laperriere	Montreal Canadiens
1966–67	Harry Howell	New York Rangers
1967–68	Bobby Orr	Boston Bruins
1968–69	Bobby Orr	Boston Bruins
1969–70	Bobby Orr	Boston Bruins
1970–71	Bobby Orr	Boston Bruins
1971–72	Bobby Orr	Boston Bruins
1972–73	Bobby Orr	Boston Bruins
1973–74	Bobby Orr	Boston Bruins
1974–75	Bobby Orr	Boston Bruins
1975–76	Denis Potvin	New York Islanders
1976–77	Larry Robinson	Montreal Canadiens
1977–78	Denis Potvin	New York Islanders
1978–79	Denis Potvin	New York Islanders
1979–80	Larry Robinson	Montreal Canadiens
1980–81	Randy Carlyle	Pittsburgh Penguins
1981–82	Doug Wilson	Chicago Black Hawks
1982–83	Rod Langway	Washington Capitals
1983–84	Rod Langway	Washington Capitals
1984–85	Paul Coffey	Edmonton Oilers

1985–86	Paul Coffey	Edmonton Oilers
1986–87	Raymond Bourque	Boston Bruins
1987–88	Raymond Bourque	Boston Bruins
1988–89	Chris Chelios	Montreal Canadiens
1989–90	Raymond Bourque	Boston Bruins
1990–91	Raymond Bourque	Boston Bruins
1991–92	Brian Leetch	New York Rangers
1992–93	Chris Chelios	Chicago Blackhawks
1993–94	Raymond Bourque	Boston Bruins
1994–95	Paul Coffey	Detroit Red Wings
1995–96	Chris Chelios	Chicago Blackhawks
1996–97	Brian Leetch	New York Rangers
1997–98	Rob Blake	Los Angeles Kings
1998–99	Al MacInnis	St. Louis Blues
1999–00	Chris Pronger	St. Louis Blues
2000–01	Nicklas Lidstrom	Detroit Red Wings
2001–02	Nicklas Lidstrom	Detroit Red Wings
2002–03	Nicklas Lidstrom	Detroit Red Wings
2003–04	Scott Niedermayer	New Jersey Devils
2004–05	no winner	
2005–06	Nicklas Lidstrom	Detroit Red Wings
2006–07	Nicklas Lidstrom	Detroit Red Wings
2007–08	Nicklas Lidstrom	Detroit Red Wings
2008–09	Zdeno Chara	Boston Bruins
2009–10	Duncan Keith	Chicago Blackhawks
2010–11	Nicklas Lidstrom	Detroit Red Wings

LESTER PATRICK TROPHY

Awarded for contributions to hockey in the United States

1965–66	Jack Adams
1966–67	Gordie Howe
	Charles F. Adams
	James Norris, Sr.
1967–68	Tommy Lockhart
	Walter A. Brown
	Gen. John R. Kilpatrick
1968–69	Bobby Hull
	Ed Jeremiah
1969–70	Eddie Shore
	Jim Hendy
1970–71	Bill Jennings

	John B. Sollenberger
	Terry Sawchuk
1971–72	Clarence Campbell
	John A. Kelly
	Cooney Weiland
	James D. Norris
1972–73	Walter Bush, Jr.
1973–74	Alex Delvecchio
	Murray Murdoch
	Weston W. Adams Sr.
	Charles L. Crovat
1974–75	Donald M. Clark
	Bill Chadwick
	Tommy Ivan
1975–76	Stan Mikita
	George Leader
	Bruce A. Norris
1976–77	Johnny Bucyk
	Murray Armstrong
	John Mariucci
1977–78	Phil Esposito
	Tom Fitzgerald
	William T. Tutt
	Bill Wirtz
1978–79	Bobby Orr
1979–80	Bobby Clarke
	Ed Snider
	Fred Shero
	1980 U.S. Olympic Hockey Team
1980–81	Charles M. Schulz
1981–82	Emile Francis
1982–83	Bill Torrey
1983–84	John A. Ziegler Jr.
	Art Ross
1984–85	Jack Butterfield
	Arthur M. Wirtz
1985–86	John MacInnes
	Jack Riley
1986–87	Hobey Baker
	Frank Mathers

1987–88	Keith Allen
	Fred Cusick
	Bob Johnson
1988–89	Dan Kelly
	Lou Nanne
	Lynn Patrick
	Bud Poile
1989–90	Len Ceglarski
1990–91	Rod Gilbert
	Mike Ilitch
1991–92	Al Arbour
	Art Berglund
	Lou Lamoriello
1992–93	Frank Boucher
	Red Dutton
	Bruce McNall
	Gil Stein
1993–94	Wayne Gretzky
	Robert Ridder
1994–95	Joe Mullen
	Brian Mullen
	Bob Fleming
1995–96	George Gund
	Ken Morrow
	Milt Schmidt
1996–97	Seymour H. Knox III
	Bill Cleary
	Pat LaFontaine
1997–98	Peter Karmanos
	Neal Broten
	John Mayasich
	Max McNab
1998–99	Harry Sinden
	1998 U.S. Olympic Women's Hockey Team
1999–00	Mario Lemieux
	Craig Patrick
	Lou Vairo
2000–01	Scotty Bowman
	David Poile
	Gary Bettman

2001–02	1960 U.S. Olympic Team
	Herb Brooks
	Larry Pleau
2002–03	Ray Bourque
	Ron DeGregorio
	Willie O'Ree
2003–04	Mike Emrick
	John Davidson
	Ray Miron
2004–05	none
2005–06	Red Berenson
	Marcel Dionne
	Reed Larson
	Glen Sonmor
	Steve Yzerman
2006–07	Brian Leetch
	Cammi Granato
	John Halligan
	Stan Fischler
2007–08	Brian Burke
	Ted Lindsay
	Phil Housley
	Bob Naegele, Jr.
2008–09	Mark Messier
	Mike Richter
	Jimmy Devellano
2009–10	Dave Andrews
	Cam Neely
	Jack Parker
	Jerry York

CONN SMYTHE TROPHY

Awarded to the most valuable player in the playoffs

* indicates played for losing team

1964–65	Jean Beliveau	Montreal Canadiens
1965–66	Roger Crozier*	Detroit Red Wings
1966–67	Dave Keon	Toronto Maple Leafs
1967–68	Glenn Hall*	St. Louis Blues
1968–69	Serge Savard	Montreal Canadiens
1969–70	Bobby Orr	Boston Bruins

1970–71	Ken Dryden	Montreal Canadiens
1971–72	Bobby Orr	Boston Bruins
1972–73	Yvan Cournoyer	Montreal Canadiens
1973–74	Bernie Parent	Philadelphia Flyers
1974–75	Bernie Parent	Philadelphia Flyers
1975–76	Reggie Leach*	Philadelphia Flyers
1976–77	Guy Lafleur	Montreal Canadiens
1977–78	Larry Robinson	Montreal Canadiens
1978–79	Bob Gainey	Montreal Canadiens
1979–80	Bryan Trottier	New York Islanders
1980–81	Butch Goring	New York Islanders
1981–82	Mike Bossy	New York Islanders
1982–83	Billy Smith	New York Islanders
1983–84	Mark Messier	Edmonton Oilers
1984–85	Wayne Gretzky	Edmonton Oilers
1985–86	Patrick Roy	Montreal Canadiens
1986–87	Ron Hextall	Philadelphia Flyers
1987–88	Wayne Gretzky	Edmonton Oilers
1988–89	Al MacInnis	Calgary Flames
1989–90	Bill Ranford	Edmonton Oilers
1990–91	Mario Lemieux	Pittsburgh Penguins
1991–92	Mario Lemieux	Pittsburgh Penguins
1992–93	Patrick Roy	Montreal Canadiens
1993–94	Brian Leetch	New York Rangers
1994–95	Claude Lemieux	New Jersey Devils
1995–96	Joe Sakic	Colorado Avalanche
1996–97	Mike Vernon	Detroit Red Wings
1997–98	Steve Yzerman	Detroit Red Wings
1998–99	Joe Nieuwendyk	Dallas Stars
1999–00	Scott Stevens	New Jersey Devils
2000–01	Patrick Roy	Colorado Avalanche
2001–02	Nicklas Lidstrom	Detroit Red Wings
2002–03	J-S Giguere*	Mighty Ducks of Anaheim
2003–04	Brad Richards	Tampa Bay Lightning
2004–05	no winner	
2005–06	Cam Ward	Carolina Hurricanes
2006–07	Scott Niedermayer	Anaheim Ducks
2007–08	Henrik Zetterberg	Detroit Red Wings
2008–09	Evgeni Malkin	Pittsburgh Penguins
2009–10	Jonathan Toews	Chicago Blackhawks
2010–11	Tim Thomas	Boston Bruins

BILL MASTERTON MEMORIAL TROPHY

Awarded to the player who best displays perseverance, sportsmanship and dedication
to the game

1967–68	Claude Provost	Montreal Canadiens
1968–69	Ted Hampson	Oakland Seals
1969–70	Pit Martin	Chicago Black Hawks
1970–71	Jean Ratelle	New York Rangers
1971–72	Bobby Clarke	Philadelphia Flyers
1972–73	Lowell MacDonald	Pittsburgh Penguins
1973–74	Henri Richard	Montreal Canadiens
1974–75	Don Luce	Buffalo Sabres
1975–76	Rod Gilbert	New York Rangers
1976–77	Ed Westfall	New York Islanders
1977–78	Butch Goring	Los Angeles Kings
1978–79	Serge Savard	Montreal Canadiens
1979–80	Al MacAdam	Minnesota North Stars
1980–81	Blake Dunlop	St. Louis Blues
1981–82	Glenn Resch	Colorado Rockies
1982–83	Lanny McDonald	Calgary Flames
1983–84	Brad Park	Detroit Red Wings
1984–85	Anders Hedberg	New York Rangers
1985–86	Charlie Simmer	Boston Bruins
1986–87	Doug Jarvis	Hartford Whalers
1987–88	Bob Bourne	Los Angeles Kings
1988–89	Tim Kerr	Philadelphia Flyers
1989–90	Gord Kluzak	Boston Bruins
1990–91	Dave Taylor	Los Angeles Kings
1991–92	Mark Fitzpatrick	New York Islanders
1992–93	Mario Lemieux	Pittsburgh Penguins
1993–94	Cam Neely	Boston Bruins
1994–95	Pat LaFontaine	Buffalo Sabres
1995–96	Gary Roberts	Calgary Flames
1996–97	Tony Granato	San Jose Sharks
1997–98	Jamie McLennan	St. Louis Blues
1998–99	John Cullen	Tampa Bay Lightning
1999–00	Ken Daneyko	New Jersey Devils
2000–01	Adam Graves	New York Rangers
2001–02	Saku Koivu	Montreal Canadiens
2002–03	Steve Yzerman	Detroit Red Wings
2003–04	Bryan Berard	Chicago Blackhawks
2004–05	no winner	
2005–06	Teemu Selanne	Mighty Ducks of Anaheim

2006–07	Phil Kessel	Boston Bruins
2007–08	Jason Blake	Toronto Maple Leafs
2008–09	Steve Sullivan	Nashville Predators
2009–10	Jose Theodore	Washington Capitals
2010–11	Ian Laperriere	Philadelphia Flyers

JACK ADAMS AWARD

Awarded to the coach of the year

1973–74	Fred Shero	Philadelphia Flyers
1974–75	Bob Pulford	Los Angeles Kings
1975–76	Don Cherry	Boston Bruins
1976–77	Scotty Bowman	Montreal Canadiens
1977–78	Bobby Kromm	Detroit Red Wings
1978–79	Al Arbour	New York Islanders
1979–80	Pat Quinn	Philadelphia Flyers
1980–81	Red Berenson	St. Louis Blues
1981–82	Tom Watt	Winnipeg Jets
1982–83	Orval Tessier	Chicago Black Hawks
1983–84	Bryan Murray	Washington Capitals
1984–85	Mike Keenan	Philadelphia Flyers
1985–86	Glen Sather	Edmonton Oilers
1986–87	Jacques Demers	Detroit Red Wings
1987–88	Jacques Demers	Detroit Red Wings
1988–89	Pat Burns	Montreal Canadiens
1989–90	Bob Murdoch	Winnipeg Jets
1990–91	Brian Sutter	St. Louis Blues
1991–92	Pat Quinn	Vancouver Canucks
1992–93	Pat Burns	Toronto Maple Leafs
1993–94	Jacques Lemaire	New Jersey Devils
1994–95	Marc Crawford	Quebec Nordiques
1995–96	Scotty Bowman	Detroit Red Wings
1996–97	Ted Nolan	Buffalo Sabres
1997–98	Pat Burns	Boston Bruins
1998–99	Jacques Martin	Ottawa Senators
1999–00	Joel Quenneville	St. Louis Blues
2000–01	Bill Barber	Philadelphia Flyers
2001–02	Bob Francis	Phoenix Coyotes
2002–03	Jacques Lemaire	Minnesota Wild
2003–04	John Tortorella	Tampa Bay Lightning
2004–05	no winner	
2005–06	Lindy Ruff	Buffalo Sabres
2006–07	Alain Vigneault	Vancouver Canucks

2007–08	Bruce Boudreau	Washington Capitals
2008–09	Claude Julien	Boston Bruins
2009–10	Dave Tippett	Phoenix Coyotes
2010–11	Dan Bylsma	Pittsburgh Penguins

LESTER B. PEARSON AWARD

Awarded to the league's most valuable player as voted on by the players

1970–71	Phil Esposito	Boston Bruins
1971–72	Jean Ratelle	New York Rangers
1972–73	Bobby Clarke	Philadelphia Flyers
1973–74	Phil Esposito	Boston Bruins
1974–75	Bobby Orr	Boston Bruins
1975–76	Guy Lafleur	Montreal Canadiens
1976–77	Guy Lafleur	Montreal Canadiens
1977–78	Guy Lafleur	Montreal Canadiens
1978–79	Marcel Dionne	Los Angeles Kings
1979–80	Marcel Dionne	Los Angeles Kings
1980–81	Mike Liut	St. Louis Blues
1981–82	Wayne Gretzky	Edmonton Oilers
1982–83	Wayne Gretzky	Edmonton Oilers
1983–84	Wayne Gretzky	Edmonton Oilers
1984–85	Wayne Gretzky	Edmonton Oilers
1985–86	Mario Lemieux	Pittsburgh Penguins
1986–87	Wayne Gretzky	Edmonton Oilers
1987–88	Mario Lemieux	Pittsburgh Penguins
1988–89	Steve Yzerman	Detroit Red Wings
1989–90	Mark Messier	Edmonton Oilers
1990–91	Brett Hull	St. Louis Blues
1991–92	Mark Messier	New York Rangers
1992–93	Mario Lemieux	Pittsburgh Penguins
1993–94	Sergei Fedorov	Detroit Red Wings
1994–95	Eric Lindros	Philadelphia Flyers
1995–96	Mario Lemieux	Pittsburgh Penguins
1996–97	Dominik Hasek	Buffalo Sabres
1997–98	Dominik Hasek	Buffalo Sabres
1998–99	Jaromir Jagr	Pittsburgh Penguins
1999–00	Jaromir Jagr	Pittsburgh Penguins
2000–01	Joe Sakic	Colorado Avalanche
2001–02	Jarome Iginla	Calgary Flames
2002–03	Markus Naslund	Vancouver Canucks
2003–04	Martin St. Louis	Tampa Bay Lightning
2004–05	no winner	
2005–06	Jaromir Jagr	New York Rangers

2006–07	Sidney Crosby	Pittsburgh Penguins
2007–08	Alexander Ovechkin	Washington Capitals
2008–09	Alexander Ovechkin	Washington Capitals

TED LINDSAY AWARD

(Formerly Lester B. Pearson Award)

| 2009–10 | Alexander Ovechkin | Washington Capitals |
| 2010–11 | Daniel Sedin | Vancouver Canucks |

FRANK J. SELKE TROPHY

Awarded to the forward who best displays defensive skills

1977–78	Bob Gainey	Montreal Canadiens
1978–79	Bob Gainey	Montreal Canadiens
1979–80	Bob Gainey	Montreal Canadiens
1980–81	Bob Gainey	Montreal Canadiens
1981–82	Steve Kasper	Boston Bruins
1982–83	Bobby Clarke	Pittsburgh Penguins
1983–84	Doug Jarvis	Washington Capitals
1984–85	Craig Ramsay	Buffalo Sabres
1985–86	Troy Murray	Chicago Black Hawks
1986–87	Dave Poulin	Philadelphia Flyers
1987–88	Guy Carbonneau	Montreal Canadiens
1988–89	Guy Carbonneau	Montreal Canadiens
1989–90	Rick Meagher	St. Louis Blues
1990–91	Dirk Graham	Chicago Blackhawks
1991–92	Guy Carbonneau	Montreal Canadiens
1992–93	Doug Gilmour	Toronto Maple Leafs
1993–94	Sergei Fedorov	Detroit Red Wings
1994–95	Ron Francis	Pittsburgh Penguins
1995–96	Sergei Fedorov	Detroit Red Wings
1996–97	Michael Peca	Buffalo Sabres
1997–98	Jere Lehtinen	Dallas Stars
1998–99	Jere Lehtinen	Dallas Stars
1999–00	Steve Yzerman	Detroit Red Wings
2000–01	John Madden	New Jersey Devils
2001–02	Michael Peca	New York Islanders
2002–03	Jere Lehtinen	Dallas Stars
2003–04	Kris Draper	Detroit Red Wings
2004–05	no winner	
2005–06	Rod Brind'Amour	Carolina Hurricanes
2006–07	Rod Brind'Amour	Carolina Hurricanes

2007–08	Pavel Datsyuk	Detroit Red Wings
2008–09	Pavel Datsyuk	Detroit Red Wings
2009–10	Pavel Datsyuk	Detroit Red Wings
2010–11	Ryan Kesler	Vancouver Canucks

WILLIAM M. JENNINGS TROPHY

Awarded to the goalie(s) with the best goals-against average in the regular season

1981–82	Rick Wamsley & Denis Herron	Montreal Canadiens
1982–83	Rollie Melanson & Billy Smith	New York Islanders
1983–84	Al Jensen & Pat Riggin	Washington Capitals
1984–85	Tom Barrasso & Bob Sauve	Buffalo Sabres
1985–86	Bob Froese & Darren Jensen	Philadelphia Flyers
1986–87	Patrick Roy & Brian Hayward	Montreal Canadiens
1987–88	Patrick Roy & Brian Hayward	Montreal Canadiens
1988–89	Patrick Roy & Brian Hayward	Montreal Canadiens
1989–90	Andy Moog & Reggie Lemelin	Boston Bruins
1990–91	Ed Belfour	Chicago Blackhawks
1991–92	Patrick Roy	Montreal Canadiens
1992–93	Ed Belfour	Chicago Blackhawks
1993–94	Dominik Hasek & Grant Fuhr	Buffalo Sabres
1994–95	Ed Belfour	Chicago Blackhawks
1995–96	Chris Osgood & Mike Vernon	Detroit Red Wings
1996–97	Martin Brodeur & Mike Dunham	New Jersey Devils
1997–98	Martin Brodeur	New Jersey Devils
1998–99	Ed Belfour & Roman Turek	Dallas Stars
1999–00	Roman Turek	St. Louis Blues
2000–01	Dominik Hasek	Buffalo Sabres
2001–02	Patrick Roy	Colorado Avalanche
2002–03	Martin Brodeur	New Jersey Devils
	Roman Cechmanek	Philadelphia Flyers
	Robert Esche	Philadelphia Flyers
2003–04	Martin Brodeur	New Jersey Devils
2004–05	no winner	
2005–06	Miikka Kiprusoff	Calgary Flames
2006–07	Manny Fernandez & Niklas Backstrom	Minnesota Wild
2007–08	Chris Osgood & Dominik Hasek	Detroit Red Wings
2008–09	Tim Thomas & Manny Fernandez	Boston Bruins
2009–10	Martin Brodeur	New Jersey Devils
2010–11	Roberto Luongo & Corey Schneider	Vancouver Canucks

KING CLANCY MEMORIAL TROPHY

Awarded to the player who best displays leadership both on and off the ice

1987–88	Lanny McDonald	Calgary Flames
1988–89	Bryan Trottier	New York Islanders
1989–90	Kevin Lowe	Edmonton Oilers
1990–91	Dave Taylor	Los Angeles Kings
1991–92	Raymond Bourque	Boston Bruins
1992–93	Dave Poulin	Boston Bruins
1993–94	Adam Graves	New York Rangers
1994–95	Joe Nieuwendyk	Calgary Flames
1995–96	Kris King	Winnipeg Jets
1996–97	Trevor Linden	Vancouver Canucks
1997–98	Kelly Chase	St. Louis Blues
1998–99	Rob Ray	Buffalo Sabres
1999–00	Curtis Joseph	Toronto Maple Leafs
2000–01	Shjon Podein	Colorado Avalanche
2001–02	Ron Francis	Carolina Hurricanes
2002–03	Brendan Shanahan	Detroit Red Wings
2003–04	Jarome Iginla	Calgary Flames
2004–05	no winner	
2005–06	Olaf Kolzig	Washington Capitals
2006–07	Saku Koivu	Montreal Canadiens
2007–08	Vincent Lecavalier	Tampa Bay Lightning
2008–09	Ethan Moreau	Edmonton Oilers
2009–10	Shane Doan	Phoenix Coyotes
2010–11	Doug Weight	New York Islanders

ROCKET RICHARD TROPHY

Awarded to the player(s) who leads the regular season in goals scored

1998–99	Teemu Selanne	Mighty Ducks of Anaheim (47 goals)
1999–00	Pavel Bure	Florida Panthers (58 goals)
2000–01	Pavel Bure	Florida Panthers (59 goals)
2001–02	Jarome Iginla	Calgary Flames (52 goals)
2002–03	Milan Hejduk	Colorado Avalanche (50 goals)
2003–04	Rick Nash	Columbus Blue Jackets (41 goals)
	Jarome Iginla	Calgary Flames (41 goals)
	Ilya Kovalchuk	Atlanta Thrashers (41 goals)
2004–05	no winner	
2005–06	Jonathan Cheechoo	San Jose Sharks (56 goals)
2006–07	Vincent Lecavalier	Tampa Bay Lightning (52 goals)
2007–08	Alexander Ovechkin	Washington Capitals (65 goals)
2008–09	Alexander Ovechkin	Washington Capitals (56 goals)
2009–10	Sidney Crosby	Pittsburgh Penguins (51 goals)
	Steve Stamkos	Tampa Bay Lightning (51 goals)
2010–11	Corey Perry	Anaheim Ducks (50 goals)

2011 HOCKEY HALL OF FAME INDUCTEES

Elections: June 28, 2011
Induction Ceremonies: November 14, 2011

PLAYER INDUCTEES

Ed Belfour

Nicknamed Eddie the Eagle, Belfour wore number 20 in honour of his childhood hero, Vladislav Tretiak. He won the Calder and Vezina trophies in 1990–91 and never looked back. Belfour remained in Chicago for eight years, but the Hawks never won the Stanley Cup. He played briefly with San Jose in 1996–97 and then signed as a free agent with Dallas, winning the Cup in 1998–99. He later played three years for the Maple Leafs, a final NHL season with Florida, and then 2007–08 with Leksand in Sweden. Belfour retired with incredible statistics, including 963 games played, 484 wins in the regular season and 76 shutouts.

Doug Gilmour

Gilmour had three sensational parts to his pro career. The first came in St. Louis, where he starred for the Blues for five years. An excellent defensive forward, he was also magnificent around the opposition goal. In 1986–87, he had 42 goals and 105 points with the Blues and later that year played on Canada's successful 1987 Canada Cup team that beat the Soviet Union in what were arguably the three best games ever played. Gilmour was traded to Calgary that summer, and over the course of the next three and a half years continued to lead the offence. He won his only Cup with the Flames in 1989, but in early 1992 was traded to the Maple Leafs in a ten-player deal. It was with Toronto that Gilmour had the finest years of his career. In parts of six seasons with the team, he became captain and leader, setting team records for most assists (95) and points in a season (127) in 1992-93. Gilmour recorded his 1,000th career point while with the Leafs, but he went on to play for four other teams. In all, he had 1,414 points in 1,474 career games, a remarkably consistent career over 20 years.

Mark Howe

Howe was no stranger to international play, either, having won a silver medal as a 16-year-old with the surprising U.S. team at the 1972 Olympics. He went on to play in the WHA with brother Marty and father Gordie for six years, and then joined the NHL in 1979 after the two leagues merged. Howe also played for the WHA at the 1974 Summit Series against the Soviet Union, a series dominated by the CCCP. Mark went on to play 16 years in the NHL, with the Hartford Whalers, Philadelphia and Detroit. He also played for the U.S. at the 1981 Canada Cup and was inducted into the U.S. Hockey Hall of Fame in 2003.

Joe Nieuwendyk

Nieuwendyk also played briefly with the Maple Leafs, but he had his best years with Calgary (when Gilmour was there) and Dallas (when Belfour was there). In Nieuwendyk's case, he was a power forward with a wicked shot, a pure scorer who had 564 goals in 1,257 career games. He is also in a rare group of players who won the Stanley Cup three times, each with a different team. His first championship came with Calgary in 1988–89, a year in which he had 51 goals for the second straight year. He won the Cup in 1999 with Dallas, and then added a third with the more defensive-minded New Jersey Devils in 2002–03, playing alongside goalie Martin Brodeur, his teammate with Canada at the 2002 Olympics. Indeed, Nieuwendyk had an excellent international career as well. He won a silver medal in 1986 with Canada's U20 team and also played briefly at the 1990 World Championship. But most impressively, he was a member of Canada's first two NHL-led Olympics, in 1998 (4th place) and in 2002, when the country won gold for the first time in half a century.

Other Notable Names Eligible but Not Inducted

Men

Viktor Tikhonov, Pat Burns, Pavel Bure, Eric Lindros, Adam Oates, Dave Andreychuk, Phil Housley, Sergei Makarov, Mike Vernon, Tom Barrasso, Arturs Irbe, Tommy Salo, Peter Bondra, Fredrik Olausson, Pierre Turgeon

Women

Fran Rider, Shirley Cameron, Cassie Campbell, Danielle Goyette, Geraldine Heaney, Nancy Drolet, France St. Louis, Ben Smith, Vicky Sunohara, Krissy Wendell, Lady Isobel Constance Mary Stanley

The Hockey Hall of Fame Selection Committee comprises Jim Gregory, Pat Quinn, Scotty Bowman, David Branch, Colin Campbell, John Davidson, Eric Duhatschek, Jan-Ake Edvinsson, Mike Emrick, Michael Farber, Mike Gartner, Igor Larionov, Lanny McDonald, Yvon Pednault, Serge Savard, Harry Sinden, Peter Stastny, Bill Torrey.

HOCKEY HALL OF FAME HONOURED MEMBERS

(member—category, year inducted)

Sid Abel—Player, 1969
Charles Adams—Builder, 1960
Jack Adams—Player, 1959
Weston Adams—Builder, 1972
Frank Ahearn—Builder, 1962
Bunny Ahearne—Builder, 1977
Sir Montagu Allan—Builder, 1945

Keith Allen—Builder, 1992
Glenn Anderson—Player, 2008
Syl Apps—Player, 1961
Al Arbour—Builder, 1996
George Armstrong—Player, 1975
Neil Armstrong—Official, 1991
John Ashley—Official, 1981

Ace Bailey—Player, 1975
Dan Bain—Player, 1945
Hobey Baker—Player, 1945
Harold Ballard—Builder, 1977
Bill Barber—Player, 1990
Marty Barry—Player, 1965
Andy Bathgate—Player, 1978
Bobby Bauer—Player, 1996
Father David Bauer—Builder, 1989
Jean Beliveau—Player, 1972
Ed Belfour—Player, 2011
Clint Benedict—Player, 1965
Doug Bentley—Player, 1964
Max Bentley—Player, 1966
Jack Bickell—Builder, 1978
Toe Blake—Player, 1966
Leo Boivin—Player, 1986
Dickie Boon—Player, 1952
Mike Bossy—Player, 1991
Butch Bouchard—Player, 1966
Frank Boucher—Player, 1958
George Boucher—Player, 1960
Ray Bourque—Player, 2004
Johnny Bower—Player, 1976
Russell Bowie—Player, 1945
Scotty Bowman—Builder, 1991
Frank Brimsek—Player, 1966
Punch Broadbent—Player, 1962
Turk Broda—Player, 1967
Herb Brooks—Builder, 2006
George Brown—Builder, 1961
Walter Brown—Builder, 1962
Frank Buckland—Builder, 1975
Johnny Bucyk—Player, 1981
Billy Burch—Player, 1974
Walter Bush—Builder, 2000
Jack Butterfield—Builder, 1980
Frank Calder—Builder, 1947
Harry Cameron—Player, 1962
Angus Campbell—Builder, 1964
Clarence Campbell—Builder, 1966
Joe Cattarinich—Builder, 1977
Bill Chadwick—Official, 1964

Gerry Cheevers—Player, 1985
Ed Chynoweth—Builder, 2008
King Clancy—Player, 1958
Dino Ciccarelli—Player, 2010
Dit Clapper—Player, 1947
Bobby Clarke—Player, 1987
Sprague Cleghorn—Player, 1958
Paul Coffey—Player, 2004
Neil Colville—Player, 1967
Charlie Conacher—Player, 1961
Lionel Conacher—Player, 1994
Roy Conacher—Player, 1998
Alex Connell—Player, 1958
Bill Cook—Player, 1952
Bun Cook—Player, 1995
Murray Costello—Builder, 2005
Art Coulter—Player, 1974
Yvan Cournoyer—Player, 1982
Bill Cowley—Player, 1968
Rusty Crawford—Player, 1962
John D'Amico—Official, 1993
Leo Dandurand—Builder, 1963
Jack Darragh—Player, 1962
Scotty Davidson—Player, 1950
Hap Day—Player, 1961
Alex Delvecchio—Player, 1977
Cy Denneny—Player, 1959
Frank Dilio—Builder, 1964
Jimmy Devellano—Builder, 2010
Marcel Dionne—Player, 1992
Gord Drillon—Player, 1975
Graham Drinkwater—Player, 1950
Ken Dryden—Player, 1983
George Dudley—Builder, 1958
Dick Duff—Player, 2006
Woody Dumart—Player, 1992
Tommy Dunderdale—Player, 1974
James Dunn—Builder, 1968
Bill Durnan—Player, 1964
Red Dutton—Player, 1958
Babe Dye—Player, 1970
Chaucer Elliott—Official, 1961
Tony Esposito—Player, 1988

Phil Esposito—Player, 1984
Art Farrell—Player, 1965
Bernie Federko—Player, 2002
Slava Fetisov—Player, 2001
Fern Flaman—Player, 1990
Cliff Fletcher—Builder, 2004
Frank Foyston—Player, 1958
Emile Francis—Builder, 1982
Ron Francis—Player, 2007
Frank Fredrickson—Player, 1958
Grant Fuhr—Player, 2003
Bill Gadsby—Player, 1970
Bob Gainey—Player, 1992
Chuck Gardiner—Player, 1945
Herb Gardiner—Player, 1958
Jimmy Gardner—Player, 1962
Mike Gartner—Player, 2001
Bernie Geoffrion—Player, 1972
Eddie Gerard—Player, 1945
Ed Giacomin—Player, 1987
Dr. Jack Gibson—Builder, 1976
Rod Gilbert—Player, 1982
Clark Gillies—Player, 2002
Billy Gilmour—Player, 1962
Doug Gilmour—Player, 2011
Moose Goheen—Player, 1952
Ebbie Goodfellow—Player, 1963
Tommy Gorman—Builder, 1963
Michel Goulet—Player, 1998
Cammi Granato—Women, 2010
Mike Grant—Player, 1950
Shorty Green—Player, 1962
Jim Gregory—Builder, 2007
Wayne Gretzky—Player, 1999
Si Griffis—Player, 1950
Frank Griffiths—Builder, 1993
George Hainsworth—Player, 1961
Glenn Hall—Player, 1975
Joe Hall—Player, 1961
William Hanley—Builder, 1986
Doug Harvey—Player, 1973
Dale Hawerchuk—Player, 2001
Charles Hay—Builder, 1974

George Hay—Player, 1958
George Hayes—Official, 1988
Jim Hendy—Builder, 1968
Riley Hern—Player, 1962
Bobby Hewitson—Official, 1963
Foster Hewitt—Builder, 1965
William Hewitt—Builder, 1947
Bryan Hextall—Player, 1969
Harry Holmes—Player, 1972
Tom Hooper—Player, 1962
Red Horner—Player, 1965
Tim Horton—Player, 1977
Harley Hotchkiss—Builder, 2006
Gordie Howe—Player, 1972
Mark Howe—Player, 2011
Syd Howe—Player, 1965
Harry Howell—Player, 1979
Bobby Hull—Player, 1983
Brett Hull—Player, 2009
Fred Hume—Builder, 1962
Bouse Hutton—Player, 1962
Harry Hyland—Player, 1962
Mike Ilitch—Builder, 2003
Punch Imlach—Builder, 1984
Mickey Ion—Official, 1961
Dick Irvin—Player, 1958
Tommy Ivan—Builder, 1974
Harvey Jackson—Player, 1971
Angela James—Women, 2010
William Jennings—Builder, 1975
Bob Johnson—Builder, 1992
Moose Johnson—Player, 1952
Ching Johnson—Player, 1958
Tom Johnson—Player, 1970
Aurel Joliat—Player, 1947
Gordon Juckes—Builder, 1979
Duke Keats—Player, 1958
Red Kelly—Player, 1969
Ted Kennedy—Player, 1966
Dave Keon—Player, 1986
Valeri Kharlamov—Player, 2005
Gen. John Reed Kilpatrick—Builder, 1960
Brian Kilrea—Builder, 2003

Seymour Knox—Builder, 1993
Jari Kurri—Player, 2001
Elmer Lach—Player, 1966
Guy Lafleur—Player, 1988
Pat LaFontaine—Player, 2003
Newsy Lalonde—Player, 1950
Rod Langway—Player, 2002
Lou Lamoriello—Builder, 2009
Jacques Laperriere—Player, 1987
Guy Lapointe—Player, 1993
Edgar Laprade—Player, 1993
Igor Larionov—Player, 2008
Jack Laviolette—Player, 1962
George Leader—Builder, 1969
Robert LeBel—Builder, 1970
Brian Leetch—Player, 2009
Hugh Lehman—Player, 1958
Jacques Lemaire—Player, 1984
Mario Lemieux—Player, 1997
Percy LeSueur—Player, 1961
Herbie Lewis—Player, 1989
Ted Lindsay—Player, 1966
Tommy Lockhart—Builder, 1965
Paul Loicq—Builder, 1961
Harry Lumley—Player, 1980
Al MacInnis—Player, 2007
Mickey MacKay—Player, 1952
Frank Mahovlich—Player, 1981
Joe Malone—Player, 1950
Sylvio Mantha—Player, 1960
John Mariucci—Builder, 1985
Jack Marshall—Player, 1965
Frank Mathers—Builder, 1992
Steamer Maxwell—Player, 1962
Lanny McDonald—Player, 1992
Frank McGee—Player, 1945
Billy McGimsie—Player, 1962
Major Frederic McLaughlin—Builder, 1963
George McNamara—Player, 1958
Mark Messier—Player, 2007
Stan Mikita—Player, 1983
Jake Milford—Builder, 1984

Hon. Hartland Molson—Builder, 1973
Dickie Moore—Player, 1974
Paddy Moran—Player, 1958
Howie Morenz—Player, 1945
Scotty Morrison—Builder, 1999
Bill Mosienko—Player, 1965
Joe Mullen—Player, 2000
Larry Murphy—Player, 2004
Monsignor Athol Murray—Builder, 1998
Cam Neely—Player, 2005
Roger Neilson—Builder, 2002
Francis Nelson—Builder, 1947
Joe Nieuwendyk—Player, 2011
Frank Nighbor—Player, 1947
Reg Noble—Player, 1962
Bruce A. Norris—Builder, 1969
James Norris Jr.—Builder, 1962
James Norris Sr.—Builder, 1958
William Northey—Builder, 1947
Ambrose O'Brien—Builder, 1962
Buddy O'Connor—Player, 1988
Harry Oliver—Player, 1967
Bert Olmstead—Player, 1985
Brian O'Neill—Builder, 1994
Bobby Orr—Player, 1979
Fred Page—Builder, 1993
Bernie Parent—Player, 1984
Brad Park—Player, 1988
Craig Patrick—Builder, 2001
Frank Patrick—Builder, 1958
Lester Patrick—Player, 1947
Lynn Patrick—Player, 1980
Matt Pavelich—Official, 1987
Gilbert Perreault—Player, 1990
Tommy Phillips—Player, 1945
Allan Pickard—Builder, 1958
Pierre Pilote—Player, 1975
Rudy Pilous—Builder, 1985
Didier Pitre—Player, 1962
Jacques Plante—Player, 1978
Bud Poile—Builder, 1990
Sam Pollock—Builder, 1978

Denis Potvin—Player, 1991
Babe Pratt—Player, 1966
Joe Primeau—Player, 1963
Marcel Pronovost—Player, 1978
Bob Pulford—Player, 1991
Harvey Pulford—Player, 1945
Bill Quackenbush—Player, 1976
Frank Rankin—Player, 1961
Jean Ratelle—Player, 1985
Sen. Donat Raymond—Builder, 1958
Chuck Rayner—Player, 1973
Ken Reardon—Player, 1966
Henri Richard—Player, 1979
Maurice Richard—Player, 1961
George Richardson—Player, 1950
Gordon Roberts—Player, 1971
John Ross Robertson—Builder, 1947
Claude Robinson—Builder, 1947
Larry Robinson—Player, 1995
Luc Robitaille—Player, 2009
Mike Rodden—Official, 1962
Art Ross—Player, 1945
Philip D. Ross—Builder, 1976
Patrick Roy—Player, 2006
Blair Russel—Player, 1965
Ernie Russell—Player, 1965
Jack Ruttan—Player, 1962
Dr. Gunther Sabetzki—Builder, 1995
Borje Salming—Player, 1996
Glen Sather—Builder, 1997
Denis Savard—Player, 2000
Serge Savard—Player, 1986
Terry Sawchuk—Player, 1971
Fred Scanlan—Player, 1965
Ray Scapinello—Official, 2008
Milt Schmidt—Player, 1961
Sweeney Schriner—Player, 1962
Daryl "Doc" Seaman—Builder, 2010
Earl Seibert—Player, 1963
Oliver Seibert—Player, 1961
Frank Selke—Builder, 1960
Eddie Shore—Player, 1947
Steve Shutt—Player, 1993

Babe Siebert—Player, 1964
Joe Simpson—Player, 1962
Harry Sinden—Builder, 1983
Darryl Sittler—Player, 1989
Cooper Smeaton—Official, 1961
Alf Smith—Player, 1962
Billy Smith—Player, 1993
Clint Smith—Player, 1991
Frank Smith—Builder, 1962
Hooley Smith—Player, 1972
Tommy Smith—Player, 1973
Conn Smythe—Builder, 1958
Ed Snider—Builder, 1988
Allan Stanley—Player, 1981
Barney Stanley—Player, 1962
Peter Stastny—Player, 1998
Scott Stevens—Player, 2007
Jack Stewart—Player, 1964
Lord Stanley of Preston—Builder, 1945
Nels Stewart—Player, 1962
Red Storey—Official, 1967
Bruce Stuart—Player, 1961
Hod Stuart—Player, 1945
Capt. James T. Sutherland—Builder, 1947
Anatoli Tarasov—Builder, 1974
Cyclone Taylor—Player, 1947
Tiny Thompson—Player, 1959
Bill Torrey—Builder, 1995
Vladislav Tretiak—Player, 1989
Harry Trihey—Player, 1950
Bryan Trottier—Player, 1997
Lloyd Turner—Builder, 1958
William Tutt—Builder, 1978
Frank Udvari—Official, 1973
Norm Ullman—Player, 1982
Andy Van Hellemond—Official, 1999
Georges Vezina—Player, 1945
Carl Voss—Builder, 1974
Fred Waghorne—Builder, 1961
Jack Walker—Player, 1960
Marty Walsh—Player, 1962
Harry E. Watson—Player, 1962
Harry Watson—Player, 1994

Cooney Weiland—Player, 1971
Harry Westwick—Player, 1962
Fred Whitcroft—Player, 1962
Phat Wilson—Player, 1962
Arthur Wirtz—Builder, 1971

Bill Wirtz—Builder, 1976
Gump Worsley—Player, 1980
Roy Worters—Player, 1969
Steve Yzerman—Player, 2009
John Ziegler—Builder, 1987

IIHF HALL OF FAME

(name, nationality, year inducted)
° denotes Referee; * denotes Builder; all others are Players

°Quido Adamec (Czech Republic), 2005
*John "Bunny" Ahearne (Great Britain),
    1997
Veniamin Alexandrov (Russia), 2007
*Ernest Aljancic, Sr. (Slovenia), 2002
Helmut Balderis (Latvia), 1998
Rudi Ball (Germany), 2004
*Father David Bauer (Canada), 1997
Art Berglund (USA), 2008
*Curt Berglund (Sweden), 2003
Sven Bergqvist (Sweden), 1999
Lars Bjorn (Sweden), 1998
Vsevolod Bobrov (Russia), 1997
Vladimir Bouzek (Czech Republic), 2007
Roger Bourbonnais (Canada), 1999
Philippe Bozon (France), 2008
*Herb Brooks (USA), 1999
*Walter Brown (USA), 1997
Vlastimil Bubnik (Czech Republic), 1997
*Mike Buckna (Canada), 2004
*Ludek Bukac (Czech Republic), 2007
Walter Bush, Jr. (USA), 2009
Karen Bye (-Dietz) (United States), 2011
*Enrico Calcaterra (Italy), 1999
Ferdinand Cattini
    (Switzerland), 1998
Hans Cattini (Switzerland), 1998
Josef Cerny (Czech Republic), 2007
*Arkady Chernyshev (Russia), 1999
Bill Christian (USA), 1998
Bill Cleary (USA), 1997

Gerry Cosby (USA), 1997
Jim Craig (USA), 1999
Mike Curran (USA), 1999
°Ove Dahlberg (Sweden), 2004
Vitali Davydov (Russia), 2004
Igor Dimitriev (Russia), 2007
Hans Dobida (Austria), 2007
Jaroslav Drobny (Czechoslovakia), 1997
Vladimir Dzurilla (Slovakia), 1998
*Rudolf Eklow (Sweden), 1999
Carl Erhardt (Great Britain), 1998
*Rickard Fagerlund (Sweden), 2010
Slava Fetisov (Russia), 2005
Anatoli Firsov (Russia), 1998
Josef Golonka (Slovakia), 1998
Cammi Granato (USA), 2008
Wayne Gretzky (Canada), 2000
*Arne Grunander (Sweden), 1997
Henryk Gruth (Poland), 2006
*Bengt-Ake Gustafsson (Sweden), 2003
Karel Gut (Czech Republic), 1998
Geraldine Heaney (Canada), 2008
Anders Hedberg (Sweden), 1997
Dieter Hegen (Germany), 2010
*Heinz Henschel (Germany), 2003
William Hewitt (Canada), 1998
Rudi Hiti (Slovenia), 2009
Ivan Hlinka (Czech Republic), 2002
Jiri Holecek (Czech Republic), 1998
Jiri Holik (Czech Republic), 1999
*Derek Holmes (Canada), 1999

Leif Holmqvist (Sweden), 1999
*Ladislav Horsky (Slovakia), 2004
Fran Huck (Canada), 1999
*Jorgen Hviid (Denmark), 2005
Arturs Irbe (Latvia), 2010
Gustav Jaenecke (Germany), 1998
Angela James (Canada), 2008
*Tore Johannessen (Norway), 1999
Mark Johnson (USA), 1999
Marshall Johnston (Canada), 1998
Tomas Jonsson (Sweden), 2000
Gord Juckes (Canada), 1997
Timo Jutila (Finland), 2003
°Yuri Karandin (Russia), 2004
Alexei Kasatonov (Russia), 2009
*Tsutomu Kawabuchi (Japan), 2004
Matti Keinonen (Finland), 2002
Valeri Kharlamov (Russia), 1998
*Anatoli Khorozov (Ukraine), 2006
Udo Kiessling (Germany), 2000
*Dave King (Canada), 2001
Jakob Kolliker (Switzerland), 2007
°Josef Kompalla (Germany), 2003
Viktor Konovalenko (Russia), 2007
*Vladimir Kostka (Czech Republic), 1997
Vladimir Krutov (Russia), 2010
Erich Kuhnhackl (Germany), 1997
Jari Kurri (Finland), 2000
Viktor Kuzkin (Russia), 2005
Jacques Lacarriere (France), 1998
Igor Larionov (Russia), 2008
*Bob Lebel (Canada), 1997
Mario Lemieux (Canada), 2008
*Harry Lindblad (Finland), 1999
Vic Lindquist (Canada), 1997
*Paul Loicq (Belgium), 1997
Konstantin Loktev (Russia), 2007
Hakan Loob (Sweden), 1998
Tord Lundstrom (Sweden), 2011
*Cesar Luthi (Switzerland), 1998
Oldrich Machac (Czech Republic), 1999
Barry MacKenzie (Canada), 1999

Sergei Makarov (Russia), 2001
Josef Malecek (Czech Republic), 2003
Alexander Maltsev (Russia), 1999
*Louis Magnus (France), 1997
Pekka Marjamaki (Finland), 1998
Seth Martin (Canada), 1997
Vladimir Martinec (Czech Republic), 2001
John Mayasich (USA), 1997
Boris Mayorov (Russia), 1999
Jack McCartan (USA), 1998
Jack McLeod (Canada), 1999
Boris Mikhailov (Russia), 2000
Bohumil Modry (Czech Republic), 2011
Lou Nanne (USA), 2004
Mats Naslund (Sweden), 2005
Vaclav Nedomansky (Czech Republic),
    1997
Riikka Nieminen-Valila (Finland), 2010
Kent Nilsson (Sweden), 2006
Nisse Nilsson (Sweden), 2002
*Kalevi Numminen (Finland), 2011
Lasse Oksanen (Finland), 1999
Terry O'Malley (Canada), 1998
Eduard Pana (Romania), 1998
*Gyorgy Pasztor (Hungary), 2001
*Peter Patton (Great Britain), 2002
Esa Peltonen (Finland), 2007
Vladimir Petrov (Russia), 2006
Ronald Pettersson (Sweden), 2004
Frantisek Pospisil (Czech Republic), 1999
Sepp Puschnig (Austria), 1999
Alexander Ragulin (Russia), 1997
Hans Rampf (Germany), 2001
*Gord Renwick (Canada), 2002
*Bob Ridder (USA), 1998
*Jack Riley (USA), 1998
Thomas Rundquist (Sweden), 2007
*Gunther Sabetzki (Germany), 1997
Borje Salming (Sweden), 1998
Laszlo Schell (Hungary), 2009
Alois Schloder (Germany), 2005
Harry Sinden (Canada), 1997

Nikolai Sologubov (Russia), 2004

*Andrei Starovoitov (Russia), 1997

Vyacheslav Starshinov (Russia), 2007

*Jan Starsi (Slovakia), 1999

Peter Stastny (Slovakia), 2000

Ulf Sterner (Sweden), 2001

Roland Stoltz (Sweden), 1999

*Arne Stromberg (Sweden), 1998

*Goran Stubb (Finland), 2000

*Miroslav Subrt (Czech Republic), 2004

Jan Suchy (Czech Republic), 2009

*Anatoli Tarasov (Russia), 1997

Frantisek Tikal (Czech Republic), 2004

*Viktor Tikhonov (Russia), 1998

*Shoichi Tomita (Japan), 2006

Richard "Bibi" Torriani (Switzerland), 1997

Vladislav Tretiak (Russia), 1997

Ladislav Trojak (Czech Republic), 2011

*Hal Trumble (USA), 1999

*Yoshiaki Tsutsumi (Japan), 1999

Sven Tumba (Sweden), 1997

Doru Tureanu (Romania), 2011

*Thayer Tutt (USA), 2002

*Xaver Unsinn (Germany), 1998

*Lou Vairo (United States), 2010

Jorma Valtonen (Finland), 1999

Valeri Vasiliev (Russia), 1998

Juhani Wahlsten (Finland), 2006

*Walter Wasservogel (Austria), 1997

Harry Watson (Canada), 1998

°Unto Wiitala (Finland), 2003

Alexander Yakushev (Russia), 2003

Urpo Ylonen (Finland), 1997

*Vldimir Yurzinov (Russia), 2002

Vladimir Zabrodsky (Czech Republic), 1997

Joachim Ziesche (Germany), 1999

INTERNATIONAL HOCKEY

TRIPLE GOLD CLUB

These 25 players and one coach form the unique group that has won the IIHF World Championship, the Olympic ice hockey tournament and the Stanley Cup. To be credited with each of these honours, the player or coach must have participated in at least one game of the event.

Players are entered chronologically by the date when they achieved the final championship of the triple. If two or more players completed their triple on the same date, priority is given to the player who was the first to win his first of the three titles. If two or more players have identical accomplishments, priority is given to the player who completes the triple at the younger age.

Legend: OG=Olympic Games; SC=Stanley Cup; WM=World Championship

1. **Tomas Jonsson** b. Falun, Sweden, April 12, 1960
   SC 1982, 1983 (New York Islanders)
   WM 1991 (Sweden)
   OG 1994 (Sweden)
   TGC member as of February 27, 1994 (Olympic final win vs. Canada)

2. **Mats Naslund** b. Timra, Sweden, October 31, 1959
   SC 1986 (Montreal Canadiens)
   WM 1991 (Sweden)
   OG 1994 (Sweden)
   TGC member as of February 27, 1994 (Olympic final win vs. Canada)

3. **Hakan Loob** b. Roma, Sweden, July 3, 1960
   WM 1987, 1991 (Sweden)
   SC 1989 (Calgary Flames)
   OG 1994 (Sweden)
   TGC member as of February 27, 1994 (Olympic final win vs. Canada)

4. **Valeri Kamensky** b. Voskresensk, Soviet Union (Russia), April 18, 1966
   WM 1986, 1989, 1990 (Soviet Union)
   OG 1988 (Soviet Union)
   SC 1996 (Colorado Avalanche)
   TGC member as of June 10, 1996 (Stanley Cup win vs. Florida)

5. **Alexei Gusarov** b. Leningrad (St. Petersburg), Soviet Union (Russia), July 8, 1964
   WM 1986, 1989, 1990 (Soviet Union)
   OG 1988 (Soviet Union)
   SC 1996 (Colorado Avalanche)
   TGC member as of June 10, 1996 (Stanley Cup win vs. Florida)

6. Peter Forsberg   b. Ornskoldsvik, Sweden, July 20, 1973
   WM 1992, 1998 (Sweden)
   OG 1994, 2006 (Sweden)
   SC 1996, 2001 (Colorado Avalanche)
   TGC member as of June 10, 1996 (Stanley Cup win vs. Florida)

7. Vyacheslav Fetisov   b. Moscow, Soviet Union (Russia), April 20, 1958
   WM 1978, 1981, 1982, 1983, 1986, 1989, 1990 (Soviet Union)
   OG 1984, 1988 (Soviet Union)
   SC 1997, 1998 (Detroit Red Wings)
   TGC member as of June 7, 1997 (Stanley Cup win vs. Philadelphia)

8. Igor Larionov (b. Voskresensk, Soviet Union (Russia), December 3, 1960)
   WM 1982, 1983, 1986, 1989 (Soviet Union)
   OG 1984, 1988 (Soviet Union)
   SC 1997, 1998, 2002 (Detroit Red Wings)
   TGC member as of June 7, 1997 (Stanley Cup win vs. Philadelphia)

9. Alexander Mogilny   b. Khabarovsk, Soviet Union (Russia), February 18, 1969
   OG 1988 (Soviet Union)
   WM 1989 (Soviet Union)
   SC 2000 (New Jersey Devils)
   TGC member as of June 10, 2000 (Stanley Cup win vs. Dallas)

10. Vladimir Malakhov   b. Ekaterinburg, Soviet Union (Russia), August 30, 1968
    WM 1990 (Soviet Union)
    OG 1992 (Russia)
    SC 2000 (New Jersey Devils)
    TGC member as of June 10, 2000 (Stanley Cup win vs. Dallas)

11. Rob Blake   b. Simcoe, Ontario, Canada, December 10, 1969
    WM 1994, 1997 (Canada)
    SC 2001 (Colorado Avalanche)
    OG 2002 (Canada)
    TGC member as of February 24, 2002 (Olympic final win vs. United States)

12. Joe Sakic   b. Burnaby, British Columbia, Canada, July 7, 1969
    WM 1994 (Canada)
    SC 1996, 2001 (Colorado Avalanche)
    OG 2002 (Canada)
    TGC member as of February 24, 2002 (Olympic final win vs. United States)

13. Brendan Shanahan b. Mimico, Ontario, Canada, January 23, 1969
WM 1994 (Canada)
SC 1997, 1998, 2002 (Detroit Red Wings)
OG 2002 (Canada)
TGC member as of February 24, 2002 (Olympic final win vs. United States)

14. Scott Niedermayer b. Edmonton, Alberta, Canada, August 31, 1973
SC 1995, 2000, 2003 (New Jersey Devils), 2007 (Anaheim Ducks)
OG 2002, 2010 (Canada)
WM 2004 (Canada)
TGC member as of May 9, 2004 (World Championship final win vs. Sweden)

15. Jaromir Jagr b. Kladno, Czechoslovakia (Czech Republic), February 15, 1972
SC 1991, 1992 (Pittsburgh Penguins)
OG 1998 (Czech Republic)
WM 2005, 2010 (Czech Republic)
TGC member as of May 15, 2005 (World Championship final win vs. Canada)

16. Jiri Slegr b. Jihlava, Czechoslovakia (Czech Republic), May 30, 1971
OG 1998 (Czech Republic)
SC 2002 (Detroit Red Wings)
WM 2005 (Czech Republic)
TGC member as of May 15, 2005 (World Championship final win vs. Canada)

17. Nicklas Lidstrom b. Vasteras, Sweden, April 28, 1970
WM 1991 (Sweden)
SC 1997, 1998, 2002 (Detroit Red Wings)
OG 2006 (Sweden)
TGC member as of February 26, 2006 (Olympic final win vs. Finland)

18. Fredrik Modin b. Sundsvall, Sweden, October 8, 1974
WM 1998 (Sweden)
SC 2004 (Tampa Bay Lightning)
OG 2006 (Sweden)
TGC member as of February 26, 2006 (Olympic final win vs. Finland)

19. Chris Pronger b. Dryden, Ontario, Canada, October 10, 1974
WM 1997 (Canada)
OG 2002, 2010 (Canada)
SC 2007 (Anaheim Ducks)
TGC member as of June 6, 2007 (Stanley Cup win vs. Ottawa)

20. **Niklas Kronwall**   b. Stockholm, Sweden, January 12, 1981
    OG 2006 (Sweden)
    WM 2006 (Sweden)
    SC 2008 (Detroit Red Wings)
    TGC member as of June 4, 2008 (Stanley Cup win vs. Pittsburgh)

21. **Henrik Zetterberg**   b. Njurunda, Sweden, October 9, 1980
    OG 2006 (Sweden)
    WM 2006 (Sweden)
    SC 2008 (Detroit Red Wings)
    TGC member as of June 4, 2008 (Stanley Cup win vs. Pittsburgh)

22. **Mikael Samuelsson**   b. Mariefred, Sweden, December 23, 1976
    OG 2006 (Sweden)
    WM 2006 (Sweden)
    SC 2008 (Detroit Red Wings)
    TGC member as of June 4, 2008 (Stanley Cup win vs. Pittsburgh)

23. **Eric Staal**   b. Thunder Bay, Ontario, Canada, October 29, 1984
    SC 2006 (Carolina Hurricanes)
    WM 2007 (Canada)
    OG 2010 (Canada)
    TGC member as of February 28, 2010 (Olympic final win vs. United States)

24. **Jonathan Toews**   b. Winnipeg, Manitoba, Canada, April 29, 1988
    WM 2007 (Canada)
    OG 2010 (Canada)
    SC 2010 (Chicago Blackhawks)
    TGC member as of June 9, 2010 (Stanley Cup win vs. Philadelphia)

25. **Patrice Bergeron**   b. L'Ancienne-Lorette, Quebec, Canada, July 24, 1985
    WM 2004 (Canada)
    OG 2010 (Canada)
    SC 2011 (Boston Bruins)
    TGC member as of June 15, 2011 (Stanley Cup win vs. Vancouver)

TRIPLE GOLD CLUB COACH

1. **Mike Babcock** (b. Saskatoon, Saskatchewan, Canada, April 29, 1963)
    WM 2004 (Canada)
    SC 2008 (Detroit Red Wings)
    OG 2010 (Canada)
    TGC member as of February 28, 2010 (Olympic final win vs. United States)

2012 WORLD U20 (JUNIOR) CHAMPIONSHIP SCHEDULE

CALGARY/EDMONTON, CANADA, December 26, 2011–January 5, 2012

Venues: Scotiabank Saddledome (Calgary) & Rexall Place (Edmonton)

Group A: Latvia, Russia, Slovakia, Sweden, Switzerland
Group B: Canada, Czech Republic, Denmark, Finland, United States

PRELIMINARY ROUND

All times local (Mountain Standard Time)

December 26	Finland–Canada	Edmonton	1:30 p.m.
December 26	Latvia–Sweden	Calgary	3:30 p.m.
December 26	Denmark–United States	Edmonton	6:00 p.m.
December 26	Switzerland–Russia	Calgary	8:00 p.m.
December 27	Czech Republic–Denmark	Edmonton	6:00 p.m.
December 27	Slovakia–Latvia	Calgary	8:00 p.m.
December 28	United States–Finland	Edmonton	1:30 p.m.
December 28	Sweden–Switzerland	Calgary	3:30 p.m.
December 28	Canada–Czech Republic	Edmonton	6:00 p.m.
December 28	Russia–Slovakia	Calgary	8:00 p.m.
December 29	Denmark–Canada	Edmonton	6:00 p.m.
December 29	Latvia–Russia	Calgary	8:00 p.m.
December 30	United States–Czech Republic	Edmonton	1:30 p.m.
December 30	Sweden–Slovakia	Calgary	3:30 p.m.
December 30	Finland–Denmark	Edmonton	6:00 p.m.
December 30	Switzerland–Latvia	Calgary	8:00 p.m.
December 31	Czech Republic–Finland	Edmonton	2:00 p.m.
December 31	Slovakia–Switzerland	Calgary	4:00 p.m.
December 31	Canada–United States	Edmonton	6:00 p.m.
December 31	Russia–Sweden	Calgary	8:00 p.m.
January 1	No games scheduled		
January 2	Relegation: A4–B5	Calgary	11:00 a.m.
January 2	Quarterfinal 1: A2–B3	Calgary	3:00 p.m.
January 2	Quarterfinal 2: B2–A3	Calgary	7:00 p.m.
January 3	Relegation: B4–A5	Calgary	11:00 a.m.
January 3	Semifinal 1: B1–Winner of QF1	Calgary	3:00 p.m.

January 3	Semifinal 2: A1–Winner of QF2	Calgary	7:00 p.m.
January 4	Relegation: B5–A5	Calgary	11:00 a.m.
January 4	Relegation: A4–B4	Calgary	3:00 p.m.
January 4	Fifth-Place Game	Calgary	7:00 p.m.
January 5	Bronze Medal Game	Calgary	1:30 p.m.
January 5	Gold Medal Game	Calgary	6:00 p.m.

2011 WORLD CHAMPIONSHIP, MEN

BRATISLAVA/KOSICE, SLOVAKIA, April 29–May 15, 2011

FINAL PLACINGS

GOLD MEDAL	Finland
SILVER MEDAL	Sweden
BRONZE MEDAL	Czech Republic
Fourth Place	Russia
Fifth Place	Canada
Sixth Place	Norway
Seventh Place	Germany
Eighth Place	United States
Ninth Place	Switzerland
Tenth Place	Slovakia
Eleventh Place	Denmark
Twelfth Place	France
Thirteenth Place	Latvia
Fourteenth Place	Belarus
Fifteenth Place	Austria
Sixteenth PLace	Slovenia

Tournament Format

Teams were divided into four groups of four teams each for the Preliminary Round. The top three teams from each group advanced to the Qualifying Round; the four last-place finishers were placed in a relegation pool, with the last two being relegated. In the Qualifying Round, the 12 teams were split into groups of six; the top four from each advanced to a crossover quarterfinal.

RESULTS & STANDINGS

Preliminary Round

Group A (Bratislava)

	GP	W	OTW	OTL	L	GF	GA	P
Germany	3	2	1	0	0	9	5	8
Russia	3	2	0	0	1	10	9	6
Slovakia	3	1	0	0	2	9	9	3
Slovenia	3	0	0	1	2	7	12	1

April 29	Germany 2/Russia 0
April 29	Slovakia 3/Slovenia 1
May 1	Russia 6/Slovenia 4

May 1	Germany 4/Slovakia 3
May 3	Germany 3/Slovenia 2 (5:00 OT/GWS—Frank Hordler)
May 3	Russia 4/Slovakia 3

Group B (Kosice)

	GP	W	OTW	OTL	L	GF	GA	P
Canada	3	2	1	0	0	17	5	8
Switzerland	3	1	1	1	0	8	5	6
France	3	0	0	1	1	3	11	3
Belarus	3	0	0	1	2	3	10	1

April 29	Switzerland 1/France 0 (Julien Vauclair 1:46 OT)
April 29	Canada 4/Belarus 1
May 1	Canada 9/France 1
May 1	Switzerland 4/Belarus 1
May 3	Canada 4/Switzerland 3 (Alex Pietrangelo 4:14 OT)
May 3	France 2/Belarus 1 (Kevin Hecquefeuille 0:46 OT)

Group C (Kosice)

	GP	W	OTW	OTL	L	GF	GA	P
Sweden	3	2	0	1	0	13	7	7
United States	3	2	0	0	1	11	9	6
Norway	3	1	1	0	1	12	8	5
Austria	3	0	0	0	3	1	13	0

April 30	United States 5/Austria 1
April 30	Norway 5/Sweden 4 (5:00 OT/GWS—Per-Age Skroder)
May 2	United States 4/Norway 2
May 2	Sweden 3/Austria 0
May 4	Norway 5/Austria 0
May 4	Sweden 6/United States 2

Group D (Bratislava)

	GP	W	OTW	OTL	L	GF	GA	P
Czech Republic	3	3	0	0	0	12	3	9
Finland	3	1	1	0	1	9	5	5
Denmark	3	0	1	0	2	4	13	2
Latvia	3	0	0	2	1	6	10	2

April 30	Finland 5/Denmark 1
April 30	Czech Republic 4/Latvia 2
May 2	Czech Republic 6/Denmark 0

May 2		Finland 3/Latvia 2 (5:00 OT/GWS—Jarkko Immonen)						
May 4		Denmark 3/Latvia 2 (5:00 OT/GWS—Mads Christensen)						
May 4		Czech Republic 2/Finland 1						

QUALIFYING ROUND

Group E (Bratislava)

	GP	W	OTW	OTL	L	GF	GA	P
Czech Republic	5	5	0	0	0	19	7	15
Finland	5	2	2	0	1	16	10	10
Germany	5	2	0	2	1	15	17	8
Russia	5	2	0	1	2	12	14	7
Slovakia	5	1	0	0	4	13	14	3
Denmark	5	0	1	0	4	9	22	2

May 5	Russia 4/Denmark 3
May 6	Finland 5/Germany 4 (5:00 OT/GWS—Mikko Koivu)
May 6	Czech Republic 3/Slovakia 2
May 7	Denmark 4/Germany 3 (5:00 OT/GWS—Mikkel Boedker)
May 7	Finland 2/Slovakia 1
May 8	Czech Republic 3/Russia 2
May 9	Slovakia 4/Denmark 1
May 9	Finland 3/Russia 2 (5:00 OT/GWS—Jarkko Immonen)
May 9	Czech Republic 5/Germany 2

Group F (Kosice)

	GP	W	OTW	OTL	L	GF	GA	P
Canada	5	3	2	0	0	23	11	13
Sweden	5	3	0	1	1	18	10	10
Norway	5	2	1	0	2	17	15	8
United States	5	2	0	1	2	15	19	7
Switzerland	5	1	1	1	2	11	12	6
France	5	0	0	1	4	5	22	1

May 5	Norway 3/Switzerland 2
May 6	Canada 4/United States 3 (5:00 OT/GWS—Jordan Eberle)
May 6	Sweden 4/France 0
May 7	Canada 3/Norway 2
May 7	United States 3/France 2
May 8	Sweden 2/Switzerland 0
May 9	Norway 5/France 2
May 9	Switzerland 5/United States 3
May 9	Canada 3/Sweden 2

RELEGATION ROUND
Group G

	GP	W	OTW	OTL	L	GF	GA	P
Latvia	3	2	0	0	1	12	9	6
Belarus	3	2	0	0	1	17	9	6
Austria	3	1	0	0	2	6	13	3
Slovenia	3	1	0	0	2	8	12	3

May 5	Bratislava	Slovenia 5/Latvia 2
May 5	Kosice	Belarus 7/Austria 2
May 7	Bratislava	Austria 3/Slovenia 2
May 7	Kosice	Latvia 6/Belarus 3
May 8	Bratislava	Belarus 7/Slovenia 1
May 8	Kosice	Latvia 4/Austria 1

PLAYOFFS (BRATISLAVA)
Quarterfinals

May 11	Czech Republic 4/United States 0
May 11	Sweden 5/Germany 2
May 12	Finland 4/Norway 1
May 12	Russia 2/Canada 1

Semifinals

May 13	Sweden 5/Czech Republic 2
May 13	Finland 3/Russia 0

Bronze Medal Game

May 15	Czech Republic 7/Russia 4

Gold Medal Game

May 15	Finland 6/Sweden 1

TEAM CANADA STATISTICS
Ken Hitchcock, coach

	GP	G	A	P	Pim
John Tavares	7	5	4	9	12
Jason Spezza	7	4	3	7	4
Jeff Skinner	7	3	3	6	8
James Neal	6	2	3	5	10
Rick Nash	7	2	3	5	2
Alex Pietrangelo	7	2	3	5	2
Jordan Eberle	7	4	0	4	2

Brent Burns	7	2	2	4	8
Chris Stewart	7	2	2	4	0
Travis Zajac	7	1	2	3	2
Dion Phaneuf	7	0	3	3	8
Marc-Andre Gragnani	6	1	1	2	2
Evander Kane	7	0	2	2	4
Mario Scalzo	3	0	2	2	0
Cal Clutterbuck	7	0	1	1	4
Luke Schenn	7	0	1	1	0
Matt Duchene	7	0	0	0	2
Andrew Ladd	7	0	0	0	2
Marc Methot	7	0	0	0	2
Carlo Colaiacovo	5	0	0	0	0
James Reimer	4	0	0	0	0
Antoine Vermette	4	0	0	0	0
Jonathan Bernier	3	0	0	0	0
Devan Dubnyk	1	0	0	0	0

In Goal	**GP**	**W-L**	**Mins**	**GA**	**SO**	**GAA**
James Reimer	4	3-0	235:24	8	0	2.04
Jonathan Bernier	3	2-1	179:00	6	0	2.01
Devan Dubnyk	1	0-0	13:50	0	0	0.00

2011 WORLD U20 (JUNIOR) CHAMPIONSHIP

BUFFALO/LEWISTON, UNITED STATES, December 26, 2010–January 5, 2011

FINAL PLACINGS

GOLD MEDAL	Russia
SILVER MEDAL	Canada
BRONZE MEDAL	United States
Fourth Place	Sweden
Fifth Place	Switzerland
Sixth Place	Finland
Seventh Place	Czech Republic
Eighth Place	Slovakia
Ninth Place	Norway
Tenth Place	Germany

All-Star Team

Goal	Jack Campbell (USA)
Defence	Ryan Ellis (CAN), Dmitri Orlov (RUS)
Forward	Yevgeni Kuznetsov (RUS), Brayden Schenn (CAN), Ryan Johansen (CAN)

Directorate Awards

Best Goalie	Jack Campbell (USA)
Best Defenceman	Ryan Ellis (CAN)
Best Forward	Brayden Schenn (CAN)
Tournament MVP	Brayden Schenn (CAN)

Tournament Format

Ten teams were placed in two groups, and each team played a round-robin series within its group. The top team from each division advanced to the semifinals, while the second- and third-place teams played for the other two semifinal spots. The second-place team from one division played the third-place team from the other, and vice versa. The two semifinal winners played for gold, while the losers played for bronze.

RESULTS & STANDINGS
Preliminary Round
Group A (Buffalo)

	GP	W	OTW	OTL	L	GF	GA	P
United States	4	3	1	0	0	15	4	11
Finland	4	3	0	1	0	17	4	10
Switzerland	4	2	0	0	2	11	13	6
Slovakia	4	0	1	0	3	7	19	2
Germany	4	0	0	1	3	5	15	1

December 26	Switzerland 4/Germany 3
December 26	United States 3/Finland 2 (Nick Bjugstad 3:08 OT)
December 27	Slovakia 2/Germany 1 (Marek Hrivik 3:39 OT)
December 28	Finland 4/Switzerland 0
December 28	United States 6/Slovakia 1
December 29	Finland 5/Germany 1
December 30	Switzerland 6/Slovakia 4
December 30	United States 4/Germany 0
December 31	Finland 6/Slovakia 0
December 31	United States 2/Switzerland 1

Group B

	GP	W	OTW	OTL	L	GF	GA	P
Sweden	4	3	1	0	0	21	9	11
Canada	4	3	0	1	0	28	12	10
Russia	4	2	0	0	2	19	13	6
Czech Republic	4	1	0	0	3	10	21	3
Norway	4	0	0	0	4	4	27	0

December 26	Buffalo	Canada 6/Russia 3
December 26	Lewiston	Sweden 7/Norway 1
December 27	Lewiston	Czech Republic 2/Norway 0
December 28	Buffalo	Canada 7/Czech Republic 2
December 28	Lewiston	Sweden 2/Russia 0
December 29	Buffalo	Canada 10/Norway 1
December 30	Lewiston	Sweden 6/Czech Republic 3
December 30	Lewiston	Russia 8/Norway 2
December 31	Buffalo	Sweden 6/Canada 5 (5:00 OT/GWS—Oscar Lindberg)
December 31	Lewiston	Russia 8/Czech Republic 3

Relegation Round (Lewiston)

	GP	W	OTW	OTL	L	GF	GA	P
Czech Republic	3	3	0	0	0	10	4	9
Slovakia	3	1	1	0	1	9	6	5
Norway	3	1	0	0	2	3	8	3
Germany	3	0	0	1	2	4	8	1

January 2	Slovakia 5/Norway 0
January 2	Czech Republic 3/Germany 2
January 4	Norway 3/Germany 1
January 4	Czech Republic 5/Slovakia 2

PLAYOFFS (BUFFALO)

Quarterfinals

January 2	Canada 4/Switzerland 1
January 2	Russia 4/Finland 3 (Yevgeni Kuznetsov 6:44 OT)

Semifinals

January 3	Russia 4/Sweden 3 (10:00 OT/GWS—Denis Golubev)
January 3	Canada 4/United States 1

Fifth-Place Game

January 4	Switzerland 3/Finland 2 (5:00 OT/GWS—Yannick Herren)

Bronze Medal Game

January 5	United States 4/Sweden 2

Gold Medal Game

January 5	Russia 5/Canada 3

TEAM CANADA STATISTICS

Dave Cameron, coach

	GP	G	A	P	Pim
Brayden Schenn	7	8	10	18	0
Ryan Ellis	7	3	7	10	2
Ryan Johansen	7	3	6	9	2
Louis Leblanc	7	3	4	7	2
Calvin de Haan	6	0	5	5	4
Erik Gudbranson	7	3	2	5	4
Quinton Howden	7	2	3	5	4
Curtis Hamilton	7	4	0	4	2
Marcus Foligno	7	2	2	4	2
Jaden Schwartz	2	1	2	3	0

Zack Kassian	5	2	1	3	27
Sean Couturier	7	2	1	3	0
Casey Cizikas	7	2	1	3	6
Cody Eakin	7	1	2	3	2
Tyson Barrie	7	1	2	3	0
Carter Ashton	7	1	2	3	6
Simon Despres	7	0	3	3	0
Brett Connolly	7	0	3	3	0
Dylan Olsen	7	0	2	2	0
Mark Visentin	4	0	1	1	0
Jared Cowen	7	1	0	1	0
Olivier Roy	3	0	0	0	0

In Goal	GP	W-L	Mins	GA	SO	GAA
Mark Visentin	4	3–1	239:05	8	0	2.01
Olivier Roy	3	2–1	185:00	11	0	3.57

2011 WORLD CHAMPIONSHIP, WOMEN

ZURICH/WINTERTHUR, SWITZERLAND, April 16–25, 2011

FINAL PLACINGS

GOLD MEDAL	United States
SILVER MEDAL	Canada
BRONZE MEDAL	Finland
Fourth Place	Russia
Fifth Place	Sweden
Sixth Place	Switzerland
Seventh Place	Slovakia
Eighth Place	Kazakhstan

Tournament Format

Eight teams were placed in two groups, and each team played a round-robin series within its group. The top two teams from each advanced to a crossover semi-final. Those winners played for the gold, and the semifinal losers played for the bronze medal.

RESULTS & STANDINGS

Preliminary Round

Group A

	GP	W	OTW	OTL	L	GF	GA	P
United States	3	3	0	0	0	27	2	9
Sweden	3	2	0	0	1	11	10	6
Russia	3	1	0	0	2	6	21	3
Slovakia	3	0	0	0	3	1	12	0

April 17	Zurich	United States 5/Slovakia 0
April 17	Zurich	Sweden 7/Russia 1
April 18	Zurich	Sweden 3/Slovakia 0
April 18	Zurich	United States 13/Russia 1
April 20	Winterthur	Russia 4/Slovakia 1
April 20	Winterthur	United States 9/Sweden 1

Group B (Winterthur)

	GP	W	OTW	OTL	L	GF	GA	P
Canada	3	3	0	0	0	21	0	9
Switzerland	3	1	1	0	1	8	14	5
Finland	3	1	0	1	1	6	7	4
Kazakhstan	3	0	0	0	3	4	18	0

April 16	Finland 5/Kazakhstan 3
April 16	Canada 12/Switzerland 0
April 17	Canada 7/Kazakhstan 0
April 17	Switzerland 2/Finland 1 (Stefanie Marty 1:50 OT)
April 19	Canada 2/Finland 0
April 19	Switzerland 6/Kazakhstan 1

Relegation Round (Winterthur)

	GP	W	OTW	OTL	L	GF	GA	P
Slovakia	2	1	1	0	0	3	1	5
Kazakhstan	2	0	0	1	1	1	3	1

| April 22 | Slovakia 1/Kazakhstan 0 |
| April 24 | Slovakia 2/Kazakhstan 1 (5:00 OT/GWS—Martina Velickova) |

PLAYOFFS (ZURICH)

Quarterfinals

| April 22 | Finland 5/Sweden 1 |
| April 22 | Russia 5/Switzerland 4 (Tatiana Burina 2:58 OT) |

Semifinals

| April 23 | Canada 4/Finland 1 |
| April 23 | United States 5/Russia 1 |

Fifth-Place Game

| April 24 | Sweden 3/Switzerland 2 (10:00 OT/GWS—Elin Holmlov) |

Bronze Medal Game

| April 25 | Finland 3/Russia 2 (Karoliina Rantamaki 2:49 OT) |

Gold Medal Game

| April 25 | United States 3/Canada 2 (Hilary Knight 7:48 OT) |

TEAM CANADA STATISTICS

Ryan Walter, coach

	GP	G	A	P	Pim
Rebecca Johnston	5	4	2	6	0
Hayley Wickenheiser	5	3	2	5	4
Jayna Hefford	5	3	2	5	2
Meghan Agosta	5	0	5	5	2
Marie-Philip Poulin-Nadeau	5	3	1	4	4
Cherie Piper	5	3	1	4	2
Haley Irwin	5	2	2	4	4

Tessa Bonhomme	5	1	3	4	0
Meaghan Mikkelson	5	3	0	3	0
Gillian Apps	5	2	1	3	0
Jennifer Wakefield	5	1	2	3	4
Caroline Ouellette	5	1	2	3	2
Natalie Spooner	5	1	2	3	0
Sarah Vaillancourt	5	0	3	3	4
Jocelyne Larocque	5	0	2	2	6
Tara Watchorn	5	0	2	2	4
Bobbi Jo Slusar	5	0	2	2	2
Catherine Ward	5	0	2	2	2
Charline Labonte	2	0	0	0	0
Shannon Szabados	2	0	0	0	0
Kim St. Pierre	1	0	0	0	0

In Goal	**GP**	**W-L**	**Mins**	**GA**	**SO**	**GAA**
Shannon Szabados	2	11	127:48	3	1	1.41
Charline Labonte	2	20	120:00	1	1	0.50
Kim St. Pierre	1	1–0	60:00	0	1	0.00

2011 WORLD U18 CHAMPIONSHIP, MEN

CRIMMITSCHAU/DRESDEN, GERMANY, April 14–24, 2011

FINAL PLACINGS

GOLD MEDAL	United States
SILVER MEDAL	Sweden
BRONZE MEDAL	Russia
Fourth Place	Canada
Fifth Place	Finland
Sixth Place	Germany
Seventh Place	Switzerland
Eighth Place	Czech Republic
Ninth Place	Norway
Tenth Place	Slovakia

Tournament Format

The ten teams were divided into two groups of five, and each team played a round-robin series within its group. The top team from each group advanced to the semifinals, while the second- and third-place teams played a crossover quarterfinal. The bottom two teams from each group played in a relegation round, the bottom two being demoted to Division I for 2012.

RESULTS & STANDINGS

Preliminary Round

Group A (Crimmitschau)

	GP	W	OTW	OTL	L	GF	GA	P
United States	4	4	0	0	0	21	8	12
Russia	4	2	1	0	1	24	13	8
Germany	4	1	0	1	2	11	17	4
Switzerland	4	1	0	0	3	8	16	3
Slovakia	4	1	0	0	3	9	19	3

April 14	Russia 8/Slovakia 2
April 14	United States 2/Switzerland 1
April 15	United States 8/Slovakia 1
April 15	Germany 4/Switzerland 1
April 16	Russia 5/Germany 4 (5:00 OT/GWS—Nikita Kucherov)
April 17	Switzerland 3/Slovakia 2
April 17	United States 4/Russia 3
April 18	Slovakia 4/Germany 0

| April 19 | Russia 8/Switzerland 3 |
| April 19 | United States 7/Germany 3 |

Group B (Dresden)

	GP	W	OTW	OTL	L	GF	GA	P
Sweden	4	3	0	0	1	20	8	9
Canada	4	3	0	0	1	17	8	9
Finland	4	2	0	0	2	16	15	6
Czech Republic	4	2	0	0	2	8	13	6
Norway	4	0	0	0	4	6	23	0

April 14	Finland 5/Norway 2
April 14	Czech Republic 2/Sweden 1
April 15	Sweden 10/Norway 2
April 15	Canada 5/Czech Republic 0
April 16	Canada 5/Finland 4
April 17	Czech Republic 3/Norway 2
April 17	Sweden 5/Finland 2
April 18	Canada 5/Norway 0
April 19	Finland 5/Czech Republic 3
April 19	Sweden 4/Canada 2

Relegation Round (Dresden)

	GP	W	OTW	OTL	L	GF	GA	P
Switzerland	3	3	0	0	0	11	5	9
Czech Republic	3	2	0	0	1	9	9	6
Norway	3	1	0	0	2	9	9	3
Slovakia	3	0	0	0	3	7	13	0

April 21	Switzerland 4/Norway 1
April 21	Czech Republic 4/Slovakia 3
April 23	Norway 6/Slovakia 2
April 23	Switzerland 4/Czech Republic 2

PLAYOFFS (CRIMMITSCHAU)

Quarterfinals

| April 21 | Russia 5/Finland 2 |
| April 21 | Canada 4/Germany 3 |

Semifinals

| April 23 | Sweden 3/Russia 1 |
| April 23 | United States 5/Canada 4 (Tyler Biggs 4:22 OT) |

Fifth-Place Game (Crimmitschau)
April 23   Finland 6/Germany 0

Bronze Medal Game
April 24   Russia 6/Canada 4

Gold Medal Game
April 24   United States 4/Sweden 3 (Connor Murphy 6:06 OT)

TEAM CANADA STATISTICS
Mike Williamson, coach

	GP	G	A	P	Pim
Ryan Murphy	7	4	9	13	2
Ryan Murray	7	3	7	10	6
Mark Schiefele	7	6	2	8	2
Nick Cousins	7	4	4	8	10
Brett Ritchie	7	4	3	7	6
Alan Quine	7	1	6	7	6
Mark McNeill	7	0	6	6	2
Colin Smith	7	2	1	3	14
Eric Locke	7	2	1	3	6
Morgan Rielly	7	2	1	3	0
Slater Koekkoek	7	1	1	2	2
Daniel Catenacci	7	0	2	2	22
Brent Andrews	7	0	1	1	14
Travis Ewanyk	7	0	1	1	4
Austen Brassard	7	0	1	1	2
Cody Ceci	7	0	1	1	2
Charles Hudon	7	0	1	1	2
Andrew D'Agostini	2	0	0	0	0
Malcolm Subban	5	0	0	0	0
Scott Harrington	7	0	0	0	8
Seth Griffith	7	0	0	0	6
Reece Scarlett	7	0	0	0	0

In Goal	GP	W-L	Mins	GA	SO	GAA
Andrew D'Agostini	2	1–1	117:30	5	1	2.55
Malcolm Subban	5	3–2	302:31	15	1	2.98

2011 WORLD U18 CHAMPIONSHIP, WOMEN

STOCKHOLM, SWEDEN, January 1–8, 2011

FINAL PLACINGS

GOLD MEDAL	United States
SILVER MEDAL	Canada
BRONZE MEDAL	Finland
Fourth Place	Czech Republic
Fifth Place	Sweden
Sixth Place	Germany
Seventh Place	Switzerland
Eighth Place	Japan

Tournament Format

The eight teams were divided into two groups of four, and each team played a round-robin series within its group. The top team in each group advanced to the semifinal, while the second- and third-place teams played a crossover quarterfinal. The fourth-place teams met in a relegation round.

RESULTS & STANDINGS

Preliminary Round

Group A

	GP	W	OTW	OTL	L	GF	GA	P
Canada	3	3	0	0	0	23	2	9
Germany	3	2	0	0	1	6	10	6
Finland	3	1	0	0	2	4	8	3
Switzerland	3	0	0	0	3	4	17	0

January 1	Canada 9/Switzerland 1
January 1	Germany 1/Finland 0
January 2	Germany 4/Switzerland 2
January 2	Canada 6/Finland 0
January 4	Finland 4/Switzerland 1
January 4	Canada 8/Germany 1

Group B

	GP	W	OTW	OTL	L	GF	GA	P
United States	3	3	0	0	0	28	1	9
Sweden	3	2	0	0	1	5	13	6
Czech Republic	3	1	0	0	2	6	15	3
Japan	3	0	0	0	3	3	13	0

January 1	United States 11/Czech Republic 0
January 1	Sweden 2/Japan 1
January 2	United States 7/Japan 1
January 2	Sweden 3/Czech Republic 2
January 4	Czech Republic 4/Japan 1
January 4	United States 10/Sweden 0

Relegation Round

	GP	W	OTW	OTL	L	GF	GA	P
Switzerland	3	2	0	0	1	10	6	6
Japan	3	1	0	0	2	6	10	3

January 5	Switzerland 4/Japan 0
January 7	Japan 5/Switzerland 1
January 8	Switzerland 5/Japan 1

PLAYOFFS

Quarterfinals

| January 5 | Czech Republic 3/Germany 1 |
| January 5 | Finland 3/Sweden 2 (Sanna Valkama 1:46 OT) |

Semifinals

| January 7 | Canada 6/Finland 1 |
| January 7 | United States 14/Czech Republic 1 |

Fifth-Place Game

| January 7 | Sweden 2/Germany 0 |

Bronze Medal Game

| January 8 | Finland 3/Czech Republic 0 |

Gold Medal Game

| January 8 | United States 5/Canada 2 |

TEAM CANADA STATISTICS

Sarah Hodges, coach

	GP	G	A	P	Pim
Nicole Kosta	5	5	3	8	6
Meghan Dufault	5	2	6	8	2
Laura Stacey	5	3	4	7	2
Emily Fulton	5	3	2	5	0
Sarah MacDonnell	5	3	2	5	2

Cayley Mercer	5	2	3	5	0
Rebecca Kohler	5	2	3	5	4
Katy Josephs	5	2	2	4	2
Cydney Roesler	5	1	3	4	0
Shelby Bram	5	2	1	3	8
Sarah Edney	5	1	2	3	2
Gabrielle Davidson	5	1	2	3	0
Katarina Zgraja	4	1	1	2	2
Sarah Robson	5	2	0	2	0
Gina Repaci	5	1	1	2	2
Jennifer Shields	5	0	2	2	0
Erin Ambrose	5	0	2	2	4
Amanda Makela	2	0	0	0	0
Ann-Renee Desbiens	3	0	0	0	0
Hailey Browne	5	0	0	0	8

In Goal	**GP**	**W-L**	**Mins**	**GA**	**SO**	**GAA**
Amanda Makela	2	2–0	120:00	2	0	1.00
Ann-Renee Desbeins	3	2–1	179:24	5	1	1.67

OLYMPICS, MEN, 1920–2010

THE GAMES OF THE VII OLYMPIAD

ANTWERP, BELGIUM, April 23–September 12, 1920
(hockey games played April 23–29, 1920)

FINAL PLACINGS

GOLD MEDAL	Canada
SILVER MEDAL	United States
BRONZE MEDAL	Czechoslovakia
Fourth Place	Sweden
Fifth Place	Switzerland
(tie)	France
(tie)	Belgium

THE FIRST OLYMPIC WINTER GAMES

CHAMONIX, FRANCE, January 28–February 3, 1924

FINAL PLACINGS

GOLD MEDAL	Canada
SILVER MEDAL	United States
BRONZE MEDAL	Great Britain
Fourth Place	Sweden
Fifth Place	Czechoslovakia
(tie)	France
Seventh Place	Belgium
(tie)	Switzerland

THE SECOND OLYMPIC WINTER GAMES

ST. MORITZ, SWITZERLAND, February 11–19, 1928

FINAL PLACINGS

GOLD MEDAL	Canada
SILVER MEDAL	Sweden
BRONZE MEDAL	Switzerland
Fourth Place	Great Britain
Fifth Place	France
(tie)	Czechoslovakia
(tie)	Austria

Eighth Place	Belgium
(tie)	Poland
(tie)	Germany
Eleventh Place	Hungary

THE THIRD OLYMPIC WINTER GAMES

LAKE PLACID, UNITED STATES, February 4–13, 1932

FINAL PLACINGS

GOLD MEDAL	Canada
SILVER MEDAL	United States
BRONZE MEDAL	Germany
Fourth Place	Poland

THE FOURTH OLYMPIC WINTER GAMES

GARMISCH-PARTENKIRCHEN, GERMANY, February 6–16, 1936

FINAL PLACINGS

GOLD MEDAL	Great Britain
SILVER MEDAL	Canada
BRONZE MEDAL	United States
Fourth Place	Czechoslovakia
Fifth Place	Germany
(tie)	Sweden
Seventh Place	Austria
(tie)	Hungary
Ninth Place	Italy
(tie)	France
(tie)	Japan
(tie)	Poland
Thirteenth Place	Belgium
(tie)	Latvia
(tie)	Switzerland

THE FIFTH OLYMPIC WINTER GAMES

ST. MORITZ, SWITZERLAND, January 30–February 8, 1948

FINAL PLACINGS

GOLD MEDAL	Canada
SILVER MEDAL	Czechoslovakia

BRONZE MEDAL	Switzerland
Fourth Place	Sweden
Fifth Place	Great Britain
Sixth Place	Poland
Seventh Place	Austria
Eighth Place	Italy
Disqualified	United States

THE SIXTH OLYMPIC WINTER GAMES

OSLO, NORWAY, February 15–25, 1952

FINAL PLACINGS

GOLD MEDAL	Canada
SILVER MEDAL	United States
BRONZE MEDAL	Sweden
Fourth Place	Czechoslovakia
Fifth Place	Switzerland
Sixth Place	Poland
Seventh Place	Finland
Eighth Place	West Germany
Ninth Place	Norway

THE SEVENTH OLYMPIC WINTER GAMES

CORTINA d'AMPEZZO, ITALY, January 26–February 4, 1956

FINAL PLACINGS

GOLD MEDAL	Soviet Union
SILVER MEDAL	United States
BRONZE MEDAL	Canada
Fourth Place	Sweden
Fifth Place	Czechoslovakia
Sixth Place	Germany
Seventh Place	Italy
Eighth Place	Poland
Ninth Place	Switzerland
Tenth Place	Austria

THE EIGHTH OLYMPIC WINTER GAMES

SQUAW VALLEY, UNITED STATES, February 19–28, 1960

FINAL PLACINGS

GOLD MEDAL	United States
SILVER MEDAL	Canada
BRONZE MEDAL	Soviet Union
Fourth Place	Czechoslovakia
Fifth Place	Sweden
Sixth Place	Germany
Seventh Place	Finland
Eighth Place	Japan
Ninth Place	Australia

THE NINTH OLYMPIC WINTER GAMES

INNSBRUCK, AUSTRIA, January 29–February 9, 1964

FINAL PLACINGS

GOLD MEDAL	Soviet Union
SILVER MEDAL	Sweden
BRONZE MEDAL	Czechoslovakia
Fourth Place	Canada
Fifth Place	United States
Sixth Place	Finland
Seventh Place	Germany
Eighth Place	Switzerland
Ninth Place	Poland
Tenth Place	Norway
Eleventh Place	Japan
Twelfth Place	Romania
Thirteenth Place	Austria
Fourteenth Place	Yugoslavia
Fifteenth Place	Italy
Sixteenth Place	Hungary

THE TENTH OLYMPIC WINTER GAMES

GRENOBLE, FRANCE, February 6–17, 1968

FINAL PLACINGS

GOLD MEDAL	Soviet Union

SILVER MEDAL	Czechoslovakia
BRONZE MEDAL	Canada
Fourth Place	Sweden
Fifth Place	Finland
Sixth Place	United States
Seventh Place	West Germany
Eighth Place	East Germany
Ninth Place	Yugoslavia
Tenth Place	Japan
Eleventh Place	Norway
Twelfth Place	Romania
Thirteenth Place	Austria
Fourteenth Place	France

THE ELEVENTH OLYMPIC WINTER GAMES

SAPPORO, JAPAN, February 5–12, 1972

FINAL PLACINGS

GOLD MEDAL	Soviet Union
SILVER MEDAL	United States
BRONZE MEDAL	Czechoslovakia
Fourth Place	Sweden
Fifth Place	Finland
Sixth Place	Poland
Seventh Place	West Germany
Eighth Place	Norway
Ninth Place	Japan
Tenth Place	Switzerland
Eleventh Place	Yugoslavia

THE TWELFTH OLYMPIC WINTER GAMES

INNSBRUCK, AUSTRIA, February 2–13, 1976

FINAL PLACINGS

GOLD MEDAL	Soviet Union
SILVER MEDAL	Czechoslovakia
BRONZE MEDAL	West Germany
Fourth Place	Finland
Fifth Place	United States
Sixth Place	Poland

Seventh Place	Romania
Eighth Place	Austria
Ninth Place	Japan
Tenth Place	Yugoslavia
Eleventh Place	Switzerland
(tie)	Norway
Thirteenth Place	Bulgaria

THE THIRTEENTH OLYMPIC WINTER GAMES

LAKE PLACID, UNITED STATES, February 12–24, 1980

FINAL PLACINGS

GOLD MEDAL	United States
SILVER MEDAL	Soviet Union
BRONZE MEDAL	Sweden
Fourth Place	Finland
Fifth Place	Czechoslovakia
Sixth Place	Canada
Seventh Place	Poland
(tie)	Romania
Ninth Place	Netherlands
(tie)	West Germany
Eleventh Place	Japan
(tie)	Norway

THE FOURTEENTH OLYMPIC WINTER GAMES

SARAJEVO, YUGOSLAVIA, February 7–19, 1984

FINAL PLACINGS

GOLD MEDAL	Soviet Union
SILVER MEDAL	Czechoslovakia
BRONZE MEDAL	Sweden
Fourth Place	Canada
Fifth Place	West Germany
Sixth Place	Finland
Seventh Place	United States
Eighth Place	Poland
Ninth Place	Italy
(tie)	Austria
Eleventh Place	Norway
(tie)	Yugoslavia

THE FIFTEENTH OLYMPIC WINTER GAMES

CALGARY, CANADA, February 13–28, 1988

FINAL PLACINGS

GOLD MEDAL	Soviet Union
SILVER MEDAL	Finland
BRONZE MEDAL	Sweden
Fourth Place	Canada
Fifth Place	West Germany
Sixth Place	Czechoslovakia
Seventh Place	United States
Eighth Place	Switzerland
Ninth Place	Austria
Tenth Place	Poland
Eleventh Place	France
Twelfth Place	Norway

THE SIXTEENTH OLYMPIC WINTER GAMES

ALBERTVILLE, FRANCE, February 8–23, 1992

FINAL PLACINGS

GOLD MEDAL	Unified Team
SILVER MEDAL	Canada
BRONZE MEDAL	Czechoslovakia
Fourth Place	United States
Fifth Place	Sweden
Sixth Place	Germany
Seventh Place	Finland
Eighth Place	France
Ninth Place	Norway
Tenth Place	Switzerland
Eleventh Place	Poland
Twelfth Place	Italy

THE SEVENTEENTH OLYMPIC WINTER GAMES

LILLEHAMMER, NORWAY, February 12–27, 1994

FINAL PLACINGS

GOLD MEDAL	Sweden
SILVER MEDAL	Canada
BRONZE MEDAL	Finland
Fourth Place	Russia
Fifth Place	Czech Republic
Sixth Place	Slovakia
Seventh Place	Germany
Eighth Place	United States
Ninth Place	Italy
Tenth Place	France
Eleventh Place	Norway
Twelfth Place	Austria

THE EIGHTEENTH OLYMPIC WINTER GAMES

NAGANO, JAPAN, February 7–22, 1998

FINAL PLACINGS

GOLD MEDAL	Czech Republic
SILVER MEDAL	Russia
BRONZE MEDAL	Finland
Fourth Place	Canada
Fifth Place	Sweden
(tie)	United States
(tie)	Belarus
(tie)	Kazakhstan
Ninth Place	Germany
Tenth Place	Slovakia
Eleventh Place	France
Twelfth Place	Italy
Thirteenth Place	Japan
Fourteenth Place	Austria

THE NINETEENTH OLYMPIC WINTER GAMES

SALT LAKE CITY, UNITED STATES, February 9–24, 2002

FINAL PLACINGS

GOLD MEDAL	Canada
SILVER MEDAL	United States
BRONZE MEDAL	Russia
Fourth Place	Belarus
Fifth Place	Sweden
(tie)	Finland
(tie)	Czech Republic
(tie)	Germany
Ninth Place	Latvia
Tenth Place	Ukraine
Eleventh Place	Switzerland
Twelfth Place	Austria
Thirteenth Place	Slovakia
Fourteenth Place	France

THE TWENTIETH OLYMPIC WINTER GAMES

TURIN, ITALY, February 15–26, 2006

FINAL PLACINGS

GOLD MEDAL	Sweden
SILVER MEDAL	Finland
BRONZE MEDAL	Czech Republic
Fourth Place	Russia
Fifth Place	Slovakia
Sixth Place	Switzerland
Seventh Place	Canada
Eighth Place	United States
Ninth Place	Kazakhstan
Tenth Place	Germany
Eleventh Place	Italy
Twelfth Place	Latvia

THE TWENTY-FIRST OLYMPIC WINTER GAMES

VANCOUVER, CANADA, February 13–28, 2010

FINAL PLACINGS

GOLD MEDAL	Canada
SILVER MEDAL	United States
BRONZE MEDAL	Finland
Fourth Place	Slovakia
Fifth Place	Sweden
Sixth Place	Russia
Seventh Place	Czech Republic
Eighth Place	Switzerland
Ninth Place	Belarus
Tenth Place	Norway
Eleventh Place	Germany
Twelfth Place	Latvia

OLYMPICS, WOMEN, 1998–2010

THE EIGHTEENTH OLYMPIC WINTER GAMES

NAGANO, JAPAN, February 8–17, 1998

FINAL PLACINGS

GOLD MEDAL	United States
SILVER MEDAL	Canada
BRONZE MEDAL	Finland
Fourth Place	China
Fifth Place	Sweden
Sixth Place	Japan

THE NINETEENTH OLYMPIC WINTER GAMES

SALT LAKE CITY, UNITED STATES, February 11–21, 2002

FINAL PLACINGS

GOLD MEDAL	Canada
SILVER MEDAL	United States
BRONZE MEDAL	Sweden
Fourth Place	Finland
Fifth Place	Russia
Sixth Place	Germany
Seventh Place	China
Eighth Place	Kazakhstan

THE TWENTIETH OLYMPIC WINTER GAMES

TURIN, ITALY, February 11–20, 2006

FINAL PLACINGS

GOLD MEDAL	Canada
SILVER MEDAL	Sweden
BRONZE MEDAL	United States
Fourth Place	Finland
Fifth Place	Germany
Sixth Place	Russia
Seventh Place	Switzerland
Eighth Place	Italy

THE TWENTY-FIRST OLYMPIC WINTER GAMES

VANCOUVER, CANADA, February 13–25, 2010

FINAL PLACINGS

GOLD MEDAL	Canada
SILVER MEDAL	United States
BRONZE MEDAL	Finland
Fourth Place	Sweden
Fifth Place	Switzerland
Sixth Place	Russia
Seventh Place	China
Eighth Place	Slovakia

WORLD CHAMPIONSHIPS, MEN, 1930–2010

JANUARY 31–FEBRUARY 10, 1930

Chamonix, France/Berlin, Germany/Vienna, Austria

GOLD MEDAL	Canada
SILVER MEDAL	Germany
BRONZE MEDAL	Switzerland
Fourth Place	Austria
Fifth Place	Poland
Sixth Place (tie)	Czechoslovakia
	France
	Hungary
	Japan
Tenth Place (tie)	Belgium
	Great Britain
	Italy

MARCH 1–8, 1931

Krynica, Poland

GOLD MEDAL	Canada
SILVER MEDAL	United States
BRONZE MEDAL	Austria
Fourth Place	Poland
Fifth Place	Czechoslovakia
Sixth Place	Sweden
Seventh Place	Hungary
Eighth Place	Great Britain
Ninth Place	France
Tenth Place	Romania

FEBRUARY 18–26, 1933

Prague, Czechoslovakia

GOLD MEDAL	United States
SILVER MEDAL	Canada
BRONZE MEDAL	Czechoslovakia
Fourth Place	Austria
Fifth Place (tie)	Germany
	Switzerland

Seventh Place (tie)	Hungary
	Poland
Ninth Place	Romania
Tenth Place	Latvia
Eleventh Place	Italy
Twelfth Place	Belgium

FEBRUARY 3–11, 1934

Milan, Italy

GOLD MEDAL	Canada
SILVER MEDAL	United States
BRONZE MEDAL	Germany
Fourth Place	Switzerland
Fifth Place	Czechoslovakia
Sixth Place	Hungary
Seventh Place	Austria
Eighth Place	Great Britain
Ninth Place	Italy
Tenth Place	Romania
Eleventh Place	France
Twelfth Place	Belgium

JANUARY 19–27, 1935

Davos, Switzerland

GOLD MEDAL	Canada
SILVER MEDAL	Switzerland
BRONZE MEDAL	Great Britain
Fourth Place	Czechoslovakia
Fifth Place	Sweden
Sixth Place	Austria
Seventh Place	France
Eighth Place	Italy
Ninth Place	Germany
Tenth Place	Poland
Eleventh Place (tie)	Hungary
	Romania
Thirteenth Place	Latvia
Fourteenth Place	Belgium
	Netherlands

FEBRUARY 17–27, 1937

London, Great Britain

GOLD MEDAL	Canada
SILVER MEDAL	Great Britain
BRONZE MEDAL	Switzerland
Fourth Place	Germany
Fifth Place	Hungary
Sixth Place	Czechoslovakia
Seventh Place	France
Eighth Place	Poland
Ninth Place (tie)	Norway
	Romania
	Sweden

FEBRUARY 11–20, 1938

Prague, Czechoslovakia

GOLD MEDAL	Canada
SILVER MEDAL	Great Britain
BRONZE MEDAL	Czechoslovakia
Fourth Place	Germany
Fifth Place	Sweden
Sixth Place	Switzerland
Seventh Place (tie)	Hungary
	Poland
	United States
Tenth Place (tie)	Austria
	Latvia
	Lithuania
Thirteenth Place (tie)	Norway
	Romania

FEBRUARY 3–12, 1939

Basel/Zurich, Switzerland

GOLD MEDAL	Canada
SILVER MEDAL	United States
BRONZE MEDAL	Switzerland
Fourth Place	Czechoslovakia
Fifth Place	Germany

Sixth Place	Poland
Seventh Place	Hungary
Eighth Place	Great Britain
Ninth Place	Italy
Tenth Place	Latvia
Eleventh Place (tie)	Belgium
	Netherlands
Thirteenth Place	Finland
	Yugoslavia

FEBRUARY 15–23, 1947

Prague, Czechoslovakia

GOLD MEDAL	Czechoslovakia
SILVER MEDAL	Sweden
BRONZE MEDAL	Austria
Fourth Place	Switzerland
Fifth Place	United States
Sixth Place	Poland
Seventh Place	Romania
Eighth Place	Belgium

FEBRUARY 12–20, 1949

Stockholm, Sweden

GOLD MEDAL	Czechoslovakia
SILVER MEDAL	Canada
BRONZE MEDAL	United States
Fourth Place	Sweden
Fifth Place	Switzerland
Sixth Place	Austria
Seventh Place	Finland
Eighth Place	Norway
Ninth Place	Belgium
Tenth Place	Denmark

MARCH 13–22, 1950

London, Great Britain

GOLD MEDAL	Canada
SILVER MEDAL	United States

BRONZE MEDAL Switzerland
Fourth Place Great Britain
Fifth Place Sweden
Sixth Place Norway
Seventh Place Belgium
Eighth Place Netherlands
Ninth Place France

MARCH 9–17, 1951

Paris, France

GOLD MEDAL Canada
SILVER MEDAL Sweden
BRONZE MEDAL Switzerland
Fourth Place Norway
Fifth Place Great Britain
Sixth Place United States
Seventh Place Finland

MARCH 6–15, 1953

Zurich/Basel, Switzerland

GOLD MEDAL Sweden
SILVER MEDAL West Germany
BRONZE MEDAL Switzerland
Fourth Place Czechoslovakia

FEBRUARY 26–MARCH 7, 1954

Stockholm, Sweden

GOLD MEDAL Soviet Union
SILVER MEDAL Canada
BRONZE MEDAL Sweden
Fourth Place Czechoslovakia
Fifth Place West Germany
Sixth Place Finland
Seventh Place Switzerland
Eighth Place Norway

FEBRUARY 25–MARCH 6, 1955

Düsseldorf, West Germany

GOLD MEDAL	Canada
SILVER MEDAL	Soviet Union
BRONZE MEDAL	Czechoslovakia
Fourth Place	United States
Fifth Place	Sweden
Sixth Place	West Germany
Seventh Place	Poland
Eighth Place	Switzerland
Ninth Place	Finland

FEBRUARY 24–MARCH 5, 1957

Moscow, Soviet Union

GOLD MEDAL	Sweden
SILVER MEDAL	Soviet Union
BRONZE MEDAL	Czechoslovakia
Fourth Place	Finland
Fifth Place	West Germany
Sixth Place	Poland
Seventh Place	Austria
Eighth Place	Japan

To protest the suppression of the Hungarian revolution by Soviet forces, Canadian Prime Minister Louis St. Laurent refused to allow a Canadian team to travel to Moscow to play at the World Championships.

FEBRUARY 25–MARCH 9, 1958

Oslo, Norway

GOLD MEDAL	Canada
SILVER MEDAL	Soviet Union
BRONZE MEDAL	Sweden
Fourth Place	Czechoslovakia
Fifth Place	United States
Sixth Place	Finland
Seventh Place	Norway
Eighth Place	Poland

MARCH 9–15, 1959

Prague, Czechoslovakia

GOLD MEDAL	Canada
SILVER MEDAL	Soviet Union
BRONZE MEDAL	Czechoslovakia
Fourth Place	United States
Fifth Place	Sweden
Sixth Place	Finland
Seventh Place	West Germany
Eighth Place	Norway
Ninth Place	East Germany
Tenth Place	Italy
Eleventh Place	Poland
Twelfth Place	Switzerland
Thirteenth Place	Romania
Fourteenth Place	Hungary
Fifteenth Place	Austria

MARCH 1–12, 1961

Geneva/Lausanne, Switzerland

GOLD MEDAL	Canada
SIVER MEDAL	Czechoslovakia
BRONZE MEDAL	Soviet Union
Fourth Place	Sweden
Fifth Place	East Germany
Sixth Place	United States
Seventh Place	Finland
Eighth Place	West Germany

MAY 8–18, 1962

Colorado Springs, United States

GOLD MEDAL	Sweden
SILVER MEDAL	Canada
BRONZE MEDAL	United States
Fourth Place	Finland
Fifth Place	Norway
Sixth Place	West Germany
Seventh Place	Switzerland
Eighth Place	Great Britain

MARCH 7–17, 1963

Stockholm, Sweden

GOLD MEDAL	Soviet Union
SILVER MEDAL	Sweden
BRONZE MEDAL	Czechoslovakia
Fourth Place	Canada
Fifth Place	Finland
Sixth Place	East Germany
Seventh Place	West Germany
Eighth Place	United States

MARCH 3–14, 1965

Tampere, Finland

GOLD MEDAL	Soviet Union
SILVER MEDAL	Czechoslovakia
BRONZE MEDAL	Sweden
Fourth Place	Canada
Fifth Place	East Germany
Sixth Place	United States
Seventh Place	Finland
Eighth Place	Norway

MARCH 3–14, 1966

Ljubljana, Yugoslavia

GOLD MEDAL	Soviet Union
SILVER MEDAL	Czechoslovakia
BRONZE MEDAL	Canada
Fourth Place	Sweden
Fifth Place	East Germany
Sixth Place	United States
Seventh Place	Finland
Eighth Place	Poland

MARCH 18–29, 1967

Vienna, Austria

GOLD MEDAL	Soviet Union
SILVER MEDAL	Sweden

BRONZE MEDAL	Canada
Fourth Place	Czechoslovakia
Fifth Place	United States
Sixth Place	Finland
Seventh Place	West Germany
Eighth Place	East Germany

MARCH 15–30, 1969

Stockholm, Sweden

GOLD MEDAL	Soviet Union
SILVER MEDAL	Sweden
BRONZE MEDAL	Czechoslovakia
Fourth Place	Canada
Fifth Place	Finland
Sixth Place	United States

To protest the ineligibility of professionals from the World Championships according to IIHF rules, Canada did not compete in IIHF sanctioned tournaments from 1970 through 1976.

MARCH 14–30, 1970

Stockholm, Sweden

GOLD MEDAL	Soviet Union
SILVER MEDAL	Sweden
BRONZE MEDAL	Czechoslovakia
Fourth Place	Finland
Fifth Place	East Germany
Sixth Place	Poland

MARCH 19–APRIL 3, 1971

Bern/Geneva, Switzerland

GOLD MEDAL	Soviet Union
SILVER MEDAL	Czechoslovakia
BRONZE MEDAL	Sweden
Fourth Place	Finland
Fifth Place	East Germany
Sixth Place	United States

APRIL 7–22, 1972

Prague, Czechoslovakia

GOLD MEDAL	Czechoslovakia
SILVER MEDAL	Soviet Union
BRONZE MEDAL	Sweden
Fourth Place	Finland
Fifth Place	East Germany
Sixth Place	Switzerland

MARCH 31–APRIL 15, 1973

Moscow, Soviet Union

GOLD MEDAL	Soviet Union
SILVER MEDAL	Sweden
BRONZE MEDAL	Czechoslovakia
Fourth Place	Finland
Fifth Place	Poland
Sixth Place	East Germany

APRIL 5–20, 1974

Helsinki, Finland

GOLD MEDAL	Soviet Union
SILVER MEDAL	Czechoslovakia
BRONZE MEDAL	Sweden
Fourth Place	Finland
Fifth Place	Poland
Sixth Place	East Germany

APRIL 3–19, 1975

Munich/Dusseldorf, West Germany

GOLD MEDAL	Soviet Union
SILVER MEDAL	Czechoslovakia
BRONZE MEDAL	Sweden
Fourth Place	Finland
Fifth Place	Poland
Sixth Place	United States

APRIL 8–25, 1976

Katowice, Poland

GOLD MEDAL	Czechoslovakia
SILVER MEDAL	Soviet Union
BRONZE MEDAL	Sweden
Fourth Place	United States
Fifth Place	Finland
Sixth Place	West Germany
Seventh Place	Poland
Eighth Place	East Germany

APRIL 21–MAY 8, 1977

Vienna, Austria

GOLD MEDAL	Czechoslovakia
SILVER MEDAL	Sweden
BRONZE MEDAL	Soviet Union
Fourth Place	Canada
Fifth Place	Finland
Sixth Place	United States
Seventh Place	West Germany
Eighth Place	Romania

APRIL 25–MAY 8, 1978

Prague, Czechoslovakia

GOLD MEDAL	Soviet Union
SILVER MEDAL	Czechoslovakia
BRONZE MEDAL	Canada
Fourth Place	Sweden
Fifth Place	West Germany
Sixth Place	USA
Seventh Place	Finland
Eighth Place	East Germany

APRIL 14–27, 1979

Moscow, Soviet Union

GOLD MEDAL	Soviet Union
SILVER MEDAL	Czechoslovakia

BRONZE MEDAL	Sweden
Fourth Place	Canada
Fifth Place	Finland
Sixth Place	West Germany
Seventh Place	United States
Eighth Place	Poland

APRIL 12–26, 1981

Gothenburg/Stockholm, Sweden

GOLD MEDAL	Soviet Union
SILVER MEDAL	Sweden
BRONZE MEDAL	Czechoslovakia
Fourth Place	Canada
Fifth Place	United States
Sixth Place	Finland
Seventh Place	West Germany
Eighth Place	Netherlands

APRIL 15–29, 1982

Helsinki/Tampere, Finland

GOLD MEDAL	Soviet Union
SILVER MEDAL	Czechoslovakia
BRONZE MEDAL	Canada
Fourth Place	Sweden
Fifth Place	Finland
Sixth Place	West Germany
Seventh Place	Italy
Eighth Place	United States

APRIL 16–MAY 2, 1983

Dortmund/Düsseldorf/Munich, West Germany

GOLD MEDAL	Soviet Union
SILVER MEDAL	Czechoslovakia
BRONZE MEDAL	Canada
Fourth Place	Sweden
Fifth Place	East Germany
Sixth Place	West Germany
Seventh Place	Finland
Eighth Place	Italy

APRIL 17–MAY 3, 1985

Prague, Czechoslovakia

GOLD MEDAL	Czechoslovakia
SILVER MEDAL	Canada
BRONZE MEDAL	Soviet Union
Fourth Place	United States
Fifth Place	Finland
Sixth Place	Sweden
Seventh Place	East Germany
Eighth Place	West Germany

APRIL 12–28, 1986

Moscow, Soviet Union

GOLD MEDAL	Soviet Union
SILVER MEDAL	Sweden
BRONZE MEDAL	Canada
Fourth Place	Finland
Fifth Place	Czechoslovakia
Sixth Place	United States
Seventh Place	East Germany
Eighth Place	Poland

APRIL 17–MAY 3, 1987

Vienna, Austria

GOLD MEDAL	Sweden
SILVER MEDAL	Soviet Union
BRONZE MEDAL	Czechoslovakia
Fourth Place	Canada
Fifth Place	Finland
Sixth Place	West Germany
Seventh Place	United States
Eighth Place	Switzerland

APRIL 15–MAY 1, 1989

Stockholm, Sweden

GOLD MEDAL	Soviet Union
SILVER MEDAL	Canada

BRONZE MEDAL	Czechoslovakia
Fourth Place	Sweden
Fifth Place	Finland
Sixth Place	United States
Seventh Place	West Germany
Eighth Place	Poland

APRIL 16–MAY 2, 1990

Bern, Switzerland

GOLD MEDAL	Soviet Union
SILVER MEDAL	Sweden
BRONZE MEDAL	Czechoslovakia
Fourth Place	Canada
Fifth Place	United States
Sixth Place	Finland
Seventh Place	West Germany
Eighth Place	Norway

APRIL 14–MAY 5, 1991

Helsinki, Finland

GOLD MEDAL	Sweden
SILVER MEDAL	Canada
BRONZE MEDAL	Soviet Union
Fourth Place	United States
Fifth Place	Finland
Sixth Place	Czechoslovakia
Seventh Place	Switzerland
Eight Place	Germany

APRIL 28–MAY 10, 1992

Prague/Bratislava, Czechoslovakia

GOLD MEDAL	Sweden
SILVER MEDAL	Finland
BRONZE MEDAL	Czechoslovakia
Fourth Place	Switzerland
Fifth Place	Russia
Sixth Place	Germany
Seventh Place	United States
Eighth Place	Canada

Ninth Place	Italy
Tenth Place	Norway
Eleventh Place	France
Twelfth Place	Poland

APRIL 18–MAY 2, 1993

Munich, Germany

GOLD MEDAL	Russia
SILVER MEDAL	Sweden
BRONZE MEDAL	Czech Republic
Fourth Place	Canada
Fifth Place	Germany
Sixth Place	United States
Seventh Place	Finland
Eighth Place	Italy
Ninth Place	Austria
Tenth Place	France
Eleventh Place	Norway
Twelfth Place	Switzerland

APRIL 25–MAY 8, 1994

Bolzano, Italy

GOLD MEDAL	Canada
SILVER MEDAL	Finland
BRONZE MEDAL	Sweden
Fourth Place	United States
Fifth Place	Russia
Sixth Place	Italy
Seventh Place	Czech Republic
Eighth Place	Austria
Ninth Place	Germany
Tenth Place	France
Eleventh Place	Norway
Twelfth Place	Great Britain

APRIL 23–MAY 7, 1995

Stockholm/Gavle, Sweden

GOLD MEDAL	Finland
SILVER MEDAL	Sweden
BRONZE MEDAL	Canada
Fourth Place	Czech Republic
Fifth Place	Russia
Sixth Place	United States
Seventh Place	Italy
Eighth Place	France
Ninth Place	Germany
Tenth Place	Norway
Eleventh Place	Austria
Twelfth Place	Switzerland

APRIL 21–MAY 5, 1996

Vienna, Austria

GOLD MEDAL	Czech Republic
SILVER MEDAL	Canada
BRONZE MEDAL	United States
Fourth Place	Russia
Fifth Place	Finland
Sixth Place	Sweden
Seventh Place	Italy
Eighth Place	Germany
Ninth Place	Norway
Tenth Place	Slovakia
Eleventh Place	France
Twelfth Place	Austria

APRIL 26–MAY 14, 1997

Helsinki/Tampere/Turku, Finland

GOLD MEDAL	Canada
SILVER MEDAL	Sweden
BRONZE MEDAL	Czech Republic
Fourth Place	Russia
Fifth Place	Finland
Sixth Place	United States

Seventh Place	Latvia
Eighth Place	Italy
Ninth Place	Slovakia
Tenth Place	France
Eleventh Place	Germany
Twelfth Place	Norway

MAY 1–17, 1998

Zurich, Switzerland

GOLD MEDAL	Sweden
SILVER MEDAL	Finland
BRONZE MEDAL	Czech Republic
Fourth Place	Switzerland
Fifth Place	Russia
Sixth Place	Canada
Seventh Place	Slovakia
Eighth Place	Belarus
Ninth Place	Latvia
Tenth Place	Italy
Eleventh Place	Germany
Twelfth Place	United States

MAY 1–16, 1999

Oslo/Hamar/Lillehammer, Norway

GOLD MEDAL	Czech Republic
SILVER MEDAL	Finland
BRONZE MEDAL	Sweden
Fourth Place	Canada
Fifth Place	Russia
Sixth Place	United States
Seventh Place	Slovakia
Eighth Place	Switzerland
Ninth Place	Belarus
Tenth Place	Austria
Eleventh Place	Latvia
Twelfth Place	Norway
Thirteenth Place	Italy
Fourteenth Place	Ukraine
Fifteenth Place	France
Sixteenth Place	Japan

APRIL 29–MAY 14, 2000

St. Petersburg, Russia

GOLD MEDAL	Czech Republic
SILVER MEDAL	Slovakia
BRONZE MEDAL	Finland
Fourth Place	Canada
Fifth Place	United States
Sixth Place	Switzerland
Seventh Place	Sweden
Eighth Place	Latvia
Ninth Place	Belarus
Tenth Place	Norway
Eleventh Place	Russia
Twelfth Place	Italy
Thirteenth Place	Austria
Fourteenth Place	Ukraine
Fifteenth Place	France
Sixteenth Place	Japan

APRIL 28–MAY 13, 2001

Hanover/Cologne/Nuremberg, Germany

GOLD MEDAL	Czech Republic
SILVER MEDAL	Finland
BRONZE MEDAL	Sweden
Fourth Place	United States
Fifth Place	Canada
Sixth Place	Russia
Seventh Place	Slovakia
Eighth Place	Germany
Ninth Place	Switzerland
Tenth Place	Ukraine
Eleventh Place	Austria
Twelfth Place	Italy
Thirteenth Place	Latvia
Fourteenth Place	Belarus
Fifteenth Place	Norway
Sixteenth Place	Japan

APRIL 26–MAY 11, 2002

Gothenburg/Karlstad/Jonkoping, Sweden

GOLD MEDAL	Slovakia
SILVER MEDAL	Russia
BRONZE MEDAL	Sweden
Fourth Place	Finland
Fifth Place	Czech Republic
Sixth Place	Canada
Seventh Place	United States
Eighth Place	Germany
Ninth Place	Ukraine
Tenth Place	Switzerland
Eleventh Place	Latvia
Tweflth Place	Austria
Thirteenth Place	Slovenia
Fourteenth Place	Poland
Fifteenth Place	Italy
Sixteenth Place	Japan

APRIL 27–MAY 11, 2003

Helsinki/Tampere/Turku, Finland

GOLD MEDAL	Canada
SILVER MEDAL	Sweden
BRONZE MEDAL	Slovakia
Fourth Place	Czech Republic
Fifth Place	Finland
Sixth Place	Germany
Seventh Place	Russia
Eighth Place	Switzerland
Ninth Place	Latvia
Tenth Place	Austria
Eleventh Place	Denmark
Twelfth Place	Ukraine
Thirteenth Place	United States
Fourteenth Place	Belarus
Fifteenth Place	Slovenia
Sixteenth Place	Japan

APRIL 24–MAY 9, 2004

Prague/Ostrava, Czech Republic

GOLD MEDAL	Canada
SILVER MEDAL	Sweden
BRONZE MEDAL	United States
Fourth Place	Slovakia
Fifth Place	Czech Republic
Sixth Place	Finland
Seventh Place	Latvia
Eighth Place	Switzerland
Ninth Place	Germany
Tenth Place	Russia
Eleventh Place	Austria
Twelfth Place	Denmark
Thirteenth Place	Kazakhstan
Fourteenth Place	Ukraine
Fifteenth Place	Japan
Sixteenth Place	France

APRIL 30–MAY 15, 2005

Vienna/Innsbruck, Austria

GOLD MEDAL	Czech Republic
SILVER MEDAL	Canada
BRONZE MEDAL	Russia
Fourth Place	Sweden
Fifth Place	Slovakia
Sixth Place	United States
Seventh Place	Finland
Eighth Place	Switzerland
Ninth Place	Latvia
Tenth Place	Belarus
Eleventh Place	Ukraine
Twelfth Place	Kazakhstan
Thirteenth Place	Slovenia
Fourteenth Place	Denmark
Fifteenth Place	Germany
Sixteenth Place	Austria

MAY 5–MAY 21, 2006

Riga, Latvia

GOLD MEDAL	Sweden
SILVER MEDAL	Czech Republic
BRONZE MEDAL	Finland
Fourth Place	Canada
Fifth Place	Russia
Sixth Place	Belarus
Seventh Place	United States
Eighth Place	Slovakia
Ninth Place	Switzerland
Tenth Place	Latvia
Eleventh Place	Norway
Twelfth Place	Ukraine
Thirteenth Place	Denmark
Fourteenth Place	Italy
Fifteenth Place	Kazakhstan
Sixteenth Place	Slovenia

APRIL 24–MAY 10, 2007

Moscow/Mytischi, Russia

GOLD MEDAL	Canada
SILVER MEDAL	Finland
BRONZE MEDAL	Russia
Fourth Place	Sweden
Fifth Place	United States
Sixth Place	Slovakia
Seventh Place	Czech Republic
Eighth Place	Switzerland
Ninth Place	Germany
Tenth Place	Denmark
Eleventh Place	Belarus
Twelfth Place	Italy
Thirteenth Place	Latvia
Fourteenth Place	Norway
Fifteenth Place	Austria
Sixteenth Place	Ukraine

MAY 2–MAY 18, 2008

Halifax/Quebec City, Canada

GOLD MEDAL	Russia
SILVER MEDAL	Canada
BRONZE MEDAL	Finland
Fourth Place	Sweden
Fifth Place	Czech Republic
Sixth Place	United States
Seventh Place	Switzerland
Eighth Place	Norway
Ninth Place	Belarus
Tenth Place	Germany
Eleventh Place	Latvia
Twelfth Place	Denmark
Thirteenth Place	Slovakia
Fourteenth Place	France
Fifteenth Place	Slovenia
Sixteenth Place	Italy

APRIL 24–MAY 10, 2009

Zurich/Bern, Switzerland

GOLD MEDAL	Russia
SILVER MEDAL	Canada
BRONZE MEDAL	Sweden
Fourth Place	United States
Fifth Place	Finland
Sixth Place	Czech Republic
Seventh Place	Latvia
Eighth Place	Belarus
Ninth Place	Switzerland
Tenth Place	Slovakia
Eleventh Place	Norway
Twelfth Place	France
Thirteenth Place	Denmark
Fourteenth Place	Austria
Fifteenth Place	Germany
Sixteenth Place	Hungary

MAY 7–23, 2010

Gelsenkirchen/Mannheim/Cologne, Germany

GOLD MEDAL	Czech Republic
SILVER MEDAL	Russia
BRONZE MEDAL	Sweden
Fourth Place	Germany
Fifth Place	Switzerland
Sixth Place	Finland
Seventh Place	Canada
Eighth Place	Denmark
Ninth Place	Norway
Tenth Place	Belarus
Eleventh Place	Latvia
Twelfth Place	Slovakia
Thirteenth Place	United States
Fourteenth Place	France
Fifteenth Place	Italy
Sixteenth Place	Kazakhstan

WORLD CHAMPIONSHIPS, WOMEN, 1990–2009

1990 WORLD CHAMPIONSHIP, WOMEN

CANADA, March 19–25, 1990

FINAL PLACINGS
GOLD MEDAL	Canada
SILVER MEDAL	United States
BRONZE MEDAL	Finland
Fourth Place	Sweden
Fifth Place	Switzerland
Sixth Place	Norway
Seventh Place	Germany
Eighth Place	Japan

1992 WORLD CHAMPIONSHIP, WOMEN

FINLAND, April 20–26, 1992

FINAL PLACINGS
GOLD MEDAL	Canada
SILVER MEDAL	United States
BRONZE MEDAL	Finland
Fourth Place	Sweden
Fifth Place	China
Sixth Place	Norway
Seventh Place	Denmark
Eighth Place	Switzerland

DIRECTORATE AWARDS
BEST GOALIE	Annica Ahlen (Sweden)
BEST DEFENCEMAN	Geraldine Heaney (Canada)
BEST FORWARD	Cammi Granato (United States)

1994 WORLD CHAMPIONSHIP, WOMEN

UNITED STATES, April 11–17, 1994

FINAL PLACINGS
GOLD MEDAL	Canada
SILVER MEDAL	United States

BRONZE MEDAL	Finland
Fourth Place	China
Fifth Place	Sweden
Sixth Place	Norway
Seventh Place	Switzerland
Eighth Place	Germany

DIRECTORATE AWARDS

BEST GOALIE	Erin Whitten (United States)
BEST DEFENCEMAN	Geraldine Heaney (Canada)
BEST FORWARD	Riikka Nieminen (Finland)

1997 WORLD CHAMPIONSHIP, WOMEN

CANADA, March 31–April 6, 1997

FINAL PLACINGS

GOLD MEDAL	Canada
SILVER MEDAL	United States
BRONZE MEDAL	Finland
Fourth Place	China
Fifth Place	Sweden
Sixth Place	Russia
Seventh Place	Switzerland
Eighth Place	Norway

DIRECTORATE AWARDS

None awarded

1999 WORLD CHAMPIONSHIP, WOMEN

FINLAND, March 8–14, 1999

FINAL PLACINGS

GOLD MEDAL	Canada
SILVER MEDAL	United States
BRONZE MEDAL	Finland
Fourth Place	Sweden
Fifth Place	China
Sixth Place	Russia
Seventh Place	Germany
Eighth Place	Switzerland

DIRECTORATE AWARDS
>   BEST GOALIE   Sami Jo Small (Canada)
>   BEST DEFENCEMAN   Kirsi Hanninen (Finland)
>   BEST FORWARD   Jenny Schmidgall (United States)

2000 WORLD CHAMPIONSHIP, WOMEN

CANADA, April 3–9, 2000

FINAL PLACINGS
>   GOLD MEDAL   Canada
>   SILVER MEDAL   United States
>   BRONZE MEDAL   Finland
>   Fourth Place   Sweden
>   Fifth Place   Russia
>   Sixth Place   China
>   Seventh Place   Germany
>   Eighth Place   Japan

DIRECTORATE AWARDS
>   BEST GOALIE   Sami Jo Small (Canada)
>   BEST DEFENCEMAN   Angela Ruggiero (United States)
>   BEST FORWARD   Katja Riipi (Finland)

2001 WORLD CHAMPIONSHIP, WOMEN

UNITED STATES, April 2–8, 2001

FINAL PLACINGS
>   GOLD MEDAL   Canada
>   SILVER MEDAL   United States
>   BRONZE MEDAL   Russia
>   Fourth Place   Finland
>   Fifth Place   Sweden
>   Sixth Place   Germany
>   Seventh Place   China
>   Eighth Place   Kazakhstan

DIRECTORATE AWARDS
>   BEST GOALIE   Kim St. Pierre (Canada)
>   BEST DEFENCEMAN   Karyn Bye (United States)
>   BEST FORWARD   Jennifer Botterill (Canada)
>   MVP   Jennifer Botterill (Canada)

2003 WORLD CHAMPIONSHIP, WOMEN

CHINA, April 3–9, 2003

CANCELLED DUE TO SARS OUTBREAK

2004 WORLD CHAMPIONSHIP, WOMEN

CANADA, March 30–April 6, 2004

FINAL PLACINGS

GOLD MEDAL	Canada
SILVER MEDAL	United States
BRONZE MEDAL	Finland
Fourth Place	Sweden
Fifth Place	Russia
Sixth Place	Germany
Seventh Place	China
Eighth Place	Switzerland
Ninth Place	Japan

DIRECTORATE AWARDS

BEST GOALIE	Kim St. Pierre (Canada)
BEST DEFENCEMAN	Angela Ruggiero (United States)
BEST FORWARD	Jayna Hefford (Canada)
MVP	Jennifer Botterill (Canada)

ALL-STAR TEAM

Goal	Pam Dreyer (United States)
Defence	Gunilla Andersson (Sweden),
	Angela Ruggiero (United States)
Forward	Jayna Hefford (Canada), Jennifer Botterill (Canada),
	Natalie Darwitz (United States)

2005 WORLD CHAMPIONSHIP, WOMEN

SWEDEN, April 2–9, 2005

FINAL PLACINGS

GOLD MEDAL	United States
SILVER MEDAL	Canada
BRONZE MEDAL	Sweden
Fourth Place	Finland

Fifth Place	Germany
Sixth Place	China
Seventh Place	Kazakhstan
Eighth Place	Russia

DIRECTORATE AWARDS
BEST GOALIE	Chanda Gunn (United States)
BEST DEFENCEMAN	Angela Ruggiero (United States)
BEST FORWARD	Jayna Hefford (Canada)
MVP	Krissy Wendell (United States)

ALL-STAR TEAM
Goalie	Natalya Turnova (Kazakhstan)
Defence	Cheryl Pounder (Canada)
	Angela Ruggiero (United States)
Forward	Hayley Wickenheiser (Canada)
	Maria Rooth (Sweden)
	Krissy Wendell (United States)

2007 WORLD CHAMPIONSHIP, WOMEN

CANADA, April 3–10, 2007

FINAL PLACINGS
GOLD MEDAL	Canada
SILVER MEDAL	United States
BRONZE MEDAL	Sweden
Fourth Place	Finland
Fifth Place	Switzerland
Sixth Place	China
Seventh Place	Russia
Eighth Place	Germany
Ninth Place	Kazakhstan

DIRECTORATE AWARDS
BEST GOALIE	Noora Raty (Finland)
BEST DEFENCEMAN	Molly Engstrom (United States)
BEST FORWARD	Hayley Wickenheiser (Canada)
MVP	Hayley Wickenheiser (Canada)

ALL-STAR TEAM

Goalie	Kim St. Pierre (Canada)
Defence	Delaney Collins (Canada)
	Angela Ruggiero (United States)
Forward	Natalie Darwitz (United States)
	Krissy Wendell (United States)
	Hayley Wickenheiser (Canada)

2008 WORLD CHAMPIONSHIP, WOMEN

CHINA, April 4–12, 2008

FINAL PLACINGS

GOLD	United States
SILVER	Canada
BRONZE	Finland
Fourth Place	Switzerland
Fifth Place	Sweden
Sixth Place	Russia
Seventh Place	Japan
Eighth Place	China
Ninth Place	Germany

ALL-STAR TEAM

Goalie	Noora Raty (Finland)
Defence	Emma Laaksonen (Finland)
	Julie Chu (United States)
Forward	Hayley Wickenheiser (Canada)
	Natalie Darwitz (United States)
	Jayne Hefford (Canada)

DIRECTORATE AWARDS

BEST GOALIE	Noora Raty (Finland)
BEST DEFENCEMAN	Angela Ruggiero (United States)
BEST FORWARD	Natalie Darwitz (United States)
MVP	Noora Raty (Finland)

2009 WORLD CHAMPIONSHIP, WOMEN

Hameenlinna, FINLAND, April 4–12, 2009

FINAL PLACINGS

GOLD	United States
SILVER	Canada
BRONZE	Finland
Fourth Place	Sweden
Fifth Place	Russia
Sixth Place	Kazakhstan
Seventh Place	Switzerland
Eighth Place	Japan
Ninth Place	China

ALL-STAR TEAM

Goalie	Jesse Vetter (USA)
Defence	Carla MacLeod (Canada)
	Angela Ruggiero (USA)
Forward	Michelle Karvinen (Finland)
	Julie Chu (USA)
	Natalie Darwitz (USA)

DIRECTORATE AWARDS

BEST GOALIE	Charline Labonte (Canada)
BEST DEFENCEMAN	Jenni Hiirikoski (Finland)
BEST FORWARD	Hayley Wickenheiser (Canada)
MVP	Carla MacLeod (Canada)

WORLD U20 (JUNIOR) CHAMPIONSHIPS, 1977–2011

ALL MEDAL WINNERS BY CUMULATIVE STANDINGS (1977–2011)

Country	Gold	Silver	Bronze	Total
Canada	15	8	4	27
Russia	5	6	5	16
Sweden	1	8	5	14
Soviet Union	8	3	2	13
Finland	2	4	6	12
Czechoslovakia	0	5	6	11
United States	2	1	4	7
Czech Republic	2	0	1	3
Slovakia	0	0	1	1
Switzerland	0	0	1	1

1977 WORLD JUNIOR CHAMPIONSHIP

CZECHOSLOVAKIA, DECEMBER 22, 1976–JANUARY 2, 1977

FINAL PLACINGS

GOLD MEDAL	Soviet Union
SILVER MEDAL	Canada
BRONZE MEDAL	Czechoslovakia
Fourth Place	Finland
Fifth Place	Sweden
Sixth Place	West Germany
Seventh Place	United States
Eighth Place	Poland*

* relegated to 'B' pool for 1978

ALL-STAR TEAM

Goal	Alexander Tyznych (Soviet Union)
Defence	Risto Siltanen (Finland)
	Lubos Oslizlo (Czechoslovakia)
Forward	Dale McCourt (Canada)
	Bengt-Ake Gustafsson (Sweden)
	Igor Romasin (Soviet Union)

DIRECTORATE AWARDS
    BEST GOALIE   Jan Hrabak (Czechoslovakia)
    BEST DEFENCEMAN   Viacheslav Fetisov (Soviet Union)
    BEST FORWARD   Dale McCourt (Canada)

1978 WORLD JUNIOR CHAMPIONSHIP

CANADA, DECEMBER 22, 1977–JANUARY 3, 1978

FINAL PLACINGS
    GOLD MEDAL   Soviet Union
    SILVER MEDAL   Sweden
    BRONZE MEDAL Canada
    Fourth Place   Czechoslovakia
    Fifth Place   United States
    Sixth Place   Finland
    Seventh Place   West Germany
    Eighth Place   Switzerland*
    * promoted from 'B' pool in 1977; relegated to 'B' pool for 1979

ALL-STAR TEAM
    Goal   Alexander Tyznych (Soviet Union)
    Defence   Risto Siltanen (Finland)
              Viacheslav Fetisov (Soviet Union)
    Forward   Wayne Gretzky (Canada)
              Mats Naslund (Sweden)
              Anton Stastny (Czechoslovakia)

DIRECTORATE AWARDS
    BEST GOALIE   Alexander Tyzhnych (Soviet Union)
    BEST DEFENCEMAN   Viacheslav Fetisov (Soviet Union)
    BEST FORWARD   Wayne Gretzky (Canada)

1979 WORLD JUNIOR CHAMPIONSHIP

SWEDEN, DECEMBER 27, 1978–JANUARY 3, 1979

FINAL PLACINGS
    GOLD MEDAL   Soviet Union
    SILVER MEDAL   Czechoslovakia
    BRONZE MEDAL Sweden
    Fourth Place   Finland

Fifth Place	Canada
Sixth Place	United States
Seventh Place	West Germany
Eighth Place	Norway*

* promoted from 'B' pool in 1978; relegated to 'B' pool for 1980

ALL-STAR TEAM

Goal	Pelle Lindbergh (Sweden)
Defence	Ivan Cerny (Czechoslovakia)
	Alexei Kasatonov (Soviet Union)
Forward	Anatoli Tarasov (Soviet Union)
	Thomas Steen (Sweden)
	Vladimir Krutov (Soviet Union)

DIRECTORATE AWARDS

BEST GOALIE	Pelle Lindbergh (Sweden)
BEST DEFENCEMAN	Alexei Kasatonov (Soviet Union)
BEST FORWARD	Vladimir Krutov (Soviet Union)

1980 WORLD JUNIOR CHAMPIONSHIP

FINLAND, DECEMBER 27, 1979–JANUARY 2, 1980

FINAL PLACINGS

GOLD MEDAL	Soviet Union
SILVER MEDAL	Finland
BRONZE MEDAL	Sweden
Fourth Place	Czechoslovakia
Fifth Place	Canada
Sixth Place	West Germany
Seventh Place	United States
Eighth Place	Switzerland*

* promoted from 'B' pool in 1979; relegated to 'B' pool for 1981

ALL-STAR TEAM

Goal	Jari Paavola (Finland)
Defence	Reijo Ruotsalainen (Finland)
	Tomas Jonsson (Sweden)
Forward	Hakan Loob (Sweden)
	Igor Larionov (Soviet Union)
	Vladimir Krutov (Soviet Union)

DIRECTORATE AWARDS
- BEST GOALIE   Jari Paavola (Finland)
- BEST DEFENCEMAN   Reijo Ruotsalainen (Finland)
- BEST FORWARD   Vladimir Krutov (Soviet Union)

1981 WORLD JUNIOR CHAMPIONSHIP

WEST GERMANY, DECEMBER 27, 1980–JANUARY 2, 1981

FINAL PLACINGS
GOLD MEDAL	Sweden
SILVER MEDAL	Finland
BRONZE MEDAL	Soviet Union
Fourth Place	Czechoslovakia
Fifth Place	West Germany
Sixth Place	United States
Seventh Place	Canada
Eighth Place	Austria*

* promoted from 'B' pool in 1980; relegated to 'B' pool for 1982

ALL-STAR TEAM
Goal	Lars Eriksson (Sweden)
Defence	Miloslav Horava (Czechoslovakia)
	Hakan Nordin (Sweden)
Forward	Ari Lahteenmaki (Finland)
	Patrik Sundstrom (Sweden)
	Jan Erixon (Sweden)

DIRECTORATE AWARDS
- BEST GOALIE   Lars Eriksson (Sweden)
- BEST DEFENCEMAN   Miloslav Horava (Czechoslovakia)
- BEST FORWARD   Patrik Sundstrom (Sweden)

1982 WORLD JUNIOR CHAMPIONSHIP

UNITED STATES, DECEMBER 22, 1981–JANUARY 2, 1982
(some games played in Canada)

FINAL PLACINGS
GOLD MEDAL	Canada
SILVER MEDAL	Czechoslovakia
BRONZE MEDAL	Finland
Fourth Place	Soviet Union

Fifth Place   Sweden
Sixth Place   United States
Seventh Place   West Germany
Eighth Place   Switzerland*

* promoted from 'B' pool in 1981; relegated to 'B' pool for 1983

ALL-STAR TEAM

Goal   Mike Moffat (Canada)
Defence   Gord Kluzak (Canada)
              Ilya Biakin (Soviet Union)

Forward   Mike Moller (Canada)
              Petri Skriko (Finland)
              Vladimir Ruzicka (Czechoslovakia)

DIRECTORATE AWARDS

BEST GOALIE   Mike Moffat (Canada)
BEST DEFENCEMAN   Gord Kluzak (Canada)
BEST FORWARD   Petri Skriko (Finland)

1983 WORLD JUNIOR CHAMPIONSHIP

SOVIET UNION, DECEMBER 26, 1982–JANUARY 4, 1983

FINAL PLACINGS

GOLD MEDAL   Soviet Union
SILVER MEDAL   Czechoslovakia
BRONZE MEDAL   Canada
Fourth Place   Sweden
Fifth Place   United States
Sixth Place   Finland
Seventh Place   West Germany
Eighth Place   Norway*

* promoted from 'B' pool in 1982; relegated to 'B' pool for 1984

ALL-STAR TEAM

Goal   Matti Rautiainen (Finland)
Defence   Ilya Biakin (Soviet Union)
              Simo Saarinen (Finland)
Forward   Tomas Sandstrom (Sweden)
              Vladimir Ruzicka (Czechoslovakia)
              German Volgin (Soviet Union)

DIRECTORATE AWARDS
- BEST GOALIE Dominik Hasek (Czechoslovakia)
- BEST DEFENCEMAN Ilya Biakin (Soviet Union)
- BEST FORWARD Tomas Sandstrom (Sweden)

1984 WORLD JUNIOR CHAMPIONSHIP

SWEDEN, DECEMBER 25, 1983–JANUARY 3, 1984

FINAL PLACINGS
- GOLD MEDAL Soviet Union
- SILVER MEDAL Finland
- BRONZE MEDAL Czechoslovakia
- Fourth Place Canada
- Fifth Place Sweden
- Sixth Place United States
- Seventh Place West Germany
- Eighth Place Switzerland*

* promoted from 'B' pool in 1983; relegated to 'B' pool for 1985

ALL-STAR TEAM
- Goal Evgeny Belosheikin (Soviet Union)
- Defence Alexei Gusarov (Soviet Union)
- Frantisek Musil (Czechoslovakia)
- Forward Petr Rosol (Czechoslovakia)
- Raimo Helminen (Finland)
- Nikolai Borschevsky (Soviet Union)

DIRECTORATE AWARDS
- BEST GOALIE Alan Perry (United States)
- BEST DEFENCEMAN Alexei Gusarov (Soviet Union)
- BEST FORWARD Raimo Helminen (Finland)

1985 WORLD JUNIOR CHAMPIONSHIP

FINLAND, DECEMBER 23, 1984–JANUARY 1, 1985

FINAL PLACINGS
- GOLD MEDAL Canada
- SILVER MEDAL Czechoslovakia
- BRONZE MEDAL Soviet Union
- Fourth Place Finland
- Fifth Place Sweden

Sixth Place	United States
Seventh Place	West Germany
Eighth Place	Poland*

* promoted from 'B' pool in 1984; relegated to 'B' pool for 1986

ALL-STAR TEAM
Goal	Timo Lehkonen (Finland)
Defence	Bobby Dollas (Canada)
	Mikhail Tatarinov (Soviet Union)
Forward	Mikko Makela (Finland)
	Michal Pivonka (Czechoslovakia)
	Esa Tikkanen (Finland)

DIRECTORATE AWARDS
BEST GOALIE	Craig Billington (Canada)
BEST DEFENCEMAN	Vesa Salo (Finland)
BEST FORWARD	Michal Pivonka (Czechoslovakia)

1986 WORLD JUNIOR CHAMPIONSHIP

CANADA, DECEMBER 26, 1985–JANUARY 4, 1986

FINAL PLACINGS
GOLD MEDAL	Soviet Union
SILVER MEDAL	Canada
BRONZE MEDAL	United States
Fourth Place	Czechoslovakia
Fifth Place	Sweden
Sixth Place	Finland
Seventh Place	Switzerland*
Eighth Place	West Germany**

* promoted from 'B' pool in 1985
** relegated to 'B' pool for 1987

ALL-STAR TEAM
Goal	Evgeny Belosheikin (Soviet Union)
Defence	Sylvain Cote (Canada)
	Mikhail Tatarinov (Soviet Union)
Forward	Shayne Corson (Canada)
	Igor Viazmikin (Soviet Union)
	Michal Pivonka (Czechoslovakia)

DIRECTORATE AWARDS
BEST GOALIE	Evgeny Belosheikin (Soviet Union)
BEST DEFENCEMAN	Mikhail Tatarinov (Soviet Union)
BEST FORWARD	Jim Sandlak (Canada)

1987 WORLD JUNIOR CHAMPIONSHIP

CZECHOSLOVAKIA, DECEMBER 26, 1986–JANUARY 4, 1987

FINAL PLACINGS
GOLD MEDAL	Finland
SILVER MEDAL	Czechoslovakia
BRONZE MEDAL	Sweden
Fourth Place	United States
Fifth Place	Poland*
Sixth Place	Switzerland**

Canada and the Soviet Union were disqualified

* promoted from 'B' pool in 1986
** relegated to 'B' pool for 1988

ALL-STAR TEAM
Goal	Sam Lindstahl (Sweden)
Defence	Jiri Latal (Czechoslovakia)
	Brian Leetch (United States)
Forward	Ulf Dahlen (Sweden)
	Juraj Jurik (Czechoslovakia)
	Scott Young (United States)

DIRECTORATE AWARDS
BEST GOALIE	Markus Ketterer (Finland)
BEST DEFENCEMAN	Calle Johansson (Sweden)
BEST FORWARD	Robert Kron (Czechoslovakia)

1988 WORLD JUNIOR CHAMPIONSHIP

RUSSIA, DECEMBER 26, 1987–JANUARY 4, 1988

FINAL PLACINGS
GOLD MEDAL	Canada
SILVER MEDAL	Soviet Union
BRONZE MEDAL	Finland
Fourth Place	Czechsloavkia
Fifth Place	Sweden

Sixth Place   United States
Seventh Place   West Germany*
Eighth Place   Poland**

* promoted from 'B' pool in 1987
** relegated to 'B' pool for 1989

ALL-STAR TEAM

Goal   Jimmy Waite (Canada)
Defence   Greg Hawgood (Canada)
           Teppo Numminen (Finland)
Forward   Theoren Fleury (Canada)
           Alexander Mogilny (Soviet Union)
           Petr Hrbek (Czechoslovakia)

DIRECTORATE AWARDS

BEST GOALIE   Jimmy Waite (Canada)
BEST DEFENCEMAN   Teppo Numminen (Finland)
BEST FORWARD   Alexander Mogilny (Soviet Union)

1989 WORLD JUNIOR CHAMPIONSHIP

UNITED STATES, DECEMBER 26, 1988–JANUARY 4, 1989

FINAL PLACINGS

GOLD MEDAL   Soviet Union
SILVER MEDAL   Sweden
BRONZE MEDAL   Czechoslovakia
Fourth Place   Canada
Fifth Place   United States
Sixth Place   Finland
Seventh Place   Norway*
Eighth Place   West Germany**

* promoted from 'B' pool in 1988
** relegated to 'B' pool for 1990

ALL-STAR TEAM

Goal   Alexei Ivashkin (Soviet Union)
Defence   Rickard Persson (Sweden)
           Milan Tichy (Czechoslovakia)
Forward   Niklas Eriksson (Sweden)
           Pavel Bure (Soviet Union)
           Jeremy Roenick (United States)

DIRECTORATE AWARDS
> BEST GOALIE   Alexei Ivashkin (Soviet Union)
> BEST DEFENCEMAN   Rickard Persson (Sweden)
> BEST FORWARD   Pavel Bure (Soviet Union)

1990 WORLD JUNIOR CHAMPIONSHIP

FINLAND, DECEMBER 26, 1989–JANUARY 4, 1990

FINAL PLACINGS
> GOLD MEDAL   Canada
> SILVER MEDAL   Soviet Union
> BRONZE MEDAL   Czechoslovakia
> Fourth Place   Finland
> Fifth Place   Sweden
> Sixth Place   Norway
> Seventh Place   United States
> Eighth Place   Poland*
>
> * promoted from 'B' pool in 1989; relegated to 'B' pool for 1991

ALL-STAR TEAM
> Goal   Stephane Fiset (Canada)
> Defence   Alexander Godynyuk (Soviet Union)
>   Jiri Slegr (Czechoslovakia)
> Forward   Dave Chyzowski (Canada)
>   Jaromir Jagr (Czechoslovakia)
>   Robert Reichel (Czechoslovakia)

DIRECTORATE AWARDS
> BEST GOALIE   Stephane Fiset (Canada)
> BEST DEFENCEMAN   Alexander Godynyuk (Soviet Union)
> BEST FORWARD   Robert Reichel (Czechoslovakia)

1991 WORLD JUNIOR CHAMPIONSHIP

CANADA, DECEMBER 26, 1990–JANUARY 4, 1991

FINAL PLACINGS
> GOLD MEDAL   Canada
> SILVER MEDAL   Soviet Union
> BRONZE MEDAL   Czechoslovakia
> Fourth Place   United States

Fifth Place	Finland
Sixth Place	Sweden
Seventh Place	Switzerland*
Eighth Place	Norway**

* promoted from 'B' pool in 1990
** relegated to 'B' pool for 1992

ALL-STAR TEAM

Goal	Pauli Jaks (Switzerland)
Defence	Dmitri Yushkevich (Soviet Union)
	Scott Lachance (United States)
Forward	Mike Craig (Canada)
	Eric Lindros (Canada)
	Martin Rucinsky (Czechoslovakia)

DIRECTORATE AWARDS

BEST GOALIE	Pauli Jaks (Switzerland)
BEST DEFENCEMAN	Jiri Slegr (Czechoslovakia)
BEST FORWARD	Eric Lindros (Canada)

1992 WORLD JUNIOR CHAMPIONSHIP

GERMANY, DECEMBER 26, 1991–JANUARY 4, 1992

FINAL PLACINGS

GOLD MEDAL	Commonwealth of Independent States
SILVER MEDAL	Sweden
BRONZE MEDAL	United States
Fourth Place	Finland
Fifth Place	Czechoslovakia
Sixth Place	Canada
Seventh Place	Germany*
Eighth Place	Switzerland**

* promoted from 'B' pool in 1991
** relegated to 'B' pool for 1993

ALL-STAR TEAM

Goal	Mike Dunham (United States)
Defence	Scott Niedermayer (Canada)
	Janne Gronvall (Finland)
Forward	Alexei Kovalev (CIS)
	Michael Nylander (Sweden)
	Peter Ferraro (United States)

DIRECTORATE AWARDS
BEST GOALIE	Mike Dunham (United States)
BEST DEFENCEMAN	Darius Kasparaitis (CIS)
BEST FORWARD	Michael Nylander (Sweden)

1993 WORLD JUNIOR CHAMPIONSHIP

SWEDEN, DECEMBER 26, 1992–JANUARY 4, 1993

FINAL PLACINGS
GOLD MEDAL	Canada
SILVER MEDAL	Sweden
BRONZE MEDAL	Czechoslovakia
Fourth Place	United States
Fifth Place	Finland
Sixth Place	Russia
Seventh Place	Germany
Eighth place	Japan*

* promoted from 'B' pool in 1992; relegated to 'B' pool for 1994

ALL-STAR TEAM
Goal	Manny Legace (Canada)
Defence	Brent Tully (Canada)
	Kenny Jonsson (Sweden)
Forward	Paul Kariya (Canada)
	Markus Naslund (Sweden)
	Peter Forsberg (Sweden)

DIRECTORATE AWARDS
BEST GOALIE	Manny Legace (Canada)
BEST DEFENCEMAN	Janne Gronvall (Finland)
BEST FORWARD	Peter Forsberg (Sweden)

1994 WORLD JUNIOR CHAMPIONSHIP

CZECH REPUBLIC, DECEMBER 26, 1993–JANUARY 4, 1994

FINAL PLACINGS
GOLD MEDAL	Canada
SILVER MEDAL	Sweden
BRONZE MEDAL	Russia

Fourth Place   Finland
Fifth Place   Czech Republic
Sixth Place   United States
Seventh Place   Germany
Eighth Place   Switzerland*

* promoted from 'B' pool in 1993; relegated to 'B' pool for 1995

ALL-STAR TEAM

Goal   Evgeny Riabchikov (Russia)
Defence   Kenny Jonsson (Sweden)
            Kimmo Timonen (Finland)
Forward   Niklas Sundstrom (Sweden)
            Valeri Bure (Russia)
            David Vyborny (Czech Republic)

DIRECTORATE AWARDS

BEST GOALIE   Jamie Storr (Canada)
BEST DEFENCEMAN   Kenny Jonsson (Sweden)
BEST FORWARD   Niklas Sundstrom (Sweden)

1995 WORLD JUNIOR CHAMPIONSHIP

CANADA, DECEMBER 26, 1994–JANUARY 4, 1995

FINAL PLACINGS

GOLD MEDAL   Canada
SILVER MEDAL   Russia
BRONZE MEDAL   Sweden
Fourth Place   Finland
Fifth Place   United States
Sixth Place   Czech Republic
Seventh Place Germany
Eighth Place   Ukraine*

* promoted from 'B' pool in 1994
Note: no team was relegated to 'B' pool from this year's tournament because in 1996 the 'A' pool expanded to ten teams and a new round-robin format

ALL-STAR TEAM

Goal   Igor Karpenko (Ukraine)
Defence   Bryan McCabe (Canada)
            Anders Eriksson (Sweden)

Forward	Jason Allison (Canada)
	Eric Daze (Canada)
	Marty Murray (Canada)

DIRECTORATE AWARDS

BEST GOALIE	Evgeny Tarasov (Russia)
BEST DEFENCEMAN	Bryan McCabe (Canada)
BEST FORWARD	Marty Murray (Canada)

1996 WORLD JUNIOR CHAMPIONSHIP

UNITED STATES, DECEMBER 26, 1995–JANUARY 4, 1996

FINAL PLACINGS

GOLD MEDAL	Canada
SILVER MEDAL	Sweden
BRONZE MEDAL	Russia
Fourth Place	Czech Republic
Fifth Place	United States
Sixth Place	Finland
Seventh Place	Slovakia*
Eighth Place	Germany
Ninth Place	Switzerland*
Tenth Place	Ukraine**

* promoted from 'B' pool in 1995
** relegated to 'B' pool for 1997

ALL-STAR TEAM

Goal	Jose Theodore (Canada)
Defence	Nolan Baumgartner (Canada)
	Mattias Ohlund (Sweden)
Forward	Jarome Iginla (Canada)
	Johan Davidsson (Sweden)
	Alexei Morozov (Russia)

DIRECTORATE AWARDS

BEST GOALIE	Jose Theodore (Canada)
BEST DEFENCEMAN	Mattias Ohlund (Sweden)
BEST FORWARD	Jarome Iginla (Canada)

1997 WORLD JUNIOR CHAMPIONSHIP

SWITZERLAND, DECEMBER 26, 1996–JANUARY 4, 1997

FINAL PLACINGS

GOLD MEDAL	Canada
SILVER MEDAL	United States
BRONZE MEDAL	Russia
Fourth Place	Czech Republic
Fifth Place	Finland
Sixth Place	Slovakia
Seventh Place	Switzerland
Eighth Place	Sweden
Ninth Place	Germany
Tenth Place	Poland*

* promoted from 'B' pool in 1996; relegated to 'B' pool for 1998

ALL-STAR TEAM

Goal	Brian Boucher (United States)
Defence	Chris Phillips (Canada)
	Mark Streit (Switzerland)
Forward	Christian Dube (Canada)
	Sergei Samsonov (Russia)
	Michael York (United States)

DIRECTORATE AWARDS

BEST GOALIE	Marc Denis (Canada)
BEST DEFENCEMAN	Joseph Corvo (United States)
BEST FORWARD	Alexei Morozov (Russia)

1998 WORLD JUNIOR CHAMPIONSHIP

FINLAND, DECEMBER 25, 1997–JANUARY 3, 1998

FINAL PLACINGS

GOLD MEDAL	Finland
SILVER MEDAL	Russia
BRONZE MEDAL	Switzerland
Fourth Place	Czech Republic
Fifth Place	United States
Sixth Place	Sweden
Seventh Place	Kazakhstan*
Eighth Place	Canada

Ninth Place	Slovakia
Tenth Place	Germany**

* promoted from 'B' pool in 1997
** relegated to 'B' pool for 1999

ALL-STAR TEAM

Goal	David Aebischer (Switzerland)
Defence	Pierre Hedin (Sweden)
	Andrei Markov (Russia)
Forward	Olli Jokinen (Finland)
	Eero Somervuori (Finland)
	Maxim Balmochnykh (Russia)

DIRECTORATE AWARDS

BEST GOALIE	David Aebischer (Switzerland)
BEST DEFENCEMAN	Pavel Skrbek (Czech Republic)
BEST FORWARD	Olli Jokinen (Finland)

1999 WORLD JUNIOR CHAMPIONSHIP

CANADA, DECEMBER 26, 1998–JANUARY 5, 1999

FINAL PLACINGS

GOLD MEDAL	Russia
SILVER MEDAL	Canada
BRONZE MEDAL	Slovakia
Fourth Place	Sweden
Fifth Place	Finland
Sixth Place	Kazakhstan
Seventh Place	Czech Republic
Eighth Place	United States
Ninth Place	Switzerland
Tenth Place	Belarus*

* promoted from 'B' pool in 1998; relegated to 'B' pool for 2000

ALL-STAR TEAM

Goal	Roberto Luongo (Canada)
Defence	Vitali Vishnevsky (Russia)
	Brian Campbell (Canada)
Forward	Daniel Tkachuk (Canada)
	Brian Gionta (United States)
	Maxim Balmochnykh (Russia)

DIRECTORATE AWARDS
BEST GOALIE	Roberto Luongo (Canada)
BEST DEFENCEMAN	Maxim Afinigenov (Russia)
BEST FORWARD	Vitali Vishnevski (Russia)

2000 WORLD JUNIOR CHAMPIONSHIP

SWEDEN, DECEMBER 25, 1999–JANUARY 4, 2000

FINAL PLACINGS
GOLD MEDAL	Czech Republic
SILVER MEDAL	Russia
BRONZE MEDAL	Canada
Fourth Place	United States
Fifth Place	Sweden
Sixth Place	Switzerland
Seventh Place	Finland
Eighth Place	Kazakhstan
Ninth Place	Slovakia
Tenth Place	Ukraine*

* promoted from 'B' pool in 1999; demoted to 'B' pool for 2001

ALL-STAR TEAM
Goal	Rick DiPietro (United States)
Defence	Mathieu Biron (Canada)
	Alexander Rjasantsev (Russia)
Forward	Milan Kraft (Czech Republic)
	Alexei Tereschenko (Russia)
	Evgeny Muratov (Russia)

DIRECTORATE AWARDS
BEST GOALIE	Rick DiPietro (United States)
BEST DEFENCEMAN	Alexander Rjasantsev (Russia)
BEST FORWARD	Milan Kraft (Czech Republic)

2001 WORLD JUNIOR CHAMPIONSHIP

RUSSIA, DECEMBER 26, 2000–JANUARY 5, 2001

FINAL PLACINGS
GOLD MEDAL	Czech Republic
SILVER MEDAL	Finland

BRONZE MEDAL	Canada
Fourth Place	Sweden
Fifth Place	United States
Sixth Place	Switzerland
Seventh Place	Russia
Eighth Place	Slovakia
Ninth Place	Belarus*
Tenth Place	Kazakhstan**

* promoted from 'B' pool in 2000
** demoted to 'B' pool for 2002

ALL-STAR TEAM

Goal	Ari Ahonen (Finland)
Defence	Rostislav Klesla (Czech Republic)
	Tuukka Mantyla (Finland)
Forward	Jason Spezza (Canada)
	Jani Rita (Finland)
	Pavel Brendl (Czech Republic)

DIRECTORATE AWARDS

BEST GOALIE	Tomas Duba (Czech Republic)
BEST DEFENCEMAN	Rostislav Klesla (Czech Republic)
BEST FORWARD	Pavel Brendl (Czech Republic)

2002 WORLD JUNIOR CHAMPIONSHIP

CZECH REPUBLIC, DECEMBER 25, 2001–JUANUARY 4, 2002

FINAL PLACINGS

GOLD MEDAL	Russia
SILVER MEDAL	Canada
BRONZE MEDAL	Finland
Fourth Place	Switzerland
Fifth Place	United States
Sixth Place	Sweden
Seventh Place	Czech Republic
Eighth Place	Slovakia
Ninth Place	Belarus
Tenth Place	France*

* promoted from 2001; demoted for 2003

ALL-STAR TEAM

Goal	Pascal Leclaire (Canada)
Defence	Jay Bouwmeester (Canada)
	Igor Knyazev (Russia)
Forward	Mike Cammalleri (Canada)
	Marek Svatos (Slovakia)
	Stanislav Chistov (Russia)

DIRECTORATE AWARDS

BEST GOALIE	Kari Lehtonen (Finland)
BEST DEFENCEMAN	Igor Knyazev (Russia)
BEST FORWARD	Mike Cammalleri (Canada)

2003 WORLD JUNIOR CHAMPIONSHIP

CANADA, DECEMBER 26, 2002–JANUARY 5, 2003

FINAL PLACINGS

GOLD MEDAL	Russia
SILVER MEDAL	Canada
BRONZE MEDAL	Finland
Fourth Place	United States
Fifth Place	Slovakia
Sixth Place	Czech Republic
Seventh Place	Switzerland
Eighth Place	Sweden
Ninth Place	Germany*
Tenth Place	Belarus**

* promoted from 2002
** demoted for 2004

ALL-STAR TEAM

Goal	Marc-Andre Fleury (Canada)
Defence	Carlo Colaiacovo (Canada)
	Joni Pitkanen (Finland)
Forward	Scottie Upshall (Canada)
	Igor Grigorenko (Russia)
	Yuri Trubachev (Russia)

DIRECTORATE AWARDS

BEST GOALIE	Marc-Andre Fleury (Canada)
BEST DEFENCEMAN	Joni Pitkanen (Finland)
BEST FORWARD	Igor Grigorenko (Russia)

2004 WORLD JUNIOR CHAMPIONSHIP

FINLAND, DECEMBER 26, 2003–JANUARY 6, 2004

FINAL PLACINGS

GOLD MEDAL	United States
SILVER MEDAL	Canada
BRONZE MEDAL	Finland
Fourth Place	Czech Republic
Fifth Place	Russia
Sixth Place	Slovakia
Seventh Place	Sweden
Eighth Place	Switzerland
Ninth Place	Austria*
Tenth Place	Ukraine**

* promoted from 2003
** demoted for 2005

ALL-STAR TEAM

Goal	Al Montoya (United States)
Defence	Dion Phaneuf (Canada)
	Sami Lepisto (Finland)
Forward	Jeff Carter (Canada)
	Valtteri Filppula (Finland)
	Zach Parise (United States)

DIRECTORATE AWARDS

BEST GOALIE	Al Montoya (United States)
BEST DEFENCEMAN	Sami Lepisto (Finland)
BEST FORWARD	Zach Parise (United States)

2005 WORLD JUNIOR CHAMPIONSHIP

UNITED STATES, December 25, 2004–January 4, 2005

FINAL PLACINGS

GOLD MEDAL	Canada
SILVER MEDAL	Russia
BRONZE MEDAL	Czech Republic
Fourth Place	United States
Fifth Place	Finland
Sixth Place	Sweden
Seventh Place	Slovakia

Eighth Place	Switzerland
Ninth Place	Germany*
Tenth Place	Belarus*

* promoted from 2004; demoted for 2006

ALL-STAR TEAM

Goal	Marek Schwarz (Czech Republic)
Defence	Dion Phaneuf (Canada)
	Gary Suter (United States)
Forward	Patrice Bergeron (Canada)
	Jeff Carter (Canada)
	Alexander Ovechkin (Russia)

DIRECTORATE AWARDS

BEST GOALIE	Marek Schwarz (Czech Republic)
BEST DEFENCEMAN	Dion Phaneuf (Canada)
BEST FORWARD	Alexander Ovechkin (Russia)

2006 WORLD JUNIOR CHAMPIONSHIP

CANADA, DECEMBER 26, 2005–JANUARY 5, 2006

FINAL PLACINGS

GOLD MEDAL	Canada
SILVER MEDAL	Russia
BRONZE MEDAL	Finland
Fourth Place	United States
Fifth Place	Sweden
Sixth Place	Czech Republic
Seventh Place	Switzerland
Eighth Place	Slovakia
Ninth Place	Latvia*
Tenth Place	Norway*

* promoted from 2005; demoted for 2007

ALL-STAR TEAM

Goal	Tuukka Rask (Finland)
Defence	Luc Bourdon (Canada)
	Jack Johnson (United States)
Forward	Steve Downie (Canada)
	Evgeni Malkin (Russia)

Lauri Tukonen (Finland)

DIRECTORATE AWARDS
BEST GOALIE	Tuukka Rask (Finland)
BEST DEFENCEMAN	Marc Staal (Canada)
BEST FORWARD	Evgeni Malkin (Russia)

2007 WORLD JUNIOR CHAMPIONSHIP

SWEDEN, DECEMBER 26, 2006–JANUARY 5, 2007

FINAL PLACINGS
GOLD MEDAL	Canada
SILVER MEDAL	Russia
BRONZE MEDAL	United States
Fourth Place	Sweden
Fifth Place	Czech Republic
Sixth Place	Finland
Seventh Place	Switzerland
Eighth Place	Slovakia
Ninth Place	Germany*
Tenth Place	Belarus*

*promoted from 2006; demoted for 2008

ALL-STAR TEAM
Goal	Carey Price (Canada)
Defence	Kristopher Letang (Canada)
	Erik Johnson (United States)
Forward	Jonathan Toews (Canada)
	Alexei Cherepanov (Russia)
	Patrick Kane (United States)

DIRECTORATE AWARDS
BEST GOALIE	Carey Price (Canada)
BEST DEFENCEMAN	Erik Johnson (United States)
BEST FORWARD	Alexei Cherepanov (Russia)
TOURNAMENT MVP	Carey Price (Canada)

2008 WORLD JUNIOR CHAMPIONSHIP

CZECH REPUBLIC, DECEMBER 26, 2007–JANUARY 5, 2008

FINAL PLACINGS

GOLD MEDAL	Canada
SILVER MEDAL	Sweden
BRONZE MEDAL	Russia
Fourth Place	United States
Fifth Place	Czech Republic
Sixth Place	Finland
Seventh Place	Slovakia
Eighth Place	Kazakhstan*
Ninth Place	Switzerland†
Tenth Place	Denmark*†

*promoted from 2006; †demoted for 2009

ALL-STAR TEAM

Goal	Steve Mason (Canada)
Defence	Drew Doughty (Canada)
	Victor Hedman (Sweden)
Forward	Viktor Tikhonov (Russia)
	Patrik Berglund (Sweden)
	James van Riemsdyk (United States)

DIRECTORATE AWARDS

BEST GOALIE	Steve Mason (Canada)
BEST DEFENCEMAN	Drew Doughty (Canada)
BEST FORWARD	Viktor Tikhonov (Russia)
TOURNAMENT MVP	Steve Mason (Canada)

2009 WORLD JUNIOR CHAMPIONSHIP

CANADA, DECEMBER 26, 2008–JANUARY 5, 2009

FINAL PLACINGS

GOLD MEDAL	Canada
SILVER MEDAL	Sweden
BRONZE MEDAL	Russia
Fourth Place	Slovakia
Fifth Place	United States
Sixth Place	Czech Republic
Seventh Place	Finland
Eighth Place	Latvia*

Ninth Place   Germany*†
Tenth Place   Kazakhstan†

*promoted from 2008; †demoted for 2010

ALL-STAR TEAM

Goal	Jaroslav Janus (SVK)
Defence	P.K. Subban (CAN), Erik Karlsson (SWE)
Forward	John Tavares (CAN), Cody Hodgson (CAN), Nikita Filatov (RUS)

DIRECTORATE AWARDS

BEST GOALIE	Jacob Markstrom (SWE)
BEST DEFENCEMAN	Erik Karlsson (SWE)
BEST FORWARD	John Tavares (CAN)
TOURNAMENT MVP	John Tavares (CAN)

2010 WORLD JUNIOR CHAMPIONSHIP

CANADA, DECEMBER 26, 2009–JANUARY 5, 2010

FINAL PLACINGS

GOLD MEDAL	United States
SILVER MEDAL	Canada
BRONZE MEDAL	Sweden
Fourth Place	Switzerland
Fifth Place	Finland
Sixth Place	Russia
Seventh Place	Czech Republic
Eighth Place	Slovakia
Ninth Place	Latvia
Tenth Place	Austria

ALL-STAR TEAM

Goal	Benjamin Conx (SUI)
Defence	Alex Pietrangelo (CAN)
	John Carlson (USA)
Forward	Jordan Eberle (CAN)
	Derek Stepan (USA)
	Nino Niederreiter (SUI)

DIRECTORATE AWARDS

Best Goalie	Benjamin Conz (SUI)
Best Defenceman	Alex Pietrangelo (CAN)
Best Forward	Jordan Eberle (CAN)
Tournament MVP	Jordan Eberle (CAN)

WORLD U18 CHAMPIONSHIPS, MEN, 1999–2010

1999 WORLD U18 CHAMPIONSHIP

Fussen/Kaufbeuren, GERMANY, April 8–18, 1999

FINAL PLACINGS

GOLD MEDAL	Finland
SILVER MEDAL	Sweden
BRONZE MEDAL	Slovakia
Fourth Place	Switzerland
Fifth Place	Czech Republic
Sixth Place	Russia
Seventh Place	United States
Eighth Place	Ukraine
Ninth Place	Germany
Tenth Place	Norway

2000 WORLD U18 CHAMPIONSHIP

Kloten/Weinfelden, SWITZERLAND, April 14–24, 2000

FINAL PLACINGS

GOLD MEDAL	Finland
SILVER MEDAL	Russia
BRONZE MEDAL	Sweden
Fourth Place	Switzerland
Fifth Place	Slovakia
Sixth Place	Czech Republic
Seventh Place	Germany
Eighth Place	United States
Ninth Place	Ukraine
Tenth Place	Belarus

2001 WORLD U18 CHAMPIONSHIP

Heinola/Helsinki/Lahti, FINLAND, April 12–22, 2001

FINAL PLACINGS

GOLD MEDAL	Russia
SILVER MEDAL	Switzerland

BRONZE MEDAL	Finland
Fourth Place	Czech Republic
Fifth Place	Germany
Sixth Place	United States
Seventh Place	Sweden
Eighth Place	Slovakia
Ninth Place	Norway
Tenth Place	Ukraine

2002 WORLD U18 CHAMPIONSHIP

Trnava/Piestany, SLOVAKIA, April 11–21, 2002

FINAL PLACINGS

GOLD MEDAL	United States
SILVER MEDAL	Russia
BRONZE MEDAL	Czech Republic
Fourth Place	Finland
Fifth Place	Belarus
Sixth Place	Canada
Seventh Place	Switzerland
Eighth Place	Slovakia
Ninth Place	Sweden
Tenth Place	Germany
Eleventh Place	Norway
Twelfth Place	Ukraine

2003 WORLD U18 CHAMPIONSHIP

Yaroslavl, RUSSIA, April 12–23 2003

FINAL PLACINGS

GOLD MEDAL	Canada
SILVER MEDAL	Slovakia
BRONZE MEDAL	Russia
Fourth Place	United States
Fifth Place	Sweden
Sixth Place	Czech Republic
Seventh Place	Finland
Eighth Place	Belarus
Ninth Place	Switzerland
Tenth Place	Kazakhstan

2004 WORLD U18 CHAMPIONSHIP

Minsk, BELARUS, April 8–18, 2004

FINAL PLACINGS

GOLD MEDAL	Russia
SILVER MEDAL	United States
BRONZE MEDAL	Czech Republic
Fourth Place	Canada
Fifth Place	Sweden
Sixth Place	Slovakia
Seventh Place	Finland
Eighth Place	Denmark
Ninth Place	Belarus
Tenth Place	Norway

2005 WORLD U18 CHAMPIONSHIP

Ceske Budejovice/Plzen, CZECH REPUBLIC, April 14–24, 2005

FINAL PLACINGS

GOLD MEDAL	United States
SILVER MEDAL	Canada
BRONZE MEDAL	Sweden
Fourth Place	Czech Republic
Fifth Place	Russia
Sixth Place	Slovakia
Seventh Place	Finland
Eighth Place	Germany
Ninth Place	Switzerland
Tenth Place	Denmark

2006 WORLD U18 CHAMPIONSHIP

Angelholm/Halmstad, SWEDEN, April 12–22, 2006

FINAL PLACINGS

GOLD MEDAL	United States
SILVER MEDAL	Finland
BRONZE MEDAL	Czech Republic
Fourth Place	Canada
Fifth Place	Russia
Sixth Place	Sweden

Seventh Place	Slovakia
Eighth Place	Germany
Ninth Place	Belarus
Tenth Place	Norway

2007 WORLD U18 CHAMPIONSHIP

Tampere/Rauma, FINLAND, April 11–22, 2007

FINAL PLACINGS

GOLD MEDAL	Russia
SILVER MEDAL	United States
BRONZE MEDAL	Sweden
Fourth Place	Canada
Fifth Place	Slovakia
Sixth Place	Switzerland
Seventh Place	Finland
Eighth Place	Germany
Ninth Place	Czech Republic
Tenth Place	Latvia

2008 WORLD U18 CHAMPIONSHIP

Kazan, RUSSIA, April 13–23, 2008

FINAL PLACINGS

GOLD MEDAL	Canada
SILVER MEDAL	Russia
BRONZE MEDAL	United States
Fourth Place	Sweden
Fifth Place	Germany
Sixth Place	Finland
Seventh Place	Slovakia
Eighth Place	Switzerland
Ninth Place	Belarus
Tenth Place	Denmark

2009 WORLD U18 CHAMPIONSHIP

Fargo/Moorhead, UNITED STATES, April 9–19, 2009

FINAL PLACINGS

GOLD MEDAL	United States
SILVER MEDAL	Russia
BRONZE MEDAL	Finland
Fourth Place	Canada
Fifth Place	Sweden
Sixth Place	Czech Republic
Seventh Place	Slovakia
Eighth Place	Switzerland
Ninth Place	Norway
Tenth Place	Germany

2010 WORLD U18 CHAMPIONSHIP

Minsk/Bobruisk, BELARUS, April 13–23, 2010

FINAL PLACINGS

GOLD MEDAL	United States
SILVER MEDAL	Sweden
BRONZE MEDAL	Finland
Fourth Place	Russia
Fifth Place	Switzerland
Sixth Place	Czech Republic
Seventh Place	Canada
Eighth Place	Slovakia
Ninth Place	Latvia
Tenth Place	Belarus

WORLD U18 CHAMPIONSHIPS, WOMEN, 2008–2010

2008 WORLD WOMEN'S U18 CHAMPIONSHIP

Calgary, CANADA, January 7–12, 2008

FINAL PLACINGS

GOLD MEDAL	United States
SILVER MEDAL	Canada
BRONZE MEDAL	Czech Republic
Fourth Place	Sweden
Fifth Place	Germany
Sixth Place	Finland
Seventh Place	Switzerland
Eighth Place	Russia

2009 WORLD WOMEN'S U18 CHAMPIONSHIP

Fussen, GERMANY, January 1–10, 2009

FINAL PLACINGS

GOLD MEDAL	United States
SILVER MEDAL	Canada
BRONZE MEDAL	Sweden
Fourth Place	Czech Republic
Fifth Place	Finland
Sixth Place	Germany
Seventh Place	Russia
Eighth Place	Switzerland

2010 WORLD WOMEN'S U18 CHAMPIONSHIP

Chicago, UNITED STATES, March 27–April 3, 2010

FINAL PLACINGS

GOLD MEDAL	Canada
SILVER MEDAL	United States
BRONZE MEDAL	Sweden
Fourth Place	Germany
Fifth Place	Finland
Sixth Place	Japan
Seventh Place	Czech Republic
Eighth Place	Russia

PRO CLASSICS RESULTS

1972 SUMMIT SERIES

Canada/Moscow, September 2–28, 1972

	GP	W	L	T	GF	GA	P
Canada	8	4	3	1	31	32	9
Soviet Union	8	3	4	1	32	31	7

Results

Game 1	September 2	Montreal	Soviet Union 7/Canada 3
Game 2	September 4	Toronto	Canada 4/Soviet Union 1
Game 3	September 6	Winnipeg	Canada 4/Soviet Union 4
Game 4	September 8	Vancouver	Soviet Union 5/Canada 3
Exhibition	September 16	Stockholm	Canada 4/Swedish Nationals 1
Exhibition	September 17	Stockholm	Canada 4/Swedish Nationals 4
Game 5	September 22	Moscow	Soviet Union 5/Canada 4
Game 6	September 24	Moscow	Canada 3/Soviet Union 2
Game 7	September 26	Moscow	Canada 4/Soviet Union 3
Game 8	September 28	Moscow	Canada 6/Soviet Union 5

(Paul Henderson scores series winner at 19:26 of 3rd)

Exhibition	September 30	Prague	Canada 3/Czech Nationals 3

1976 CANADA CUP

Canada, September 2–15, 1976

Series MVP: Bobby Orr (Canada)

Team MVPs

Canada	Rogie Vachon
Czechoslovakia	Milan Novy
Soviet Union	Alexander Maltsev
Sweden	Borje Salming
United States	Robbie Ftorek
Finland	Matti Hagman

Final Standings Round Robin

	GP	W	L	T	GF	GA	P
Canada	5	4	1	0	22	6	8
Czechoslovakia	5	3	1	1	19	9	7
Soviet Union	5	2	2	1	23	14	5
Sweden	5	2	2	1	16	18	5
United States	5	1	3	1	14	21	3
Finland	5	1	4	0	16	42	2

Results

September 2	Ottawa	Canada 11/Finland 2
September 3	Toronto	Sweden 5/United States 2
	Montreal	Czechoslovakia 5/Soviet Union 3
September 5	Montreal	Canada 4/United States 2
	Montreal	Soviet Union 3/Sweden 3
	Toronto	Czechoslovakia 8/Finland 0
September 7	Toronto	Canada 4/Sweden 0
	Montreal	Soviet Union 11/Finland 3
	Philadelphia	Czechoslovakia 4/United States 4
September 9	Montreal	Czechoslovakia 1/Canada 0
	Winnipeg	Finland 8/Sweden 6
	Philadelphia	Soviet Union 5/United States 0
September 11	Toronto	Canada 3/Soviet Union 1
	Quebec City	Sweden 2/Czechoslovakia 1
	Montreal	United States 6/Finland 3

FINALS (best two-of-three)

September 13	Toronto	Canada 6/Czechoslovakia 0
September 15	Montreal	Canada 5/Czechoslovakia 4
		(Sittler 11:33 OT)

1981 CANADA CUP

Canada, September 1–13, 1981

Tournament MVP: Vladislav Tretiak
Team Canada MVP: Mike Bossy

All-Star Team

Goal	Vladislav Tretiak (Soviet Union)
Defence	Alexei Kasatonov (Soviet Union)
	Arnold Kadlec (Czechoslovakia)

Forward   Gil Perreault (Canada)
                 Mike Bossy (Canada)
                 Sergei Shepelev (Soviet Union)

Final Standings Round Robin

	GP	W	L	T	GF	GA	P
Canada	5	4	0	1	32	13	9
Soviet Union	5	3	1	1	20	13	7
Czechoslovakia	5	2	1	2	21	13	6
United States	5	2	2	1	17	19	5
Sweden	5	1	4	0	13	20	2
Finland	5	0	4	1	6	31	1

Results

September 1	Edmonton	Canada 9/Finland 0
	Edmonton	United States 3/Sweden 1
	Winnipeg	Czechoslovakia 1/Soviet Union 1
September 3	Edmonton	Canada 8/United States 3
	Edmonton	Czechoslovakia 7/Finland 1
	Winnipeg	Soviet Union 6/Sweden 3
September 5	Winnipeg	Canada 4/Czechoslovakia 4
	Winnipeg	Sweden 5/Finland 0
	Edmonton	Soviet Union 4/United States 1
September 7	Montreal	Canada 4/Sweden 3
	Winnipeg	Soviet Union 6/Finland 1
	Montreal	United States 6/Czechoslovakia 2
September 9	Montreal	Canada 7/Soviet Union 3
	Ottawa	Czechoslovakia 7/Sweden 1
	Montreal	Finland 4/United States 4

Semifinals

September 11	Montreal	Canada 4/United States 1
	Ottawa	Soviet Union 4/Czechoslovakia 1

Finals

September 13	Montreal	Soviet Union 8/Canada 1

1984 CANADA CUP

Canada, September 1–18, 1984
Tournament MVP: John Tonelli

All-Star Team

Goal	Vladimir Myshkin (Soviet Union)
Defence	Paul Coffey (Canada)
	Rod Langway (United States)
Forward	Wayne Gretzky (Canada)
	John Tonelli (Canada)
	Sergei Makarov (Soviet Union)

Final Standings Round Robin

	GP	W	L	T	GF	GA	P
Soviet Union	5	5	0	0	22	7	10
United States	5	3	1	1	21	13	7
Sweden	5	3	2	0	15	16	6
Canada	5	2	2	1	23	18	5
West Germany	5	0	4	1	13	29	1
Czechoslovakia	5	0	4	1	10	21	1

Results

September 1	Montreal	Canada 7/West Germany 2
	Halifax	United States 7/Sweden 1
September 2	Montreal	Soviet Union 3/Czechoslovakia 0
September 3	Montreal	Canada 4/United States 4
September 4	London	Czechoslovakia 4/West Germany 4
	Calgary	Soviet Union 3/Sweden 2
September 6	Vancouver	Sweden 4/Canada 2
	Edmonton	Soviet Union 8/West Germany 1
	Buffalo	United States 3 /Czechoslovakia 2
September 8	Calgary	Canada 7/Czechoslovakia 2
	Calgary	Sweden 4/West Germany 2
	Edmonton	Soviet Union 2/United States 1
September 10	Edmonton	Soviet Union 6/Canada 3
	Vancouver	Sweden 4/Czechoslovakia 2
	Calgary	United States 6/West Germany 4

Semifinals

September 12	Edmonton	Sweden 9/United States 2
September 13	Calgary	Canada 3/Soviet Union 2 (Bossy 12:29 OT)

Finals (best two-of-three)

September 16	Calgary	Canada 5/Sweden 2
September 18	Edmonton	Canada 6/Sweden 5

1987 CANADA CUP

Canada, August 28–September 15, 1987

Tournament All-Star Team

Goal	Grant Fuhr (Canada)
Defence	Ray Bourque (Canada)
	Viacheslav Fetisov (Soviet Union)
Forward	Mario Lemieux (Canada)
	Wayne Gretzky (Canada)
	Vladimir Krutov (Soviet Union)

Final Standings Round Robin

	GP	W	L	T	GF	GA	P
Canada	5	3	0	2	19	13	8
Soviet Union	5	3	1	1	22	13	7
Sweden	5	3	2	0	17	14	6
Czechoslovakia	5	2	2	1	12	15	5
United States	5	2	3	0	13	14	4
Finland	5	0	5	0	9	23	0

Results

August 28	Calgary	Canada 4/Czechoslovakia 4
	Hartford	United States 4/Finland 1
August 29	Calgary	Sweden 5/Soviet Union 3
August 30	Hamilton	Canada 4/Finland 1
August 31	Regina	Soviet Union 4/Czechoslovakia 0
	Hamilton	United States 5/Sweden 2
September 2	Halifax	Soviet Union 7/Finland 4
	Hamilton	Canada 3/United States 2
	Regina	Sweden 4/Czechoslovakia 0
September 4	Hartford	Soviet Union 5/United States 1
	Sydney	Czechoslovakia 5/Finland 2
	Montreal	Canada 5/Sweden 3
September 6	Sydney	Sweden 3/Finland 1
	Sydney	Czechoslovakia 3/United States 1
	Hamilton	Canada 3/Soviet Union 3
September 8	Hamilton	Soviet Union 4/Sweden 2
	Montreal	Canada 5/Czechoslovakia 3

Finals (best two-of-three)

September 11	Montreal	Soviet Union 6/Canada 5 (Semak 5:33 OT)
September 13	Hamilton	Canada 6/Soviet Union 5 (Mario Lemieux 30:07 OT)
September 15	Hamilton	Canada 6/Soviet Union 5 (Lemieux scores winner at 18:34 of 3rd)

1991 CANADA CUP

Canada, August 31–September 16, 1991

Tournament All-Star Team

Goal	Bill Ranford (Canada)
Defence	Al MacInnis (Canada)
	Chris Chelios (United States)
Forward	Wayne Gretzky (Canada)
	Jeremy Roenick (United States)
	Mats Sundin (Sweden)

Final Standings Round Robin

	GP	W	L	T	GF	GA	P
Canada	5	3	0	2	21	11	8
United States	5	4	1	0	19	15	8
Finland	5	2	2	1	10	13	5
Sweden	5	2	3	0	13	17	4
Soviet Union	5	1	3	1	14	14	3
Czechoslovakia	5	1	4	0	11	18	2

Results

August 31	Toronto	Canada 2/Finland 2
	Saskatoon	Czechoslovakia 5/Soviet Union 2
	Pittsburgh	United States 6/Sweden 3
September 2	Hamilton	Canada 6/United States 3
	Montreal	Sweden 3/Soviet Union 2
	Saskatoon	Finland 1/Czechoslovakia 0
September 5	Toronto	Canada 4/Sweden 1
	Hamilton	Soviet Union 6/Finland 1
	Detroit	United States 4/Czechoslovakia 2
September 7	Montreal	Canada 6/Czechoslovakia 2
	Toronto	Finland 3/Sweden 1
	Chicago	United States 2/Soviet Union 1
September 9	Quebec City	Canada 3/Soviet Union 3
	Toronto	Sweden 5/Czechoslovakia 2
	Chicago	United States 4/Finland 3

Semifinals

September 11	Hamilton	United States 7/Finland 3
September 12	Toronto	Canada 4/Sweden 0

Finals (best two-of-three)

September 14	Montreal	Canada 4/United States 1
September 16	Hamilton	Canada 4/United States 2

WORLD CUP OF HOCKEY 1996

Canada/Europe/United States, August 30–September 14, 1996

FINAL STANDINGS ROUND ROBIN

North American Pool

	GP	W	L	T	GF	GA	P
United States	3	3	0	0	19	8	6
Canada	3	2	1	0	11	10	4
Russia	3	1	2	0	12	14	2
Slovakia	3	0	3	0	9	19	0

European Pool

	GP	W	L	T	GF	GA	P
Sweden	3	3	0	0	14	3	6
Finland	3	2	1	0	17	11	4
Germany	3	1	2	0	11	15	2
Czech Republic	3	0	3	0	4	17	0

Results

August 26	Stockholm	Sweden 6/Germany 1
August 27	Helsinki	Finland 7/Czech Republic 3
August 28	Helsinki	Finland 8/Germany 3
	Prague	Sweden 3/Czech Republic 0
	Vancouver	Canada 5/Russia 3
August 31	Philadelphia	United States 5/Canada 3
	Garmisch	Germany 7/Czech Republic 1
	Montreal	Russia 7/Slovakia 4
September 1	Ottawa	Canada 3/Slovakia 2
	Stockholm	Sweden 5/Finland 2
September 2	New York	United States 5/Russia 2
September 3	New York	United States 9/Slovakia 3

Quarter-finals

September 5	Montreal	Canada 4/Germany 1
September 6	Ottawa	Russia 5/Finland 0

Semifinals

September 7	Philadelphia	Canada 3/Sweden 2 (Fleury 39:47 OT)
September 8	Ottawa	United States 5/Russia 2

Finals (best two-of-three)

September 10	Philadelphia	Canada 4/United States 3 (Yzerman 19:53 OT)
September 12	Montreal	United States 5/Canada 2
September 14	Montreal	United States 5/Canada 2

WORLD CUP OF HOCKEY 2004

August 30–September 14, 2004
Tournament MVP: Vincent Lecavalier (CAN)

All-Tournament Team

Goal	Martin Brodeur (CAN)
Defence	Adam Foote (CAN)
	Kimmo Timonen (FIN)
Forward	Vincent Lecavalier (CAN)
	Fredrik Modin (SWE)
	Saku Koivu (FIN)

PRELIMINARY ROUND STANDINGS

European Pool

	GP	W	L	T	GF	GA	P
Finland	3	2	0	1	11	4	5
Sweden	3	2	0	1	13	9	5
Czech Republic	3	1	2	0	10	10	2
Germany	3	0	3	0	4	15	0

August 30	Helsinki	Finland 4/Czech Republic 0
August 31	Stockholm	Sweden 5/Germany 2
September 1	Stockholm	Sweden 4/Czech Republic 3
September 2	Cologne	Finland 3/Germany 0
September 3	Prague	Czech Republic 7/Germany 2
September 4	Helsinki	Finland 4/Sweden 4 (5:00 OT)

North American Pool

	GP	W	L	T	GF	GA	P
Canada	3	3	0	0	10	3	6
Russia	3	2	1	0	9	6	4
USA	3	1	2	0	5	6	2
Slovakia	3	0	3	0	4	13	0

August 31	Montreal	Canada 2/USA 1
September 1	Montreal	Canada 5/Slovakia 1
September 2	St. Paul	Russia 3/USA 1
September 3	St. Paul	USA 3/Slovakia 1
September 4	Toronto	Canada 3/Russia 1
September 5	Toronto	Russia 5/Slovakia 2

Quarter-finals

September 6	Helsinki	Finland 2/Germany 1
September 7	Stockholm	Czech Republic 6/Sweden 1
September 7	St. Paul	USA 5/Russia 2
September 8	Toronto	Canada 5/Slovakia 1

Semifinals

September 11	St. Paul	Finland 2/USA 1
September 12	Toronto	Canada 4/Czech Republic 3 (Vincent Lecavalier 3:45 OT)

Finals

September 14	Toronto	Canada 3/Finland 2

WOMEN'S PRO HOCKEY LEAGUES, 1999–2011

1999–2000

NATIONAL WOMEN'S HOCKEY LEAGUE (NWHL) REGULAR-SEASON STANDINGS

Eastern Division

	GP	W	L	T	GF	GA	P
Sainte Julie Pantheres	35	20	8	7	109	68	47
Montreal Wingstar	35	18	7	10	116	62	46
Ottawa Raiders	35	9	20	6	61	109	24
Laval Le Mistral	35	7	23	5	78	177	19

Western Division

	GP	W	L	T	GF	GA	P
Beatrice Aeros	40	35	3	2	217	37	72
Brampton Thunder	40	29	5	6	208	64	64
Mississauga Chiefs	40	21	13	6	133	79	48
Clearnet Lightning	40	4	33	3	44	249	11
Scarborough Sting	40	3	34	3	49	170	9

CHAMPIONSHIP FINALS

March 18   Sainte Julie Pantheres 2/Beatrice Aeros 2
March 19   Beatrice Aeros 1/Sainte Julie Pantheres 0
Beatrice wins championship 3–1 in points

2000–01

NWHL REGULAR-SEASON STANDINGS

Eastern Division

	GP	W	L	T	GF	GA	P
Montreal Wingstar	40	30	6	4	163	63	64
Sainte Julie Pantheres	40	22	15	3	168	102	47
Ottawa Raiders	40	11	25	4	78	150	26
Laval Le Mistral	40	5	33	2	68	261	12

Western Division

	GP	W	L	T	GF	GA	P
Beatrice Aeros	40	35	2	3	222	46	73
Brampton Thunder	40	30	7	3	223	82	63
Mississauga Ice Bears	40	21	16	3	107	97	45
Toronto Sting	40	8	29	3	82	168	19

Clearnet Lightning	40	5	34	1	77	219	11
Vancouver Griffins	18	14	4	0	91	43	28

CHAMPIONSHIP FINALS

Beatrice Aeros 2/Sainte Julie Pantheres 2
Beatrice Aeros 8/Sainte Julie Pantheres 1
Beatrice wins championship 3–1 in points

2001–02

NWHL REGULAR-SEASON STANDINGS

Eastern Division

	GP	W	L	T	GF	GA	P
Ottawa Raiders	30	14	10	6	71	72	34
Montreal Wingstar	30	11	14	5	66	78	27
Le Cheyenne de la Metropol	30	11	15	4	73	85	26

Western Division

	GP	W	L	T	GF	GA	P
Beatrice Aeros	30	23	2	5	149	39	51
Mississauga Ice Bears	30	12	10	8	82	81	32
Brampton Thunder	30	8	14	8	73	97	24
Telus Lightning	30	4	18	8	59	120	16

Pacific Division

	GP	W	L	T	GF	GA	P
Vancouver Griffins	31	27	4	0	84	14	54

CHAMPIONSHIP FINALS

Beatrice Aeros 3/Brampton Thunder 2 (OT)

2002–03

NWHL REGULAR-SEASON STANDINGS

Eastern Division

	GP	W	L	T	OTL	GF	GA	P
Montreal Wingstar	36	18	15	3	0	83	81	39
Ottawa Raiders	36	13	20	1	2	96	122	29
Quebec Avalanche	36	10	20	5	1	87	120	26

Central Division

	G	W	L	T	OTL	GF	GA	P
Beatrice Aeros	36	32	3	1	0	201	54	65
Brampton Thunder	36	27	9	0	0	152	71	54
Mississauga Ice Bears	36	19	13	3	1	122	111	42
Telus Lightning	36	0	34	1	1	54	236	2

Western Division

	G	W	L	T	OTL	GF	GA	P
Calgary X-Treme	24	23	1	0	0	144	37	46
Vancouver Griffins	24	10	13	0	1	82	92	21
Edmonton Chimos	24	3	20	0	1	35	132	7

CHAMPIONSHIP FINALS
Calgary X-Treme 3/Beatrice Aeros 0

2003–04

NWHL REGULAR-SEASON STANDINGS

Eastern Division

	G	W	L	T	OTL	GF	GA	P
Montreal Axion	36	20	10	5	1	113	84	46
Ottawa Raiders	36	9	23	4	0	85	144	22
Quebec Avalanche	36	4	28	2	2	65	163	12

Central Division

	G	W	L	T	OTL	GF	GA	P
Toronto Aeros	36	33	2	1	0	197	42	67
Brampton Thunder	36	28	6	2	0	190	72	58
Oakville Ice	36	17	17	2	0	118	99	36
Telus Lightning	36	8	28	0	0	66	224	16

Western Division

	G	W	L	T	OTL	GF	GA	P
Calgary X-Treme	12	11	1	0	0	64	9	22
Edmonton Chimos	12	1	11	0	0	9	64	2

CHAMPIONSHIP FINALS
Calgary X-Treme 5/Brampton Thunder 4 (OT/SO)

2004–05

NWHL REGULAR-SEASON STANDINGS

Eastern Division

	G	W	L	T	OTL	GF	GA	P
Montreal Axion	36	24	9	2	1	140	85	51

	G	W	L	T	OTL	GF	GA	P
Ottawa Raiders	36	14	19	2	1	101	128	31
Quebec Avalanche	36	5	25	4	2	53	132	16

Central Division

	G	W	L	T	OTL	GF	GA	P
Brampton Thunder	36	30	3	2	1	165	70	63
Toronto Aeros	36	24	6	4	2	142	68	54
Oakville Ice	36	13	15	6	2	97	99	34
Telus Lightning	36	4	28	4	0	72	189	12

CHAMPIONSHIP FINALS
Toronto Aeros 5/Montreal Axion 4 (OT)

2005–06

NWHL REGULAR-SEASON STANDINGS
Eastern Division

	G	W	L	T	OTL	GF	GA	P
Ottawa Raiders	36	21	8	4	3	122	77	49
Montreal Axion	36	14	17	3	2	100	122	33
Quebec Avalanche	36	4	28	2	2	58	135	12

Central Division

	G	W	L	T	OTL	GF	GA	P
Durham Lightning	36	23	6	5	2	107	74	53
Brampton Thunder	36	19	12	5	0	113	97	43
Oakville Ice	36	20	14	1	1	118	100	42
Toronto Aeros	36	13	17	4	2	114	127	32

CHAMPIONSHIP FINALS
April 15   Montreal Axion 1/Brampton Thunder 0

2006–07

NWHL REGULAR-SEASON STANDINGS

	G	W	L	T	OTL	GF	GA	P
Etobicoke Dolphins	20	15	1	2	2	87	66	64
Mississauga Aeros	21	15	5	0	1	107	51	31
Brampton Thunder	16	8	8	0	0	71	66	16
Oakville Ice	17	6	8	1	2	40	53	15
Montreal Axion	13	6	6	0	0	66	56	13
Quebec Avalanche	12	2	8	2	0	41	91	6
Ottawa Raiders	11	2	8	0	0	25	54	5

CHAMPIONSHIP FINALS
April 14   Brampton Thunder 4/Montreal Axion 0
Note: the NWHL was replaced by the CWHL in 2007

2007–08

NWHL REGULAR-SEASON STANDINGS

Central Division

	GP	W	L	OT	GF	GA	P
Brampton Canadette-Thunder	30	22	7	1	111	59	45
Mississauga Chiefs	30	21	8	1	115	61	43
Vaughan Flames	30	12	16	2	69	101	26
Burlington Barracudas	30	11	18	1	76	98	23

Eastern Division

	GP	W	L	OT	GF	GA	P
Montreal Stars	28	21	6	1	112	55	43
Ottawa Capital-Canucks	28	8	17	3	58	102	19
Quebec Phoenix	28	8	21	1	56	121	17

PLAYOFFS
Burlington 2 at Ottawa 1
(Burlington advanced)

Mississauga 6 at Vaughan 2
Mississauga 6 at Vaughan 2

Mississauga 4 at Montreal 3
Mississauga 1 at Montreal 4
(Mississauga won tie-breaker)

Burlington 2 at Brampton 5
Burlington 3 at Brampton 3
(Brampton advanced)

CHAMPIONSHIP FINALS
Mississauga Chiefs 3/Brampton Canadette-Thunder 2 (OT)

2008–09*

CANADIAN WOMEN'S HOCKEY LEAGUE (CWHL) REGULAR-SEASON STANDINGS

	GP	W	L	P
Montreal Stars	28	24	3	49
Brampton Thunder	26	19	6	39
Mississauga Chiefs	26	16	8	34
Burlington Barracudas	25	10	13	22
Vaughan Flames	25	4	19	10
Ottawa Senators	24	4	20	8

League Playoffs
(best-of-two plus sudden-death OT in case of tie)

March 14	Brampton 3/Mississauga 2
March 15	Mississauga 4/Brampton 1

OT tie-breaker: Brampton, Jayna Hefford
Brampton Thunder advance to Clarkson Cup finals

March 14	Montreal 6/Burlington 1
March 15	Burlington3/Montreal 1

OT tie-breaker: Montreal, Noemie Marin
Montreal Stars advance to Clarkson Cup finals

WESTERN WOMEN'S HOCKEY LEAGUE (WWHL) REGULAR-SEASON STANDINGS

	GP	W	L	OTL	P
Calgary Oval X-Treme	23	20	2	1	42
Minnesota Whitecaps	22	18	3	1	38
Edmonton Chimos	24	14	10	0	28
Strathmore Rockies	23	6	16	1	13
B.C. Breakers	24	0	22	2	2

League Playoffs
Semifinals

March 7	Calgary 9/Strathmore 0
March 7	Minnesota 4/Edmonton 0

Finals

March 8	Minnesota 2/Calgary 0

Both finalists advance to Clarkson Cup finals

*In 2008, the National Women's Hockey League split into the Canadian Women's Hockey League and the Western Women's Hockey League.

CLARKSON CUP FINALS
Kingston, Ontario

Round Robin

March 19	Minnesota 4/Montreal 3
March 19	Brampton 4/Calgary 3

Semifinals

March 20	Montreal 4/Brampton 1
March 20	Minnesota 2/Calgary 1

Finals

March 21	Montreal 3 Minnesota 1

2009–10

CWHL REGULAR-SEASON STANDINGS

	GP	W	L	OTL	GF	GA	Pts
*Montreal Stars	30	23	5	2	122	70	48
*Mississauga Chiefs	30	21	8	1	94	60	43
Burlington Barracudas	30	19	8	3	94	80	41
Brampton Thunder	29	12	14	3	76	78	27
Vaughan Flames	29	9	19	1	77	111	19
Ottawa Senators	30	5	23	2	61	125	12

*advanced to Clarkson Cup as top two teams

Playoffs (winner advances to Clarkson Cup)

March 20	Brampton 4/Vaughan 1
March 20	Burlington 4/Ottawa 3 (OT)
March 21	Brampton 2/Burlington 1

WWHL REGULAR-SEASON STANDINGS

	GP	W	L	T	OTL	GF	GA	Pts
*Minnesota Whitecaps	12	10	2	0	0	44	24	20
Edmonton Chimos	18	7	7	0	4	40	48	18
Strathmore Rockies	18	7	10	0	1	43	55	15
Calgary Oval X-Treme	0	0	0	0	0	0	0	0
British Columbia Breakers		DID NOT PLAY						

*advanced to Clarkson Cup for finishing in first place

CLARKSON CUP FINALS
Richmond Hill, Ontario

Semifinals
| March 27 | Brampton 3/Montreal 2 |
| March 27 | Minnesota 3/Mississauga 1 |

Finals
| March 28 | Minnesota 4/Brampton 0 |

2010-11

CWHL REGULAR-SEASON STANDINGS
	GP	W	L	T	GF	GA	Pts
Montreal Stars	26	22	2	2	125	70	46
Brampton Thunder	26	19	6	1	111	69	39
Boston Blades	26	10	15	1	73	101	21
Toronto Aeros	26	8	13	5	83	98	21
Burlington Barracudas	26	6	18	2	54	108	14

Clarkson Cup Qualification
March 11	Toronto 4/Boston 2
March 11	Brampton 1/Montreal 2 (SO)
March 12	Toronto 3/Boston 1
March 12	Brampton 3/Montreal 4

(Boston eliminated from Clarkson Cup competition)

WWHL REGULAR-SEASON STANDINGS
	GP	W	L	T	OTL	GF	GA	Pts
*Minnesota Whitecaps	18	17	0	0	1	120	43	35
Edmonton Chimos	17	11	5	0	1	56	41	23
Manitoba Maple Leafs	12	1	11	0	0	31	80	2
Strathmore Rockies	11	0	10	0	1	21	64	1

*advanced to Clarkson Cup round-robin

CLARKSON CUP FINALS
Barrie, Ontario

Round-Robin Standings & Results

	GP	W	L	T	GF	GA	Pts
Montreal	3	3	0	0	14	6	6
Toronto	3	2	1	0	10	4	4
Brampton	3	1	2	0	13	12	2
Minnesota	3	0	3	0	3	18	0

March 24	Toronto 3/Brampton 2
March 24	Montreal 5/Minnesota 1
March 25	Toronto 6/Minnesota 0
March 25	Montreal 7/Brampton 4
March 26	Brampton 7/Minnesota 2
March 26	Montreal 2/Toronto 1

Finals

| March 26 | Montreal 5/Toronto 0 |

HOCKEY POOL NOTES

HOCKEY POOL NOTES

HOCKEY POOL NOTES